When Justice Fails

When Justice Fails
Causes and Consequences of Wrongful Convictions

SECOND EDITION

Robert J. Norris
GEORGE MASON UNIVERSITY

Catherine L. Bonventre
NORTH CAROLINA A&T STATE UNIVERSITY

James R. Acker
UNIVERSITY AT ALBANY, SUNY

CAROLINA ACADEMIC PRESS
Durham, North Carolina

Library of Congress Cataloging-in-Publication Data

Names: Norris, Robert J., author. | Bonventre, Catherine L., author. |
  Acker, James R., 1951- author.
Title: When justice fails : causes and consequences of wrongful convictions
  / by Robert J. Norris, Catherine L. Bonventre, James R. Acker.
Description: Second edition. | Durham, North Carolina : Carolina Academic
  Press, LLC, [2021] | Includes index.
Identifiers: LCCN 2021028862 | ISBN 9781531023638 (paperback) | ISBN
  9781531023645 (ebook)
Subjects: LCSH: Criminal justice, Administration of--United States. |
  Judicial error--United States.
Classification: LCC HV9950 .N67 2021 | DDC 345.73/0122--dc23
LC record available at https://lccn.loc.gov/2021028862

Carolina Academic Press
700 Kent Street
Durham, North Carolina 27701
Telephone (919) 489-7486
www.cap-press.com

To Saundra Westervelt, an incredible teacher, scholar, mentor, and friend, who sparked my interest in wrongful convictions more than a decade ago. And to Kirk Bloodsworth, who cemented my desire to be an ally in the fight for justice. May this work and these stories do the same for others.
—RJN

To Vin, my mother, and my brothers. And to justice.
—CLB

To three generations of family—Jenny, Elizabeth, Anna, and Ethan— and to the continuing quest for justice in the courts and well beyond.
—JRA

Contents

Acknowledgments

We first wish to thank the good folks at Carolina Academic Press, who have been a pleasure to work with. Beth Hall has shepherded us through the process from the outset with enthusiasm and unwavering support. We also gratefully acknowledge the careful and thorough assistance provided by TJ Smithers in helping prepare our manuscript for publication. Any remaining errors, of course, are ours alone.

We also are thankful to our many colleagues in wrongful conviction scholarship and teaching, whose work has inspired this book and made it possible.

We are particularly indebted to Andrew Madrigal and Clayton Drummond, whose research assistance helped greatly in getting this manuscript across the finish line.

Finally, we must acknowledge those whose stories are covered in this volume and the thousands of others like them. Individuals who experience wrongful conviction and the many others affected by errors in the criminal legal system withstand harm that is difficult to capture in words. Yet they manage to survive and endure with grace and humility. We hope this book will help educate students, scholars, practitioners, advocates, and the public and be a small contribution toward reducing further injustices. And to those who advocate on behalf of the wrongly convicted and are in the trenches fighting to ensure our system is one of justice, we continue to admire your work and hope this volume will help accelerate needed reforms.

RJN, CLB, & JRA

When Justice Fails

Chapter 1

Wrongful Convictions: Introduction and Overview

Learning Objectives

After reading this chapter, you should be able to:

- Distinguish "wrong person" and "no-crime" wrongful convictions.
- Understand how "exoneration" is defined.
- Discuss why the known number of wrongful convictions is considered the "tip of the iceberg."
- Appreciate the unrepresentative nature of known wrongful convictions and the consequent limitations on our knowledge of the universe of wrongful convictions.
- Sketch the challenges faced by wrongfully accused and convicted defendants at various stages in the criminal process from arrest through appeals.

Case Study: The Scottsboro Boys

On March 25, 1931, nine young African Americans, ages 13 to 19, were rousted off a freight train by sheriff's deputies and armed white citizens at a northern Alabama train station. They were taken into custody because several white youths had reported being ejected from the moving train after fighting with a gang of Blacks. Two young white women were on the same train. Like the young men and many others during the Great Depression, they had been riding the rails in search of jobs and a better life. On being detected as stowaways when the train came to a stop, Victoria Price and Ruby Bates

3

claimed that they had been raped by multiple Black assailants. These incendiary charges fueled angry lynch mobs, which gathered soon after the young men were locked up in jail in the nearby town of Scottsboro. Within the space of two weeks, eight of the nine defendants—who would become known throughout the country and internationally as the Scottsboro Boys—were convicted of rape and sentenced to death (a mistrial was declared for the youngest boy because the jury failed to reach agreement about his capital punishment).

The trials and surrounding atmosphere presented a host of ingredients that were liable to produce grave miscarriages of justice. The trial venue was awash with racial prejudice that was inflamed by vitriolic and condemning pretrial publicity. The youths were represented by attorneys who were appointed the morning of the trial and were woefully unprepared. Forensic evidence of dubious reliability was introduced at the trial through medical testimony. A distant eyewitness claimed to have observed details of the assault as the train traveled past his farm. In a desperate attempt to avoid conviction, some of the defendants, while denying personal involvement with the assaults, maintained that they had witnessed others ravage the women. In the aftermath of the youths' convictions, Ruby Bates, one of the alleged victims, recanted her accusing trial testimony. She admitted having engaged in sexual relations prior to the reported attack, but declared that none of the defendants had touched her. She claimed that law enforcement officers had pressured her into accusing the boys of the rapes (Acker, 2008; Carter, 1979).

The Scottsboro Boys' original convictions were vacated by the United States Supreme Court (*Powell v. Alabama*, 1932), thus sparing them from execution. Over the next several years they were subjected to multiple retrials and suffered a series of new convictions. Although the new trials exposed numerous inconsistencies and weaknesses in the prosecution's case that undermined the rape allegations, Victoria Price stood by her accusations, and the all-white Alabama juries continued to find the defendants guilty. Most of the young men remained incarcerated deep into the 1930s and 1940s. In 1937, prosecutors dropped the rape charges against five of the original defendants—Olen Montgomery, Ozie Powell, Willie Roberson, Eugene Williams, and Roy Wright—and they were released from prison. The other four languished in prison, although Haywood Patterson eventually escaped, only to be convicted of committing manslaughter in Michigan and imprisoned there. The last of the defendants was freed from prison in Alabama in 1950 (Acker, 2008; Carter, 1979).

Collectively, the Scottsboro Boys served more than 90 years behind bars for the charged rapes, with eight of the nine experiencing lengthy terms under sentence of death. With the passage of time, their convictions were officially recognized as gross miscarriages of justice. In 1976, Alabama Governor George Wallace pardoned Clarence Norris, the last living of the Scottsboro Boys. In 2013, the Alabama Board of Pardons and Paroles issued posthumous pardons to Haywood Patterson, Charles Weems, and Andy Wright, the remaining three defendants whose convictions had not been overturned (Acker, 2008; Blinder, 2013).

Wrongful Convictions in the United States

Our subject matter involves the **wrongful conviction** of factually innocent people. Although serious and worthy of concern, our focus does not encompass convictions plagued by **procedural error** only, such as the admission at trial of illegally seized evidence or of a confession obtained in violation of a defendant's *Miranda* rights. We instead limit our consideration to cases in which individuals are innocent of wrongdoing and have erroneously been convicted: (a) for crimes committed by someone else (**"wrong-person" cases**); or (b) when no crime at all actually was committed (**"no-crime" cases**).

Most people probably think about "wrong-person" cases when they hear that an innocent person has been convicted of a crime. In such cases, a guilty party commits a crime that is blamed on someone who is free of wrongdoing but is nevertheless convicted and punished. For example, in 1985, Rolando Cruz and Alejandro Hernandez were sentenced to death in Illinois for the 1983 kidnapping, rape, and murder of a 10-year-old girl. The convictions were supported by expert testimony concerning a bootprint found on the door of the victim's home, police officers' testimony attributing incriminating statements to both defendants, the testimony of jailhouse informants, and other evidence (*Buckley v. Fitzsimmons*, 1993; Center on Wrongful Convictions, 2001a, 2001b). The Illinois Supreme Court reversed the convictions of both men on procedural grounds in 1988 (*People v. Cruz*, 1988; *People v. Hernandez*, 1988). Cruz was convicted and again sentenced to death at his 1990 retrial. A second trial for Hernandez resulted in a hung jury, but a third trial produced another conviction and a sentence of 80 years imprisonment.

Cruz appealed his second conviction and again was awarded a new trial by the Illinois Supreme Court (*People v. Cruz*, 1994). Hernandez's second conviction also was overturned on appeal. In 1995, the judge presiding at Cruz's third trial directed a not guilty verdict, and Cruz finally was released from prison. Hernandez's conviction also was vacated, and the charges against him were dismissed. Meanwhile, another man, Brian Dugan, had confessed to the murder and rape for which Cruz and Hernandez had originally been convicted. DNA evidence confirmed Dugan's guilt. Dugan, who had raped and murdered other victims, ultimately pled guilty to the crimes for which Cruz and Hernandez had each spent more than a decade behind bars, including long stretches on death row (Frisbie & Garrett, 2005; Gutowski & Mills, 2014).

"No-crime" cases are wrongful convictions in which no one is truly guilty because no crime has been committed. The Scottsboro Boys' cases described earlier represent "no-crime" wrongful convictions; the young men who were convicted and sentenced to death in Alabama were falsely accused of rapes that never occurred. The earliest known wrongful conviction in the United States occurred in Vermont in 1819, involving Jesse and Stephen Boorn. The Boorn brothers were found guilty of murdering their brother-in-law, Russell Colvin, who had mysteriously disappeared after witnesses reported that the three men had argued. Both brothers eventually confessed to the slaying, although Jesse recanted his confession and Stephen maintained that he delivered the fatal blow to Colvin while defending himself as the two men fought. Just three weeks before Stephen Boorn was scheduled to be hanged, Colvin turned up very much alive. The Boorns had been convicted of a murder that never happened (McFarland, 1993; Warden, n.d.).

Surprisingly, perhaps, "no-crime" cases account for more than one-third (37.2%) of the known wrongful convictions reported on the National Registry of Exonerations through April 2021. Nearly half (82 out of 172, or 47.7%) of the wrongful convictions exposed in 2018 involved no-crime cases. We will explore no-crime wrongful convictions more fully in chapter 10.

How Common Are Wrongful Convictions?

The criminal justice systems administered by the federal government and the 50 states are busy. An estimated 13 million misdemeanor cases are processed annually in the nation's courts (Mayson & Stevenson, 2020; Natapoff, 2018; Stevenson & Mayson, 2018). Approximately 1.1 million adults were convicted of a felony in state courts in 2004 (Durose & Langan, 2007). Federal law enforcement officers made more than 165,000 arrests in 2014, and the federal courts imposed sentence in more than 64,000 criminal cases during fiscal year 2020 (Motivans, 2017; United States Sentencing Commission, 2021). At year-end 2018, more than 6.4 million people — approximately 1 in 40 adults in the United States — were under some form of correctional supervision or custody throughout the nation, including more than 2.1 million experiencing incarceration and approximately 4.4 million under community supervision, probation, or parole (Maruschak & Minton, 2020).

Particularly in light of such a large volume of cases, extraordinary optimism would be required to believe that justice systems are error-free. Consider the difficulties involved in trying to reconstruct who did what to whom, and why, when a crime is reported or discovered. Information may be scarce, ambiguous, and of uncertain reliability. The police, prosecutors, defense lawyers, crime witnesses, judges, jurors, and everyone else associated with the administration of justice are human, and humans make mistakes. Some will be careless or grossly negligent. Others will attempt to conceal the truth, and some will lie. As a result, people who are innocent of wrongdoing may be arrested, prosecuted, convicted, and punished for crimes they did not commit.

Even if criminal justice systems function with remarkable accuracy, the sheer number of cases processed suggests that tens of thousands of innocents are apt to suffer wrongful conviction and punishment annually. For example, an **error rate** in guilty verdicts as small as 1% (or, alternatively, an accuracy rate of 99%) would mean that more than 21,000 people incarcerated in the United States are innocent, along with nearly 44,000 under community supervision. It is impossible to know how good this estimate is, although it is consistent with (actually, somewhat lower than) those made by experienced attorneys, judges, and academics (Gross et al., 2014; Loeffler et al., 2019; Risinger, 2007; Zalman, 2012; Zalman et al., 2008).

The estimates made by criminal justice officials and academics about how often innocent people are convicted of crimes are estimates only. No one knows what the true incidence may be. This is so because wrongful convictions escape notice when they take place (if it were known that the accused person was innocent, the case would never have gone to court or resulted in a guilty verdict). Once wrongful convictions happen there is no guarantee that they will be discovered. A precise estimate of the rate of wrongful conviction thus remains elusive; "a 'dark figure'… that is not merely unknown but unknowable" (Gross et al., 2014, p. 7230, quoting Bedau & Radelet, 1987).

We can, however, identify cases in which convictions have been overturned after evidence points to or demonstrates a defendant's innocence. The **National Registry of Exonerations (NRE)**, founded in 2012, "collects, analyzes and disseminates information about all known exonerations of innocent criminal defendants in the United States, from 1989 to the present" (National Registry of Exonerations, n.d.a). The NRE stands as the most comprehensive collection of known exonerations that exists. As of February 2021, the NRE database includes 2,737 exonerations in the United States since 1989. To qualify for inclusion, a case must meet the following criteria:

> **Exoneration**—A person has been exonerated if he or she was convicted of a crime and later was either: (1) declared to be factually innocent by a government official or agency with the authority to make that declaration; or (2) relieved of all the consequences of the criminal conviction by a government official or body with the authority to take that action. The official action may be: (i) a complete pardon by a governor or other competent authority, whether or not the pardon is designated as based on innocence; (ii) an acquittal of all charges factually related to the crime for which the person was originally convicted; or (iii) a dismissal of all charges related to the crime for which the person was originally convicted, by a court or by a prosecutor with the authority to enter that dismissal. The pardon, acquittal, or dismissal must have been the result, at least in part, of evidence of innocence that either (i) was not presented at the trial at which the person was convicted; or (ii) if the person pled guilty, was not known to the defendant and the defense attorney, and to the court, at the time the plea was entered. The evidence of innocence need not be an explicit basis for the official action that exonerated the person. A person who otherwise qualifies has not been exonerated if there is unexplained physical evidence of that person's guilt (National Registry of Exonerations, n.d.b).

Of the **exonerees** in the NRE database, nearly 20% (n = 533) were exonerated with the assistance of DNA evidence. More than 20% (n = 558) were convicted via a guilty plea (rather than at trial; we explore false guilty pleas in chapter 5), and nearly 5% (n = 131) were sentenced to death. Combined, the NRE exonerees lost more than 24,770 years of their lives while incarcerated.

There are two other lists of known exonerations that are often cited. First, the **Innocence Project** (IP) maintains a roster of the individuals convicted of crimes who later were exonerated "where DNA results were central to establishing [their] innocence" (West & Meterko, 2015/2016, p. 718). Their list includes exonerations since 1989, the year of the first DNA-based exoneration in the U.S. Second, the **Death Penalty Information Center** (DPIC) maintains a list of individuals who were exonerated after being sentenced to death, beginning in 1973. Due to their focus on specific subsets of cases (DNA-based exonerations and death row exonerations), both the IP and DPIC lists are less inclusive than the more comprehensive NRE database, although the DPIC list of death row exonerees extends farther back in time (1973) than the NRE list with its 1989 starting point.

The lists just described shed some light on wrongful convictions as a whole, but it is important to remember that these known instances of exoneration are a highly imperfect measure of all wrongful convictions that have occurred (Gross, 2017). In fact, the NRE is not even likely to be an all-inclusive list of exonerations, let alone all wrongful convictions. Therefore, we cannot rely on reported exonerations to provide a complete and accurate account of all cases in which innocent people have been convicted of crimes. In the first place, no database systematically captures exonerations that take place in the thousands of local, state, and federal courts that hear criminal cases. An unknown number of exonerations thus will likely escape detection (Gross, 2017). Yet this problem is far less fundamental than others. In short, no one seriously maintains that the wrongful convictions that come to light and culminate with an exoneration represent the entire universe of innocent people convicted of crimes.

Untold numbers of innocents will never be able to demonstrate that they have erroneously been convicted. The needed evidence may never surface, courts may not accept or credit the evidence that does, and advocates—be they family members, friends, attorneys, journalists, or other supporters—may not be able or willing to help champion their cause. Many thus will continue to suffer the onus of punishment and the stigma of a criminal record. This threat of under-inclusiveness, or missing a portion of the wrongful convictions that take place, may be especially acute with respect to less serious crimes. In misdemeanor cases and in felony cases that do not result in lengthy incarceration, the considerable time, effort, and resources required to unearth a wrongful conviction are unlikely to be invested by organizations devoted to innocence work, or by the affected individuals themselves (Acker, 2017; Gross & O'Brien, 2008). Phrases such as "tip of the iceberg" and "the dark figure of innocence" are commonly used to describe the gulf between the exonerations we know about, and the considerably larger body of wrongful convictions that almost certainly exists (Bedau & Radelet, 1987, p. 87; Garrett, 2011, pp. 6, 11).

On the other hand, we must be mindful that the fact of an exoneration—as defined by criteria such as those used by the National Registry of Exonerations, above—does not always guarantee that the person whose conviction was overturned is factually innocent. Consider, for example, the case of a defendant whose original conviction was reversed on appeal and then was found not guilty after receiving a new trial. The not guilty verdict signifies only that the prosecution failed to establish guilt "beyond a reasonable doubt." Although relying on jury verdicts, prosecutors' dismissals, and executive pardons may be the best we can do to establish that a defendant has been wrongfully convicted (Findley, 2010/2011), such authoritative actions do not conclusively establish the defendant's actual innocence. Indeed, it would be naïve to believe that factually guilty parties never benefit by acquittals (Forst, 2010/2011; Marquis, 2005; Schmidle, 2012). Still, these errors of over-inclusion — that is, of classifying the guilty among exonerees who are presumed to be innocent — almost certainly are dwarfed by the converse problem of failing to identify truly innocent people who have been wrongfully convicted (Gross, 2008).

Wrongful Convictions: Contributing Factors

The lack of reliable information concerning how many innocent people have been wrongfully convicted severely hampers our understanding of why wrongful convictions occur and how we can help prevent them. Since we cannot be confident that the wrongful convictions we know about are representative of all cases in which innocent persons suffer conviction, we cannot safely assume that the factors that appear to have contributed to the known wrongful convictions are similarly influential more generally. To illustrate this concern, consider the problems we would encounter if we studied the exoneration cases identified by the Innocence Project with the hope of understanding what normally leads to innocent people being convicted of crimes. On doing so, we would learn that 91% of the wrongful convictions on the IP list occurred in cases involving a sexual assault, including many which resulted in a homicide. We additionally would note that eyewitness identification errors were far and away the most common contributing factor, occurring in 72% of the IP exoneration cases (West & Meterko, 2015/2016, pp. 725, 733). Would these observations justify us in concluding that most wrongful convictions occur in sex offense cases and that eyewitness errors are the leading cause of wrongful convictions? The answer to these questions is an emphatic no.

When we recall that the Innocence Project exoneration list is confined to cases in which DNA was instrumental in overturning convictions, it should not surprise us that such a high proportion of the cases involve sexual assault — the very type of crime for which biological evidence such as semen is likely to be available for DNA analysis. Moreover, we might expect that the victims of sexual assault will commonly be asked if they can identify their assailant and will have named the person who has been tried and convicted for the offense. Only later will DNA evidence help demonstrate that a misidentification was made. What we do not know, of course, is how many wrongful convictions occur in other types of cases, including the many for which no DNA evidence exists. We would be on remarkably thin ice if we made inferences about the types of cases in which wrongful convictions are most likely to occur, and about why they occur, in reliance on information extracted from the Innocence Project data. Even a cursory glance at the more comprehensive exoneration list compiled by the National Registry of Exonerations would tell us that we cannot trust that the IP cases are representative of exoneration cases that do not rely on DNA evidence.

Our problems are not solved by studying the more expansive set of exoneration cases identified by the NRE. We still cannot assume that those cases are representative of wrongful convictions in general, and thus we cannot safely draw conclusions from them about how often innocent people are convicted, for what types of offenses, and why. Nor is it a simple matter to separate the factors that produce wrongful convictions from those that simply coincide with them, i.e., to distinguish between causes and correlates of such miscarriages of justice. Moreover, it is challenging to try to pinpoint the sources of error in cases, since wrongful convictions almost invariably involve multiple contributing factors rather than a single definitive cause (Gould et al., 2014). On the brighter side, owing to an outpouring of scholarly research by social scientists and members of the legal community, we know considerably more about wrongful convictions today than we once did.

An Abbreviated History of the Innocence Movement

The publication of Edwin Borchard's *Convicting the Innocent* in 1932 is often defined as the dawning of the era of wrongful conviction scholarship. In this book, Borchard, a Yale Law School professor, described 65 "prosecutions and convictions of completely innocent people," and he catalogued "[t]he particular errors" which plagued these cases (p. 367). He was motivated to do so as "a refutation of [the] supposition" voiced by a prosecutor and presumably shared by others, that "'Innocent men are never convicted. Don't worry about it, it never happens in the world. It is a physical impossibility'" (p. v). Borchard's tack of collecting individual cases of wrongful conviction, detailing their antecedents, and making the accounts accessible to a broad readership, served as a model for other writers over the next several decades. One such author was lawyer and novelist Erle Stanley Gardner, creator of the popular fictional defense lawyer, Perry Mason, whose clients almost invariably proved to have been wrongly accused of crimes (Gardner, 1952; Leo, 2005).

More refined scholarly analysis ensued later. A groundbreaking 1987 study by Hugo Adam Bedau and Michael Radelet identified 350 instances of wrongful conviction in the United States between 1900 and 1985. Their report focused exclusively on cases that could have ended or actually did result in death sentences. It included 23 individuals who were executed but, in the authors' judgment, were factually innocent (Bedau & Radelet, 1987). Meanwhile, organizations devoted to assisting men and women who had been convicted of crimes yet claimed to be innocent began investigating cases and pursuing court action to free them. **Centurion Ministries**, founded by Jim McCloskey in the 1980s, helped pioneer such efforts (Norris, 2017). The Innocence Project was later co-founded by attorneys Peter Neufeld and Barry Scheck. The IP opened its doors at Cardozo Law School in New York City in 1992. DNA evidence was first used in American criminal courts in the late 1980s to help free the wrongly convicted, and the Innocence Project limited its exoneration work to cases in which DNA analysis would be instrumental in upsetting convictions. In the ensuing decades, an **Innocence Network**, consisting of numerous law school clinical programs and organizations in the United States and internationally, has developed to carry on such work.

The forensic use of DNA demonstrated unequivocally that innocent people are sometimes victims of wrongful convictions. The emergence of DNA evidence and its impact on public perceptions regarding the plight of the wrongfully convicted greatly accelerated the **Innocence Movement** (Norris, 2017; Zalman, 2010/2011). A report issued by the United States Department of Justice's National Institute of Justice (1996) stimulated additional attention to problems in the administration of justice that were exposed by DNA evidence. Researchers redoubled their efforts to study the causes and consequences of errors of justice (Gould & Leo, 2010), and policymakers began considering and implementing responsive safeguards and reforms (Hicks et al., 2021; Kent & Carmichael, 2015; Norris et al., 2017). As the twenty-first century began, the Innocence Movement, hailed by some as a "revolution" (Marshall, 2004) and by others as a new "civil rights movement" (Medwed, 2008, p. 1550; see Norris, 2017, p. 28) gained increased momentum.

Administering Justice:
Arrest, Prosecution, and Adjudication

Criminal convictions take place when courts enter judgment following a defendant's guilty plea or the return of a guilty verdict at the conclusion of a trial. But guilty pleas and trials are neither the first nor the last stage in the administration of justice. All decisions made as a case evolves from the first time a crime is reported to the final review of a conviction by the courts or a governor (or another executive official or agency) authorized to grant clemency, can be instrumental in producing, detecting, or correcting a wrongful conviction.

Crimes, or suspected crimes, come to the attention of authorities when citizens report them or when the police directly observe them or infer that they have occurred. The criminal justice process formally begins in most cases with the arrest of a suspected offender. An arrest lawfully can be made on probable cause to believe that the suspect has committed a crime. Probable cause is a relatively low threshold showing. The Supreme Court has defined the term as follows (*Brinegar v. United States*, 1949, pp. 175–176):

> In dealing with probable cause, ... as the very name implies, we deal with probabilities. These are not technical; they are the factual and practical considerations of everyday life on which reasonable and prudent men, not legal technicians, act. The standard of proof is accordingly correlative to what must be proved.
>
> "The substance of all the definitions" of probable cause "is a reasonable ground for belief of guilt." And this "means less than evidence which would justify condemnation" or conviction.... [I]t has come to mean more than bare suspicion: Probable cause exists where "the facts and circumstances within their [the officers'] knowledge and of which they had reasonably trustworthy information [are] sufficient in themselves to warrant a man of reasonable caution in the belief that" an offense has been or is being committed.
>
> These long-prevailing standards seek to safeguard citizens from rash and unreasonable interferences with privacy and from unfounded charges of crime. They also seek to give fair leeway for enforcing the law in the community's protection. Because many situations which confront officers in the course of executing their duties are more or less ambiguous, room must be allowed for some mistakes on their part. But the mistakes must be those of reasonable men, acting on facts leading sensibly to their conclusions of probability. The rule of probable cause is a practical, nontechnical conception affording the best compromise that has been found for accommodating these often opposing interests. Requiring more would unduly hamper law enforcement. To allow less would be to leave law-abiding citizens at the mercy of the officers' whim or caprice.

An arrested suspect can be taken into custody and then booked and held in jail. A first appearance, or arraignment, before a judge or a magistrate will follow shortly thereafter. The judicial officer will review the sufficiency of the

criminal complaint, advise the arrestee of their rights, consider whether to appoint an attorney, and often set bail or authorize the suspect's release on a
promise to appear for later proceedings. An arrest can be a crucial step in producing a wrongful conviction. It not only sets the machinery of justice in
motion against a suspect, but it also usually means that the police will no longer
investigate the possibility that someone else has committed the crime. It may
additionally signal to later decision-makers that the arrestee is probably guilty
(Findley & Scott, 2006).

Sometime after the suspect has been arrested and arraigned, a prosecutor
will review the case and decide whether to proceed with formal charges. Cases
can be terminated if the prosecutor determines there is insufficient evidence
or for other reasons. Otherwise, cases will move forward. For more serious
charges (felonies), the accused may be entitled to a preliminary hearing before
a judge, where the prosecutor must present evidence establishing probable
cause to support the accusation. In some jurisdictions, felony prosecutions
must be authorized by an indictment returned by a grand jury. Other jurisdictions allow charges to be based on a prosecutor's allegations (an "information"), followed by a preliminary hearing.

Discussions and negotiations concerning guilty pleas that take place may
curtail a trial. A defendant's decision to plead guilty might entail a prosecutor's
agreement to reduce the charges or recommend a lower sentence than might
otherwise be imposed, but not all guilty pleas involve such bargaining. Cases
not resolved by guilty pleas will be scheduled for trial before a judge (a **bench
trial**) or a jury. Unless and until a defendant pleads guilty or is found guilty at
a trial, the legal presumption of innocence remains in effect. This presumption
requires, in contested trials, that the prosecution must prove all elements of
the charged crime beyond a reasonable doubt. If the defendant is convicted,
however, the presumption of innocence is lost. The defendant thereafter will
be required to demonstrate why a conviction should be overturned or vacated.
This shifting of the burden of persuasion has significant implications for individuals who seek redress from a wrongful conviction.

Defendants who plead guilty often (although not invariably) forgo the right
to have their conviction reviewed on appeal. Defendants who have been found
guilty after a contested trial are entitled to appeal their convictions. For the
most part, however, appellate courts are concerned with correcting mistakes
of law that may have occurred during a trial. Only in extreme cases will they
review the sufficiency of the evidence, or the facts that support a guilty verdict.
Claims of innocence typically fall on deaf ears on appeal. Unless there is
virtually no evidence in the trial court record that supports a guilty verdict —
i.e., so that no reasonable juror could have concluded that the defendant com-

mitted the crime beyond a reasonable doubt—appellate courts will not nullify the conviction of a defendant who claims "only" to be innocent.

Some errors may not be apparent from the trial transcript or other evidence included in the record that forms the basis of an appeal. For example, a defendant might claim that their lawyer failed to investigate and present evidence critical to their defense. Or the defense might have learned after the trial ended that the prosecutor withheld important exculpatory evidence. Or, through no one's fault, evidence that was unknown at the time of trial may have come to light that strongly suggests that the defendant is innocent. In circumstances such as these, defendants who have been found guilty at trial will be allowed to seek a hearing on post-conviction review in order to present evidence and argue for a new trial. If the court hearing the petition for post-conviction relief denies the claim, the defendant typically will be entitled to appeal that decision to a higher court.

Defendants whose convictions are upheld on appeal and following post-conviction hearings face increasingly steep obstacles to gain relief. In most jurisdictions, a defendant who has taken advantage of the right to appeal from a conviction or the denial of post-conviction relief has no further entitlement to judicial review. The jurisdiction's highest court (e.g., a state supreme court), might exercise its discretion to hear a case through a petition for a writ of certiorari, but such review is infrequently granted. Discretionary review by the U.S. Supreme Court is extraordinarily rare. The Supreme Court typically gets about 7,000 to 8,000 requests annually from parties seeking review of lower court decisions, yet the justices hear only a small fraction (roughly 1%) of them (SCOTUSblog, 2017). Defendants convicted in the state courts are authorized to ask a federal district court to review claims that their constitutional rights were violated by filing a petition for a writ of habeas corpus. However, defendants who cannot afford to hire a lawyer must usually pursue such relief on their own. Appellate review in the federal system is not automatic when a district court denies relief on habeas corpus. And as noted, review by the Supreme Court on a petition for writ of certiorari is rare, indeed.

Evidence suggesting that an innocent person has been convicted of a crime may surface well after the appeals and other normal avenues of judicial review have run their course. In such cases, the defendants may be allowed to petition for a new trial based on newly discovered evidence if they can satisfy requirements such as demonstrating that they could not have produced the evidence earlier by exercising due diligence, and that the evidence is strong enough to cast significant doubt on their guilt. Such claims are often met with resistance by prosecutors and with skepticism by the courts. Only by surmounting the formidable practical and legal challenges associated with demonstrating their likely innocence can individuals who have been convicted of crimes succeed in having courts overturn their conviction.

The last avenue of relief available to correct a miscarriage of justice typically resides in the executive branch. In most states, the governor, or the governor in concert with a pardons board, is empowered to issue executive clemency. In the federal system, the president is given such authority. One form of clemency, a commutation, is the reduction of sentence (such as from death to life imprisonment). This form of relief leaves a conviction intact. A more complete form of executive clemency is a pardon, which forgives and often nullifies a conviction. An incarcerated defendant who is pardoned will be released from prison. In such cases, their innocence often (but not always) will be formally recognized.

Learning Objectives and Volume Preview

The issues explored in this volume are important, complex, and multi-dimensional. Miscarriages of justice in the form of wrongful convictions are devastating for the innocent persons who are erroneously found guilty of crimes and then must suffer punishment. Yet, the harms are not restricted only to the exoneree, but inevitably spill more widely, creating what some have called a "web of impact" (Westervelt & Cook, 2012, p. 84) or "circle of harm" (Thompson & Baumgartner, 2018). That is, wrongful convictions not only affect the innocent person convicted, but their family, friends, and communities, as well original crime victims, legal actors, and beyond. Meanwhile, in "wrong-person" cases, the true criminal remains at large, having escaped apprehension, perhaps to claim new victims (Baumgartner et al., 2017/2018; Norris et al., 2020). Wrongful convictions also may tarnish and undermine confidence in systems of justice (Acker, 2012/2013, p. 1631; Norris & Mullinix, 2020; Simon-Kerr, 2019; Zalman et al., 2012). They often are rooted in deeper societal inequities that skew the administration of justice more broadly, through racial bias, other forms of discrimination, depressed socioeconomic status, and related matters. Our hope is that in the pages that follow readers will gain a deeper appreciation of the multi-faceted issues associated with wrongful convictions — not only *that* they occur, but *how* and *why* they occur, how to help *prevent*, *detect*, and *correct* them, and what *redress* can and should be made following their discovery.

In chapter 2, we discuss the broad social context surrounding wrongful convictions in the United States, including issues related to race and gender in the criminal legal system. Chapters 3 through 9 canvass the factors most commonly identified as contributing to wrongful convictions: eyewitness misidentification, false confessions and guilty pleas, flawed and overstated conclusions drawn from the forensic sciences, informant testimony, the errors and misconduct of police and prosecutors, and inadequate representation by defense counsel. Chapter 10 examines "no-crime" wrongful convictions, offering several examples of them and reconstructing how they occurred. Chapters 11 and 12 address how miscarriages of justice can be uncovered and corrected, and what is owed and should be provided to the individuals who endure wrongful conviction and punishment in the aftermath of these errors of justice. Chapter 13 focuses on an important issue that sometimes is overlooked in wrongful conviction cases: that when an innocent person is convicted of a crime someone else has committed, the guilty party not only escapes justice, but may also commit new crimes that could have been prevented had the original investigation and prosecution not been misguided. Our concluding chapter highlights a series of challenges that are likely to confront practitioners, researchers, and policy makers in the future.

Key Terms and Concepts

- **Wrongful conviction**: cases in which individuals are innocent of wrongdoing and have erroneously been convicted
- **No-crime case**: a case in which a factually innocent person is erroneously convicted, but no actual crime ever occurred
- **Wrong-person case**: a case in which a factually innocent person is erroneously convicted for crimes committed by someone else
- **Procedural error**: an error of process or procedure made in a court case, such as the denial of a fair hearing or an irregularity in the manner of enforcing a substantive legal right; a procedural error may be grounds for reversing a conviction but does not necessarily mean that a factual error has occurred or that a defendant has been wrongfully convicted
- **Error rate**: the rate at which innocent people are convicted, or the proportion of all convictions that involve innocent persons; estimates generally fall between 1 and 5%
- **National Registry of Exonerations (NRE)**: a project founded in 2012 that provides information about wrongful convictions and exonerations in the United States; currently, the largest collection of known exonerations
- **Exoneration**: an official declaration that a person is innocent of the crimes for which they were convicted and/or relieved of the consequences of the criminal conviction

- **Exoneree**: a person who has met the criteria for an exoneration as described above
- **The Innocence Project**: a non-profit organization founded in 1992 that works to secure exonerations through post-conviction DNA testing and advocates for criminal justice reform
- **Death Penalty Information Center**: a non-profit organization that compiles and analyzes information related to capital punishment
- **Innocence Movement**: the collection of international advocacy efforts centered on wrongful convictions and exonerations; includes casework, policy reform, public education, and popular culture
- **Centurion Ministries**: the first innocence organization in the United States, founded in 1983, that works to secure the exoneration of innocent defendants
- **Innocence Network**: an international affiliation of organizations that provide legal services to the wrongly convicted and work to reform justice systems
- **Bench trial**: a trial in which the judge serves as the fact-finder and determines guilt or innocence in criminal cases

Discussion Questions

1. What is the definition of a "wrongful conviction" as used in this volume? Can you provide an example of a procedural error that might result in a conviction being overturned? Can an innocent person be convicted in a trial that contains procedural errors? Can an innocent person be convicted in a trial that is free from procedural error?

2. Do the wrongful convictions of the Scottsboro Boys represent "wrong-person" or "no-crime" cases? What is the difference between "wrong-person" and "no-crime" wrongful convictions? Which type do you think occurs more often, and why?

3. Why are the lists of cases of individuals who were wrongfully convicted that are maintained by the National Registry of Exonerations and the Innocence Project so different? Is either one a complete listing of wrongful convictions?

4. If we do not have a complete listing, or at least a representative sample of all the wrongful convictions that have occurred, what are the implications for our ability to understand the types of problems that most likely help produce wrongful convictions?

5. In percentage terms (from 0% to 100%), how often do you believe factually innocent people are convicted of crimes in the nation's courts? What is the basis for your estimate? If your estimate is accurate, how many innocent people (in absolute numbers) would be serving prison sentences today?

6. Do you believe that people are less skeptical today than they were when Edwin Borchard's *Convicting the Innocent* was published in 1932 that innocent people sometimes are convicted of crimes? If so, what reasons might help account for the changes in public perception and opinion between then and now?

References

Acker, J. R. (2008). *Scottsboro and its legacy: The cases that challenged American legal and social justice*. Praeger.

Acker, J. R. (2012/2013). The flipside injustice of wrongful convictions: When the guilty go free. *Albany Law Review, 76*, 1629–1712.

Acker, J. R. (2017). Taking stock of innocence: Movements, mountains, and wrongful convictions. *Journal of Contemporary Criminal Justice, 33*, 8–25.

Baumgartner, F. R., Grigg, A., Ramirez, R., & Lucy, J. S. (2017/2018). The mayhem of wrongful liberty: Documenting the crimes of true perpetrators in cases of wrongful incarceration. *Albany Law Review, 81*, 1263–1288.

Bedau, H. A., & Radelet, M. L. (1987). Miscarriages of justice in potentially capital cases. *Stanford Law Review, 40*, 21–173.

Blinder, A. (2013, November 21). Alabama pardons 3 'Scottsboro Boys' after 80 years. *New York Times*. http://www.nytimes.com/2013/11/22/us/with-last-3-pardons-alabama-hopes-to-put-infamous-scottsboro-boys-case-to-rest.html.

Borchard, E. M. (1932). *Convicting the innocent: Sixty-five actual errors of criminal justice*. Garden City Publishing Co.

Brinegar v. United States, 338 U.S. 160 (1949).

Buckley v. Fitzsimmons, 509 U.S. 259 (1993).

Carter, D. T. (1979). *Scottsboro: A tragedy of the American south*. Louisiana State University Press.

Center on Wrongful Convictions. (2001a). *Case study: Rolando Cruz*. Bluhm Legal Clinic, Pritzker School of Law, Northwestern University. http://www.law.northwestern.edu/legalclinic/wrongfulconvictions/exonerations/documents/ilcruzchart.pdf.

Center on Wrongful Convictions. (2001b). *Case study: Alejandro Hernandez*. Bluhm Legal Clinic, Pritzker School of Law, Northwestern University. http://www.law.northwestern.edu/legalclinic/wrongfulconvictions/exonerations/documents/ilHernandezChart.pdf.

Death Penalty Information Center. (n.d.). *Innocence: List of those freed from death row*. https://deathpenaltyinfo.org/innocence-list-those-freed-death-row.

Durose, M. R., & Langan, P. A. (2007). *Felony sentences in state courts, 2004*. U.S. Department of Justice, Bureau of Justice Statistics. https://www.bjs.gov/content/pub/pdf/fssc04.pdf.

Findley, K. A. (2010/2011). Defining innocence. *Albany Law Review, 74,* 1157–1208.

Findley, K. A., & Scott, M. S. (2006). The multiple dimensions of tunnel vision in criminal cases. *Wisconsin Law Review, 2006,* 291–397.

Forst, B. (2010/2011). Managing miscarriages of justice from victimization to reintegration. *Albany Law Review, 74,* 1209–1275.

Frisbie, T., & Garrett, R. (2005). *Victims of justice revisited*. Northwestern University Press.

Gardner, E. S. (1952). *The court of last resort*. Pocket Books.

Garrett, B. L. (2011). *Convicting the innocent: Where criminal prosecutions go wrong*. Harvard University Press.

Gould, J. B., Carrano, J., Leo, R. A., & Hail-Jares, K. (2014). Predicting erroneous convictions. *Iowa Law Review, 99,* 471–522.

Gould, J. B., & Leo, R. A. (2010). One hundred years later: Wrongful convictions after a century of research. *Journal of Criminal Law & Criminology, 100,* 825–868.

Gross, S. R. (2008). Convicting the innocent. *Annual Review of Law and Social Science, 4,* 173–192.

Gross, S. R. (2017). What we think, what we know and what we think we know about false convictions. *Ohio State Journal of Criminal Law, 14,* 753–786.

Gross, S. R., & O'Brien, B. (2008). Frequency and predictors of false conviction: Why we know so little, and new data on capital cases. *Journal of Empirical Legal Studies, 5,* 927–962.

Gross, S. R., O'Brien, B., Hu, C., & Kennedy, E. H. (2014). Rate of false conviction of criminal defendants who are sentenced to death. *Proceedings of the National Academy of Sciences of the United States of America, 111,* 7230–7235.

Gutowski, C., & Mills, S. (2014, December 13). Serial killer Brian Dugan gives 1st prison interview: 'I could not stop.' *Chicago Tribune.* http://www.

chicagotribune.com/news/ct-brian-dugan-serial-killer-interview-met-201 41212-story.html.

Hicks, W. D., Mullinix, K. J., & Norris, R. J. (2021). The politics of wrongful conviction legislation. *State Politics & Policy Quarterly*. Advance online publication. http://doi.org/10.1017/spq.2020.4.

Kent, S. L., & Carmichael, J. T. (2015). Legislative responses to wrongful conviction: Do partisan principals and advocacy efforts influence state-level criminal justice policy? *Social Science Research, 52*, 147–160.

Leo, R. A. (2005). Rethinking the study of miscarriages of justice: Developing a criminology of wrongful conviction. *Journal of Contemporary Criminal Justice, 21*, 201–223.

Loeffler, C. E., Hyatt, J., & Ridgeway, G. (2019). Measuring self-reported wrongful convictions among prisoners. *Journal of Quantitative Criminology, 35*, 259–286.

Marquis, J. (2005). The myth of innocence. *Journal of Criminal Law & Criminology, 95*, 501–522.

Marshall, L. C. (2004). The innocence revolution and the death penalty. *Ohio State Journal of Criminal Law, 1*, 1573–1584.

Maruschak, L. M., & Minton, T. D. (2020). *Correctional populations in the United States, 2017–2018*. U.S. Department of Justice, Bureau of Justice Statistics. https://www.bjs.gov/content/pub/pdf/cpus1718.pdf.

Mayson, S. G., & Stevenson, M. T. (2020). Misdemeanors by the numbers. *Boston College Law Review, 61*, 971–1044.

McFarland, G. M. (1993). *The "counterfeit" man: The true story of the Boorn-Colvin murder case*. University of Massachusetts Press.

Medwed, D. (2008). Innocentrism. *University of Illinois Law Review, 2008*, 1549–1572.

Motivans, M. (2017). *Federal justice statistics, 2013–2014*. U.S. Department of Justice, Bureau of Justice Statistics. https://www.bjs.gov/content/pub/pdf/fjs1314.pdf.

Natapoff, A. (2018). *Punishment without crime: How our massive misdemeanor system traps the innocent and makes America more unequal*. Basic Books.

National Institute of Justice. (1996). *Convicted by juries, exonerated by science: Case studies in the use of DNA evidence to establish innocence after trial*. United States Department of Justice. https://www.ncjrs.gov/pdffiles/dnaevid.pdf.

National Registry of Exonerations. (n.d.a). *Our mission*. https://www.law.umich.edu/special/exoneration/Pages/mission.aspx.

National Registry of Exonerations. (n.d.b). *Glossary*. https://www.law.umich.edu/special/exoneration/Pages/glossary.aspx.

National Registry of Exonerations. (2017). *Exonerations in 2016*. https://www. law.umich.edu/special/exoneration/Pages/Exonerations-in-2016.aspx.

Norris, R. J. (2017). Framing DNA: Social movement theory and the foundations of the innocence movement. *Journal of Contemporary Criminal Justice, 33*, 26–42.

Norris, R. J., Bonventre, C. L., Redlich, A. D., Acker, J. R., & Lowe, C. (2017). Preventing wrongful convictions: An analysis of state investigation reforms. *Criminal Justice Policy Review*. http://doi.org/10.1177/0887403416687359.

Norris, R. J., & Mullinix, K. J. (2020). Framing innocence: An experimental test of the effects of wrongful convictions on public opinion. *Journal of Experimental Criminology, 16*, 311–334.

Norris, R. J., Weintraub, J. N., Acker, J. R., Redlich, A. D., & Bonventre, C. L. (2020). The criminal costs of wrongful convictions: Can we reduce crime by protecting the innocent? *Criminology & Public Policy, 19*, 367–388.

People v. Cruz, 521 N.E.2d 18 (Ill. 1988).

People v. Cruz, 643 N.E.2d 646 (Ill. 1994).

People v. Hernandez, 521 N.E.2d 25 (Ill. 1988).

Powell v. Alabama, 287 U.S. 45 (1932).

Risinger, D. M. (2007). Innocents convicted: An empirically justified factual wrongful conviction rate. *Journal of Criminal Law & Criminology, 97*, 761–806.

Schmidle, N. (2012, November 14). Three trials for murder. *The New Yorker*. http://www.newyorker.com/magazine/2011/11/14/three-trials-for-murder.

SCOTUSblog. (2017). *Supreme Court procedure*. http://www.scotusblog.com/reference/educational-resources/supreme-court-procedure/.

Simon-Kerr, J. (2019). Public trust and police deception. *Northeastern University Law Review, 11*, 625–693.

Stevenson, M. T., & Mayson, S. G. (2018). The scale of misdemeanor justice. *Boston University Law Review, 98*, 731–777.

Thompson, J. E., & Baumgartner, F. R. (2018, April 3). An American epidemic: Crimes of wrongful liberty. Injustice Watch. https://www.injusticewatch.org/commentary/2018/an-american-epidemic-crimes-of-wrongful-liberty/.

United States Sentencing Commission. (2021, April). *Overview of federal criminal cases fiscal year 2020*. https://www.ussc.gov/sites/default/files/pdf/research-and-publications/research-publications/2021/FY20_Overview_Federal_Criminal_Cases.pdf.

Warden, R. (n.d.). First wrongful conviction: Jesse Boorn and Stephen Boorn. Center on Wrongful Convictions, Bluhm Legal Clinic, Pritzker School of Law, Northwestern University. http://www.law.northwestern.edu/legalclinic/wrongfulconvictions/exonerations/vt/boorn-brothers.html.

West, E., & Meterko, V. (2015/2016). Innocence Project: DNA exonerations, 1989–2014: Review of data and findings from the first 25 years. *Albany Law Review*, *79*, 717–795.

Westervelt, S. D., & Cook, K. J. (2012). *Life after death row: Exonerees' search for community and identity*. Rutgers University Press.

Zalman, M. (2010/2011). An integrated justice model of wrongful convictions. *Albany Law Review*, *74*, 1465–1524.

Zalman, M. (2012). Qualitatively estimating the incidence of wrongful convictions. *Criminal Law Bulletin*, *48*, 229–279.

Zalman, M., Larson, M. J., & Smith, B. (2012). Citizens' attitudes toward wrongful convictions. *Criminal Justice Review*, *37*, 51–69.

Zalman, M., Smith, B., & Kiger, A. (2008). Officials' estimates of the incidence of "actual innocence" convictions. *Justice Quarterly*, *25*, 72–100.

Chapter 2

Wrongful Convictions and Criminal Justice in Social Context

Learning Objectives

After reading this chapter, you should be able to:

- Understand the importance of social, cultural, and political context for the practice of criminal justice.
- Be aware of the racialized history of criminal justice in the United States.
- Recognize racial and gender disparities in wrongful convictions and critically assess their potential sources.

Case Study: The Central Park Five

Just before 9:00 p.m. on April 19, 1989, Trisha Meili went for a jog in New York City's Central Park. Meili, a white 28-year-old investment banker, had made plans with a coworker, Pat Garrett, to meet at 10:00 that evening, giving her enough time to complete her run before meeting him. When Garrett appeared at her apartment at the designated time, Meili did not open the door. Garrett called her phone, but there was no answer.

Around the time that Meili left for her run, a group of about 30 teenagers entered the northern end of Central Park. The group was engaged in what was referred to in the sensationalized media accounts that followed as "wilding." Some members of the group vandalized and damaged cars, harassed joggers and cyclists, and assaulted several people. When police responded to calls about teenagers causing trouble in the park, two detectives encountered a young man named Matias Reyes, whom they knew from the neighborhood. Reyes said he had not seen the group of teens and went on his way. Police arrested several youths in connection with the reported behavior, including Kevin Richardson and Raymond Santana. Three others—Antron McCray, Yusef Salaam, and Korey Wise—were later implicated as participants in the events and brought to the police station for questioning.

In the early morning hours of April 20, Trisha Meili was found unconscious in a secluded, wooded area of Central Park. She had been raped, stabbed, and badly beaten. She had lost more than seventy-five percent of her blood, suffered hypothermia and severe brain damage, and had lapsed into a coma, which would endure for 12 days. Meili was injured beyond recognition; Pat Garrett ultimately identified her based on the ring she wore.

The police investigation into the assault focused on five teenagers: Richardson (14 years old), Santana (14), McCray (15), Salaam (15), and Wise (16). The youths were detained and individually questioned for long periods of time. Detectives used a variety of techniques to encourage the young men to confess their guilt to the rape and assault of Meili. Police aggressively questioned and accused them, and employed the classic "good cop/bad cop" routine. They also used a technique known as the "prisoner's dilemma," whereby detectives told each suspect that the others were talking and had implicated them in the crime (see Norris & Redlich, 2014). Following the lengthy interrogations, four of the five boys confessed to participating in the crime; Yusef Salaam did not, as his mother stopped the questioning by demanding a lawyer.

The teenagers' statements were inconsistent with one another and with details about the crime that were known to the police. In addition, no physical evidence linked the five youths to the assault; in fact, the initial forensic analysis failed to produce evidence matching any of the suspects and appeared to suggest that Meili had been assaulted by a single person. Still, investigators focused their attention on the five teens.

The investigation and ensuing prosecution occurred amidst a cultural firestorm that surrounded the case. In a city struggling with high levels of violent crime and racial tension, brimming with social and economic anxieties, the story of a young, successful white woman who was brutally attacked—supposedly by five Black and Latino teens—sparked local outrage and made headlines nationwide (Burns, 2011).

In this setting, despite the lack of physical evidence linking the teenagers to the attack, all five were convicted based largely on their incriminating statements. Their sentences ranged from 5 to 15 years in prison. The four younger men — Richardson, Santana, Salaam, and McCray — were released on parole after about six years. Wise, the oldest of the young men at age 16, was sentenced as an adult and remained in prison after the others were freed.

While incarcerated, Wise had a run-in with Matias Reyes, who was serving time in the same prison for a separate offense. Reyes eventually told officials that he had committed the rape and assault of Meili alone and that the five teenagers were innocent. Reyes gave a full confession that included details that were unknown to others involved in the case. DNA evidence from the case was tested and came back with a match for Reyes. In December 2002, the convictions of the Central Park Five were overturned. Wise was released from prison after serving almost 12 years. Santana, who had been convicted for selling drugs following his release on parole and sentenced as a repeat offender because of his previous conviction for the attack on Meili, was also released.

Politics, Social Structural Conditions, and the Criminal Legal System

As with all human endeavors, context is key when considering criminal legal practices and the outcomes they produce. In the United States, systems of justice are fundamentally political in nature. The actors and organizations that compose those systems exist as an element of, rather than being insulated from, our broader culture. Thus, sociopolitical factors and cultural forces play key roles in shaping the formation and practice of law and the administration of criminal justice. While many of these forces can be difficult to measure with precision — it is challenging (if not impossible) to accurately measure the direct effects of racism on wrongful convictions, for example, or how a suspect's socioeconomic status influenced a police investigation — we can draw upon the available data and research to raise important questions about how broad social and cultural factors influence miscarriages of justice.

Contextualizing Wrongful Convictions

In chapter 1, we noted that wrongful convictions are not new; to the contrary, they have existed as long as there have been systems of criminal justice. Throughout most of this volume, we nevertheless focus on errors of justice in the contemporary United States. Miscarriages of justice do not occur in isolation, and we must understand the broader social context in which they take place. As Lofquist (2014, p. 23) explains, discussions of wrongful convictions (as with many other topics in criminal justice) "must proceed from the recognition of three closely related and defining features of [the American criminal justice] system: that the United States has the largest penal system in history; that approximately 90% of all felony defendants are represented by indigent counsel; and that more than 95% of all felony convictions are produced by guilty pleas."

The United States incarcerates more people, and more per capita, than virtually any other country in the world. The Bureau of Justice Statistics reports that, in 2019, more than 1.4 million people were incarcerated in prisons (Carson, 2020) and more than 730,000 in jails (Zeng & Minton, 2021) throughout the United States. In addition, nearly 4.4 million people were under **community supervision** (Maruschak & Minton, 2020). Collectively, this means that approximately 6.5 million people, or roughly 1 in 47 individuals in the U.S. over the age of five, were under correctional supervision.[1]

It was not always this way. Fifty years ago, fewer than 200,000 people were imprisoned in the U.S. (Lofquist, 2014). Since the 1970s, a series of conscious decisions made by federal, state, and local lawmakers led to policies that have dramatically increased the size of the incarcerated population. The history of **mass incarceration** does not begin in the 1970s, however. Rather, the current era is the product of historical processes, including systems of racial control in the post-Civil War era, concerns about immigration and urbanization, political rhetoric that capitalized on the fear and unease of citizens, and more (e.g., Alexander, 2010; Beckett, 1997; Beckett & Sasson, 2004; Garland, 2001; Hinton, 2016). These processes and the policies that grew from them were not simply innocuous and organic, but instead were strategically developed. In the wake of the American Civil Rights Movement, politicians and cultural commentators took advantage of the concerns and fears of citizens, particularly whites, that involved race and social upheaval. They drew on historical stereotypes about Black criminality and developed a "social construction of crime" (Lofquist, 2014, p. 25) as a major threat to white society. This was part of what has been termed the "**Southern Strategy,**" which involved racialized images of not just who commits crimes, but also who de-

---

1. The U.S. Census estimates that the U.S. population age five and older was over 308 million in 2019.

pends most heavily on welfare and who benefits most from government support. The Southern Strategy became a core element of the political movement to redirect resources from social support to law enforcement and criminal justice, and was a driving force behind the wars on crime and drugs (Lofquist, 2014; Simon, 2007).

From the 1970s through the 2000s, criminal justice in the United States became increasingly punitive; law-and-order and crime control came to the fore, while the rights and protections of criminal defendants were cut back and social support systems seemingly fell to the wayside. From stepped-up police practices to criminalization of marginalized populations and harsher sentencing laws, including expanded use of the death penalty, the states and the federal government significantly enlarged the scope of the criminal legal system. As part of this process, issues that arguably are best considered as social, economic, and/or health problems — for example, drug addiction, homelessness, and mental health — were defined as criminal justice problems. As the reach of criminal justice actors and organizations expanded, the impact was disproportionately felt by already-marginalized individuals and communities, including the poor and racial minorities. These trends are perhaps seen most clearly through the lens of race, which permeates virtually every aspect of the criminal legal system in the United States. Racial and ethnic disparities are evident through the entirety of the criminal justice process. Cultural stereotypes have historically emphasized images of minorities, particularly Blacks, as criminals; lawmakers have targeted Black Americans and other minorities in determining what behaviors are criminalized; much research suggests that the police are more likely to stop, search, and arrest Blacks than whites; and sentencing outcomes have been found to be disproportionately harsh for minority defendants in many cases, particularly young Black men (e.g., Alexander, 2010; Epp et al., 2014; Gaston, 2019; Steffensmeier et al., 1998, 2017). Racialized perceptions and practices in the criminal legal system have had particularly negative consequences for communities of color. Indeed, the Sentencing Project reports that while 1 in 17 white men born in 2001 are likely to experience imprisonment in their lifetime, the odds are significantly higher for Latino men (1-in-6) and Black men (1-in-3) (Sentencing Project, n.d.).

Vice President Kamala Harris articulated the deep-rooted historical and social contexts relating to these issues when she spoke following the murder conviction of former Minneapolis police officer Derek Chauvin in April 2021. Chauvin, who is white, had knelt on the neck of George Floyd, a Black man, for more than nine minutes as Floyd repeatedly protested, "I can't breathe. I can't breathe." Floyd's death sparked national protests about police brutality, particularly affecting people of color. In the immediate aftermath of the jury's guilty verdict in Chauvin's trial, Vice President Harris said:

> America has a long history of systemic racism. Black Americans and Black men in particular have been treated throughout the course of our history as less than human. Black men are fathers and brothers and sons and uncles and grandfathers and friends and neighbors. Their lives must be valued in our education system, in our health care system, in our housing system, in our economic system, in our criminal justice system, in our nation. Full stop (*New York Times*, 2021).

To the extent that marginalized individuals and groups are disproportionately likely to come into contact with the criminal justice system and face legal sanctions, it stands to reason that the same individuals and groups are at greater risk of wrongful conviction. In the following sections, we discuss issues that relate specifically to race and miscarriages of justice.

The Racial History of American Criminal Justice

The **Thirteenth Amendment** to the United States Constitution was ratified in 1865 and states: "Neither slavery nor involuntary servitude, *except as a punishment for crime* whereof the party shall have been duly convicted, shall exist within the United States, or any place subject to their jurisdiction" (emphasis added). In the decades following the Thirteenth Amendment's passage, criminal punishments were often used to replace slave labor, such as through the use of penal farms, convict-leasing systems, and industrial prisons. Thus, as with many criminal legal practices in the United States, mass incarceration cannot be separated from broader social concerns about race, politics, and power.

- *The New Jim Crow*—A book by Michelle Alexander that traces the racialized history of criminal justice in the United States. Alexander argues that through practices and policies tied, for example, to the War on Drugs and mass incarceration, criminal justice operates as a modern form of a racial caste system.

- *13th*—A documentary directed by Ava DuVernay that features commentary from a number of scholars, politicians, and activists about the rise of mass incarceration and the criminal legal system's targeting of the Black community.

Race and Wrongful Convictions

United States Census estimates for 2019 indicate that 60.1% of the population identifies as white alone (not Hispanic or Latino), 13.4% identify as Black or African American, and 18.5% identify as Hispanic or Latino (United

States Census, n.d.). However, of the first 2,755 exonerations captured in the National Registry of Exonerations database, 49.7% involved a Black defendant, while whites accounted for 36.1%, Hispanics for 11.7%, and members of other racial groups for the remaining 2.3%.[2] The greatest disparity clearly exists for Blacks, who are vastly overrepresented among exonerees compared to the make-up of the general population. What accounts for such a large gap?

In part, the disproportionate number of Black exonerees is likely a function of other widespread disparities in criminal justice, some of which were highlighted above. The racialized patterns in exonerations mirror more general patterns within justice systems. For example, African Americans are more likely to be victims of homicide and are more likely to be imprisoned for murder than white Americans. To the extent that African Americans are more often arrested and convicted for murder, it follows that they also are more likely to be *wrongly* convicted of murder. Nevertheless, these broader racial disparities in criminal justice do not fully account for the vast differences we observe among exonerations. A 2017 report by the National Registry of Exonerations revealed that African Americans then accounted for 40% of persons incarcerated for murder, but 50% of murder exonerations. The discrepancy was even greater for sexual assault cases, in which Blacks accounted for 22% of those incarcerated but 59% of exonerees. The NRE report concluded that, compared to white suspects, Black suspects are approximately seven times more likely to be wrongly convicted of murder and three-and-a-half times more likely to be wrongly convicted of sexual assault than whites (Gross et al., 2017).

The reasons why Black suspects face an enhanced likelihood of wrongful conviction are numerous and varied. Core police practices may be contributors. Some research has shown that, for several reasons, including systemic practices and individual biases, Blacks are more likely than whites to be stopped, searched, and arrested by the police (Figures & Legewie, 2019; Epp et al., 2014). Several studies have demonstrated differential treatment of Blacks in charging, prosecution, conviction, and sentencing decisions (Steffensmeier et al., 1998, 2017). This research exists outside of the wrongful convictions context, but, as suggested above, it can be instructive regarding the explanations for racial disparities in the erroneous outcomes produced by justice systems. The broader

---

2. At the time of this writing, there were five NRE cases for which the race of the exoneree is not reported. We also note that we use the phrases "Hispanic" and/or "Latino" as used in the original sources, and thus do not refer to the gender-inclusive, "Latinx."

penal culture in which cases occur also may be relevant. One study that compared wrongful convictions to **"near misses"**—cases in which innocent individuals were arrested or charged with crimes but ultimately were not convicted—found that "[d]efendants in punitive states appear to be at an increased risk of erroneous convictions once indicted" (Gould et al., 2014, p. 497). It is possible that a link between punitiveness and wrongful convictions also increases racial disparities in wrongful convictions, since, as discussed above, punitive penal practices have historically been linked with racialized politics and social attitudes (Alexander, 2010).

Within the innocence literature, a number of issues (which are discussed in more depth throughout this book) also provide insight into racial disparities in exonerations. For example, psychological research has consistently found that cross-racial identifications—situations in which the victim and the perpetrator are members of different racial groups—are more likely to result in misidentifications (see chapter 3 of this book). Other scholarship has explored stereotype threat, which influences the way individuals may act when they feel as though they are being treated differently because of their social group identity. Such actions, in turn, may be interpreted as indicators of suspicion or deception, thus heightening the risk that they will be erroneously arrested (see chapter 4 of this book). As we discuss in the following chapters, understanding issues of this nature can lead to concrete policy suggestions to help alleviate some of the individualized sources of racial disparities, even if they do not fully eliminate the effects of race on wrongful convictions.

The known wrongful convictions for child sex abuse reveal an interesting and atypical pattern related to racial disparities. A majority of the exonerations, 181 of 294 (61.6%) in child sexual abuse cases currently reported in the NRE involved white defendants. The reasons for this imbalance are unclear, but one explanation may be that several of the cases involved group exonerations in which the wrongful convictions stemmed from the same or overlapping investigations involving primarily or exclusively white suspects. Another possible explanation is that while many stereotypes about criminality in the United States have involved Black men, middle-aged white men tend to fit cultural conceptions of sex offenders who prey upon children (e.g., Socia & Stamatel, 2010). Indeed, while much research has documented racial disparities in sentencing outcomes for Black defendants, whites may be more harshly sentenced for certain types of offenses, particularly, sexual battery and child abuse (Lehmann, 2020).

In addition to the race of the individuals suspected or convicted of criminal offenses, we must also consider how the race of victims might factor into wrongful convictions. The majority of violent crime in the U.S. is intra-racial — involving a perpetrator and victim of the same race — rather than inter-racial — involving a perpetrator and victim of different races. Yet, inter-racial crimes appear more likely to generate wrongful convictions. For example, the NRE report noted above revealed that although 42% of murder victims in the United States are white, 52% of the exonerees in murder cases were convicted of killing white victims. In addition, there may be an important interaction between the race of defendants and the race of victims; while only 15% of murders committed by Black individuals involved white victims, nearly one-third of Black exonerees in murder cases were convicted of killing whites (Gross et al., 2017). Such patterns, which suggest a race-of-victim-bias that is exacerbated in crimes allegedly involving Black defendants and white victims, are seen elsewhere in the criminal legal system, perhaps most notably in capital cases (Hoag, 2020; Phillips & Marceau, 2020). Since 1976, 296 Black defendants have been executed for the murder of white victims, while only 21 white defendants have been executed for the murder of Black victims (Death Penalty Information Center, n.d.).

Some of the racial patterns observed in exonerations also speak to another important issue — how the intersection of race and gender might further skew the administration of justice and contribute to wrongful convictions in the criminal legal process.

Intersections: Race, Gender, and the Lessons of History

Recall from chapter 1 the story of the Scottsboro Boys, nine Black teenagers who were wrongly convicted of raping two white women in 1931 (Acker, 2008). Consider, as well, the story of the Central Park Five described at the beginning of this chapter, involving five Black and Latino teens convicted of raping a white woman in 1989. These sets of cases, occurring decades apart, were both awash in racialized and gendered narratives concerning young men of color and white women. How is it that cases separated by more than a half-century (including the American Civil Rights Movement) bear such similarities? These occurrences are not exceptional; a number of prominent cases involved one or more Black defendants wrongly convicted of crimes against white victims, including those of George Whitmore, Jr. (convicted of attempted rape and assault in 1967 and linked with the infamous "Career Girl Murders") and the Ford Heights Four (four young Black men convicted of rape and murder in 1978).

Key Cases: George Whitmore, Jr. and the Ford Heights Four

- George Whitmore, Jr. falsely confessed to the 1964 assault and attempted rape of a Puerto Rican woman in Brooklyn, New York. He was convicted in 1966 and not exonerated until 1973. According to the National Registry of Exonerations (Warden, n.d.), "[t]he case probably would not have been prosecuted had Whitmore not also confessed to a sensational crime that occurred eight months earlier," the murder of two white women in what famously became known as the "Career Girl Murders." Those charges were dropped when the real killer was apprehended. The case was an inspiration for *Kojak*, a popular television show in the 1970s, and Whitmore's treatment served as an example in the U.S. Supreme Court's 1966 decision in *Miranda v. Arizona* (for more on *Miranda*, see chapter 4). Whitmore passed away in October 2012. For more on Whitmore, the Career Girl Murders, and the social and racial context surrounding the events, readers are referred to the book, *The Savage City: Race, Murder, and a Generation on the Edge*, by T. J. English.

- The Ford Heights Four refers to the 1978 wrongful convictions of four Black men, ages 20 to 25, in Chicago, Illinois. Dennis Williams, Verneal Jimerson, Kenneth Adams, and Willie Rainge were convicted of kidnapping a recently engaged white couple, raping the woman, and murdering both. Williams and Jimerson were sentenced to death, Rainge to life imprisonment, and Adams to 75 years in prison. The convictions were based largely on the statements of Paula Gray, an intellectually disabled 17-year-old who, after being held for two days, confessed to participating in the crimes and implicated the four men. Gray was also convicted and sentenced to 50 years. The four men were exonerated in 1996, and Gray was exonerated in 2002. For more on the case, readers are referred to the book, *A Promise of Justice*, by David Protess and Rob Warden.

We cannot say with certainty why such patterns continue to emerge in the American criminal legal system. As law professor Brandon Garrett (2011, p. 73) has observed, there is "evidence that prosecutors may pursue more serious charges in cases involving white victims and [B]lack men. There is evidence that white jurors may be less sympathetic to [B]lack defendants, and may be more likely to convict [B]lack defendants in crimes involving white victims." Yet, the explanations may run far deeper, rooted as they are in historical constructions of race, gender, and crime. Particularly troubling is the legacy of discrimination and abuses in cases involving Black men and white women in the United States. This legacy is perhaps best exemplified by the lynching era.

The height of the lynching era occurred in the United States during the late nineteenth and early twentieth centuries. Although lynchings took place throughout the country, they predominated in the South. And although lynchings were not exclusively carried out against Blacks, the overwhelming majority were. According to the NAACP (n.d.), more than 4,700 people were lynched from 1882 to 1968, and nearly three-fourths of the victims were Black. Similarly, Tolnay and Beck (1995) identified 2,805 lynchings between 1882 and 1930, most of which involved Black victims lynched at the hands of white mobs. Such extralegal actions were often justified as community responses to crimes that actually were committed, but the historical record suggests that in a great many cases they were not. Many lynchings were instead driven by narratives based on suspicion and fear, in particular, by sentiments harbored in white communities threatened by the image of predatory Black men. Tolnay and Beck (1995) categorized the justifications offered for lynchings in their analysis and concluded that in more than 80% of cases in which the lynching victim was Black, the reasons given were that the individual supposedly committed murder, assault, or engaged in some type of sexual transgression. These patterns appear to have driven lynchings in the South and elsewhere, including Colorado, Arizona, California, Illinois, New York, and other states, where allegations of a Black man's sexual transgressions against a white woman were especially damning (Leonard, 2002).

Lynchings typically were local affairs, reflecting the sentiment of whites in the community who perceived Black men as animalistic, sexual predators and white women as pure, virtuous, and in need of protection. While lynchings as traditionally conceived are largely events of the past, criminal justice in the United States is still highly localized, and the underlying perceptions and stereotypes that influenced lynchings — fundamental ideas about white superiority and Black inferiority, and about Black criminality and sexuality in particular — have endured throughout history. Both classic and contemporary writing have highlighted the pervasiveness of the "myth of the Black rapist," the "bestial Black man," or the "criminal Blackman" (Duru, 2004; Rome, 2004; Russell-Brown, 1998). Despite the fact that Black-on-white sexual crimes have always been relatively uncommon, such stereotypes were often maintained and spread through popular culture and media outlets (Gunning, 1996; Rome, 2004; Tolnay & Beck, 1995), continuing throughout the Civil Rights Movement and into the twenty-first century (Barak, 1996; Garland, 2010; Rome, 2004).

Fear and anxiety about crime in general, and about race and crime in particular, have long been a part of American culture. As a part of that culture, the criminal legal system has not been insulated from such forces. Racialized perceptions of crime have consequences; for example, neighborhoods with more Black residents may be perceived as dangerous independently of the actual incidence of crime (Quillian & Pager, 2001). In addition, the explanations offered by many white citizens for racially disparate outcomes in criminal justice, and their support for punitive law enforcement and sentencing policies, may be influenced by their more fundamental views about race and race relations (e.g., Hurwitz & Peffley, 1997; Mullinix & Norris, 2019; Peffley & Hurwitz, 2007). Racial stereotypes about crime are likely to influence more than public opinion, affecting criminal justice systems in matters including police investigations and arrests (e.g., Welch, 2007) and jurors' decision-making (e.g., Vogelman, 1993). Research also has shown that attitudes about race, gender, and age might interact to influence sentencing outcomes (e.g., Steffensmeier et al., 1998, 2017).

To the extent that views about race and gender influence public attitudes and criminal legal practices, they may also affect the production of wrongful convictions. Duru (2004) has argued that wrongful convictions are rooted in the racial history of the United States and its continuing legacy of unfairness and discrimination. While such a claim is difficult to examine empirically, some of the patterns we observe in the contemporary cases discussed above, as well as the wealth of empirical research on race and criminal justice more generally, suggest that there is an important element of truth in this argument.

Key Case: The Duke Lacrosse Case

The Duke lacrosse case provides something of a contrast to what has been discussed throughout this chapter. In 2006, three white lacrosse players from Duke University were accused of raping a young Black woman at a party. The men were never convicted—the North Carolina attorney general dropped all charges against them in 2007 and declared them innocent (CNN, 2007)—but the discourse surrounding the case addressed issues of race, class, privilege, politics, due process, sexual violence, and more. Coverage of the case initially portrayed the defendants as rich, privileged white men who took advantage of a young Black woman (Cauterucci, 2016). The prosecutor in the case, interim-District Attorney Mike Nifong, was running for reelection and may have used the case to try to gain favor with Black constituents (Block, 2016). On the other end, the defendants' privileged position as white student-athletes from an elite university who were able to secure high-quality defense counsel—privileges not available to most criminal defendants—may have saved them from wrongful conviction and incarceration. Regardless, Nifong was disbarred "for a battery of ethics violations" in the case after the North Carolina bar's disciplinary panel found him guilty of fraud, making false statements before a judge and before bar investigators, lying about evidence, and more (Setrakian & Francescani, 2009).

- *Fantastic Lies*—An ESPN *30 for 30* documentary released in 2016 about the Duke lacrosse case.

A Note on Gender and Wrongful Convictions

Our knowledge about wrongful convictions has grown tremendously in recent decades, but most of it has come from the most serious cases involving predominantly male defendants. This aligns with general patterns in criminal activity and incarceration, both of which are heavily skewed toward men, but an increasing proportion of the incarcerated population in the United States is composed of women. The Sentencing Project (n.d.) reports that "[b]etween 1980 and 2019, the number of incarcerated women increased by more than 700%," from approximately 26,000 to more than 222,000.

Currently, at least 245 of the 2,774 National Registry of Exonerations cases involve female exonerees. More interesting than the overall number, however, are some of the patterns among these cases. While women constitute less than 9% of the NRE cases overall, they account for nearly 13% of child sex abuse exonerations (38 of 294) and more than half of the child abuse exonerations that do not include allegations of sexual abuse (6/11). Furthermore, 10 of the 19 **Shaken Baby Syndrome (SBS)** cases — all murder or child abuse convictions — in the NRE involved female exonerees. The science around SBS has developed significantly in recent years, leading to a number of exonerations in cases of suspected SBS or Abusive Head Trauma, although there have been some concerns raised about the accuracy of available data and validity of their analyses (Johnson et al., 2020; Tuerkheimer, 2009; Weiner et al., 2021), an issue we revisit in chapter 14.

It also is important to consider the potential influence of race in the wrongful convictions of women. For example, of the 245 female exonerees, 57.1% are white and 28.7% are Black. However, of the 63 women wrongly convicted of drug possession or sale, 27 of them (42.9%) were Black. This may speak to much broader issues of economic disadvantage, drug use, and the disproportionate impact of the War on Drugs on Black communities in general, and on Black women in particular (e.g., Bush-Baskette, 2013; Sudbury, 2002).

Battered woman syndrome is a psychological construct predicated on a theory that began to receive prominence with the publication in 1979 of Dr. Lenore Walker's book, *The Battered Woman*. Walker posited that some women endure repeat cycles of violence from intimate partners, consisting of three stages — a tension-building stage, an acute-battering incident, and then a period in which the abuser is contrite and pledges to mend their ways. As a result, Walker theorized, the abused women can experience a sense of "learned helplessness," or psychological paralysis, which severely limits their ability to leave the battering relationship (Walker, 1979; see also Walker, 2009). The theory is controversial, with some critics claiming that it is not grounded in rigorous science (e.g., Angel, 2015; Coughlin, 1994; Faigman & Wright, 1997). Testimony about the battered woman syndrome began to be admissible in some state courts in the early 1980s in connection with self-defense claims raised by women who were charged with the murder or manslaughter of their intimate partner. The testimony was considered relevant to explain to jurors why a woman who had suffered repeated abuse at the hands of the deceased (alleged) batterer would stay year after year in the relationship and not leave. If jurors could not understand why a woman would remain and endure repeated beatings, they might be inclined to disbelieve her testimony that she was forced to kill her partner in self-defense, rather than in anger or retaliation, as the prosecution might claim. Psychologists or other professionals thus were permitted to offer expert testimony to educate jurors about the battered woman syndrome, and thus bolster the credibility of the woman claiming self-defense. In some jurisdictions the testimony also was admissible to help jurors understand why the accused woman might reasonably fear that she was in imminent danger when she took her partner's life (e.g., *State v. Allery*, 1984; *State v. Kelly*, 1984; *State v. Leidholm*, 1983; *Witt v. State*, 1995).

Expert testimony about the battered woman syndrome now is admissible in courts in all of the states to buttress claims of self-defense (Champaign, 2010). However, before the theory was developed and expert testimony concerning the "learned helplessness" phenomenon was admitted in court, countless women who faced murder or manslaughter charges lacked the opportunity to support their self-defense claims when they killed an intimate partner who allegedly had repeatedly abused them. We cannot know how many juries erroneously convicted women of homicide charges when they rejected legitimate self-defense claims. We do know that some women have been wrongfully convicted, and later exonerated, when juries failed to believe that they acted in self-defense and instead found them guilty of serious crimes. This happened to Lydia Salce, in New York (National Registry of Exonerations, n.d.a), and Teresa Thomas, in Ohio (National Registry of Exonerations, n.d.b), and well could have happened to many others (Acker & Wu, 2020). In a somewhat related vein, Ohio Governor Richard Celeste commuted the prison sentences of multiple individuals as he was leaving office in late 1990, including 25 women who had been convicted of killing or assaulting their alleged abusers (Kobil, 1991).

As with race, sex and gender play a pivotal role in criminal justice, including wrongful convictions. Yet, only recently has scholarship begun to truly focus on the role gender might play in the production, detection, and remediation of errors. It is important that work of this nature continues, especially given the recent growth and development of feminist scholarship in law and criminology, "which theorizes how gender shapes the organization of crime, law, and criminal justice" (Webster & Miller, 2014/2015, p. 978). This research is ongoing (e.g., Konvisser, 2012; Lewis & Sommervold, 2014/2015), but much remains to be learned about the factors that contribute to the wrongful conviction of women and the ensuing consequences.

Women on Death Row

As with incarceration in general, the vast majority of individuals on death row in the U.S. are men. As of October 2020, 51 women were on death rows nationwide. Two women previously sentenced to death have been exonerated.

- Sabrina Butler was convicted in 1990 of killing her nine-month-old son in Mississippi and sentenced to death. Her conviction was reversed on appeal, and she was acquitted at her retrial in 1995, making her the first woman to be exonerated after receiving a death sentence. Her case is discussed in more detail in chapter 10 of this book.

- Debra Milke was convicted in Arizona in 1990 of murder, child abuse, kidnapping, and conspiracy. The case revolved around the death of her four-year-old son, Christopher, who went to a shopping mall with a family friend, James Styers. The boy allegedly disappeared at the mall and was later found about 20 miles away in the Phoenix desert. He had been shot to death. A friend of Styers, Roger Scott, was an alcoholic who suffered brain damage. Scott had shown up at the mall and helped police find the body. He said that Styers and Milke killed Christopher to cash in on a life insurance policy. Despite a lack of physical evidence linking Milke to the murder, she was convicted and sentenced to death. An intensive reinvestigation uncovered evidence of misconduct by the lead investigator who had testified about Milke's supposed confession. Milke was released on bond in 2013, and she was exonerated in 2015.

Moving Forward:
Further Exploring the Structural
Sources of Wrongful Convictions

Throughout the remainder of this book, we will focus on specific issues that contribute to wrongful convictions (e.g., eyewitness misidentification, false confessions, forensic errors), examine legal issues involving how errors are discovered and overturned, and explore the consequences of wrongful convictions for exonerees and others. There is good reason for concentrating on these issues; research has uncovered much information about how and why errors of justice occur, and the Innocence Movement has helped generate a number of specific reforms to improve the accuracy of the criminal legal process. However, we must bear in mind that none of these issues—police investigatory practices, courtroom procedures, reentry after incarceration, and many others—exists in a vacuum. Rather, they are connected to fundamental and deeply rooted social, cultural, and political systems. More specifically, as we have discussed throughout this chapter, criminal legal practices in the United States cannot be divorced from issues of race, power, and politics.

We also might ponder the role that the Innocence Movement can potentially play in wider criminal and social justice reform efforts. Many wrongful conviction cases can be viewed as civil rights cases, as they often deal with issues of race, poverty, mental health, disparate resources, and more (Norris, 2017). These cases thus may serve as a springboard for innocence advocates to address criminal justice issues that extend beyond factual errors. For example, the Innocence Project has supported reform on issues such as bail (Innocence Project, 2020) and police accountability and transparency (Innocence Project, n.d.). These issues are related to wrongful convictions in important ways, but are not exclusively the domain of the Innocence Movement. They instead concern broadly targeted reforms that are designed to address core disparities in the justice system based on poverty, class, and race. To the extent that wrongful conviction cases provide a lens through which to view more widespread problems in the criminal legal process, the Innocence Movement can provide an important platform for advocates seeking to make progress on issues involving fundamental civil rights and social justice.

Key Terms and Concepts

- **Community supervision**: also referred to as community corrections, this refers to sentences that involve supervision in the community, rather than incarceration in a prison or jail; includes probation and parole
- **Mass incarceration**: the phrase used to rely on the United States' extensive use of incarceration as a form of criminal sanction
- **Southern Strategy**: a strategy used largely by Republican politicians in the mid-twentieth century to appeal to Southern white voters by emphasizing issues of racial threat and states' rights
- **Thirteenth Amendment**: the amendment to the U.S. Constitution that abolished the practice of slavery and did away with involuntary servitude, "except as a punishment for crime"

- **Near misses:** cases in which innocent individuals were arrested or charged with crimes but ultimately were not convicted
- **Shaken Baby Syndrome (SBS):** a form of child abuse that may result in severe brain damage; also referred to as "abuse head trauma"
- **Battered woman syndrome:** a psychological construct predicated on a controversial theory that posits that some women endure repeat cycles of violence from intimate partners and can experience a sense of psychological paralysis which severely limits their ability to leave the battering relationship

Discussion Questions

1. What do you see as the key similarities and differences between the cases of the Scottsboro Boys and the Central Park Five?

2. What do you make of the argument of scholars like Michelle Alexander that the criminal justice system in the United States evolved as a form of racial control?

3. What types of reforms to policy and practice do you think might help alleviate the influence of cultural stereotypes in the criminal legal system?

4. What role, if any, do you think the Innocence Movement will play in the broader fight for equality and civil rights in the United States?

References

Acker, J. R. (2008). *Scottsboro and its legacy: The cases that challenged American legal and social justice*. Praeger.

Acker, J. R., & Wu, S. (2020). "I did it but … I didn't": When rejected affirmative defenses produce wrongful convictions. *Nebraska Law Review, 98*, 578–642.

Alexander, M. (2010). *The new Jim Crow: Mass incarceration in the age of colorblindness*. The New Press.

Angel, M. (2015). The myth of battered woman syndrome. *Temple Political & Civil Rights Law Review, 24*, 301–312.

Barak, G. (1996). *Media, criminal justice, and mass culture*. Criminal Justice Press.

Beckett, K. (1997). *Making crime pay*. Oxford University Press.

Beckett, K., & Sasson, T. (2004). *The politics of injustice: Crime and punishment in America* (2nd ed.). Sage.

Block, J. (2016, December 29). 10 years later, the Duke lacrosse rape case still stings. *HuffPost*. https://www.huffpost.com/entry/duke-lacrosse-rape-espn-30-for-30_n_56e07e33e4b065e2e3d486f7.

Burns, S. (2011). *The Central Park Five: A chronicle of a city wilding*. Alfred A. Knopf.

Bush-Baskette, S. (2013). The war on drugs as a war against Black women. In M. Chesney-Lind & L. Pasko (Eds.), *Girls, women, and crime: Selected readings* (pp. 175–184). Sage.

Carson, E. A. (2020). *Prisoners in 2019*. U.S. Department of Justice, Bureau of Justice Statistics. https://www.bjs.gov/content/pub/pdf/p19.pdf.

Cauterucci, C. (2016, March 11). An new ESPN doc exposes the real villains in the Duke lacrosse case. *Slate*. https://slate.com/human-interest/2016/03/a-new-espn-film-exposes-the-real-villains-in-the-duke-lacrosse-case.html.

Champaign, L. (2010). Eleventh annual review of gender and sexuality law: Criminal law chapter: Battered woman syndrome. *Georgetown Journal of Gender & Law, 11*, 59–76.

Coughlin, A. M. (1994). Excusing women. *California Law Review, 82*, 1–93.

CNN. (2007, April 11). N.C. attorney general: Duke players 'innocent.' CNN. https://www.cnn.com/2007/LAW/04/11/cooper.transcript/index.html#:~:text=RALEIGH%2C%20North%20Carolina%20(CNN),the%20charges%20are%20being%20dropped.

Death Penalty Information Center. (n.d.). *Race and the death penalty by the numbers*. https://deathpenaltyinfo.org/policy-issues/race/race-and-the-death-penalty-by-the-numbers.

Duru, N. J. (2004). The Central Park Five, the Scottsboro Boys, and the myth of the bestial Black man. *Cardozo Law Review, 25*, 1315–1346.

Epp, C. R., Maynard-Moody, S., & Haider-Markel, D. P. (2014). *Pulled over: How police stops define race and citizenship*. The University of Chicago Press.

Faigman, D. L., & Wright, A. J. (1997). The battered woman syndrome in the age of science. *Arizona Law Review, 39*, 67–115.

Figures, K. D., & Legewie, J. (2019). Visualizing police exposure by race, gender, and age in New York City. *Socius, 5*, 1–2.

Garland, D. (2001). *The culture of control: Crime and social order in contemporary society*. University of Chicago Press.

Garland, D. (2010). *Peculiar institution: America's death penalty in an age of abolition*. Belknap Press.

Garrett, B. L. (2011). *Convicting the innocent: Where criminal prosecutions go wrong*. Harvard University Press.

Gaston, S. (2019). Enforcing race: A neighborhood-level explanation of Black-white differences in drug arrests. *Crime & Delinquency, 65*, 499–526.

Gould, J. B., Carrano, J., Leo, R. A., & Hail-Jares, K. (2014). Predicting erroneous convictions. *Iowa Law Review, 99*, 471–522.

Gross, S. R., Possley, M., & Stephens, K. (2017, March 7). *Race and wrongful convictions in the United States.* National Registry of Exonerations. https:// www.law.umich.edu/special/exoneration/Documents/Race_and_ Wrongful_Convictions.pdf.

Gunning, S. (1996). *Race, rape, and lynching: The red record of American literature, 1890–1912.* Oxford University Press.

Hinton, E. (2016). *From the war on poverty to the war on crime: The making of mass incarceration in America.* Harvard University Press.

Hoag, A. (2020). Valuing Black lives: A case for ending the death penalty. *Columbia Human Rights Law Review, 51*, 983–1007.

Hurwitz, J., & Peffley, M. (1997). Public perceptions of race and crime: The role of racial stereotypes. *American Journal of Political Science, 41*, 375–401.

The Innocence Project. (n.d.). Fight for police accountability and transparency in all 50 states. https://innocenceproject.org/petitions/police-accountability/.

The Innocence Project. (2020, January 3). Innocence Project statement on New York's new pretrial laws. https://innocenceproject.org/innocence-project-statement-on-new-yorks-new-pretrial-laws/.

Johnson, M. B., Baker, C., Prempeh, B., & Lewis, S. R. (2020). Shaken baby syndrome/abusive head trauma: Wrongful conviction risks, mis-information effects, and psychological consultation. *Journal of Forensic Psychology Research and Practice, 20*, 290–304.

Kobil, D. T. (1991). Do the paperwork or die: Clemency, Ohio style? *Ohio State Law Journal, 52*, 655–704.

Konvisser, Z. D. (2012). Psychological consequences of wrongful conviction in women and the possibility of positive change. *DePaul Journal for Social Justice, 5*, 221–294.

Lehmann, P. S. (2020). Race, ethnicity, crime type, and the sentencing of violent felony offenders. *Crime & Delinquency, 66*, 770–805.

Leonard, S. J. (2002). *Lynching in Colorado 1859–1919.* University Press of Colorado.

Lewis, A. L., & Sommervold, S. L. (2014/2015). Death, but is it murder? The role of stereotypes and cultural perceptions in the wrongful convictions of women. *Albany Law Review, 78*, 1035–1058.

Lofquist, W. S. (2014). Finding the causes in the contexts: Structural sources of wrongful convictions. In A. D. Redlich, J. R. Acker, R. J. Norris, & C. L. Bonventre (Eds.), *Examining wrongful convictions: Stepping back, moving forward* (pp. 19–33). Carolina Academic Press.

Maruschak, L. M., & Minton, T. D. (2020). *Correctional populations in the United States, 2017–2018.* U.S. Department of Justice, Bureau of Justice Statistics. https://www.bjs.gov/content/pub/pdf/cpus1718.pdf.

Mullinix, K. J., & Norris, R. J. (2019). Pulled-over rates, causal attributions, and trust in police. *Political Research Quarterly, 72,* 420–434.

NAACP. (n.d.). *History of lynchings.* https://www.naacp.org/history-of-lynchings/.

National Registry of Exonerations. (n.d.a). Lydia Salce. http://www.law.umich.edu/special/exoneration/Pages/casedetail.aspx?caseid=4691.

National Registry of Exonerations. (n.d.b). Teresa Thomas. http://www.law.umich.edu/special/exoneration/Pages/casedetail.aspx?caseid=4124.

The New York Times. (2021, April 20). Biden and Harris on the Chauvin trial verdict. https://www.nytimes.com/2021/04/20/us/politics/biden-harris-chauvin-verdict-transcript.html?action=click&module=Spotlight&pgtype=Homepage.

Norris, R. J. (2017). *Exonerated: A history of the innocence movement.* NYU Press.

Norris, R. J., & Redlich, A. D. (2014). Seeking justice, compromising truth? Criminal admissions and the prisoner's dilemma. *Albany Law Review, 77,* 1005–1038.

Peffley, M., & Hurwitz, J. (2007). Persuasion and resistance: Race and the death penalty in America. *American Journal of Political Science, 51,* 996–1012.

Phillips, S., & Marceau, J. (2020). Whom the State kills. *Harvard Civil Rights-Civil Liberties Law Review, 55,* 585–656.

Quillian, L., & Pager, D. (2001). Black neighbors, higher crime? The role of racial stereotypes in evaluations of neighborhood crime. *American Journal of Sociology, 107,* 717–767.

Rome, D. (2004). *Black demons: The media's depiction of the African American male criminal stereotype.* Praeger.

Russell-Brown, K. (1998). *The color of crime: Racial hoaxes, white fear, Black protectionism, police harassment, and other macroaggressions.* NYU Press.

The Sentencing Project. (n.d.). *Criminal justice facts.* https://www.sentencingproject.org/criminal-justice-facts/.

Setrakian, L., & Francescani, C. (2009, February 10). Former Duke prosecutor Nifong disbarred. ABC News. https://abcnews.go.com/TheLaw/story?id=3285862&page=1.

Simon, J. (2007). *Governing through crime: How the war on crime transformed American democracy and created a culture of fear.* Oxford University Press.

Socia, K. M., & Stamatel, J. P. (2010). Assumptions and evidence behind sex offender laws: Registration, community notification, and residence restrictions. *Sociology Compass, 4,* 1–20.

State v. Allery, 682 P.2d 312 (Wash. 1984).

State v. Kelly, 478 A.2d 364 (N.J. 1984).

State v. Leidholm, 334 N.W.2d 811 (N.D. 1983).

Steffensmeier, D., Painter-Davis, N., & Ulmer, J. (2017). Intersectionality of race, ethnicity, gender, and age on criminal punishment. *Sociological Perspectives, 60*, 810–833.

Steffensmeier, D., Ulmer, J., & Kramer, J. (1998). The interaction of race, gender, and age in criminal sentencing: The punishment cost of being young, Black, and male. *Criminology, 36*, 763–798.

Sudbury, J. (2002). Celling Black bodies: Black women in the global prison industrial complex. *Feminist Review, 70*, 57–74.

Tolnay, S. E., & Beck, E. M. (1995). *A festival of violence: An analysis of Southern lynchings, 1882–1930.* University of Illinois Press.

Tuerkheimer, D. (2009). The next innocence project: Shaken baby syndrome and the criminal courts. *Washington University Law Review, 87*, 1–58.

United States Census. (n.d.). *Quick facts.* https://www.census.gov/quickfacts/fact/table/US/PST045219.

Vogelman, L. (1992). The Big Black Man Syndrome: The Rodney King trial and the use of racial stereotypes in the courtroom. *Fordham Urban Law Journal, 20*, 570–578.

Walker, L. E. (1979). *The battered woman.* Harper & Row.

Walker, L. E. A. (2009). *The battered woman syndrome* (3rd ed). Springer Publishing Co.

Warden, R. (n.d.). George Whitmore, Jr. The National Registry of Exonerations. https://www.law.umich.edu/special/exoneration/Pages/casedetailpre1989.aspx?caseid=358.

Webster, E., & Miller, J. (2014/2015). Gendering and racing wrongful conviction: Intersectionality, "normal crimes," and women's experiences of miscarriage of justice. *Albany Law Review, 78*, 973–1033.

Weiner, M., Groisberg, S., Diah, P., Mariano, M., & Romalin, J. (2021). A commentary on Johnson et al.'s "Shaken baby syndrome/abusive head trauma: Wrongful conviction risks, mis-information effects, and psychological consultation." *Journal of Forensic Psychology Research and Practice.* http://doi.org/10.1080/24732850.2021.1892439.

Welch, K. (2007). Black criminal stereotypes and racial profiling. *Journal of Contemporary Criminal Justice, 23*, 276–288.

Witt v. State, 892 P.2d 132 (Wyo. 1995).

Zeng, Z., & Minton, T. D. (2021). *Jail inmates in 2019.* U.S. Department of Justice, Bureau of Justice Statistics. https://www.bjs.gov/content/pub/pdf/ji19.pdf.

Chapter 3

Eyewitness Identification

Learning Objectives

After reading this chapter, you should be able to:

- Distinguish, in general, which variables related to eyewitness identifications are under the control of the criminal justice system and which are not.
- Understand the implications for an accurate identification when the eyewitness and the culprit are of different races.
- Appreciate how the design and administration of suspect lineups influence identification accuracy.
- Appreciate the malleability of eyewitness confidence and the fallibility of human memory and the implications of both for accurate identifications.
- Understand the extent (and limitations) of the Sixth Amendment right to counsel at corporeal and non-corporeal identifications.
- List the reliability criteria set forth by the U.S. Supreme Court for determining the admissibility of identification testimony.
- Appreciate that while Supreme Court cases interpreting the U.S. Constitution determine the minimal legal requirements governing the admissibility of eyewitness identifications, other sources of law, including legislation, can establish additional procedural guidelines or requirements to help bolster reliability.
- Discuss the recommended changes to police identification procedures.

Case Study: Robert Foxworth

On May 23, 1991, a group of men entered the apartment of Kenneth McLean in Boston, Massachusetts. They bound him with duct tape, but he escaped and ran. Two men chased him into the street, and one shot him. Two teenagers, Derek Hobson and Anthony McAfee, were on the street at the time of the shooting and described two Black men as being involved. The shooter apparently had a "long curl down the center of his hair down the nape of his neck" (Otterbourg, 2021).

A detective received a separate tip that four men were involved and put together a photo array to show the 15-year-old Hobson. On June 17, Hobson picked out 23-year-old Robert Foxworth, the only individual in the photos with long hair, as the shooter. Weeks later, Hobson was shown another photo array. He again selected Foxworth, whose photo was the only one repeated from the initial array and who once again was the only person shown with a long strand of hair. Foxworth was arrested on July 11.

Police later arrested two other men, Troy Logan and Ronnie Christian. Foxworth's trial was delayed so the three men could be tried together. Logan earlier had identified Foxworth in a photo array and told police that he, Foxworth, and another man had gone to McLean's apartment to purchase drugs. According to Logan's story, Foxworth and McLean argued, and Logan left, but he saw Foxworth leave the apartment and then reenter with a gun. Logan said he heard shots but that he did not see the shooting.

Hobson served as the key witness for the prosecution, despite the fact that he had not accurately described Foxworth to the police. He "fail[ed] to mention, for example, that Foxworth had noticeable protruding teeth." He also admitted that he had not seen the shooter's face, only his back, and that he selected Foxworth because of the "tail," in reference to the long strand of hair he had observed on the shooter. Hobson's testimony was inconsistent, in that he initially stated that he had only seen the shooter's back, but then claimed that he had a side-view that allowed him to make an identification. He ultimately said that he was "80 percent sure" in making his identification (Otterbourg, 2021). McAfee, the other teen who was on the street at the time of the shooting, said that Logan had handed a black object to the shooter. Logan's statements were read to the jury, but instead of naming Foxworth as the man with the gun, Foxworth's name was redacted from the statement and "Mr. X" was substituted. Foxworth's name was redacted because Logan did not take the witness stand at the joint trial, so the defense did not have an opportunity to cross-examine him.

Several alibi witnesses testified on Foxworth's behalf, but Foxworth nevertheless was convicted of second-degree murder. He was sentenced to life in prison in March 1992. The other men tried with him, Logan and Christian, were both acquitted.

Throughout the lengthy appellate process, the defense uncovered new information which suggested that McLean's killing was part of a dispute between cocaine dealers. In addition, McAfee recanted his testimony, and Hobson recanted his identification of Foxworth, stating that police and prosecutors pressured him into making it. Additional information was uncovered suggesting that Logan was involved in the shooting, but not Foxworth. After a protracted battle, Foxworth's motion for a new trial was granted in January 2021 and the district attorney's office dismissed the charges. Foxworth had been incarcerated for nearly 30 years.

Eyewitness Errors: Overview and Research

According to the National Registry of Exonerations, nearly 30% of the 2,749 exonerations documented through February 2021 involved a mistaken eyewitness identification. Furthermore, the Innocence Project reports that almost 70% of the first 375 DNA-based exoneration cases involved an eyewitness misidentification. These numbers suggest that eyewitnesses are less reliable than one might think, a conclusion that is also supported by scientific research. A recent review of eyewitness research summarized the findings of both laboratory studies — those in which voluntary participants are exposed to a simulated crime and researchers know the identity of the "culprit" — and field studies — examinations of lineup results in real cases. In lab studies, the overall rate at which witnesses identified a **filler**, or a person in the lineup who is *not* the culprit, was nearly 28%. Across 11 published field studies, the overall rate of filler identifications was nearly 24%. In other words, almost one-in-four witnesses who viewed a lineup chose an innocent person (Wells et al., 2020).

As psychologist and prominent eyewitness researcher Gary Wells noted, while the "discoveries of wrongful convictions from mistaken identifications ... have been a surprise and shock to the legal system and the public, psychological scientists have been less surprised. This is because psychological scientists were 'blowing the whistle' on the eyewitness identification problem for decades prior to forensic DNA testing" (Wells, 2020, p. 1316). Wells is correct, of course; knowledge about eyewitness errors is not new. In fact, psychologist Hugo Munsterberg (1908) wrote about how unreliable witnesses may be and how they can have a negative effect on the outcomes of trials in the early 1900s. Systematic research since the 1970s has uncovered many of the factors that generate mistaken identifications. Some of these factors — for example, whether a crime occurred in the dark of night or under a brilliant sun, whether a witness has 20/20 vision and was standing five feet from the offender or instead is hopelessly nearsighted and was 50 feet away, or whether a suspect is quickly located and an identification attempt is made within minutes of the crime or several months pass before an attempted identification is possible — are beyond the control of the justice system. Such factors are called "**estimator variables**." On the other hand, some factors may be under the control of the justice system. Examples of so-called "**system variables**" (Wells, 1978) include the size of a lineup and the number of pictures used in a photo array, what the police say to a witness before and after an attempted identification, and whether a defense lawyer is allowed to be present during an identification procedure. Both estimator and system variables are vital to understanding how and why witnesses make mistakes and what can be done to improve witness accuracy.

Estimator Variables

Estimator variables are factors that are beyond the control of the criminal justice system. Many characteristics of a situation can influence the likelihood of a witness making an error, but cannot be controlled by those who work in the system. These characteristics include obvious visual issues such as the lighting, the distance from which a witness viewed an event, or the length of time a witness was exposed to the perpetrator. For instance, a witness who sees a crime at night from 100 yards away may be more likely to make an error than one who witnesses a crime up close in broad daylight. But other details of a criminal event may alter a witness's ability to accurately remember and recall information in important ways. For example, much research has explored the "**weapon-focus effect**," which suggests that in crimes involving a weapon, witnesses may have difficulty remembering characteristics of the perpetrator because their focus is on the weapon rather than on remembering details of the offender's appearance. Indeed, while some research has not found evidence of a weapon-focus effect, several studies have found that the presence of a weapon may negatively affect the accuracy of identifications as well as the accuracy of a witness's descriptions of the perpetrator (Carlson et al., 2017; Kocab & Sporer, 2016).

The presence of a weapon in addition to other situational characteristics, such as the type and severity of the crime, may increase the fear a witness feels and thus the stress they are under. A number of research studies have found that witnessing violent events can adversely affect human memory (Deffenbacher et al., 2004).

In addition to characteristics of the crime and the situation, individual characteristics of the witness may affect the reliability of an identification. One such factor is the witness's age. A review of psychological studies on this topic found that, when the suspect was present in the lineup, young adults were more accurate in their identifications than both children and older adults. Importantly, they were also better at *not* making identifications in lineups when the suspect was *not* present; in other words, they were less likely to make a false identification when the culprit was not included in the lineup. The review also found similar age-related differences among children: older children were more accurate in their identifications than younger ones (Fitzgerald & Price, 2015).

Another important characteristic is the race of both the witness and the culprit. Many researchers have studied what is often called the "own-race bias" (Meissner & Brigham, 2001) or the "other-race effect" (Wells & Olson, 2001), both of which refer to the tendency of people to be better at remembering, distinguishing between, and identifying faces of individuals of the same race. This means that witnesses may be more likely to make an error when the culprit is someone of a different race than they are. In fact, of the first 235 DNA exonerations that involved an eyewitness error reported by the Innocence Project, 41% were **cross-racial identifications**, despite the fact that inter-racial crime is relatively uncommon (West & Meterko, 2016). While the exact reasons are unclear, research has generally found that, when identifying culprits of the same race, witnesses have higher rates of accurate identifications and lower rates of "false alarms" (identifications of the wrong suspects). Some studies also suggest that white witnesses may be more likely than witnesses of other racial groups to show an own-race bias (Meissner & Brigham, 2001).

Finally, there also may be differences in how men and women remember events that they have witnessed. A recent lab study in which participants viewed a video involving an encounter with a stranger found that females more accurately recalled details about the individual stranger, but males more accurately remembered details about the surrounding environment (Longstaff & Belz, 2020).

System Variables

Imagine the following scenario: Police receive word that a young, African-American man with a dark complexion committed a robbery. After arresting a suspect who fits the general description of the perpetrator, they place him in a lineup. There are six men in the lineup: one is Hispanic; two are African-

American but are significantly older than the described perpetrator; two are African-American but have significantly lighter skin than the suspect; and one is the young arrestee. In this situation, which person is a witness most likely to choose from the lineup?

While it is impossible to say for sure, it can reasonably be predicted that the young Black man arrested by the police will be chosen as the perpetrator, owing to nothing other than the composition of the lineup and how it was structured. How a lineup is structured is one of the many factors under the control of the criminal justice system that can influence an identification. Such factors are referred to as system variables.

The importance of lineup structure for understanding eyewitness identification errors owes, in part, to how witnesses tend to make judgments when they attempt to identify a perpetrator from the lineup's participants. Specifically, witnesses often make a "**relative judgment,**" meaning they are apt to choose the person in the lineup who most closely resembles the offender relative to the other individuals presented (Lindsay & Wells, 1985; Wells, 1984). If it turns out that the suspect in the lineup is the actual perpetrator, relative judgment may not lead to a misidentification. If, however, the actual offender is not in the lineup, using relative judgment might lead a witness to mistakenly identify a lineup member who is *not* actually the perpetrator, simply because the individual selected looks *most like* the person that the witness remembers seeing. Thus, in the above scenario, a witness might be inclined to pick the arrestee not because he matches their actual memory of the perpetrator, but simply because he looks more like the perpetrator than the other members of the lineup. Such a tendency is clearly problematic, as there will always be one lineup member who more closely resembles the perpetrator than the others.

Due to these decision-making tendencies, the way a lineup is designed and implemented can influence the reliability of an identification. Traditionally, lineups were conducted with the suspect and fillers presented simultaneously and a witness viewing all members in the lineup at the same time. A **simultaneous lineup** in which the suspect stands out from the fillers might encourage the witness to choose the suspect, even if they do not match the witness's recollection of the offender. A review of research on the issue of suspect-filler similarity found that lineups characterized by relatively low similarity were more likely to result in witnesses making an identification of the suspect, regardless of whether or not the suspect was guilty. Furthermore, identifications of guilty suspects were approximately the same for moderate and high-similarity lineups, but identifications of innocent suspects were reduced when similarity was the highest (Fitzgerald et al., 2013). This suggests that if police have mistakenly arrested an innocent person and conduct a lineup in which the innocent suspect stands out from the fillers, the procedure is more likely to result in a mistaken identification.

Another important system variable that may affect an identification is the behavior of the officer who administers the lineup. In particular, how an officer asks questions, provides information or feedback, or even makes gestures may influence the thinking and decision-making of a witness. For example, imagine a situation where the suspect is placed in the fifth position in a lineup but the witness chooses number three. The officer administering the lineup then says to the witness, "Are you sure? Take your time. Look again." This type of feedback might plant a seed of doubt in the witness's mind and encourage them to change course. On the other hand, consider a scenario in which the witness did choose number five, and the officer responded by saying, "Good, that's who we thought it was." Rather than instilling doubt, the officer is likely to have boosted the witness's confidence in their choice, which may carry over into future identifications, including their testimony if the case goes to trial. Thus, the behavior of the law enforcement officials administering the lineup can have a major impact on the outcome of an identification that continues beyond the immediate procedure. Interestingly, at least one recent study has found that administering lineups online via a computer, rather than in-person, may help reduce such biases. Such an approach may also help promote blind administration, an important safeguard we discuss later, which ensures that the officer overseeing the identification procedure does not know who the actual suspect is, thus preventing even inadvertent positive or negative feedback being delivered to the witness (Pica et al., 2018).

It also is worth noting that identifications may be conducted "live," sometimes called "corporeal" administration, in which the witness views lineup members in-person. Alternatively, identifications can be conducted using several photographs (often called "**photo-arrays**") or with computer-simulated images. While some have suggested that **live lineups** are superior — known as the "live-superiority hypothesis" — scientific evidence does not support such a conclusion (Wells et al., 2020, p. 7). For this reason, and due to the practical challenges associated with properly conducting and controlling a live lineup, Fitzgerald and colleagues (2018, p. 307) concluded, "live lineups are rarely the best option in practice."

Witness Confidence

Witness confidence has been a widely researched aspect of eyewitness identification and can be considered both a system and estimator variable. A witness will go into an identification with some degree of confidence in their ability to pick out the perpetrator; this pre-identification confidence is beyond the control of the justice system. On the other hand, as noted earlier, the nature of the identification procedure and the behavior of the officials involved may serve to increase or decrease the witness's confidence. Research generally suggests that witnesses' pre-identification confidence is a poor predictor of whether their identifications in fact are accurate, while witnesses who are highly confident after making an identification generally tend to be somewhat more accurate in their selections. However, confidence is malleable and may be affected by a number of outside factors, including the timing of the identification and when confidence is assessed, the nature of the lineup and its composition, and the behaviors of law enforcement personnel. Furthermore, changes in a witness's confidence over time may have important consequences for later stages in a case. For instance, jurors have been shown to believe that witnesses who express confidence in making identifications are, in fact, more likely to be accurate (Wells et al., 1998).

False Memories

One other individual factor over which the justice system has no control is worth mentioning: the general fallibility of human memory. Research has shown that even the most confident of witnesses, who believe they remember every detail, can be mistaken due to the simple fact that human memories are not wholly reliable. In fact, humans can create false memories that will fill in details about past experiences or construct events that never occurred in the first place. This can happen in response to information obtained after an event occurs (Loftus & Pickrell, 1995). Research suggests that both visual information, such as photographs, as well as narrative information can lead to the development of false memories. In one interesting study, psychologists manipulated people's childhood memories of their experiences at Disneyland; based on the information provided, some remembered an experience in which the character, Pluto, uncomfortably licked their ear, while others remembered the same interaction as a playful, positive experience. Not surprisingly, the researchers also found that false beliefs can alter people's behavior (Berkowitz et al., 2008).

In regards to wrongful convictions, false memories have seemingly played a part in several sexual assault cases. For example, Jennifer Thompson was assaulted at knifepoint in her Burlington, North Carolina, apartment in 1984. Unable to escape, Thompson made a conscious effort to study the man's face and voice to ensure that if she survived, she would be able to help the police identify her assailant. Thompson worked with police to develop a composite sketch of her attacker, and on August 1, 1984, police arrested an African-American man named Ronald Cotton. Cotton's photograph was placed in a photo array, and Thompson identified Cotton as the perpetrator. Shortly thereafter, she viewed a live lineup, and again chose Ronald Cotton. Thompson was told she had picked the same person both times, and she was sure that she had identified the man who had attacked her. In January 1985, Cotton was convicted of rape and burglary (he would later be convicted of a second rape that occurred the same night as Thompson's attack). In 1995, DNA from the investigation was tested. It did not match Cotton, and when the DNA profile was run through the state database, it matched a man named Bobby Poole, who had been incarcerated for other sexual assaults and served time in the same prison with Cotton. Ronald Cotton was cleared of both rape convictions and was released from prison in June 1995. Although Thompson had been attacked by Bobby Poole, she had nightmares about being attacked by Ronald Cotton, despite the fact that he was not the actual perpetrator. After choosing Cotton out of two lineups, Thompson's memory was constructed such that in her mind he was the attacker. The false memory phenomenon has also been seen with children, whose memories may be particularly malleable, in cases of alleged sexual abuse.

A Closer Look: Ronald Cotton and Jennifer Thompson

- *Picking Cotton: Our Memoir of Injustice and Redemption* (2009) — a memoir co-authored by Thompson and Cotton, with Erin Torneo. The book helps readers understand the case from the perspective of those who were involved in it.

- *I Didn't Do It*, Episode 3, "Ronald Cotton: Shadow of Doubt" — *I Didn't Do It* is a documentary series that began airing in 2012 and was produced by Canadian production company Lively Media for the Investigation Discovery cable channel. Episode 3 recounts the Cotton case through dramatic recreations and interviews with Cotton, Thompson, and others involved in the case.

- *What Jennifer Saw* (1997) — a PBS FRONTLINE documentary on the case, featuring interviews with Thompson and Cotton, as well as police involved in the case and leading researchers who discuss the psychology of identification errors.

Eyewitness Identification and the Law

The law cannot require eyewitnesses to a crime to be 100% accurate in their perceptions of who did what to whom, retain what they saw over time without forgetting or altering any details, or describe to the police and testify in court precisely what they originally witnessed. If it could, the likelihood of wrongful convictions caused by witnesses' misidentifying a crime's true perpetrator would be dramatically reduced or eliminated. Unfortunately, as discussed above, estimator variables, which are likely to affect the reliability of an eyewitness identification, are beyond the law's control.

In contrast, some system variables relating to eyewitness identification procedures can be controlled and, at least in principle, regulated by the law. As we consider the law governing eyewitness identification, we must be careful to distinguish what the Constitution requires (i.e., the minimum safeguards which must be observed) and what additional regulations might be imposed through legislation, rules of evidence, or administratively because they are desirable from a policy perspective. We begin by offering an overview of Supreme Court decisions which establish the constitutional requirements for procedures which must be followed to allow eyewitness identification testimony to be admissible in evidence. We then give an example of how legislation can reinforce and go beyond the constitutional minima to try to help ensure the reliability of identification testimony.

Constitutional Rules Governing the Admissibility of Eyewitness Identification Testimony

The Supreme Court has made several constitutional rulings addressing the admissibility of eyewitness identification testimony. Note that an *admissibility* decision concerns a threshold determination that the fact-finder in a criminal trial (the jury, or the judge in a bench trial) is allowed to consider the evidence. Some identification testimony may be so highly unreliable that it is inadmissible as evidence, meaning that the jury will never hear about it. Even when identification testimony is admitted into evidence, however, that does not necessarily mean that the fact-finder will decide that it should be considered trustworthy or believable. The jury or judge is free to give whatever *weight* it deems appropriate to identification testimony after it is admitted into evidence. Thus, for example, a defendant always remains free to argue that a witness's identification of him as the perpetrator of a crime is simply mistaken.

Witnesses might be asked to identify a suspect in a lineup (involving, for example, a witness viewing five or six different people, one of whom is the actual suspect), or at a one-on-one **show-up** (at which a single suspect is displayed to the witness). Both lineups and show-ups are known as "corporeal" identification procedures. A "corporeal" identification simply means that a witness is viewing "the body" of one or more possible suspects. We will see that different rules may apply to corporeal identifications and those which do not make use of "live" suspects but instead rely on photographs, computer-generated images, and the like. The Supreme Court decided three cases presenting constitutional issues important to corporeal eyewitness identification procedures on the same day in 1967. These seminal cases are commonly referred to as "**the *Wade* trilogy.**"

In *United States v. Wade* (1967), a man affixed a small strip of tape to each side of his face, entered a bank, pointed a gun at the teller and the bank's vice president, and ordered the teller to "put the money in the bag." The teller complied, and the robber escaped in an awaiting vehicle. The bank robbery occurred in September 1964. Six months later, in March 1965, Billy Joe Wade was indicted for the crime. He was arrested 10 days later. An attorney was appointed to represent him in late April. Roughly two weeks later, an FBI agent brought Wade from jail to another building, where he was displayed in a lineup with five or six other men, each of whom wore strips of tape fashioned after the bank robber's appearance. Wade's lawyer was not notified and was not present at the lineup. The bank teller and the vice president observed as each man in the lineup stepped forward and spoke the words, "Put the money in the bag." Both witnesses identified Wade as the bank robber. When Wade was brought to trial, the prosecutor asked the two witnesses whether the man who had robbed the bank was present in the courtroom. Over objection, each of them identified Wade as the robber. On cross-examination, the witnesses each testified that they had also identified Wade at the earlier lineup, and each acknowledged that they had observed an FBI agent escorting Wade through the building before he was placed in the lineup with the other men. The jury found Wade guilty as charged.

When the case reached the U.S. Supreme Court, the justices ruled that Wade's Sixth Amendment right to the assistance of counsel had been violated when he was required to participate in the lineup without his lawyer being present. Justice Brennan's opinion for the Court noted that a defense lawyer's role is not limited to what takes place at trial. Some matters that occur before a trial begins — such as a witness's identification of a suspect at a lineup — can so fundamentally influence a trial's outcome that a lawyer's assistance is necessary.

> [T]he confrontation compelled by the State between the accused and the victim or witnesses to a crime to elicit identification evidence is peculiarly riddled with innumerable dangers and variable factors which might seriously, even crucially, derogate from a fair trial. The vagaries of eyewitness identification are well-known; the annals of criminal law are rife with instances of mistaken identification....
>
> Moreover, "[i]t is a matter of common experience that, once a witness has picked out the accused at the line-up, he is not likely to go back on his word later on, so that in practice the issue of identity may (in the absence of other relevant evidence) for all practical purposes

be determined there and then, before the trial." Williams & Hammel-mann, Identification Parades, Part I, (1963) *Crim. L. Rev.* 479, 482....

[R]isks of suggestion ... increase the dangers inhering in eyewitness identification. But ... there is serious difficulty in depicting what transpires at line-ups and other forms of identification confrontations.... [T]he defense can seldom reconstruct the manner and mode of line-up identification for judge or jury at trial.... [N]either witnesses nor line-up participants are apt to be alert for conditions prejudicial to the suspect. And if they were, it would likely be of scant benefit to the suspect since neither witnesses nor line-up participants are likely to be schooled in the detection of suggestive influences.... In short, the accused's inability effectively to reconstruct at trial any unfairness that occurred at the line-up may deprive him of his only opportunity meaningfully to attack the credibility of the witness' courtroom identification....

Insofar as the accused's conviction may rest on a courtroom identification in fact the fruit of a suspect pretrial identification which the accused is helpless to subject to effective scrutiny at trial, the accused is deprived of that right of cross-examination which is an essential safeguard to his right to confront the witnesses against him. And even though cross-examination is a precious safeguard to a fair trial, it cannot be viewed as an absolute assurance of accuracy and reliability. Thus in the present context, where so many variables and pitfalls exist, the first line of defense must be the prevention of unfairness and the lessening of the hazards of eyewitness identification at the line-up itself. The trial which might determine the accused's fate may well not be that in the courtroom but that at the pretrial confrontation, with the State aligned against the accused, the witness the sole jury, and the accused unprotected against the overreaching, intentional or unintentional, and with little or no effective appeal from the judgment there rendered by the witness—"that's the man."

Since it appears that there is grave potential for prejudice, intentional or not, in the pretrial line-up, which may not be capable of reconstruction at trial, and since presence of counsel itself can often avert prejudice and assure a meaningful confrontation at trial, there can be little doubt that for Wade the post-indictment line-up was a critical stage of the prosecution at which he was "as much entitled to such aid (of counsel) ... as at the trial itself." *Powell v. Alabama*, 287 U.S. 45, 57 [(1932)]. Thus both Wade and his counsel should have been notified of the impending line-up, and counsel's presence should have been a requisite to conduct of the lineup, absent an "intelligent waiver."....

In our view counsel can hardly impede legitimate law enforcement; on the contrary, for the reasons expressed, law enforcement may be assisted by preventing the infiltration of taint in the prosecution's identification evidence. That result cannot help the guilty avoid conviction but can only help assure that the right man has been brought to justice.

Having established that Wade's Sixth Amendment right to counsel had been violated at the lineup identification, the Court then turned to the consequence of the constitutional violation. In fashioning a remedy, the justices distinguished testimony concerning the witnesses' "out-of-court" identification of Wade, meaning when the bank teller and vice president picked him out of the pretrial lineup, and their "in-court" identification, meaning whether they could testify at the trial that the man who robbed the bank was present in court and indeed was the defendant, Billy Joe Wade. In *Gilbert v. California* (1967), the second case in the *Wade* trilogy, the Court ruled that when a lineup is conducted in violation of a defendant's Sixth Amendment right to counsel, witnesses are strictly prohibited from testifying about having made a prior out-of-court identification. This *per se* or automatic rule requiring the exclusion of out-of-court identification testimony was designed in large part to deter the police from violating defendants' rights by conducting lineups without their lawyers being present. The Court in *Wade* had to decide whether that same policy should govern witnesses' ability to make an in-court identification after they had viewed a lineup conducted in violation of the defendant's right to counsel.

We come now to the question whether the denial of Wade's ... [right to] counsel at the lineup required ... [the witnesses' courtroom identification testimony] to be excluded. We do not think this disposition can be justified without first giving the Government the opportunity to establish by clear and convincing evidence that the in-court identifications were based upon observations of the suspect other than the lineup identification. Where, as here, the admissibility of evidence of the lineup identification itself is not involved, a per se rule of exclusion of courtroom identification would be unjustified. A rule limited solely to the exclusion of testimony concerning identification at the lineup itself, without regard to admissibility of the courtroom identification, would render the right to counsel an empty one. The lineup is most often used, as in the present case, to crystallize the witnesses' identification of the defendant for future reference.... Since counsel's presence at the lineup would equip him to attack not only the lineup identification but the courtroom identification as well, limiting the impact of violation of the right to counsel to exclusion of evidence only of identification at the lineup itself disregards a critical element of that right.

We think it follows that the proper test to be applied in these situations is that quoted in *Wong Sun v. United States*, 371 U.S. 471, 488 [(1963)], "[W]hether, granting establishment of the primary illegality, the evidence to which instant objection is made has been come at by exploitation of that illegality or instead by means sufficiently distinguishable to be purged of the primary taint." Application of this test in the present context requires consideration of various factors; for example, the prior opportunity to observe the alleged criminal act, the existence of any discrepancy between any pre-lineup description and the defendant's actual description, any identification prior to lineup of another person, the identification by picture of the defendant prior to the lineup, failure to identify the defendant on a prior occasion, and the lapse of time between the alleged act and the lineup identification. It is also relevant to consider those facts which, despite the absence of counsel, are disclosed concerning the conduct of the lineup....

On the record now before us we cannot make the determination whether the in-court identifications had an independent origin.... That inquiry is most properly made in the District Court. We therefore think the appropriate procedure to be followed is to vacate the conviction pending a hearing to determine whether the in-court identifications had an independent source....

The *Wade* Court thus declined to adopt a *per se* rule excluding witnesses' in-court identification of a defendant in the aftermath of a lineup conducted in violation of the accused's right to counsel. The justices instead opted to allow such identification testimony to be introduced at the defendant's trial, but only if the prosecution could prove by clear and convincing evidence that the in-court identification was not tainted or corrupted by what transpired at the lineup (i.e., that the in-court identification had an "independent source" from the lineup viewing). This resolution attempted to balance competing interests: respecting the defendant's constitutional right to the assistance of counsel, while also acknowledging the importance of admitting reliable evidence to help determine the truth at a criminal trial. Justice Brennan's opinion noted several factors that might be useful to help determine whether a witness's courtroom identification is likely to be influenced by or instead is independent of their prior exposure to the defendant in a lineup. We will return to the difficult question of how to make such a determination when we consider later court decisions.

The last case making up the *Wade* trilogy, *Stovall v. Denno* (1967), concerned Theodore Stovall's conviction in a New York state court for the 1961 murder of Dr. Paul Behrendt. Mrs. Behrendt suffered multiple stab wounds from her husband's assailant during the same incident. She survived following emergency surgery, and she remained hospitalized when, just two days after the attack, several police officers escorted the handcuffed Stovall into her room. Mrs. Behrendt responded affirmatively when one of the officers asked her if Stovall "was the man." When Stovall was brought to trial, she testified that she had identified Stovall as the man who had stabbed her husband and herself when he was brought to her hospital room (the "out-of-court" identification), and she also made an in-court identification of him.

When Stovall's challenges to the identification testimony reached the Supreme Court, the justices ruled that the Sixth Amendment right to counsel — which was at issue in *Wade* and *Gilbert* — would not be applied retroactively to the identification made in his case, which occurred in 1961. The majority opinion nevertheless considered whether Stovall's Fourteenth Amendment Due Process rights had been violated when testimony concerning the out-of-court and in-court identifications was admitted into evidence at his trial. Agreeing with the lower court's opinion, the Supreme Court found no Due Process violation had occurred under the circumstances.

We turn now to the question whether petitioner, although not entitled to the application of *Wade* and *Gilbert* to his case, is entitled to relief on his claim that in any event the confrontation conducted in this case was so unnecessarily suggestive and conducive to irreparable mistaken identification that he was denied due process of law. This is a recognized ground of attack upon a conviction independent of any right to counsel claim. The practice of showing suspects singly to persons for the purpose of identification, and not as part of a line-up, has been widely condemned. However, a claimed violation of due process of law in the conduct of a confrontation depends on the totality of the circumstances surrounding it, and the record in the present case reveals that the showing of Stovall to Mrs. Behrendt in an immediate hospital confrontation was imperative. The Court of Appeals, [(355 F.2d. 731, 735 (2d Cir. 1966) (*en banc*)], stated,

"Here was the only person in the world who could possibly exonerate Stovall. Her words, and only her words, 'He is not the man' could have resulted in freedom for Stovall. The hospital was not far distant from the courthouse and jail. No one knew how long Mrs. Behrendt might live. Faced with the responsibility of identifying the attacker, with the need for immediate action and with the knowledge that Mrs. Behrendt could not visit the jail, the police followed the only feasible procedure and took Stovall to the hospital room. Under these circumstances, the usual police station line-up, which Stovall now argues he should have had, was out of the question."

The justices' recognition of a Due Process basis for challenging the admissibility of eyewitness identification testimony in *Stovall v. Denno*, even though unsuccessful in that case, would prove to be highly important in light of the later limitations the Court placed on the reach of the right to counsel at corporeal identifications. The lineups at issue in both *Wade* and *Gilbert* were conducted after each defendant had been indicted by a grand jury. In contrast, the defendant in *Kirby v. Illinois* (1972) was identified by a witness during a show-up conducted at a police station shortly after he was arrested but before he had been formally charged and prior to his appearance before a judge to be arraigned on a criminal complaint. A badly divided Supreme Court (Justice Stewart's plurality opinion was joined by three other members of the Court, Justice Powell concurred in the judgment, and four justices dissented) ruled that the Sixth Amendment does not require the presence of counsel at an identification that takes place at such an early point in the criminal justice process.

The Sixth Amendment, in part, provides: "In all criminal prosecutions, the accused shall enjoy the right ... to have the Assistance of Counsel for his defence." Justice Stewart's opinion in *Kirby* explained that the right to counsel attaches only when a "**critical stage**" of a criminal case has been reached, which is to say, "at or after the time that adversary judicial proceedings have been initiated." Since Kirby had only been placed under arrest, his case had not reached a critical stage of the criminal justice process, and he had no right to counsel at the show-up. The rules recognized in *Wade* and *Gilbert* were consequently inapplicable in his case.

> This is not to say that a defendant in a criminal case has a constitutional right to counsel only at the trial itself. [*Powell v. Alabama*, 287 U.S. 45 (1932)] makes clear that the right attaches at the time of arraignment, and the Court has recently held that it exists also at the time of a preliminary hearing. But ... all of [the cases in which the Court has recognized the existence of the right to counsel] have involved points of time at or after the initiation of adversary judicial criminal proceedings — whether by way of formal charge, preliminary hearing, indictment, information, or arraignment....

The initiation of judicial criminal proceedings is far from a mere formalism. It is the starting point of our whole system of adversary criminal justice. For it is only then that the government has committed itself to prosecute, and only then that the adverse positions of government and defendant have solidified. It is then that a defendant finds himself faced with the prosecutorial forces of organized society, and immersed in the intricacies of substantive and procedural criminal law. It is this point, therefore, that marks the commencement of the "criminal prosecutions" to which alone the explicit guarantees of the Sixth Amendment are applicable.

In this case we are asked to import into a routine police investigation an absolute constitutional guarantee historically and rationally applicable only after the onset of formal prosecutorial proceedings. We decline to do so.

In his dissenting opinion, Justice Brennan, the author of the majority opinions in *Wade* and *Gilbert*, complained:

Wade did not require the presence of counsel at pretrial confrontations for identification purposes simply on the basis of an abstract consideration of the words "criminal prosecutions" in the Sixth Amendment. Counsel is required at those confrontations because 'the dangers inherent in eyewitness identification and the suggestibility inherent in the context of the pretrial identification,' mean that protection must be afforded to the 'most basic right (of) a criminal defendant — his right to a fair trial at which the witnesses against him might be meaningfully cross-examined.'... Hence, 'the initiation of adversary judicial criminal proceedings,' is completely irrelevant to whether counsel is necessary at a pretrial confrontation for identification in order to safeguard the accused's constitutional rights to confrontation and the effective assistance of counsel at his trial.

... [T]here inhere in a confrontation for identification conducted after arrest the identical hazards to a fair trial that inhere in such a confrontation conducted "after the onset of formal prosecutorial proceedings." ... An arrest evidences the belief of the police that the perpetrator of a crime has been caught. A post-arrest confrontation for identification is not "a mere preparatory step in the gathering of the prosecution's evidence." *Wade*, [388 U.S.,] at 227. A primary, and frequently sole, purpose of the confrontation for identification at that stage is to accumulate proof to buttress the conclusion of the police that they have the offender in hand. The plurality offers no reason, and

I can think of none, for concluding that a post-arrest confrontation for identification, unlike a post-charge confrontation, is not among those "critical confrontations of the accused by the prosecution at pretrial proceedings where the results might well settle the accused's fate and reduce the trial itself to a mere formality." *Id.*, at 224.

The police typically use lineups and show-ups as an investigative tool to determine whether witnesses to a crime are able to identify a suspect in their custody. In the overwhelming majority of cases, identification procedures take place before a suspect has been formally charged, arraigned, or a "critical stage" of a criminal prosecution otherwise has been reached. The Court's ruling in *Kirby* thus greatly reduces the availability of the right to counsel at corporeal identifications and elevates Due Process concerns to prominence for defendants who seek to challenge the admissibility of eyewitness identification testimony at their trials. As the Court ruled in *Stovall v. Denno*, such a challenge requires attention to "the totality of the circumstances" and will succeed only if the defendant can establish that the procedures were "so unnecessarily suggestive and conducive to irreparable mistaken identification" as to violate Due Process.

The Supreme Court addressed two aspects of a Due Process challenge to the admissibility of identification testimony in its important ruling in *Manson v. Brathwaite* (1977). The first issue concerned whether the police's use of *unnecessarily* suggestive identification procedures should require the exclusion of identification testimony, irrespective of the likely reliability of the identification. Acting in an undercover capacity, Officer Glover of the Connecticut State Police went to an apartment building where he bought heroin from a man he did not previously know. The officer returned to the police station and described the seller to a colleague, Officer D'Onofrio. Believing that the description fit Nowell Brathwaite, D'Onofrio subsequently retrieved a file photograph of Brathwaite and left it on Glover's desk. When Glover returned to his desk two days later and saw the photograph, he identified Brathwaite as the man who had sold him the heroin. Glover later testified about his out-of-court photo identification at Brathwaite's trial, and also identified Brathwaite at the trial. Brathwaite was convicted and on appeal argued that his Due Process rights had been violated by the admission of Glover's identification testimony into evidence.

Brathwaite sought to distinguish the Court's holding in *Stovall v. Denno* because in that case the witness's critical medical condition justified an urgent although highly suggestive identification procedure, whereas in his case there was no immediacy. He argued that the suggestive, one-photo display was simply bad police work and that excluding Glover's testimony was necessary to deter the police from carelessly or deliberately compromising the integrity of identifications. Justice Blackmun's majority opinion rejected the argument. The Court ruled that "reliability is the linchpin for determining the admissibility of identification testimony," and took precedence over deterring the police from employing suggestive identification procedures. This holding gave rise to the second critical issue in the case, which concerned whether Glover's identification of Brathwaite was sufficiently reliable to be admitted in evidence notwithstanding the suggestive identification procedure involving the single photograph. Determining that the reliability threshold had been satisfied, Justice Blackmun's opinion highlighted several factors that courts should consider to arrive at an admissibility decision.

1. The opportunity to view. Glover testified that for two to three minutes he stood at the apartment door, within two feet of the respondent [Brathwaite]. The door opened twice, and each time the man stood at the door. The moments passed, the conversation took place, and payment was made. Glover looked directly at his vendor. It was near sunset, to be sure, but the sun had not yet set, so it was not dark or even dusk or twilight. Natural light from outside entered the hallway through a window. There was natural light, as well, from inside the apartment.

2. The degree of attention. Glover was not a casual or passing observer, as is so often the case with eyewitness identification. Trooper Glover was a trained police officer.... Glover himself was a Negro and unlikely to perceive only general features of "hundreds of Hartford [B]lack males," as the Court of Appeals stated. It is true that Glover's duty was that of ferreting out narcotics offenders and that he would be expected in his work to produce results. But it is also true that, as a specially trained, assigned, and experienced officer, he could be expected to pay scrupulous attention to detail, for he knew that subsequently he would have to find and arrest his vendor. In addition, he knew that his claimed observations would be subject later to close scrutiny and examination at any trial.

3. The accuracy of the description. Glover's description was given to D'Onofrio within minutes after the transaction. It included the vendor's race, his height, his build, the color and style of his hair, and the high cheekbone facial feature. It also included clothing the vendor wore. No claim has been made that respondent did not possess the physical characteristics so described. D'Onofrio reacted positively at once. Two days later, when Glover was alone, he viewed the photograph D'Onofrio produced and identified its subject as the narcotics seller.

4. The witness' level of certainty. There is no dispute that the photograph in question was that of respondent. Glover, in response to a question whether the photograph was that of the person from whom he made the purchase, testified: "There is no question whatsoever." This positive assurance was repeated.

5. The time between the crime and the confrontation. Glover's description of his vendor was given to D'Onofrio within minutes of the crime. The photographic identification took place only two days later. We do not have here the passage of weeks or months between the crime and the viewing of the photograph.

These indicators of Glover's ability to make an accurate identification are hardly outweighed by the corrupting effect of the challenged identification itself. Although identifications arising from single-photograph displays may be viewed in general with suspicion, we find in the instant case little pressure on the witness to acquiesce in the suggestion that such a display entails. D'Onofrio had left the photograph at Glover's office and was not present when Glover first viewed it two days after the event. There thus was little urgency and Glover could view the photograph at his leisure. And since Glover examined the photograph alone, there was no coercive pressure to make an identification arising from the presence of another. The identification was made in circumstances allowing care and reflection....

Surely, we cannot say that under all the circumstances of this case there is "a very substantial likelihood of irreparable misidentification." [*Simmons v. United States*, 390 U.S. 377, 384 (1968)]. Short of that point, such evidence is for the jury to weigh. We are content to rely upon the good sense and judgment of American juries, for evidence with some element of untrustworthiness is customary grist for the jury mill. Juries are not so susceptible that they cannot measure intelligently the weight of identification testimony that has some questionable feature....

Justice Marshall, joined by Justice Brennan, dissented in *Brathwaite*.

In light of the eyewitness research described in the previous section, do the considerations listed in Justice Blackmun's opinion for courts to use in determining the admissibility of eyewitness identification testimony—the so-called "***Brathwaite* factors**"—appear to be good indicators of the reliability, or accuracy, of a witness's identification of a crime suspect? Some of the factors (the witness's opportunity to view the suspect at the time of the crime, the witness's degree of attention, and the witness's level of certainty in making the identification) rely heavily or exclusively on the witness's own account, which itself might be influenced (even if subconsciously) by later events or otherwise be inaccurate. Additionally, if the true identity of a crime's perpetrator is disputed, how is "the accuracy of the description" provided by the witness to be determined? In *Brathwaite*, two days lapsed between Officer Glover's seeing the man who sold him heroin and his identifying Brathwaite's photograph. Should this amount of "time between the crime and the confrontation" be considered relatively short or long? Is the witness's "level of certainty" a good measure of the reliability or accuracy of an identification? After the *Brathwaite* factors (and other aspects of "the totality of the circumstances") are considered, how are they to be weighed against the suggestiveness of an identification procedure to determine whether there exists "a very substantial likelihood of irreparable misidentification"?

Some state court decisions, in reliance on state constitutional provisions or evidentiary principles, have departed from the criteria used by the Supreme Court in *Brathwaite* and have imposed somewhat different tests for determining the admissibility of identification testimony (e.g., *State v. Harris*, 2018; *State v. Henderson*, 2011; *State v. Lawson*, 2012; *Young v. State*, 2016). If identification testimony is admitted into evidence, courts in almost all states now allow expert testimony about factors that may affect the reliability of eyewitness identification to be introduced at criminal trials to help educate jurors about potential sources of error and hence what weight they might choose to assign to witness's identification testimony (e.g., *People v. Boone*, 2017 [cross-racial identifications]; *People v. LeGrand*, 2007; *People v. Lerma*, 2016; *State v. Clopten*, 2009; *State v. Guilbert*, 2012; see Hunt, 2011).

The Supreme Court last gave prominent attention to corporeal eyewitness identification issues in *Perry v. New Hampshire* (2012). The justices ruled that a prerequisite to a Due Process challenge to the admissibility of identification testimony is a showing that the suggestive identification procedures involved in a case were arranged by the police. A witness's exposure to a suggestive identification standing alone, absent conduct attributable to the police, does not require a pretrial hearing regarding the admissibility of the identification testimony.

In *Perry*, the police responded to a call that a man was breaking into cars in the parking lot of an apartment complex. While a police officer spoke with a witness to the incident in her apartment, the witness "spontaneously" looked out her window and saw a man standing next to another police officer in the parking lot. She identified the man, Barion Perry, as the person who had been breaking into cars. The judge at Perry's trial admitted testimony about the witness's out-of-court identification without conducting a pre-trial hearing to consider Perry's Due Process challenge to its reliability. Perry had requested a hearing, arguing that the witness's identification of him was so highly suggestive that it should be considered unreliable and hence inadmissible. Justice Ginsburg's majority opinion concluded that the police had not arranged for or orchestrated the identification of Perry, and consequently Due Process did not require the trial judge to conduct an admissibility hearing: "The fallibility of eyewitness evidence does not, without the taint of improper state conduct, warrant a due process rule requiring a trial court to screen such evidence for reliability before allowing the jury to assess its creditworthiness."

> We have not extended pretrial screening for reliability to cases in which the suggestive circumstances were not arranged by law enforcement officers. [Perry] requests that we do so because of the grave risk that mistaken identification will yield a miscarriage of justice. Our decisions, however, turn on the presence of state action and aim to deter police from rigging identification procedures, for example, at a lineup, showup, or photograph array. When no improper law enforcement activity is involved, we hold, it suffices to test reliability through the rights and opportunities generally designed for that purpose, notably, the presence of counsel at postindictment lineups, vigorous cross-examination, protective rules of evidence, and jury instructions on both the fallibility of eyewitness identification and the requirement that guilt be proved beyond a reasonable doubt.

Justice Sotomayor dissented. She argued that eyewitness identification testimony presents special concerns implicating the integrity of criminal convictions, which the majority opinion ignored.

> [T]he majority points to no other type of evidence that shares the rare confluence of characteristics that makes eyewitness evidence a unique threat to the fairness of trial....
>
> It would be one thing if the passage of time had cast doubt on the empirical premises of our precedents. But just the opposite has happened. A vast body of scientific literature has reinforced every concern our precedents articulated nearly a half-century ago, though it merits barely a parenthetical mention in the majority opinion. Over the past three decades, more than two thousand studies related to eyewitness identification have been published....
>
> The empirical evidence demonstrates that eyewitness misidentification is "'the single greatest cause of wrongful convictions in this country.'" [*State v. Henderson*, 27 A.3d 872, 885 (N.J. 2011).] Researchers have found that a staggering 76% of the first 250 convictions

overturned due to DNA evidence since 1989 involved eyewitness misidentification. [B. Garrett, *Convicting the Innocent: Where Criminal Prosecutions Go Wrong* 9, 48, 279 (2011)]. Study after study demonstrates that eyewitness recollections are highly susceptible to distortion by postevent information or social cues; that jurors routinely overestimate the accuracy of eyewitness identifications; that jurors place the greatest weight on eyewitness confidence in assessing identifications even though confidence is a poor gauge of accuracy; and that suggestiveness can stem from sources beyond police-orchestrated procedures. The majority today nevertheless adopts an artificially narrow conception of the dangers of suggestive identifications at a time when our concerns should have deepened.

Agreeing with the position taken by Justice Sotomayor and relying on common law evidentiary principles, the Massachusetts Supreme Judicial Court has ruled that state trial judges may conduct pretrial admissibility hearings and exclude unreliable identification evidence even if the police are not responsible for the suggestive procedures (*Commonwealth v. Johnson*, 2016).

Most of the Supreme Court decisions we have considered thus far have concerned corporeal identification procedures. For various reasons, including the difficult logistical challenges in assembling a multi-person lineup composed of individuals who resemble the described suspect, and the suggestiveness inherent in conducting one-person show-ups, the police instead frequently ask witnesses to view photographs or computer-generated composites when they attempt to identify crime suspects. As discussed earlier, the witness in *Manson v. Brathwaite*, Officer Glover, viewed a single photograph and thereafter confirmed that the subject (Brathwaite) was the man who had sold him heroin. Presenting a witness with the photo of only one person to determine if a suspect can be identified is clearly far more suggestive than providing photographs of several different people. However, even a **photo array** with pictures of multiple individuals can be suggestive. For example, the police might have displayed the photos in a way that made the true suspect stand out, or inadvertently suggested through a gesture or a verbal cue which photo should be picked.

In *United States v. Ash* (1973), the Supreme Court considered "whether the Sixth Amendment grants an accused the right to have counsel present whenever the Government conducts a post-indictment photographic display, containing a picture of the accused, for the purpose of allowing a witness to attempt an identification of the offender." Justice Blackmun's majority opinion concluded that no such right exists. In doing so, the opinion first distinguished *United States v. Wade* (1967) and its ruling that the Sixth Amendment right to the assistance of counsel requires defense counsel's presence at a post-in-dictment lineup.

> The function of counsel in rendering "Assistance" [is important in situations such as] ... the lineup under consideration in *Wade*.... Although the accused was not confronted there with legal questions, the lineup offered opportunities for prosecuting authorities to take advantage of the accused. Counsel was seen by the Court as being more sensitive to, and aware of, suggestive influences than the accused himself, and as better able to reconstruct the events at trial. Counsel present at lineup would be able to remove disabilities of the accused in precisely the same fashion that counsel compensated for the disabilities of the layman at trial. Thus, the Court mentioned that the accused's memory might be dimmed by "emotional tension," that the accused's credibility at trial would be diminished by his status as defendant, and that the accused might be unable to present his version effectively without giving up his privilege against compulsory self-incrimination. It was in order to compensate for these deficiencies that the Court found the need for the assistance of counsel....
>
> Although *Wade* did discuss possibilities for suggestion and the difficulty for reconstructing suggestivity, this discussion occurred only after the Court had concluded that the lineup constituted a trial-like confrontation, requiring the "Assistance of Counsel" to preserve the adversary process by compensating for advantages of the prosecuting authorities....
>
> The structure of *Wade*, viewed in light of the careful limitation of the Court's language to "confrontations," makes it clear that lack of scientific precision and inability to reconstruct an event are not the tests for requiring counsel in the first instance. These are, instead, the tests to determine whether confrontation with counsel at trial can serve as a substitute for counsel at the pretrial confrontation. If accurate reconstruction is possible, the risks inherent in any confrontation still remain, but the opportunity to cure defects at trial causes the confrontation to cease to be "critical."....
>
> A substantial departure from the historical test would be necessary if the Sixth Amendment were interpreted to give Ash a right to counsel at the photographic identification in this case. Since the accused himself is not present at the time of the photographic display, and asserts no right to be present, no possibility arises that the accused might be misled by his lack of familiarity with the law or overpowered by

his professional adversary. Similarly, the counsel guarantee would not be used to produce equality in a trial-like adversary confrontation.... That adversary mechanism remains as effective for a photographic display as [in other contexts involving pretrial witness interviews]. No greater limitations are placed on defense counsel in constructing displays, seeking witnesses, and conducting photographic identifications than those applicable to the prosecution. Selection of the picture of a person other than the accused, or the inability of a witness to make any selection, will be useful to the defense in precisely the same manner that the selection of a picture of the defendant would be useful to the prosecution.... Although we do not suggest that equality of access to photographs removes all potential for abuse, it does remove any inequality in the adversary process itself and thereby fully satisfies the historical spirit of the Sixth Amendment's counsel guarantee....

We are not persuaded that the risks inherent in the use of photographic displays are so pernicious that an extraordinary system of safeguards is required.

We hold, then, that the Sixth Amendment does not grant the right to counsel at photographic displays conducted by the Government for the purpose of allowing a witness to attempt an identification of the offender.

Note that although the photos used in an identification array can be preserved to help determine whether the defendant's picture was markedly different from the others, it is not possible to reconstruct the entirety of the procedure, including how the photos were presented and precisely what the police and the witness may have discussed. Cross-examination may not be able to expose subtle suggestive cues, particularly those eluding the witness and police's awareness. We consider procedures designed to help minimize the risk of suggestiveness in both photo and corporeal identification procedures in the next section.

Legislative Guidelines for Eyewitness Identification

While legislation and administrative regulations cannot weaken constitutional safeguards, they can provide directives or guidelines that complement or go beyond what is constitutionally required. Many states now have adopted statutory measures, typically in the form of nonbinding guidelines, that relate to eyewitness identification procedures (see Norris et al., 2019, pp. 603–605). Although legislative guidelines may be helpful in identifying best practices, violation of the specified procedures in such measures does not alone require that identification testimony be excluded from evidence. The "eyewitness identification procedures" statute enacted in Connecticut, is illustrative. The statute requires police departments to develop guidelines for conducting eyewitness identifications that conform to designated standards, yet it does not mandate suppression of identification testimony if the statutory procedures are violated. The identification procedures outlined in the Connecticut statute are as follows:

Conn. Gen. Stat. Ann. §54-1p (c) (2012)

(1) Whenever a specific person is suspected as the perpetrator of an offense, the photographs included in a photo lineup or the persons participating in a live lineup shall be presented sequentially so that the eyewitness views one photograph or one person at a time ...;

(2) The identification procedure shall be conducted in such a manner that the person conducting the procedure does not know which person in the photo lineup or live lineup is suspected as the perpetrator of the offense, except that, if it is not practicable to conduct a photo lineup in such a manner, the photo lineup shall be conducted by the use of a folder shuffle method, computer program or other comparable method so that the person conducting the procedure does not know which photograph the eyewitness is viewing during the procedure;

(3) The eyewitness shall be instructed prior to the identification procedure:

(A) That the eyewitness will be asked to view an array of photographs or a group of persons, and that each photograph or person will be presented one at a time;

(B) That it is as important to exclude innocent persons as it is to identify the perpetrator;

(C) That the persons in a photo lineup or live lineup may not look exactly as they did on the date of the offense because features like facial or head hair can change;

(D) That the perpetrator may or may not be among the persons in the photo lineup or live lineup;

(E) That the eyewitness should not feel compelled to make an identification;

(F) That the eyewitness should take as much time as needed in making a decision; and

(G) That the police will continue to investigate the offense regardless of whether the eyewitness makes an identification;

....

(5) The photo lineup or live lineup shall be composed so that the fillers generally fit the description of the person suspected as the perpetrator and, in the case of a photo lineup, so that the photograph of the person suspected as the perpetrator resembles his or her appearance at the time of the offense and does not unduly stand out;

(6) If the eyewitness has previously viewed a photo lineup or live lineup in connection with the identification of another person suspected of involvement in the offense, the fillers in the lineup in which the person suspected as the perpetrator participates or in which the photograph of the person suspected as the perpetrator is included shall be different from the fillers used in any prior lineups;

(7) At least five fillers shall be included in the photo lineup and at least four fillers shall be included in the live lineup, in addition to the person suspected as the perpetrator;

(8) In a photo lineup, no writings or information concerning any previous arrest of the person suspected as the perpetrator shall be visible to the eyewitness;

(9) In a live lineup, any identification actions, such as speaking or making gestures or other movements, shall be performed by all lineup participants;

(10) In a live lineup, all lineup participants shall be out of the view of the eyewitness at the beginning of the identification procedure;

(11) The person suspected as the perpetrator shall be the only suspected perpetrator included in the identification procedure;

(12) Nothing shall be said to the eyewitness regarding the position in the photo lineup or the live lineup of the person suspected as the perpetrator;

(13) Nothing shall be said to the eyewitness that might influence the eyewitness's selection of the person suspected as the perpetrator;

(14) If the eyewitness identifies a person as the perpetrator, the eyewitness shall not be provided any information concerning such person prior to obtaining the eyewitness's statement regarding how certain he or she is of the selection; and

(15) A written record of the identification procedure shall be made that includes the following information:

(A) All identification and nonidentification results obtained during the identification procedure, signed by the eyewitness, including the eyewitness's own words regarding how certain he or she is of the selection;

(B) The names of all persons present at the identification procedure;

(C) The date and time of the identification procedure;

(D) In a photo lineup, the photographs presented to the eyewitness or copies thereof;

(E) In a photo lineup, identification information on all persons whose photograph was included in the lineup and the sources of all photographs used; and

(F) In a live lineup, identification information on all persons who participated in the lineup.

Reducing Witness Error: Eyewitness Identification Policy Reforms

Although we highlighted earlier in this chapter a number of factors that may undermine the reliability of eyewitness evidence, this does not mean that all eyewitness evidence is necessarily poor. Eyewitnesses may provide highly reliable evidence, even though their recollections can become contaminated and otherwise influenced (Wixted et al., 2018). How might we ensure, then, that eyewitness evidence is as reliable as possible?

As discussed in the previous section, the law provides some basic protections for suspects from mistaken eyewitness identifications, but these protections are far from foolproof. Experts have developed a set of recommended changes to police practices that may help reduce mistaken identifications and increase the overall reliability of eyewitness evidence. Many of these recommendations have been incorporated into legislative guidelines, as illustrated in the Connecticut statute reproduced above, or in analogous administrative regulations. A recent scientific review, or "white paper," on the topic offered nine specific recommendations related to system variables (Wells et al., 2020), some of which are discussed below.

Pre-Lineup Suggestions

Wells and colleagues (2020) suggest that a person should only be included in a lineup as a suspect if there are *evidence-based grounds that they are guilty of the crime* being investigated. More specifically, they suggest that there should be "articulable evidence that leads to a reasonable inference that a particular person, to the exclusion of most other people, likely committed the crime in question" (p. 12). They also note that any such evidence should be documented prior to conducting the lineup. A key motivation for this suggestion is to increase the "base rate" of culprit-present lineups (that is, lineups in which the suspect is actually guilty) and thus reduce the potential for misidentifications that may lead to wrongful convictions.

Another suggestion is for police to conduct a *pre-lineup interview* of eyewitnesses to document their self-reported description of the person they witnessed committing the crime, as well as the environmental conditions under which they saw the events, their prior familiarity with the culprit (if any), and more.

Finally, before the identification procedure takes place, the witness should be provided with specific *instructions*. Upon entering an identification procedure, witnesses often fail to fully comprehend the procedures and the purpose of their participation. They may assume that the police would not go through the trouble of an identification procedure if they did not already have a likely suspect in custody. Witnesses may therefore feel obliged to identify someone, even if they do not have a strong inclination to do so. One way to partially solve this problem is to provide witnesses with specific instructions that may help clarify the purpose of the identification and the expectations of the witness.

First, witnesses should be informed that the suspect may or may not be present in the lineup, and that they should not feel compelled to make an identification. Research has found that witnesses are less likely to select the wrong person when given this instruction (Steblay, 1997). In addition, some suggest that witnesses should be told that the investigation will continue whether or not they make an identification, and that in addition to identifying a criminal, it is equally important to clear any innocent persons.

Other experts also suggest that witnesses should be instructed that the officer conducting the identification procedure does not know the identity of the suspect. Doing so will discourage the witness from looking to the officer for guidance or confirmation, and thus will not be influenced by the officer to make any particular decision. This instruction, along with the recommendation for blind procedures discussed in the next section, is designed to prevent the police from providing feedback to the witness that may taint the reliability of an identification.

Suggestions for Conducting the Lineup

As discussed earlier in this chapter, the officer(s) conducting the identification procedure may influence the eyewitness in important ways that may reduce the reliability of any identification that is made. In some cases, the officer administering the lineup is involved in the investigation and is aware of the suspect's identity. This officer then interacts with the witness before, during, and after the identification procedure, and may influence the witness intentionally or unintentionally. The officer, with or without realizing that it is occurring, may give the witness audio or visual cues that influence the decision of the witness and their confidence in that decision (Steblay et al., 2014).

In order to avoid these potential problems, experts suggest using "**blind**" or "**double-blind**" lineups. This means that the officer administering the lineup does not know who the suspect is and thus cannot provide confirming or disconfirming feedback. Research has shown that influential cues do affect witness behavior, and blind procedures may help reduce this unwanted influence (Wells et al., 1998, 2020). Further, double-blind procedures may also ensure that reports about the identification procedure are more complete and more accurate, as pre-existing knowledge will not influence perceptions of events and what information is recorded and how.

A number of other factors related to *lineup composition* may influence the accuracy of identification procedures. The construction of a lineup or a photo array—how many people or pictures are in it and what they look like—can have a significant impact on a witness's identification. For example, if the photo of the suspect looks significantly different than the other photos, the witness may be drawn to and become inclined to pick the suspect, even if that person does not fit the witness's memory of the criminal. Therefore, experts suggest constructing lineups and photo arrays in a way that ensures that the suspect does not unfairly stand out. In particular, there should only be *one suspect* in any given lineup or photo array and there should be *at least five appropriate fillers*—again, the people in the lineup or array who are *not* the suspect. The fillers should match the witness's description of the offender as closely as possible, and the suspect should resemble the fillers. This helps ensure that the witness carefully evaluates the members of the lineup or all of the pictures in a photo array before making an identification. Finally, when a case involves multiple witnesses, different lineups or photo arrays should be constructed for each witness, and the suspect should be placed in different positions to make sure that the different witnesses are not biased by the same factors (Wells et al., 1998).

Experts suggest *avoiding show-up procedures* whenever it is possible. It is generally agreed that show-ups, where a single suspect is shown to a witness, are suggestive, and that a live lineup or a photo array are preferable identification procedures. Research has shown that show-up procedures increase the likelihood of a misidentification.

Another potential change, although one less universally agreed-upon, concerns the presentation of lineup members or pictures in a photo array. When witnesses are confronted with a lineup or photo array and asked to make an identification, they may rely on "relative judgment." As we noted earlier, this means that they look at all of the individuals presented and try to determine which one looks *most like* the person they remember. This is likely to happen with a "simultaneous" lineup or photo array where all of the people or photos are presented together at the same time. When this process occurs, witnesses may be more likely to attempt an identification, because there will always be one person who looks more like who they remember seeing than the others. To reduce mistaken identifications, it may be preferable for witnesses to rely on "**absolute judgment**," which means that they look at each person or photo separately and respond whether that individual matches their memory of the culprit (Wells et al., 1998).

To help promote the use of absolute judgment, some advocates and experts suggest using "**sequential**" lineups and photo arrays, where each person or photo is presented one at a time, rather than all at once. In a sequential procedure, the witness views each person or photo individually, and must make a decision about that person before moving on to the next. Even if a witness identifies someone as the perpetrator, it usually is suggested that they be asked to view all of the lineup members or pictures in the photo array before any decisions are finalized.

Post-Lineup Suggestions

Several practices that occur after a lineup procedure takes place may help promote reliability and the later evaluation of any identification that was made. First, Wells et al. (2020) suggest that investigators should *avoid repeating an identification* that involves the same eyewitness and same suspect, whether or not an identification was made during the first lineup.

A witness's level of confidence should be recorded as soon as they make their identification decision, whether that decision is positive or negative. The witness's expressed level of confidence in making their decision should take place *before* they are given any feedback whatsoever. An officer's feedback can influence how confident the witness is in their decision. This may influence the perceived strength of the evidence; a judge or jury may place more weight on the testimony of witnesses who are confident in their identification than ones who express a measure of doubt about their decision. Having an immediate confidence statement may be useful insofar as it allows the judge or jury to determine if there were any changes in the witness's confidence from the time of the original identification to the time of trial, and help them evaluate the significance of any such changes.

Recording Identification Procedures

The final major suggestion for reform is to video-record the entire identification procedure, including the pre-lineup interview, the witness instructions, the identification procedure itself, and the witness's confidence statement. Doing so creates a record of the process and may assist all involved — prosecutors, defense attorneys, judges, and juries — in evaluating the reliability of eyewitness identification evidence.

Conclusion

The fallibility of human memory, recall, and recognition has long been recognized, but recent exonerations have brought to light the problems associated with an overreliance on eyewitness testimony to secure convictions. Psychological research has uncovered several of the underlying factors that contribute to witness errors, and while the law provides some protections for defendants, a number of additional changes to policy and practice may help avoid and overcome misidentification errors and improve the overall accuracy of the justice system.

Key Terms and Concepts

- **Estimator variables**: factors that may influence the accuracy of eyewitness identifications, but are beyond the control of the justice system
- **System variables**: factors that may influence the accuracy of eyewitness identifications and are subject to control by actors in the justice system
- **Weapon-focus effect**: the phenomenon whereby the presence of a weapon used in the commission of a crime commands the attention of a witness and thus threatens to undermine the accuracy of an identification
- **Cross-racial identification**: identifications in which the witness and perpetrator are of different races; tend to be less reliable than identifications within racial groups, a phenomenon often referred to as "own-race bias" or "the other-race effect"
- **Relative judgment**: when a witness decides which subject in a lineup or photo array most closely resembles the offender they saw compared to other

members of the lineup or photo array, rather than basing an identification
on the witness's recollection of the person viewed at the time of the crime

- **Absolute judgment**: when a witness evaluates each lineup or photo array
member individually to determine if that person matches their recollection
of the offender
- **Show-up**: a one-on-one identification procedure in which the witness is
presented with a single person and asked if that person is the offender
- **Photo array**: a display constructed of multiple photographs, rather than in-
dividuals presented in an in-person lineup, for purposes of identification
- **Live lineup**: the presentation of multiple individuals, in-person, for purposes
of identification
- **Fillers**: the members of a lineup or photo array who are not the suspect
- **The *Wade* trilogy**: three Supreme Court cases (*United States v. Wade,
Gilbert v. California*, and *Stovall v. Denno*) that decided important consti-
tutional issues related to in-person eyewitness identification procedures
- **Critical stage**: according to *Kirby v. Illinois*, a stage of the criminal process
in which formal adversarial proceedings have begun, thus triggering the defendant's right to the assistance of counsel
- **The *Brathwaite* factors**: from *Manson v. Brathwaite*, the factors
considered by courts in determining the admissibility of eyewitness identification testimony
- **Blind/double-blind procedure**: an identification procedure in which the
officials administering the lineup or photo array do not know which person
is the actual suspect
- **Simultaneous lineup/photo array**: an identification procedure in which all
lineup members or pictures in a photo array are viewed at the same time
- **Sequential lineup/photo array**: an identification procedure in which lineup
members or the pictures in a photo array are viewed one at a time and the
witness is asked as each is presented to make an identification decision

Discussion Questions

1. What are the key differences between "estimator" and "system" variables?
Which do you think are most influential in shaping eyewitness identifications and why?

2. Thinking about your own memory and ability to remember and recall what
you have seen, how well do you think you would fare as an eyewitness? In
general, how accurate do you believe eyewitnesses are?

3. In *Manson v. Brathwaite*, what factors did the Supreme Court identify as important in determining the admissibility of identifications? What do you think about these factors? Are they good indicators of an accurate and reliable identification? Are there other factors that might be worth considering?

4. As discussed throughout this chapter, several of the reasons explaining the reliability or unreliability of eyewitness identifications are related to basic human functioning, including imperfect and malleable memory. What types of policy reforms might help overcome these issues? How can police departments, legislatures, or the courts help prevent and respond to problems such as false memories?

References

Berkowitz, S. R., Laney, C., Morris, E. K., Garry, M., & Loftus, E. F. (2008). Pluto behaving badly: False beliefs and their consequences. *American Journal of Psychology, 121*, 643–660.

Carlson, C. A., Dias, J. L., Weatherford, D. R., & Carlson, M. A. (2017). An investigation of the weapon focus effect and the confidence-accuracy relationship for eyewitness identification. *Journal of Applied Research in Memory and Cognition, 6*, 82–92.

Commonwealth v. Johnson, 45 A.3d 83 (Mass. 2016).

Deffenbacher, K. A., Bornstein, B. H., Penrod, S. D., & McGorty, E. K. (2004). A meta-analytic review of the effects of high stress on eyewitness memory. *Law and Human Behavior, 28*, 687–706.

Fitzgerald, R. J., & Price, H. L. (2015). Eyewitness identification across the life span: A meta-analysis of age differences. *Psychological Bulletin, 141*, 1228–1265.

Fitzgerald, R. J., Price, H. L., Oriet, C., & Charman, S. D. (2013). The effect of suspect-filler similarity on eyewitness identification decisions: A meta-analysis. *Psychology, Public Policy, and Law, 19*, 151–164.

Fitzgerald, R. J., Price, H. L., & Valentine, T. (2018). Eyewitness identification: Live, photo, and video lineups. *Psychology, Public Policy, and Law, 24*(3), 307–325.

Gilbert v. California, 388 U.S. 263 (1967).

Hunt, S. S. (2011). The admissibility of eyewitness-identification expert testimony in Oklahoma. *Oklahoma Law Review, 63*, 511–551.

Kirby v. Illinois, 406 U.S. 682 (1972).

Kocab, K., & Sporer, S. L. (2016). The weapon focus effect for person identifications and descriptions: A meta-analysis. In M. K. Miller & B. H. Bornstein (Eds.), *Advances in Psychology and Law* (pp. 71–117). Springer International.

Lindsay, R. C. L., & Wells, G. L. (1985). Improving eyewitness identifications from lineups: Simultaneous versus sequential lineup presentation. *Journal of Applied Psychology, 70*, 556–564.

Loftus, E. F., & Pickrell, J. E. (1995). The formation of false memories. *Psychiatric Annals, 25*, 720–725.

Longstaff, M. G., & Belz, G. K. (2020). Sex differences in eyewitness memory: Females are more accurate than males for details related to people and less accurate for details surrounding them and feel more anxious and threatened in a neutral but potentially threatening context. *Personality and Individual Differences, 164*, 1–6.

Manson v. Brathwaite, 432 U.S. 98 (1977).

Meissner, C. A., & Brigham, J. C. (2001). Thirty years of investigating the own-race bias in memory for faces: A meta-analytic review. *Psychology, Public Policy, and Law, 7*, 3–35.

Munsterberg, H. (1908). *On the witness stand.* McClure.

Norris, R. J., Bonventre, C. L., Redlich, A. D., Acker, J. R., & Lowe, C. (2019). Preventing wrongful convictions: An analysis of state investigation reforms. *Criminal Justice Policy Review, 30*, 597–626.

Otterbourg, K. (2021). Robert Foxworth. National Registry of Exonerations. http://www.law.umich.edu/special/exoneration/Pages/casedetail.aspx?caseid=5920.

People v. Boone, 91 N.E.3d 1194 (N.Y. 2017).

People v. LeGrand, 867 N.E.2d 374 (N.Y. 2007).

People v. Lerma, 47 N.E.3d 985 (Il. 2016).

Perry v. New Hampshire, 565 U.S. 228 (2012).

Pica, E., Pozzulo, J., & Sheahan, C. L. (2018). Dance like no one's watching: The influence of demand characteristics when examining lineups via computer or in-person. *Journal of Police and Criminal Psychology*, 1–11. http://doi.org/10.1007/s11896-018-9270-4.

State v. Clopten, 223 P.3d 1103 (Utah 2009).

State v. Guilbert, 49 A.3d 705 (Ct. 2012).

State v. Harris, 191 A.3d 119 (Ct. 2018).

State v. Henderson, 27 A.3d 872 (N.J. 2011).

State v. Lawson, 291 P.3d 673 (Ore. 2012).

Steblay, N. K. (1997). Social influence in eyewitness recall: A meta-analytic review of lineup instruction effects. *Law and Human Behavior, 21*, 283–297.

Steblay, N. K., Wells, G. L., & Douglass, A. B. (2014). The eyewitness post identification feedback effect 15 years later: Theoretical and policy implications. *Psychology, Public Policy, and Law, 20*, 1–18.

Stovall v. Denno, 388 U.S. 293 (1967).

Thompson-Cannino, J., Cotton, R., & Torneo, E. (2009). *Picking Cotton: Our memoir of injustice and redemption.* St. Martin's Press.

United States v. Ash, 413 U.S. 300 (1973).

United States v. Wade, 388 U.S. 218 (1967).

Wells, G. L. (1978). Eyewitness-testimony research: System variables and estimator variables. *Journal of Personality and Social Psychology, 36*, 1546–1557.

Wells, G. L. (1984). The psychology of lineup identifications. *Journal of Applied Social Psychology, 14*, 89–103.

Wells, G. L., Kovera, M. B., Douglass, A. B., Brewer, N., Meissner, C. A., & Wixted, J. T. (2020). Policy and procedure recommendations for the collection and preservation of eyewitness identification evidence. *Law and Human Behavior, 44*(1), 3–36.

Wells, G. L., & Olson, E. A. (2001). The other-race effect in eyewitness identification: What do we do about it? *Psychology, Public Policy, and Law, 7*, 230–246.

Wells, G. L., Small, M., Penrod, S., Malpass, R. S., Fulero, S. M., & Brimacome, C. A. E. (1998). Eyewitness identification procedures: Recommendations for lineups and photospreads. *Law and Human Behavior, 22*, 1–39.

West, E., & Meterko, V. (2016). Innocence Project: DNA exonerations, 1989–2014: Review of data and findings from the first 25 years. *Albany Law Review, 79*, 717–795.

Wixted, J. T., Mickes, L., & Fisher, R. P. (2018). Rethinking the reliability of eyewitness memory. *Perspectives on Psychological Science, 13*(3), 324–335.

Young v. State, 374 P.3d 395 (Alaska 2016).

Chapter 4

False Admissions: Interrogations and Confessions

Learning Objectives

After reading this chapter, you should be able to:

- Distinguish voluntary, compliant, and internalized false confessions.
- Discuss the three-step pathway to police-induced false confessions.
- List and discuss the situational and dispositional factors related to false confessions.
- Appreciate the influence of confessions on decision-making in the criminal process.
- Discuss U.S. Supreme Court doctrine governing confessions.
- Discuss the benefits to both law enforcement and defendants of recording custodial interrogations.
- Compare and contrast confrontational interrogation with investigative interviewing.

Case Study: Frances Choy

In April 2003, Frances Choy, a 17-year-old high school senior, reported a fire at her family's Massachusetts home. Firefighters rescued Choy and her 16-year-old nephew, Kenneth, from the blaze. Her mother was pronounced dead at the scene, and her father was taken to the hospital.

Police initially questioned Choy at the hospital while she was being treated with oxygen. They questioned her again later that morning when she returned to her home. Her father was transferred to a different hospital, and two officers questioned her as they drove her there so she could see him. Following her arrival at the hospital, Choy authorized removal of her father's life support, and he passed away.

That evening, Choy was told to meet an officer at the house where the fire had occurred. The police then transported her to the police station to view items that had been taken from the scene. At the station, police officers questioned Choy for more than three hours. They repeatedly asked her how gasoline had gotten on her sweatpants, even though the crime lab's tests on the pants had not yet been conducted. The interrogation was not recorded, and the interrogators destroyed their notes after preparing a report.

In the meantime, police found notes under Kenneth's bed that set forth plans to burn the house with gasoline. Kenneth initially denied any knowledge of the crime, but later changed his story. He said he did not intend to kill anyone, and when police suggested that he had not acted alone, he blamed the idea on Choy. He claimed that on the night of the fire, he saw Choy preparing the gasoline, but he refused to help and returned to his room. Kenneth claimed "he heard a 'fooh' sound — the sound of a fire starting" (Possley, 2020). Police brought Kenneth to confront Choy, and although she initially denied any involvement, she eventually said, "Fine, I did it," after police said they would take her to booking (Possley, 2020). A detective claimed that while awaiting booking, Choy made more admissions, but she immediately recanted them. Choy moved to suppress her statements in 2005, but the motion was denied.

Choy went to trial in 2008, charged with two counts of murder and one count of arson. The prosecution claimed that she felt burdened by her parents and wanted the $100,000 payout from their life insurance policy. The crux of the commonwealth's case was the testimony of investigators who claimed that Choy had admitted involvement in setting the fire. They said she had shown little emotion and had no explanation for the gasoline on her pants. Other witnesses for the commonwealth, including a state trooper who claimed that he and his K-9 were "certified" in detecting accelerants, testified regarding the presence of gasoline. Another state trooper testified about the starting point of the fire — a mattress in the basement — but said no gasoline was found there, on the couch, or on the wooden stairs leading from the living room to the second floor. This witness did note that there was a towel near Kenneth's bedroom door, potentially placed there to block the smoke.

When Choy's jury failed to reach a unanimous verdict, a mistrial was declared. In a separate trial, Kenneth was acquitted of murder. Choy's motion to bar a retrial was denied, and she was again brought to trial in January 2011.

Kenneth testified for the prosecution after being granted immunity. The jury again failed to reach a unanimous verdict, and a second mistrial was declared. Choy was tried a third time in May 2011. Kenneth had since departed for China so he did not appear at the trial, but his statements from the second trial were read to the jury. This time, the jury convicted Choy of all three counts, and she was sentenced to life imprisonment without parole.

Through a lengthy legal battle conducted with the assistance of the Boston College Law School's Innocence Program, Choy's defense lawyers uncovered evidence of anti-Asian racism and sexually demeaning comments made by prosecutors in the case. In addition, review of the original trial testimony by a chemist suggested that there was not a credible scientific basis for the conclusion that Choy's sweatpants contained gasoline. The defense additionally discovered a witness who stated that Kenneth admitted to planning and carrying out the crime. The prosecution also had failed to disclose the fact that other fires occurred at the Choy home after Frances was arrested, that Kenneth had other drug charges that had been dismissed, and that Kenneth's mother, to whom he had returned in China, was mad at the Choy family because they repeatedly asked for money. A variety of other issues, including the discovery of an interrogator's original notes, which had allegedly been destroyed and which contained information inconsistent with his testimony, led to a motion for a new trial, which was granted. On September 29, 2020, the district attorney's office dismissed the charges, and Frances Choy was exonerated. As is generally the case, multiple factors contributed to Frances Choy's wrongful convictions. Yet the false confession she made during her interrogation, "Fine, I did it," and subsequent incriminating admissions—all of which she promptly retracted—represented some of the most damning evidence leading to her wrongful convictions for arson and murder.

False Admissions:
Overview and Research

False admissions encompass two related but distinct issues: confessions and guilty pleas. Although they are among the most widely researched factors that contribute to wrongful convictions, they remain counterintuitive; after all, why would anyone admit to a crime they did not commit?

For many people, both in the general public and within the criminal justice system, moving beyond this obvious question is difficult. Indeed, a number of officials have made comments suggesting that anyone who is innocent simply would not admit to something they did not do. At the heart of this belief is the assumption that people do not act in self-destructive ways (Leo, 2008). However, the Innocence Movement and DNA exonerations have shown definitively that people do sometimes admit to crimes even though they are entirely innocent.

Although interrogations and plea bargaining occur at different points in the criminal justice process, they are closely related in some important ways. The logic behind both is "remarkably similar" (Leo, 2008, p. 31). At their core, each is designed to encourage a person to admit being guilty of a crime. During an interrogation, police seek to obtain a confession from a suspect, which will be used as evidence against them going forward. During plea bargaining, the prosecution offers defendants a break on their charge and/or sentence in exchange for an admission of guilt, thereby avoiding a contested trial.

Both interrogations and plea bargaining are guilt-presumptive. That is, police often will not interrogate someone unless they believe the person to be guilty. The goal of the interrogation thus is to secure a confession, rather than simply to collect information (Kassin et al., 2010). Similarly, the state's push to secure a guilty plea is based on the prosecutor's belief in the defendant's guilt. Importantly, the prosecutor's view of the crime and of the defendant is likely to be heavily shaped by the information provided by the police. Interrogations and plea bargaining consequently may be "closely linked in practice, in that the former can strongly influence the latter." (Norris & Redlich, 2014, p. 1013). For these reasons, interrogations have been referred to as "plea bargaining without defense counsel" (Kamisar, 1980, p. 40) and "pre-plea bargaining" (Leo, 2008, p. 32). In effect, both guilt-presumptive interrogations and plea negotiations serve to increase the efficiency of the criminal justice process, but may be at odds with the search for truth that is so vital to the American adversarial system.

Despite their substantial overlap, interrogations and plea bargaining are distinct practices. In this chapter, we focus on the former: police interrogations and false confessions. In the next chapter, we will explore wrongful convictions that occur as a result of guilty pleas.

Interrogations and False Confessions

False confessions are not new to justice systems. For example, the case discussed in chapter 1 of Stephen and Jesse Boorn, who were convicted in 1819 and who were among the first known wrongfully convicted individuals in the United States, involved false confessions. As noted earlier, patterns found in modern exonerations suggest that false confessions occur with some regularity.

Of the first 325 DNA exonerations reported by the Innocence Project, 88 (27.1%) involved some type of false confession (West & Meterko, 2016). Further, according to the National Registry of Exonerations, 337 of the first 2,754 exonerations (12.2%) involved a false confession. Interestingly, among known exonerations, false confessions appear to be especially prevalent in homicide cases, as 246 of the 1,108 murder and manslaughter cases (22.2%) in the NRE database involved a false confession.

It is important to note that the above figures do not represent the rate, prevalence, or incidence of false confessions; that is, they are not indicative of the proportion of all confessions that are false, nor do they indicate what percentage of innocent people who are interrogated ultimately confess to a crime. Such exact figures are unknowable. However, a meta-analysis of laboratory studies encompassing 19 published articles found that approximately 47% of "innocent" participants confessed (Stewart et al., 2018), although rates varied depending on several factors. Of course, such an estimate should be taken with a grain of salt, as it is the product of laboratory studies, rather than based on the stressful conditions of real-world interrogations. Still, this body of research clearly demonstrates that under some conditions, innocent people are prone to falsely admit guilt, and psychological science has helped us understand much more about why this is so.

Psychologists have developed categories to describe different types of false confessions. Generally speaking, there are three primary types: (a) voluntary false confessions, (b) compliant false confessions, and (c) internalized or persuaded false confessions.[1]

Voluntary false confessions are those situations in which an innocent person "claim[s] responsibility for crimes they did not commit without prompting or pressure from the police" (Kassin et al., 2010, p. 14). The most common reason for such confessions is purported to be a desire to protect the identity of the actual offender; other reasons include issues related to mental illness, feelings of guilt that lead to a desire for self-punishment, and a longing for notoriety. Gudjonsson (2003) even describes a case in which a man was

---

1. It is worth noting that writers use slightly different language or naming schemes for the various types of false confessions. For example, Kassin and Wrightsman (1985) described the categories of voluntary, coerced-compliant, and coerced-internalized false confessions. Leo (2008) notes that some scholars have divided compliant confessions into "coerced-compliant" and "stress-compliant" confessions. Further, some have suggested adding a fourth category of "coerced-reactive" confessions, or those that are induced, but outside of the police custodial context (McCann, 1998; Stridbeck, 2020). For the sake of brevity and clarity, we focus on the broad naming schemes that capture the essence of each of the three primary categories.

angry at police and wanted to mislead them, so he confessed to a crime to throw them off track.

Unlike voluntary false confessions, the other types are induced through police interrogation. A **compliant false confession** represents what most people likely imagine when they think of a false admission of guilt. These confessions are prompted by interrogation.

Under the pressure and stress of a custodial interrogation, the suspect acquiesces and provides a confession in order to escape the situation, avoid punishment, and/or receive an implied reward. For example, in the Central Park Jogger case (discussed in chapter 2), five teenagers were arrested for the rape and attempted murder of a woman in New York City. Four of the five youths ultimately confessed, after hours upon hours of intense interrogation at the police station. The case stands as one of the most well-known examples of compliant false confessions.

The third type of false confession, often referred to as **internalized** false confessions, occurs when innocent suspects not only admit guilt, but also come to believe that they actually committed the crime. Because innocent persons are unlikely to fully internalize a belief in their own guilt, but instead are persuaded that they may actually have committed the crime, Ofshe and Leo (1997) have called such admissions "persuaded false confessions." Such confessions may result from suspects distrusting their memory and their consequent susceptibility to coercive or suggestive interrogation tactics (e.g., the police stating that they have clear evidence of the person's guilt) (Kassin et al., 2010). As discussed in the previous chapter, false memories might also contribute to this type of incriminating admission.

While voluntary false confessions are interesting and important to understand, we focus here on the situations in which the police helped induce, or were somehow involved in producing, the false confession. Leo (2008) has described a three-step pathway to such false confessions.

The Curious Case of Henry Lee Lucas

The case of Henry Lee Lucas remains a fascinating one in the annals of American criminal justice. Lucas had a difficult upbringing and was convicted of a number of burglaries in the 1950s in Virginia. Then, in 1960, he was convicted of killing his mother in Michigan, though he claimed it was self-defense. After serving more than a decade in prison, he was released. He was convicted of attempted kidnap in 1971 and was incarcerated until 1975. In 1983, Lucas was questioned in relation to the murder of two women in Texas. He confessed to the killings and supposedly led police to the victims' remains. Shortly thereafter, Lucas began admitting to a number of unsolved murders, leading to the establishment of the Lucas Task Force in Texas. As he worked with investigators to solve the murders he claimed to have committed, Lucas received national attention and was given preferential treatment by Texas officials. At one point, Lucas claimed to have committed as many as 600 killings across the United States, although some of these included admissions to acts that were not possible. He was ultimately convicted of 11 murders and sentenced to death in 1984. His death sentence was commuted in 1998 by Governor George W. Bush—the only time Bush commuted a death sentence during his time in office. Lucas died of a heart attack in prison in 2001. While none of Lucas's cases is considered a "wrongful conviction," it is beyond doubt that some, perhaps most, of his confessions were false. His admissions seem to carry elements of both compliant and voluntary false confessions—he freely offered some information while also responding to incentives from law enforcement— and his case remains an intriguing one for those interested in criminal interrogations and confessions (Gajanan, 2019).

- *The Confession Killer*—a Netflix documentary examining the Lucas case, including original footage of Lucas and Texas investigators, and interviews with officials and journalists involved in the case.

Misclassification

A police-induced false confession begins with what Leo (2008, p. 225) calls a "misclassification error." This occurs when detectives err in deciding that an innocent suspect is in fact guilty and thus pursue an intensive interrogation designed to secure an admission. Such an erroneous assumption occurs for several reasons. One key is that the police often believe, based in part on their training, that they can accurately discern when a person is lying. However, a significant body of research on deception-detection has found that many people, including police officers and other law enforcement officials, are poor at determining when others are being truthful or dishonest (e.g., Bond & DePaulo, 2006; Vrij, 2004). Nevertheless, interrogation training often counsels that specific cues are telltale signs that a person is lying, despite the fact that such cues do not reliably exist. In addition, people respond quite differently when interacting with law enforcement, and these differences may have implications for how interrogators perceive them. For example, research suggests that Black suspects may experience "stereotype threat," or "concern about being judged and treated unfairly by police" because of generalizations based on their social group identity (Najdowski et al., 2015, p. 463). Such perceptions may result in attitudinal and behavioral cues (e.g., anxiety, nervousness, etc.) that can be interpreted by police as indicators of suspicion, deception, and/or guilt. This increases the likelihood that innocent Black suspects will erroneously be perceived as being guilty (Najdowski, 2014, 2016; Najdowski et al., 2015).

Importantly, police are often inordinately confident in their judgments about a suspect's guilt, leading to "investigator response bias" (Meissner & Kassin, 2002). With a mistaken belief that they can detect when a person is lying, police may accept unreliable cues as indicators of guilt, thus enhancing their confidence that the suspect committed the crime being investigated, and then subject the suspect to an accusatory interrogation designed to secure an admission rather than probe for the truth. As discussed earlier, interrogations are largely guilt-presumptive, and thus the misclassification error is an important starting point for police-induced false confessions. To make matters worse, innocent suspects may be at a particular disadvantage in the early stages of questioning, as they are more likely than guilty parties to exhibit "a naïve mindset that leads them to believe they have nothing to hide or fear," and as a result waive legal protections including the right to have an attorney present and to remain silent (Scherr et al., 2020).

Coercion

Once police conclude that a suspect is likely guilty, they may pursue their interrogation aggressively, relying on accusatory and manipulative tactics in the hope of securing a confession. Factors related to the interrogation tactics being used and to the characteristics of the suspect being questioned may affect the likelihood of a false confession. These characteristics are generally referred to as **situational risk factors** and **dispositional risk factors**.

Situational Risk Factors

Various characteristics of the situation — in this case, a criminal interrogation — may affect the likelihood that a suspect will make a false admission of guilt. Although interrogations can be physically demanding, law enforcement officers have largely moved beyond the overtly physical, sometimes torturous "third degree" tactics of the past. Instead, modern interrogations are apt to involve psychological tactics and pressures (Janzen, 2019).

Suspects undergoing custodial interrogation are physically isolated in an environment that is controlled entirely by the police. This alone may have a profound psychological impact, particularly when the individual is isolated for a long period of time. Although most interrogations last less than two hours, one study of known false confessions found that the average interrogation length in those cases was 16 hours (Drizin & Leo, 2004). Such lengthy periods of time secluded from others, without social support, can be highly stressful.

Lengthy interrogations may also involve sleep deprivation, which impairs cognitive abilities and can make individuals more vulnerable to influential interrogation tactics (Harrison & Horne, 2000).

A number of specific tactics may also be used by interrogators to elicit statements from suspects. Officials may regularly interrupt the suspect, refute their statements, or claim the suspect is in denial. They may also use **maximization** and **minimization** tactics. The police might seek to maximize the benefit of confessing, for example, by implying that significantly harsher consequences will befall suspects who do not confess. Minimization tactics, on the other hand, minimize the suspect's involvement in or responsibility for the crime. The police might, for example, offer moral justifications or excuses for the presumed offender's actions, or sympathize with the suspect. Minimization tactics, which may carry with them implications for leniency in exchange for a confession, may be particularly effective when used on innocent suspects who feel they have little choice but to admit guilt (Kassin et al., 2010).

One other tactic that may help stimulate false confessions is confronting the suspect with false evidence. When interrogators have actual evidence of a suspect's guilt, they may present that information to the suspect to secure a confession. However, even when such evidence does *not* exist, officers may lie to a suspect and claim that they have incontrovertible evidence that the suspect was involved in the crime. This tactic is generally allowed by law, although psychological research suggests that it may induce innocent suspects — who already feel vulnerable and powerless, and are experiencing extreme levels of stress — to falsely admit guilt. Indeed, laboratory studies that used false evidence ploys have generally found increased rates of false confessions (Stewart et al., 2018).

Dispositional Risk Factors

In addition to circumstances characterizing the interrogation, the particular attributes of suspects might make them more or less likely to falsely confess.

Several of these dispositional risk factors are tied to core tenets of human psychology. For example, people tend to act in their own self-interest, and thus make decisions that maximize their well-being. Furthermore, people generally are social beings and consequently are susceptible to influence by others who seek to persuade them. Finally, human memory is faulty, at best. People regularly misremember details and misreport events, and as a result are susceptible to the creation of false memories.

In addition, particular characteristics may make some individuals more likely to confess than others. Indeed, certain groups are overrepresented among known cases of false confession, suggesting that they are particularly at risk to make false self-incriminating statements (Mogavero, 2020; Norris & Redlich, 2012). These vulnerable populations include juveniles, as seen in a number of prominent wrongful conviction cases, including the Central Park Jogger case discussed previously (see Waxman, 2020, for a general discussion of juvenile false confessions). Furthermore, individuals with intellectual or developmental disabilities and those suffering from mental illness may also be particularly susceptible to manipulative interrogation tactics (Schatz, 2018). In general, those who tend to be more suggestible and susceptible to influence, more obedient to authority, more likely to engage in risky behaviors, and less likely to consider the long-term consequences of decisions are more likely to falsely confess (Kassin et al., 2010). More recently, research has suggested that other subgroups may be at increased risk of falsely confessing, including individuals suffering from depression or Attention-Deficit/Hyperactivity Disorder (ADHD) (Gudjonsson et al., 2006, 2012). An analysis of NRE data suggests that false confessions are more common among females and in cases involving multiple suspects (Mogavero, 2020).

Contamination

Leo (2008, p. 234) identifies the third step in the progression from false confession to wrongful conviction as the "contamination error." Once a suspect admits guilt, the next step typically is to develop a complete narrative. That is, police may work with the suspect to construct a full account of what occurred. This process, during which details may be added or adjusted to provide a clearer and more complete picture of the crime, makes the confession seem more authentic and accurate.

A number of consequences follow after a confession is obtained and a narrative of the events is developed. The confession may contaminate the ensuing investigation by essentially determining its course and eventual outcome (Scherr et al., 2020). Not only might investigators stop pursuing other leads, but the confession may alter their interpretation of existing evidence. Believing that the guilty offender has been captured and admitted guilt, police, prosecutors, defense attorneys, and other officials may consciously or subconsciously adjust their thinking to support that version of events and make subsequent decisions accordingly. They will have been influenced, in other words, by confirmation and disconfirmation biases and belief perseverance. Furthermore, studies have shown that information about confessions can even affect experts' opinions, for example, in the interpretation of fingerprint evidence (Dror & Charlton, 2006), and influence the testimony of eyewitnesses (Hasel & Kassin, 2009). This contamination effect often helps explain why false confessions can seem so reliable and are supported by other evidence. A suspect's false confession, which "appears to be intrinsically corroborated by accurate crime details and extrinsically corroborated by lay and expert witnesses," can essentially "predetermine[] the outcome of adjudication" (Scherr et al., 2020, p. 354).

Strength of Confession Evidence

One reason false confessions are so damaging owes to the impressive strength of confession evidence at trial. Studies have shown that the presence of a confession significantly increases the likelihood of conviction, even when fact-finders are informed that the confession was coerced or reported second-hand via informants (e.g., Kassin & Neumann, 1997; Neuschatz et al., 2008; Redlich et al., 2008; see also, chapter 7 in this book for more on informants). In short, a confession is arguably the most powerful piece of evidence at trial. Even when obtained under questionable circumstances, a defendant's confession may influence a jury to return a guilty verdict. Jurors may also be hesitant to believe or accept a defendant's claim that their confession was false; a recent study found that jurors treat such claims more skeptically than witness recantations (Bernhard & Miller, 2018).

Wrongful Convictions in Popular Culture: Interrogations and Confessions

- *The Wrong Guys: Murder, False Confessions, and the Norfolk Four* (2008) — a book by author Tom Wells and law professor Richard Leo provides an in-depth analysis of the Norfolk Four case, in which four Navy sailors were convicted of rape and murder in Norfolk, Virginia. All four of the men falsely confessed to the crime, although their stories were inaccurate and inconsistent. The authors describe the crime and recount how investigators altered their interpretation of events to persuade the suspects to confess, fit new evidence to the admissions, and maintain the guilt of the four men, ultimately leading to their wrongful convictions.

- *The Confessions* (2011) — a PBS FRONTLINE documentary written, produced, and directed by Ofra Bickel about the Norfolk Four convictions, featuring interviews with the four defendants, as well as Richard Leo and others involved in the case.

- *Making a Murderer* (2015) — a 10-episode Netflix documentary series produced by Moira Demos and Laura Ricciardi that focuses largely on the case of Steven Avery, who was convicted of murder in 2007. Avery was allegedly assisted by his nephew, Brendan Dassey, who also was convicted after confessing under interrogation. Dassey's conviction was overturned in 2016, although it was reinstated the following year when the full complement of judges on the Seventh Circuit Court of Appeals reconsidered that decision (*Dassey v. Dittmann*, 2017). Dassey consequently remains in service of his sentence of life imprisonment in Wisconsin.

- *The Confession* (2010) — a novel by famed lawyer-turned-novelist John Grisham. The plot centers on a young man wrongly convicted of a rape and murder whose execution is pending, and the guilty man, suffering from a brain tumor, and his decision to do what's right and try to convince officials that they are on the verge of executing an innocent man.

Interrogations, Confessions, and the Law

To this point, our focus has been on accepting and understanding the reality that sometimes individuals who are completely innocent of wrongdoing will falsely confess that they have committed a crime when interrogated by the police. It is indeed counterintuitive that a person who has done nothing wrong will claim just the opposite. On the other hand, we might also wonder with some justification why a person who *has* committed a crime would admit as much to the police, and thereby provide a potentially persuasive piece of inculpatory evidence. Even if guilty, it is not difficult to understand why a person intent on avoiding a criminal record and being fined, incarcerated, or even executed might be expected to deny committing a crime or maintain silence so as not to provide the police or prosecutor with damning evidence. If we posit that suspects are not likely to volunteer that they are guilty when questioned by the police or when asked to respond to an accusation in court, we might inquire what license (if any) the authorities should be given to break down or overcome their predictable resistance to admitting guilt. Conversely, we must ask what protections the suspect is owed to guard against official overreaching, including pressures that might lead to a false admission of guilt.

Few U.S. Supreme Court cases have penetrated American culture as deeply as *Miranda v. Arizona* (1966), a decision made famous by the relentless recitation of "*Miranda* rights" in television shows, movies, and novels that feature crime, police investigation, and courtroom drama. *Miranda* has been a part of the country's legal landscape for more than a half-century. Before probing the contours of this famous ruling and considering its relationship to the subject of false confessions, we examine the law that governed police interrogation of criminal suspects prior to *Miranda*. Many aspects of earlier legal doctrine remain relevant today.

In relevant part, the Fifth Amendment to the United States Constitution provides: "No person shall ... be compelled in any criminal case to be a witness against himself." As with other provisions of the Bill of Rights—the first ten amendments to the Constitution, which were adopted in 1791—the Fifth Amendment originally applied only against *federal* governmental officials and thus did not constrain state or local law enforcement officers. Nor did this amendment govern the admissibility of confession evidence in state court proceedings, where the overwhelming majority of criminal cases are resolved. Prior to the mid-1960s, the only limitations placed by the federal Constitution on state and local police officers in their interrogation of criminal suspects, and on the admissibility of confessions in state courts, were those implicit in the Fourteenth Amendment's Due Process guarantee.

The Fourteenth Amendment, ratified in 1868, is binding on *state* governmental officials. Its initial section provides: "nor shall any State deprive any person of life, liberty, or property, without due process of law." In *Brown v. Mississippi* (1936), the Supreme Court relied on the Fourteenth Amendment's Due Process Clause to overturn convictions and death sentences resulting from a state court trial in which law enforcement officers testified that they had beaten, whipped, and choked the defendants to secure their confessions to murder. Chief Justice Hughes's opinion denounced the methods used to obtain the confessions as "revolting" and impossible to square with "fundamental principles of liberty and justice" (p. 286). It further seems clear that confessions "extorted by officers of the state by brutality and violence" are of dubious reliability. Indeed, the defendants in *Brown* "testified that the confessions were false" (p. 279).

The Due Process Clause was interpreted to bar the use of "involuntary" confessions, defined as statements obtained through official coercion rather than being the product of an individual's "rational intellect and a free will" (*Reck v. Pate*, 1961, p. 440). The imprecision of the involuntariness test, with its reliance on concepts such as "coercion," "rational intellect," and "free will," offered scant concrete guidance to the police or to the courts who were charged with applying it. Its meaning was all the more elusive because its enforcement depended on the "totality of the circumstances" of individual cases, including the specific interrogation tactics employed by the police and the unique characteristics of the suspect being questioned. Compounding these difficulties, the test required courts to reconstruct the events culminating in a confession, which often left them having to resolve diametrically opposing factual accounts offered by the police and the suspect.

The numerous problems associated with the Due Process "involuntariness" test became painfully clear over time. Concurrently, the police use of physically coercive tactics to secure confessions, such as those involved in *Brown v. Mississippi*, had increasingly given way to psychological ploys and strategies. The frustrating challenges of how to "police the police" in their interrogation of suspected criminals form the important backdrop to the Supreme Court's decision in *Miranda*. During the tumultuous decade of the 1960s, with Earl Warren serving as its Chief Justice, the Supreme Court ruled that almost all of the Bill of Rights safeguards pertaining to criminal procedure must be observed by state law enforcement officers and in state courts. The Bill of Rights protections were said to be "incorporated" through the Fourteenth Amendment Due Process Clause and thus were applicable to the states. In *Malloy v. Hogan* (1964), the Court announced that the Fifth Amendment right against compelled self-incrimination was binding on the states. Two years later, the Court relied on the Fifth Amendment to decide *Miranda*.

On its surface, *Miranda* offers precisely the sort of clear and straightforward framework the Court majority deemed necessary to govern the admissibility of confessions in criminal cases. The police must advise suspects of their rights (to remain silent, to an attorney, to court-appointed counsel if they cannot afford to hire a lawyer) and the consequences of forgoing them (anything they say can be used against them). Statements made to the police are admissible in court if and only if suspects thereafter choose to relinquish, or waive those protections. No longer would the admissibility of confessions depend on their "voluntariness" under the "totality of the circumstances," and after divining whether a suspect's "free will" had been overborne.

But embedded in the *Miranda* ruling were numerous vexing issues that would belie the decision's promised clarity and straightforward application. The *Miranda* rights applied only when suspects were in police *custody* and *interrogated*— important and uncertain limitations on the ruling's scope. Nor was it clear how the required "knowing, intelligent, and voluntary waiver" of the *Miranda* rights would be demonstrated, or how a suspect could successfully invoke the right to remain silent, or to an attorney, and thus take advantage of the promised protections.

In many respects, the safeguards envisioned by the *Miranda* Court arguably have been watered down by later decisions. For example, in *Duckworth v. Eagan* (1989), the justices approved of the police administering an altered form of the venerable *Miranda* warnings, which instructed that "We have no way of giving you a lawyer, but one will be appointed for you, if you wish, if and when you go to court." In *Davis v. United States* (1994), the Court ruled that to successfully invoke *Miranda's* right to counsel, suspects must "unambiguously" assert that they want a lawyer, holding that the suspect's statement, "Maybe I should talk to a lawyer," did not suffice. In *Berghuis v. Thompkins*

(2010), the justices further backtracked from *Miranda*, ruling that a waiver of *Miranda* rights can be inferred from a suspect's agreement to talk to the police after being advised of and acknowledging that they understood their rights, and that a more explicit indication of a willingness to forgo their protections is not required. In *Oregon v. Elstad* (1985), the Court held that even though the police secured an initial confession from a suspect in violation of *Miranda*, thus rendering the confession inadmissible, a subsequent confession obtained after proper *Miranda* warnings are given is admissible, and that the police are not required to tell the suspect that the previous confession could not have been used as evidence. In *Missouri v. Seibert* (2004), the Court ruled that the police cannot deliberately employ this "cat out of the bag" strategy to capitalize on a prior *Miranda* violation. And in *Harris v. New York* (1971), the justices authorized the use of a statement obtained in violation of *Miranda* for impeachment purposes, that is, to undermine the credibility of a defendant whose trial testimony deviated from the otherwise inadmissible statement earlier made to the police. In due course, the Court even recognized a "public safety exception" to *Miranda*, which authorizes the police to secure and make use of incriminating statements in court without first administering the standard warnings based on a reasonable belief that information is needed in the interests of public safety (*New York v. Quarles*, 1984).

The *Miranda* rights can certainly offer protection against the pressures that help produce false confessions by suspects who undergo custodial police interrogation. Yet because the safeguards are not always required, and because they often are relinquished even when available, the *Miranda* rights are a decidedly imperfect barrier against false confessions. Ironically, perhaps, courts continue to scrutinize many of the factors contributing to false confessions under the Due Process "voluntariness" principles, which preceded *Miranda*. The analysis involves the same uncertainties and difficulties that plagued the test at its inception.

Under current law, the police may not threaten individuals they are questioning (*Lynumn v. Illinois*, 1963), nor make promises such as for immunity from prosecution or judicial leniency (*Haynes v. Washington*, 1961), but they are not forbidden from using many other forms of trickery and deceit in their attempts to elicit incriminating statements from suspects. Thus, for example, the Supreme Court has found confessions to be admissible despite the police falsely telling a suspect that an accomplice already had implicated him in a murder (*Frazier v. Cupp*, 1969), and lying to another suspect that his fingerprints had been found in a burglarized home (*Oregon v. Mathiason*, 1977). Courts have found acceptable many other police ruses, such as falsely telling suspects that they have failed a polygraph exam, that gunpowder residue has been detected on their hands, that tire tracks left at the crime scene match their car, and that eyewitnesses have identified them (*Commonwealth v. Selby*, 1995; *Lincoln v. State*, 2005; *State v. Kelekolio*, 1993; *Whittington v. State*, 2002). While tactics of this sort might help persuade a guilty party to throw in the towel and confess wrongdoing, they also risk inducing a frightened or vulnerable individual to falsely admit guilt. State courts occasionally have found that police trickery and deception designed to secure confessions go too far, presenting too great of a risk of inducing false confessions or otherwise being offensive to legal principles (see, e.g., *State v. Baker*, 2020; *State v. Cayward*, 1989). As long as the tactics employed are not so overbearing as to render a confession involuntary, and assuming that *Miranda*'s threshold requirements have been satisfied, the courts generally find that a suspect's incriminating statements are admissible in evidence. And as we have noted, once a jury or judge (or a prosecutor, or even a defense lawyer) hears that a defendant has confessed, it may be very difficult to convince them that the admission is untrue.

As we discussed in connection with the admissibility of eyewitness identifications, court decisions which interpret and apply constitutional provisions, including the Fifth Amendment's right against compelled self-incrimination, and the Fifth and Fourteenth Amendments' Due Process rights, establish the minimum legal protections which governmental officials must observe. Legislation and administrative regulations cannot restrict constitutional protections, but they can extend additional safeguards to individuals. Many states have enacted statutes that govern police interrogation of suspected criminals to help guard against false confessions and ensure that the police do not overstep their lawful authority. One important initiative has been the movement to require interrogations to be video-recorded, a requirement usually limited to serious crimes and interrogations that take place in custodial settings. We discuss the benefits of video-recording interrogation sessions and related research later in this chapter. The following New York statute, which addresses involuntary confessions, includes a section which became effective in 2018 that requires the video-recording of police interrogation under specified circumstances.

––––––––––

New York Criminal Procedure Law § 60.45
Rules of evidence; admissibility of statements of defendants

1. Evidence of a written or oral confession, admission, or other statement made by a defendant with respect to his participation or lack of participation in the offense charged, may not be received in evidence

against him in a criminal proceeding if such statement was involuntarily made.

2. A confession, admission or other statement is "involuntarily made" by a defendant when it is obtained from him:

(a) By any person by the use or threatened use of physical force upon the defendant or another person, or by means of any other improper conduct or undue pressure which impaired the defendant's physical or mental condition to the extent of undermining his ability to make a choice whether or not to make a statement; or

(b) By a public servant engaged in law enforcement activity or by a person then acting under his direction or in cooperation with him:

(i) by means of any promise or statement of fact, which promise or statement creates a substantial risk that the defendant might falsely incriminate himself; or

(ii) in violation of such rights as the defendant may derive from the constitution of this state or of the United States.

3. (a) Where a person is subject to custodial interrogation by a public servant at a detention facility, the entire custodial interrogation, including the giving of any required advice of the rights of the individual being questioned, and the waiver of any rights by the individual, shall be recorded by an appropriate video recording device if the interrogation involves a class A-1 felony, [subject to various exceptions], or a felony offense defined [under other specified sections of the Penal Law]. For purposes of this paragraph, the term "detention facility" shall mean a police station, correctional facility, holding facility for prisoners, prosecutor's office or other facility where persons are held in detention in connection with criminal charges that have been or may be filed against them.

(b) No confession, admission or other statement shall be subject to a motion to suppress … based solely upon the failure to video record such interrogation in a detention facility as defined in paragraph (a) of this subdivision. However, where the people offer into evidence a confession, admission or other statement made by a person in custody with respect to his or her participation or lack of participation in an offense specified in paragraph (a) of this subdivision, that has not been video recorded, the court shall consider the failure to record as a factor, but not as the sole factor, in accordance with paragraph (c) of this subdivision in determining whether such confession, admission or other statement shall be admissible.

(c) Notwithstanding the requirement of paragraph (a) of this subdivision, upon a showing of good cause by the prosecutor, the custodial interrogation need not be recorded. Good cause shall include, but not be limited to:

(i) If electronic recording equipment malfunctions.

(ii) If electronic recording equipment is not available because it was otherwise being used.

(iii) If statements are made in response to questions that are routinely asked during arrest processing.

(iv) If the statement is spontaneously made by the suspect and not in response to police questioning.

(v) If the statement is made during an interrogation that is conducted when the interviewer is unaware that a qualifying offense has occurred.

(vi) If the statement is made at a location other than the "interview room" because the suspect cannot be brought to such room, e.g., the suspect is in a hospital or the suspect is out of state and that state is not governed by a law requiring the recordation of an interrogation.

(vii) If the statement is made after a suspect has refused to participate in the interrogation if it is recorded, and appropriate effort to document such refusal is made.

(viii) If such statement is not recorded as a result of an inadvertent error or oversight, not the result of any intentional conduct by law enforcement personnel.

(ix) If it is law enforcement's reasonable belief that such recording would jeopardize the safety of any person or reveal the identity of a confidential informant.

(x) If such statement is made at a location not equipped with a video recording device and the reason for using that location is not to subvert the intent of the law. For purposes of this section, the term "location" shall include those locations specified in paragraph (b) of subdivision four of section 305.2 of the family court act.

(d) In the event the court finds that the people have not shown good cause for the non-recording of the confession, admission, or other statement, but determines that a non-recorded confession, admission or other statement is nevertheless admissible because it was voluntarily made then, upon request of the defendant, the court must instruct the jury that the people's failure to record the defendant's confession, admission, or other statement as required by this section may be weighed as a factor, but not as the sole factor, in determining whether such confession, admission, or other statement was voluntarily made, or was made at all.

(e) Video recording as required by this section shall be conducted in accordance with standards established by rule of the division of criminal justice services.

Reforming Interrogations

As discussed throughout this chapter, research has highlighted many of the factors underlying false confessions and the law has several safeguards in place designed to protect suspects under investigation. However, a number of additional policy reforms have been suggested that might reduce the occurrence of false admissions.

Recording Custodial Interrogations

As discussed in the previous section, the primary reform suggested by most experts is the electronic recording of all **custodial interviews and interrogations** conducted by the police. This recommendation is designed to "lift the veil of secrecy from the interrogation process" (Kassin et al., 2010, p. 25), which has historically occurred behind closed doors. Such a policy has been supported by scholars in psychology, law, and other disciplines, as well as individual practitioners and organizations like the American Bar Association.

A recording of the interrogation provides an objective record of the process used to obtain a confession and has a number of benefits for many people involved in the adjudication of criminal cases. It may serve to discourage investigators from using the most coercive and potentially illegal tactics that are known to generate false confessions, and provide the defense with evidence if a claim of coerced confession is raised. The recording may also benefit law enforcement personnel by protecting them from frivolous or inaccurate claims of coercion or abuse. Furthermore, the recording is useful for judges, who may be tasked with evaluating whether statements made by the defendant were voluntary, or juries, who must weigh confessions as evidence in determining guilt or innocence. The relatively objective and accurate record of the interrogation helps in these matters, rather than relying solely on the memories and accounts of those involved, which may be incomplete, tainted, or biased.

Although most experts support the recording of custodial interrogations in general, the specific policies suggested may vary. Almost all supporters suggest that the entire process, including the reading of the suspect's rights, be recorded in order to assist judges in evaluating whether the waiver of rights was voluntary and whether matters that occurred prior to an admission of guilt may have elicited or influenced the suspect's statement. Another specific suggestion deals with the positioning of the camera used to record interrogations. Most experts support an "equal focus" perspective wherein the camera equally captures both the interrogator(s) and the suspect. Research suggests that when viewing a recording focused only on the suspect, people may judge the situation as less coercive, potentially leading jurors to underestimate the pressure suspects are under. In other words, a camera angle that also includes the interrogator allows viewers to better assess the conditions under which the confession occurred, which in turn allows them to make better determinations about voluntariness and, ultimately, the statement's reliability.

Other aspects of interrogation recording policies have not yielded such clear-cut recommendations. For example, the specific situations that require recording may vary, as policies try to account for exigencies that may render recording impractical. The New York statute, reproduced above, identifies several reasons, including the malfunction of equipment, that would excuse the authorities from recording an interrogation session. Finally, the consequences for non-compliance with recording requirements vary. In some jurisdictions, an unrecorded statement is excluded as evidence unless there is a valid reason for non-compliance; in others, a failure to record does not preclude the admission of a statement, but the jury may be given a cautionary instruction to encourage skepticism and careful evaluation of the confession. The New York legislation offers an example of this latter approach.

A number of states now require that some or all custodial interrogations be recorded, and many police agencies have initiated the practice without being mandated by the state. Initially, many law enforcement officers were reluctant to embrace the practice. However, interviews with officials suggest that after implementing recording procedures, most police departments prefer the practice. They identify a number of benefits to recording including being able to focus on the suspect rather than note-taking, reducing the time spent in court to defend interrogation tactics, and increasing the public's trust in law enforcement, among others. Most departments have also reported that recording interrogations has not affected the willingness of suspects to speak with police and potentially incriminate themselves (Sullivan, 2004). Indeed, a recent study found that in the state surveyed, most departments followed the state law mandating recording and in many cases went beyond the law's requirements (Zalman et al., 2019).

Reforming Interrogation Practices

Of course, recording interrogations will not, on its own, prevent psychologically coercive tactics from producing false confessions from innocent suspects. To help respond to some of the issues discussed in the earlier research overview, in addition to recording procedures, some experts have suggested altering specific interrogation practices, specifically those that are deemed coercive and are known to contribute to false confessions. For example, some scholars and practitioners suggest limiting the amount of time suspects are isolated and interrogated. As noted earlier, while most interrogations are relatively short, those in known false confession cases tend to be significantly longer; generally, experts suggest that interrogations that last more than four to six hours might presumptively be considered coercive (e.g., Blair, 2005). Other suggestions include prohibiting or limiting techniques such as the presentation of false evidence and minimization tactics that might include implications of leniency in exchange for a confession (Kassin et al., 2010).

Rather than reform individual interrogation practices, there is some support for working toward wholesale changes in the culture of interrogation as it exists in the United States. As we discussed earlier, American interrogations tend to be guilt-presumptive and accusatorial, with the goal of securing a confession. Some have advocated for a change in this model, moving from confrontational interrogation to **investigative interviewing**. The suggested approach generally follows the PEACE model used in Britain, which stands for "Preparation and Planning," "Engage and Explain," "Account," "Closure," and "Evaluate." This method of questioning suspects focuses more on fact-finding and less on simply obtaining an admission of guilt. Some research has shown that this type of investigative interviewing does not lead to a decrease in convictions, as the methods used allow officers to gather information that can clear innocent suspects yet also build cases against those who are guilty (for a discussion, see Kassin et al., 2010). This approach has been adopted outside of Britain, including in New Zealand and Norway. Several techniques associated with the PEACE model also are taught in the United States, as the idea of using less accusatorial and more investigative techniques has gained increased traction. For example, at least one large consulting firm for police agencies in the United States recently announced that its instructors will stop teaching the "Reid technique," which has been the most widely used interrogation strategy for decades, due to the risks associated with confrontational interrogations and false confessions (Hager, 2017; Kassin et al., 2010).

Protecting Vulnerable Suspects

As noted earlier, certain groups, including juveniles and suspects suffering from mental illness, developmental or intellectual disabilities, and cognitive or psychological disorders, tend to be particularly vulnerable to coercive interrogation tactics and therefore are overrepresented among known false confessors. Several suggested reforms may help alleviate this problem. The first is to restrict or limit the use of certain tactics that are especially manipulative, such as false evidence ploys and minimization tactics, when suspects from vulnerable populations are interrogated. It additionally has been recommended that law enforcement officials receive special training regarding the interviewing and interrogation of suspects from these groups. Specialized training and education may help officers understand the vulnerabilities of certain suspects, and what types of tactics should be used and which should be avoided to guard against unreliable admissions of guilt.

Another potential reform is to require the presence of an attorney when a suspect known to be a member of a vulnerable population undergoes interrogation. Such suspects generally may have more difficulty understanding that they are in legal jeopardy and in comprehending their rights, and may be likely to waive their rights without a clear understanding of the consequences (Norris & Redlich, 2012). While some jurisdictions require a parent or guardian to be present when police interrogate juveniles, research suggests that the presence of an interested adult may not actually benefit the suspect (e.g., Cohen, 2020; Oberlander & Goldstein, 2001). Thus, according to some experts and advocates, juveniles, individuals with mental illness, and other vulnerable suspects should "be accompanied and advised by a professional advocate, preferably an attorney, trained to serve in this role" (Kassin et al., 2010, p. 30).

While no single reform can fully address the myriad challenges associated with the interrogation of vulnerable suspects, what appears to be clear is that standard existing legal protections do not effectively protect those who are particularly susceptible to the psychologically intense practices associated with police interrogations (see Fabiszewski, 2020).

Conclusion

Interrogations are integral to criminal investigations. There is good cause for this: confessions secured from guilty parties help the police solve crimes and aid prosecutors in convicting offenders. However, the problems associated with modern interrogation practices and the ways in which innocent suspects can be led to falsely admit guilt must be acknowledged, understood, and addressed. Following this recognition, the courts, practitioners, and policymakers must continue to work to improve interrogation practices and reduce resulting miscarriages of justice in which false confessions are contributing factors.

Key Terms and Concepts

- **Custodial interview and interrogation**: questioning that occurs after a suspect is taken into custody, or when their liberty has been constrained in a significant way
- **Confession**: an admission of guilt; in this chapter, referring to the admission of a person to a criminal act that is made to police officers either voluntarily or as the result of police interrogation
- **Voluntary false confession**: a false confession made without prompting or pressure from police
- **Compliant false confession**: a false confession prompted by the pressure and stress of police interrogation
- **Internalized/persuaded false confession**: a false confession in which an innocent suspect comes to believe that they actually committed the crime
- **Situational risk factors**: characteristics of the situation, or the criminal interrogation, that may affect the likelihood of a suspect giving a false statement
- **Dispositional risk factors**: characteristics of the suspect that may affect the likelihood of the suspect giving a false statement
- **Minimization**: interrogation techniques that involve downplaying the seriousness of the offense or the suspect's role in it
- **Maximization**: interrogation techniques that involve exaggerating the strength of evidence against the suspect or the seriousness of the charges, and thus the benefit of confessing
- *Miranda v. Arizona*: a 1966 Supreme Court case announcing the procedures required to protect suspects' rights against compelled self-incrimination during custodial interrogation; requires law enforcement to advise suspects of their rights and secure a waiver of them
- **Investigative interviewing**: a non-confrontational approach to suspect questioning that focuses on gathering information, rather than securing an admission of guilt

Discussion Questions

1. Could you ever imagine confessing to a crime you did not commit? Do you think you could withstand the psychologically intense nature of a police interrogation? Why or why not?

2. What are "situational" and "dispositional" risk factors for false confessions?

3. How might we protect populations that are most vulnerable to police interrogation and most likely to falsely confess?

4. What rights must police advise suspects of according to *Miranda v. Arizona*? Are these rights clear? Do you think most people fully understand the meaning of these rights and the consequences of waiving them? Does *Miranda* provide an effective protection against false confessions?

References

Berghuis v. Thompkins, 560 U.S. 370 (2010).

Bernhard, P. A., & Miller, R. S. (2018). Juror perceptions of false confessions versus witness recantations. *Psychiatry, Psychology, & Law, 25*(4), 539–549.

Blair, J. P. (2005). A test of the unusual false confession perspective using cases of proven false confessions. *Criminal Law Bulletin, 41*, 127–144.

Bond, C. F., & DePaulo, B. M. (2006). Accuracy of deception judgments. *Personality & Social Psychology Review, 10*, 214–234.

Brown v. Mississippi, 297 U.S. 278 (1936).

Cohen, L. (2020). When parents are not enough: The case for counsel in juvenile interrogations. *Criminal Justice, 34*(4), 55–56.

Commonwealth v. Selby, 651 N.E.2d 843 (Mass. 1995).

Dassey v. Dittmann, 877 F.3d 297 (7th Cir. 2017) (*en banc*), cert. den. 138 S.Ct. 2677 (2018).

Davis v. United States, 512 U.S. 452 (1994).

Drizin, S. A., & Leo, R. A. (2004). The problem of false confessions in the post-DNA world. *North Carolina Law Review, 82*, 891–1008.

Dror, I. E., & Charlton, D. (2006). Why experts make errors. *Journal of Forensic Identification, 56*, 600–616.

Duckworth v. Eagan, 492 U.S. 195 (1989).

Fabiszewski, M. J. (2020). Major reforms for minors' confessions: Rethinking self-incrimination protections for juveniles. *Boston College Law Review, 61*(7), 2643–2694.

Frazier v. Cupp, 394 U.S. 731 (1969).

Gajanan, M. (2019, December 6). The story of Henry Lee Lucas, the notorious subject of Netflix's *The Confession Killer*. *TIME*. https://time.com/5745028/the-confession-killer-henry-lee-lucas-netflix/.

Gudjonsson, G. H. (2003). *The psychology of interrogations and confessions*. Wiley.

Gudjonsson, G. H., Sigurdsson, J. F., Asgeirsdottir, B. B., & Sigfusdottir, I. D. (2006). Custodial interrogation, false confession, and individual differences: A national study among Icelandic youth. *Personality and Individual Differences, 41*, 49–59.

Gudjonsson, G. H., Sigurdsson, J. F., Sigfusdottir, I. D., & Young, S. (2012). False confessions to police and their relationship with conduct disorder, ADHD, and life adversity. *Personality and Individual Differences, 52*, 696–701.

Hager, E. (2017, March 7). The seismic change in police interrogations. The Marshall Project. https://www.themarshallproject.org/2017/03/07/the-seismic-change-in-police-interrogations?utm_medium=email&utm_campaign=newsletter&utm_source=opening-statement&utm_term=newsletter-20170308-708#.q1WyaTGld.

Harris v. New York, 401 U.S. 222 (1971).

Harrison, Y., & Horne, J. A. (2000). The impact of sleep deprivation on decision making: A review. *Journal of Experimental Psychology: Applied, 6*, 236–249.

Hasel, L. E., & Kassin, S. M. (2009). On the presumption of evidentiary independence: Can confessions corrupt eyewitness identifications? *Psychological Science, 20*, 122–126.

Haynes v. Washington, 373 U.S. 503 (1961).

Janzen, K. (2019). Coerced fate: How negotiation models lead to false confessions. *Journal of Criminal Law & Criminology, 109*(1), 71–101.

Kamisar, Y. (1980). *Police interrogation and confessions: Essays in law and policy*. University of Michigan Press.

Kassin, S. M., Drizin, S. A., Grisso, T., Gudjonsson, G. H., Leo, R. A., & Redlich, A. D. (2010). Police-induced confessions: Risk factors and recommendations. *Law and Human Behavior, 34*, 3–38.

Kassin, S. M., & Neumann, K. (1997). On the power of confession evidence: An experimental test of the "fundamental difference" hypothesis. *Law and Human Behavior, 21*, 469–484.

Leo, R. A. (2008). *Police interrogation and American justice*. Harvard University Press.

Lincoln v. State, 882 A.2d 944 (Md. App. 2005).

Lynumn v. Illinois, 372 U.S. 528 (1963).

Malloy v. Hogan, 378 U.S. 1 (1964).

McCann, J. T. (1998). A conceptual framework for identifying various types of confessions. *Behavioral Sciences & the Law, 16*(4), 441–453.

Meissner, C. A., & Kassin, S. M. (2002). "He's guilty!": Investigator bias in judgments of truth and deception. *Law and Human Behavior, 26,* 469–480.

Miranda v. Arizona, 384 U.S. 436 (1966).

Missouri v. Seibert, 542 U.S. 600 (2004).

Mogavero, M. C. (2020). An exploratory examination of intellectual disability and mental illness associated with alleged false confessions. *Behavioral Sciences & the Law, 38*(4), 299–316.

Najdowski, C. J. (2014). Interactions between African Americans and police officers: How cultural stereotypes create a wrongful conviction pipeline for African Americans. In A. D. Redlich, J. R. Acker, R. J. Norris, & C. L. Bonventre (Eds.), *Examining wrongful convictions: Stepping back, moving forward* (pp. 55–70). Carolina Academic Press.

Najdowski, C. J. (2016, February 8). Stereotype threat in police encounters: Implications for miscarriages of justice. *Behavioral Scientist.* https://behavioralscientist.org/stereotype-threat-in-police-encounters-implications-for-miscarriages-of-justice/.

Najdowski, C. J., Bottoms, B. L., & Goff, P. A. (2015). Stereotype threat and racial differences in citizens' experiences of police encounters. *Law and Human Behavior, 39*(5), 463–477.

Neuschatz, J. S., Lawson, D. S., Swanner, J. K., Meissner, C. A., & Neuschatz, J. S. (2008). The effects of accomplice witnesses and jailhouse informants on jury decision making. *Law and Human Behavior, 32,* 137–149.

New York v. Quarles, 467 U.S. 649 (1984).

Norris, R. J., & Redlich, A. D. (2012). At-risk populations under investigation and at trial. In B. L. Cutler (Ed.), *Conviction of the innocent: Lessons from psychological research* (pp. 13–32). American Psychological Association.

Norris, R. J., & Redlich, A. D. (2014). Seeking justice, compromising truth? Criminal admissions and the prisoner's dilemma. *Albany Law Review, 77,* 1005–1038.

Oberlander, L. B., & Goldstein, N. E. (2001). A review and update on the practice of evaluating Miranda comprehension. *Behavioral Sciences and the Law, 19,* 453–471.

Ofshe, R. J., & Leo, R. A. (1997). The social psychology of police interrogation: The theory and classification of true and false confessions. *Studies in Law, Politics, and Society, 16,* 189–251.

Oregon v. Elstad, 470 U.S. 298 (1985).

Oregon v. Mathiason, 429 U.S. 492 (1977).

Possley, M. (2020). Frances Choy. National Registry of Exonerations. http://www.law.umich.edu/special/exoneration/Pages/casedetail.aspx?caseid=5815.

Reck v. Pate, 367 U.S. 433 (1961).

Redlich, A. D. (2010). False confessions and false guilty pleas: Similarities and differences. In G. D. Lassiter & C. Meissner (Eds.), *Interrogations and confessions: Current research, practice, and policy* (pp. 49–66). American Psychological Association.

Redlich, A. D., Quas, J. A., & Ghetti, S. (2008). Perceptions of children during a police interview: Guilt, confessions, and interview fairness. *Psychology, Crime, and Law, 14,* 201–223.

Schatz, S. J. (2018). Interrogated with intellectual disabilities: The risks of false confession. *Stanford Law Review, 70*(2), 643–690.

Scherr, K. C., Redlich, A. D., & Kassin, S. M. (2020). Cumulative disadvantage: A psychological framework for understanding how innocence can lead to confession, wrongful conviction, and beyond. *Perspectives on Psychological Science, 15*(2), 353–383. https://doi.org/10.1177/1745691619896608.

State v. Baker, 465 P.3d 860 (Haw. 2020).

State v. Cayward, 552 So.2d 971 (Fla. App. 1989).

State v. Kelekolio, 849 P.2d 58 (Haw. 1993).

Stewart, J. M., Woody, W. D., & Pulos, S. (2018). The prevalence of false confessions in experimental laboratory simulations: A meta-analysis. *Behavioral Sciences & the Law, 36*(1), 12–31.

Stridbeck, U. (2020). Coerced-reactive confessions: The case of Thomas Quick. *Journal of Forensic Psychology Research & Practice, 20*(4), 305–322.

Sullivan, T. P. (2004). *Police experiences with recording custodial interrogations.* Northwestern University School of Law Center on Wrongful Convictions.

Vrij, A. (2004). Why professionals fail to catch liars and how they can improve. *Legal & Criminological Psychology, 9,* 159–181.

Waxman, S. P. (2020). Innocent juvenile confessions. *Journal of Criminal Law & Criminology, 110*(1), 1–8.

West, E., & Meterko, V. (2016). Innocence Project: DNA exonerations, 1989–2014: Review of data and findings from the first 25 years. *Albany Law Review, 79,* 717–795.

Whittington v. State, 809 A.2d 721 (Md. App. 2002).

Zalman, M., Rubino, L. L., & Smith, B. (2019). Beyond police compliance with electronic recording of interrogation legislation: Toward error reduction. *Criminal Justice Policy Review, 30*(4), 627–655.

Chapter 5

False Admissions: Guilty Pleas and Plea Bargaining

Learning Objectives

After reading this chapter, you should be able to:

- Appreciate the similarities and differences between police interrogations and plea bargaining.
- Understand the prevalence of guilty pleas and plea bargaining as a means of case adjudication in the United States.
- Evaluate some of the factors that influence defendants in their decisions to plead guilty.
- Discuss U.S. Supreme Court doctrine governing guilty pleas and plea bargaining.

Case Study: Corruption in Cook County, Illinois

In January 2003, when Marc Giles entered his girlfriend's apartment building in Chicago, he encountered several people being detained by the police. An officer stopped Giles and searched him. Although no contraband was found on him or any of the other people, Giles was handcuffed and detained with the others. Sergeant Ronald Watts walked each person outside one at a time. When he took Giles outside, Watts asked if Giles could find guns for him. Giles responded that he could not, explaining that he did not know where to get any guns. Watts eventually went upstairs in the housing complex and returned with several bundles of drugs. In November 2003, Giles pled guilty to possession of a controlled substance. He said that although he was innocent, he agreed to plead guilty and be sentenced to eight years in prison "because I was afraid I would be sentenced to an even lengthier jail term" if he pled not guilty and was convicted following a trial (Possley, 2021).

Nearly two years later, in March 2005, Sgt. Watts arrested Ben Baker in the same Chicago housing complex for possession of heroin and cocaine with intent to deliver. Baker was released on bond and filed a complaint claiming that the police had planted the drugs. Baker and his wife, Clarissa Glenn, were again arrested in December 2005 when the same officers said they found cocaine in their car. Baker elected to have a bench trial before Judge Michael Toomin. Baker's defense attorney requested information pertaining to misconduct allegations against the police officers in the case. Judge Toomin reviewed several relevant files, including statements from drug dealers at the housing complex where Baker was arrested. The statements were to the effect that the informants had given Sgt. Watts thousands of dollars to be allowed to avoid arrest and continue dealing drugs. Judge Toomin did not disclose the statements to the defense. Based largely on the testimony from police officers, Baker was convicted of the charges stemming from the March 2005 arrest and was sentenced to 18 years in prison (later reduced to 14 years). In September 2006, Baker and Glenn both pled guilty to the charges resulting from the December 2005 arrest. Baker agreed to a four-year prison sentence in exchange for his guilty plea, and Glenn agreed to plead guilty on the condition that she would be placed on probation to allow her to care for the couple's children (Possley, 2018a, 2018b).

Meanwhile, in March 2006, Sgt. Watts led a team of officers on a raid of the apartment of Lionel White, Sr. The officers searched White's apartment but did not find any drugs. The following month, Watts and another officer returned to the apartment, physically assaulted White, and then arrested him for aggravated battery. White also was charged with possession of heroin. Because he had previous felony convictions, White was faced with a sentence of life imprisonment without parole upon being convicted again. In June 2006, the prosecution offered to allow White to plead guilty and receive a five-year prison term. White accepted the offer but told the judge, "This is wrong. I am pleading guilty because I'm scared" (Possley, 2017). The next month, Sgt. Watts arrested White's son, Lionel White, Jr., who was charged with drug possession.

White, Jr. pled guilty in October 2006, and he was sentenced to two years of probation (Possley, 2019).

In 2012, Sgt. Watts and another police officer, Kallatt Mohammed, were caught stealing money from a man they thought was a drug courier, but who was actually an FBI informant. Both officers pled guilty; Watts was sentenced to 22 months in prison, and Mohammed to 18 months. The Chicago-based Exoneration Project then assisted in the cases of several individuals who were convicted based on investigations and arrests made by Sgt. Watts. They detailed Watts's corruption, noting that he had been under investigation by the FBI and the Chicago Police Department at the time of Baker's trial, and that he was receiving weekly payments from drug dealers.

Clarissa Glenn was granted a gubernatorial pardon in January 2015, but she was initially denied a certificate of innocence. The Cook County State's Attorney's Office Conviction Integrity Unit (CIU) reinvestigated the cases. In January 2016, the prosecution agreed to vacate Ben Baker's conviction from the March 2005 case. He was granted a certificate of innocence the next month. In March 2016, the convictions of both Baker and Glenn from the December 2005 case were vacated and the charges were dismissed. Glenn eventually received her certificate of innocence in 2018. Baker was arrested for selling heroin to an undercover informant in April 2018.

Lionel White, Sr.'s convictions were vacated, and the charges were dismissed in December 2016. He was awarded a certificate of innocence in January 2017. Lionel White, Jr.'s conviction was vacated and the charge was dismissed in November 2017, along with the convictions and charges of 14 other defendants who were prosecuted following investigations involving Sgt. Watts.

Finally, in February 2021, after another CIU investigation, the convictions of nine individuals, including Marc Giles, were vacated, and the charges against them were dismissed.

In the end, nearly 100 convictions that involved Sgt. Watts and his tactical unit were vacated. Joshua Tepfer of the Exoneration Project estimated that the members of that unit were responsible for at least 500 additional convictions (Possley, 2018). While it is highly unlikely that all of these individuals are innocent, these cases highlight the widespread damage that may be caused by individual and organizational wrongdoing (see chapter 8 for more on police misconduct). The specific cases described above demonstrate how legal pressures and perceived threats can encourage the innocent to plead guilty.

Innocence, Guilty Pleas, and Plea Bargaining: Overview and Research

In the previous chapter, we examined false confessions, primarily those made in response to police interrogation. Here, we look at the distinct but related issues concerning guilty pleas and plea bargaining and their contributions to wrongful convictions.

Most cases that result in formal criminal charges never proceed to trial. Sometimes charges are dismissed, bringing an end to cases before they reach adjudication. Defendants who continue to face charges must eventually appear in court, where they will be asked to enter a **plea**. Here, their choices vary. One option, of course, is to plead not guilty and proceed to trial, putting the prosecution to its obligation to establish guilt beyond a reasonable doubt in order to secure a conviction. Yet, as we will see, most defendants forgo their right to a trial by pleading guilty, which normally involves a sworn admission that they committed the offense and are in fact guilty. Surprisingly, perhaps, sometimes defendants are allowed to plead guilty while maintaining their innocence (typically called entering an "*Alford* **plea**," as we will discuss). Defendants often receive some concession, in the form of a reduced charge or an agreement for a recommended sentence short of the maximum, in exchange for their agreement to plead guilty. Such arrangements are produced by plea bargaining between defendants (typically negotiated by their attorneys) and prosecutors. A close companion to a guilty plea is a plea of no contest (sometimes called *nolo contendere*). Such pleas normally require the prosecution's agreement. A no contest plea authorizes the court to enter a guilty verdict but does not require defendants to admit their guilt. Throughout this chapter we generally will use the term "guilty plea" to encompass no contest pleas as well as traditional guilty pleas and *Alford* pleas.

As we have already discussed, while interrogations and plea bargaining occur at distinct points in the criminal legal process, they are related in important ways. Both practices are guilt-presumptive and are driven by a similar logic, in that the primary function is to encourage a suspect or defendant to admit to their presumptive wrongdoing. Although there is some overlap in the issues and the research concerning interrogations and negotiated guilty pleas, the practices are quite different and warrant individualized attention (Redlich, 2010a). In this chapter, we focus on guilty pleas.

Wrongful Convictions and Guilty Pleas

Despite the right to a trial as provided in the Sixth Amendment to the United States Constitution, relatively few criminal defendants, once formally charged, exercise that right. Instead, the overwhelming majority of criminal cases that result in convictions are settled through guilty pleas. In most states, guilty pleas account for 90% or more of criminal convictions. In the federal court system, rates are especially high; in 2019, more than 97% of convictions resulted from guilty pleas rather than contested trials (United States Sentencing Commission, 2020).

Because overwhelming numbers of criminal convictions are the product of guilty pleas, it almost certainly is true that the number of wrongful convictions resulting from them far outweighs the number of wrongful trial convictions. Yet, the available evidence concerning exonerations presents a starkly different picture. Of the first 325 DNA exonerations reported by the Innocence Project, only 31 (9.5%) involved a false guilty plea (West & Meterko, 2016). As of this writing, just over 20% of cases (569/2,754) reported by the National Registry of Exonerations resulted from guilty pleas. Of these 569 guilty plea cases, more than half (52%) of the exonerations involved drug-related charges (compared to just 4% in contested cases), while only 9% of the guilty plea exonerations involved murder (compared to 46% in cases that went to trial) (National Registry of Exonerations, n.d.).

What might account for the wide discrepancy between the proportion of criminal convictions that are secured through guilty pleas (90% to 95% or more) and the relatively low proportion of exoneration cases that involved guilty pleas (approximately 20%)? We consider various explanations, which are not mutually exclusive. We discuss these possibilities in turn.

One possible explanation is that false guilty pleas by innocent defendants are rare; that is, few defendants who are not in fact guilty will admit guilt and consent to being convicted without a trial. Although some legal commentators and scholars have speculated or implied that wrongful convictions produced by guilty pleas likely occur at relatively low rates (e.g., Gross & O'Brien, 2008; Hoffman, 2007), these suggestions are based primarily on assumptions rather than firm evidence, and psychological and other social science research paints a different picture.

We cannot know with certainty the rate at which innocent defendants plead guilty, but various laboratory studies and experimental methods — using hypothetical situations or vignettes, for example, or scenarios in which participants are told they made an error when they did not — have found rates in these "non-real world" settings that typically range between 20% and 50%

(Wilford & Khairalla, 2019). In addition, one self-report study found that approximately 19% of adults who pled guilty in actual criminal cases claimed to be innocent (Zottli et al., 2016). Regardless of the exact figure, we have incontrovertible evidence, through DNA analysis and other sources, that some innocent defendants have pled guilty to crimes they did not commit. The question, of course, is why this occurs.

Guilty pleas are frequently entered in connection with **plea bargaining**, which involves negotiations between the prosecution and defense to reach an agreement about terms important to a defendant's conviction and/or punishment. In many cases, defendants have strong incentives to plead guilty, whether or not that plea reflects that they actually are guilty.

Consider, for instance, the following scenario:

A defendant is charged with a relatively minor drug offense and is denied bail or is unable to post it. They consequently must remain in jail until brought to trial, which may be scheduled months in the future. They risk losing education and/or employment opportunities, they are separated from and cannot care for children and other family members, and otherwise remain deprived of their freedom and isolated from their communities as they await trial. Eventually, they are offered a deal — plead guilty to a misdemeanor offense, and be released with a sentence of time already served, with a year or two probation term. And even if they are not incarcerated and they receive no promised concessions in the form of a charge reduction or a lesser sentence, some defendants will plead guilty gambling that they will not be severely punished, simply to avoid the expense and aggravation of making multiple court appearances and the corresponding disruption to their employment, familial, and other obligations. Such outcomes may be especially prevalent in misdemeanor cases, which entail a much lower risk of incarceration than felonies and are disposed of in court proceedings that may place speed and efficiency above accurate fact-finding and procedural regularity (see Acker, 2017; Appleman, 2012; Gross, 2013).

Whether or not they are strongly incentivized by **pretrial incarceration**, innocent defendants may have other reasons to plead guilty. Their decisions might be made through acquiescence with their defense attorney's advice to accept a guilty plea (Bordens & Bassett, 1985; Henderson & Levett, 2018; Viljoen et al., 2005). The decision may also be practical, as defendants may perceive a high likelihood of conviction at trial and resulting severe sanctions. Guilty pleas often, although not invariably, entail reduced charges, lower sentences, and mitigate other potential adverse consequences (Redlich, 2010b; Wilford et al., 2020; Zimmerman & Hunter, 2018). Indeed, a large enough plea discount (or severe enough trial penalty) may be enough to persuade defendants to give up their right to a trial and enter a guilty plea (Wilford & Khairalla, 2019). For example, as discussed in the next section, Henry Alford, the man after whom the *Alford* plea is named, denied being guilty of the murder he was charged with committing, but pled guilty to avoid a possible death sentence if he were convicted at trial (*North Carolina v. Alford*, 1970). Prosecutors may increase the pressure on defendants to plead guilty by manipulating the value of a plea, or the difference between the negotiated recommended plea sentence and a potential trial sentence. The Supreme Court sanctioned such a practice in *Bordenkircher v. Hayes* (1978), a case we discuss in the following section. And some have suggested that prosecutors may be more likely to offer the best deals during plea negotiations when they have the least confidence in their ability to secure a conviction at trial. That is, prosecutors may offer the greatest inducements for pleading guilty in the "weakest cases," and it is reasonable to assume that defendants are especially likely to be innocent in cases in which there is relatively weak evidence of guilt (Bibas, 2014; Gazal-Ayal, 2006).

Other issues associated with false guilty pleas dovetail with reasons that help explain false confessions. For example, Russano and colleagues (2005) found that when minimization tactics were used and incentives to plead guilty were offered, innocent subjects were willing to admit to cheating on a task they had completed honestly. Norris and Redlich (2014) used the Prisoner's Dilemma paradigm — in which two co-suspects are separated and pitted against one another by being provided with options to plead guilty or maintain innocence and presented with corresponding incentives for doing so — to examine the willingness of subjects in a hypothetical case to make false admissions of guilt. They found that innocent subjects, under certain conditions, would accept an offered deal and plead guilty at a rate similar to guilty subjects.

Also related to the research bearing on false confessions is the notion that specific subsets of defendants are likely to be more susceptible to enter false guilty pleas than other defendants. These particularly vulnerable populations, which may overlap, include juveniles, individuals suffering from mental illness, and those with developmental or intellectual disabilities. We noted above a study in which 19% of adults who pled guilty claimed to be innocent; in that same study, 26% of juveniles claimed to be innocent (Zottoli et al., 2016), although other studies have reported lower rates (Wilford & Khairalla, 2019). In a large-scale study of defendants with mental illness, self-reported false guilty plea rates ranged from 27% to 41% (Redlich et al., 2010). The reasons for the similarities between those vulnerable in the interrogation and plea-bargaining contexts are related, involving developmental limitations, heightened suggestibility, hampered decision-making processes, and diminished legal competence (e.g., Helm et al., 2018; NeMoyer et al., 2018). At least one recent study found that, in a laboratory context, female participants were more likely to falsely plead guilty than males, owing to their perceptions of the strength of the case against them (Zimmerman & Hunter, 2018).

The studies relating to guilty pleas just considered are far from definitive and additional research is needed. However, it is clear that some innocent defendants do plead guilty, and the frequency with which this practice occurs may be significantly higher than is often assumed. In fact, legal scholar Albert Alschuler (2015/2016, p. 919) has described plea bargaining as "a nearly perfect system for convicting the innocent."

This brings us to other potential explanations for the discrepancy between the high rate of convictions obtained by guilty pleas and the much lower percentage of guilty pleas represented in exoneration cases—the difficulty of overturning convictions obtained through guilty pleas.

Initially, challenging convictions that result from guilty pleas is not always possible. Negotiated guilty pleas often require defendants to waive their right of appeal (Reimelt, 2010). And even if defendants are able to pursue appeals, they will have forfeited the opportunity to challenge most evidentiary and procedural issues in their cases, and the appellate process is ill-equipped to address claims of factual accuracy (Brooks et al., 2015/2016).

On top of the legal hurdles is the issue of practicality. Guilty pleas are commonly entered in cases involving lower-level offenses and often result in relatively short jail or non-incarceration sentences. Defendants given such sentences are less likely to have their cases thoroughly reinvestigated to find evidence needed to support their exoneration. There may be less motivation to investigate potential errors in these cases; innocence organizations, defense attorneys, and investigators are more likely to channel their limited resources and focus their time and energy on potentially innocent defendants who are facing lengthy incarceration or awaiting execution. It also may be more difficult to reinvestigate convictions that result from guilty pleas, as there is often less physical evidence and a shorter paper trail. Finally, defendants who plead guilty may simply be ineligible to have their cases reinvestigated by an innocence project or other such organization. Indeed, for practical and other understandable reasons, a number of innocence organizations restrict the cases they accept based on sentence length, time remaining on a sentence, and convictions resulting from trials rather than those based on guilty pleas (Krieger, 2011).

Plea Bargaining and the Law

Criminal defendants who plead guilty relinquish a host of fundamental constitutional protections they would enjoy if they pled not guilty and proceeded to trial. By admitting guilt, they give up rights against self-incrimination, to confront and cross-examine accusing witnesses, to trial by jury, to require the prosecution to establish all elements of the charged crime beyond a reasonable doubt, and often the right to appeal, among others. It thus is imperative that their decision to enter a guilty plea be made voluntarily, and with knowledge of the rights they are giving up and the punishment they may endure. Judges are required to engage in a dialogue with defendants in open court to ensure that guilty pleas are made knowingly, intelligently, and voluntarily (*Boykin v. Alabama*, 1969). During this exchange, defendants typically, although not invariably, are required to respond to the question, "Are you in fact guilty?" With such procedures observed, we might justifiably wonder how a guilty plea could ever be entered by an innocent person and produce a wrongful conviction. Yet, such wrongful convictions do occur; as we have discussed, as of this writing, in March 2021, roughly one out of five (20.7%) known wrongful convictions were supported by guilty pleas, according to the National Registry of Exonerations, and this figure could well represent a conservative estimate (Alschuler, 2015/2016; Bibas, 2014).

The law requires that guilty pleas be made voluntarily, but what distinguishes an involuntary decision and an exceedingly difficult, albeit voluntary decision made under extreme pressure, may be unclear. For example, if defendants charged with murder are told that if they plead guilty they will receive a prison sentence but if they plead not guilty the prosecution will seek the death penalty, will a decision to forgo a trial truly be voluntary? If defendants are offered a five-year prison sentence in exchange for pleading guilty to a crime, but are told that they will be punished by life imprisonment if convicted following a jury trial, owing to their status as a habitual felon with two prior felony convictions, would a decision to plead guilty be considered voluntary?

The Supreme Court has ruled that "a plea of guilty is not invalid merely because entered to avoid the possibility of a death penalty" (*Brady v. United States*, 1970, p. 755). More generally, "[t]he choice occasioned by the possibility of a harsher sentence, even in the case in which the choice may in fact be 'difficult,' does not place an impermissible burden" on criminal defendants (*Chaffin v. Stynchcombe*, 1973, p. 35). This premise explained the Court's approval of the prosecutor's negotiating tactic in *Bordenkircher v. Hayes* (1978), the case envisioned above in which a defendant was required to choose between pleading guilty to the felony of uttering a forged check in the amount of $88.30 in exchange for a five-year prison sentence, or risk going to trial and receiving a life sentence on conviction because the prosecutor vowed to re-indict him under the state's Habitual Criminal Act. While acknowledging that criminal defendants cannot be punished for exercising their constitutional rights to plead not guilty and proceed to trial, Justice Stewart's majority opinion disputed that this principle had been violated:

> To punish a person because he has done what the law plainly allows him to do is a due process violation of the most basic sort, and for an agent of the State to pursue a course of action whose objective is to penalize a person's reliance on his legal rights is "patently unconstitutional." *Chaffin v. Stynchcombe*, 412 U.S. [17], 32–33, n. 20 [(1973)]. But in the "give-and-take" of plea bargaining, there is no such element of punishment or retaliation so long as the accused is free to accept or reject the prosecution's offer.
>
> Plea bargaining flows from "the mutuality of advantage" to defendants and prosecutors, each with his own reasons for wanting to avoid trial. *Brady v. United States*, 397 U.S. [742], 752 [(1970)]. Defendants advised by competent counsel and protected by other procedural safeguards are presumptively capable of intelligent choice in response to prosecutorial persuasion, and unlikely to be driven to false self-condemnation. Indeed, acceptance of the basic legitimacy of plea bargaining necessarily implies rejection of any notion that a guilty plea is involuntary in a constitutional sense simply because it is the end result of the bargaining process. By hypothesis, the plea may have been induced by promises of a recommendation of a lenient sentence or a reduction of charges, and thus by fear of the possibility of a greater penalty upon conviction after a trial.
>
> While confronting a defendant with the risk of more severe punishment clearly may have a "discouraging effect on the defendant's assertion of his trial rights, the imposition of these difficult choices [is] an inevitable" — and permissible — "attribute of any legitimate system which tolerates and encourages the negotiation of pleas." *Chaffin v. Stynchcombe*, 412 U.S., at 31. It follows that, by tolerating and encouraging the negotiation of pleas, this Court has necessarily accepted as constitutionally legitimate the simple reality that the prosecutor's interest at the bargaining table is to persuade the defendant to forgo his right to plead not guilty.

Factors in addition to avoiding a harsher punishment might motivate defendants — even innocent ones — to plead guilty. Particularly with respect to lower-level offenses, as we have discussed, a guilty plea may be the ticket out of jail for defendants who are unable to post bail to secure release prior to trial. The consequences of conviction, including acquiring a criminal record and accepting punishment, may be preferable to the disruption of family life, employment, and other important matters compromised by pre-trial incarceration (Acker, 2017; Natapoff, 2018, 2012; Roberts, 2013). The attorneys representing criminal defendants, moreover, may be burdened with such heavy caseloads that they are hard-pressed to investigate cases and mount defenses, even meritorious ones (Green, 2013; Roberts, 2011; see *Lafler v. Cooper*, 2012; *Missouri v. Frye*, 2012). This latter problem is compounded by the fact that prosecutors are under no constitutional obligation pursuant to *Brady v. Maryland* (1963) to reveal at least some types of potentially exculpatory evidence before the defendant is required to decide whether to plead guilty (*United States v. Ruiz*, 2002, involving nondisclosure of evidence that might be used to impeach a witness's credibility).

In addition, as illogical as it may seem, most jurisdictions allow judges to accept guilty pleas even when defendants insist that they are innocent. Such "*Alford* pleas" owe their name to the Supreme Court decision in *North Carolina v. Alford* (1970), which authorized that practice. Henry Alford was indicted for first-degree murder, a crime punishable by death under North Carolina law. Substantial evidence supported that charge against Alford, including testimony from witnesses who saw Alford with a gun and heard him declare his intention to kill the victim, and later heard him affirm that he had accomplished his mission. Alford pled guilty to second-degree murder, a non-capital crime, but did so while professing his innocence.

> After giving his version of the events of the night of the murder, Alford stated:
>> "I pleaded guilty on second degree murder because they said there is too much evidence, but I ain't shot no man, but I take the fault for the other man. We never had an argument in our life and I just pleaded guilty because they said if I didn't they would gas me for it, and that is all."
>
> In response to questions from his attorney, Alford affirmed that he had consulted several times with his attorney and with members of his family and had been informed of his rights if he chose to plead not guilty. Alford then reaffirmed his decision to plead guilty to second-degree murder:

"Q. (by Alford's attorney). And you authorized me to tender a plea of guilty to second degree murder before the court?

"A. Yes, sir.

"Q. And in doing that, that you have again affirmed your decision on that point?

"A. Well, I'm still pleading that you all got me to plead guilty. I plead the other way, circumstantial evidence; that the jury will prosecute me on — on the second. You told me to plead guilty, right. I don't — I'm not guilty but I plead guilty."

Justice White's majority opinion concluded that while state courts are not obligated to accept guilty pleas that are unaccompanied by the defendant's admission of guilt, nor are they constitutionally prohibited from doing so.

[Courts in several jurisdictions have] concluded that they should not "force any defense on a defendant in a criminal case," particularly when advancement of the defense might "end in disaster...." *Tremblay v. Overholser*, 199 F. Supp. 569, 570 (D. D.C. 1961). They have argued that, since "guilt, or the degree of guilt, is at times uncertain and elusive," "[a]n accused, though believing in or entertaining doubts respecting his innocence, might reasonably conclude a jury would be convinced of his guilt and that he would fare better in the sentence by pleading guilty...." *McCoy v. United States*, 363 F.2d 306, 308 (D. C. Cir. 1966). As one state court observed nearly a century ago, "[r]easons other than the fact that he is guilty may induce a defendant to so plead, ... [and he] must be permitted to judge for himself in this respect." *State v. Kaufman*, 2 N.W. 275, 276 (Iowa 1879) (dictum).

Thus, while most pleas of guilty consist of both a waiver of trial and an express admission of guilt, the latter element is not a constitutional requisite to the imposition of criminal penalty. An individual accused of crime may voluntarily, knowingly, and understandingly consent to the imposition of a prison sentence even if he is unwilling or unable to admit his participation in the acts constituting the crime.

Nor can we perceive any material difference between a plea that refuses to admit commission of the criminal act and a plea containing a protestation of innocence when, as in the instant case, a defendant intelligently concludes that his interests require entry of a guilty plea and the record before the judge contains strong evidence of actual guilt. Here the State had a strong case of first-degree murder against Alford. Whether he realized or disbelieved his guilt, he insisted on his plea because in his view he had absolutely nothing to gain by a trial and much to gain by pleading. Because of the overwhelming evidence against him, a trial was precisely what neither Alford nor his attorney desired. Confronted with the choice between a trial for first-degree murder, on the one hand, and a plea of guilty to second-degree murder, on the other, Alford quite reasonably chose the latter and thereby limited the maximum penalty to a 30-year term. When his plea is viewed in light of the evidence against him, which substantially negated his claim of innocence and which further provided a means by which the judge could test whether the plea was being intelligently entered, its validity cannot be seriously questioned. In view of the strong factual basis for the plea demonstrated by the State and Alford's clearly expressed desire to enter it despite his professed belief in his innocence, we hold that the trial judge did not commit constitutional error in accepting it.

Almost all jurisdictions accept *Alford* pleas — they are prohibited only in Indiana, Michigan, and New Jersey (Schneider, 2013, p. 283) — and they are entered with some regularity. A 1997 survey reported that approximately 3% of federal correctional inmates and 6.5% of state correctional inmates had been convicted following *Alford* pleas (Bibas, 2003, p. 1375). Although the prevalence of wrongful convictions resulting from *Alford* pleas is uncertain, several such cases have been uncovered (see Rose, 2017). For example, in Georgia, 12-year-old Jonathan Adams falsely confessed to murdering an 8-year-old girl and subsequently entered an *Alford* plea to that offense after being charged in juvenile court proceedings. His conviction was vacated when, nearly two years after the murder, another youth confessed to the crime. Ironically, charges against the latter youth, who suffered from compromised mental health, were later dismissed after his confession failed to match other evidence associated with the crime (National Registry of Exonerations, n.d.a). In Virginia, Robert Davis entered *Alford* pleas in 2004 to two counts of murder and served 12 years in prison before being released after others implicated in the crimes recanted their accusations against him and an investigation supported Davis's contention that he had falsely confessed to the killings. Governor Terry McAuliffe pardoned Davis based on actual innocence in 2016 (National Registry of Exonerations n.d.b).

Wrongful Convictions in Popular Culture: The Problem with Pleas

- *The Plea* (2005) — a PBS FRONTLINE documentary written, produced, and directed by Ofra Bickel that highlights four cases in which false guilty pleas led to miscarriages of justice. Cases include a large drug bust in Texas, two murders in New York, and a rape-murder in Texas ending in an *Alford* plea. The film features interviews with the defendants, their families, officials involved in the cases, and legal experts.

- *Paradise Lost* (1996, 2001, 2011) — a three-part documentary by directors Joe Berlinger and Bruce Sinofsky that covers the case of the West Memphis Three. Teenagers Jessie Misskelly, Damien Echols, and Jason Baldwin were convicted of murdering and sexually mutilating three boys in 1993. Released over the course of more than a decade, the films chronicle the crime, trials, imprisonment, and eventual release of the three men. They eventually settled with *Alford* pleas to murdering the three boys and have not been exonerated as of this writing.

- *West of Memphis* (2012) — another documentary by filmmaker Amy Berg that tells the story of the West Memphis Three. The film includes interviews with Misskelly, Echols, and Baldwin, as well as their families, journalists, lawyers, and judges.

- *Life After Death* (2012) — a memoir written by Damien Echols, one of the teenagers convicted of murder in the West Memphis Three case. Echols was thought to be the leader of the group and spent nearly 18 years on death row before being released following his *Alford* plea to the murder charges. The book chronicles Echols's experiences.

Suggested Reforms

At one end of the spectrum of possible reforms to the problems we have noted is the recommendation to abolish plea bargaining altogether. While such a drastic step might seem extreme, dispensing with this practice could entail potential benefits. For instance, without the ability to rely on guilty pleas to settle a large number of cases with relative efficiency, lawmakers might be persuaded to rethink more fundamental issues, such as what behaviors should be made criminal in the first place. Doing so might be advantageous for various reasons, including reducing the detrimental effects of criminal justice contact on already-marginalized communities, allowing law enforcement to focus additional time and resources on more serious criminal activities, and reducing the overall reach of the criminal legal system. Plea bargaining also raises fundamental questions about justice, particularly concerning whether gains in expediency and the conservation of resources outweigh whatever is sacrificed when offenders are allowed to plead guilty to reduced charges and/or avoid the punishment they arguably deserve for their conduct. Prosecutors also wield inordinate power in the dynamics of plea bargaining, power that some argue detracts from decisions that are better made by the legislative and judicial branches regarding criminal activity and punishment. However, given the modern legal system's heavy reliance on plea bargaining to help inspire guilty pleas, it is unlikely that plea bargaining will be abandoned anytime soon. Moreover, the elimination of plea bargaining would have to be accompanied by a host of additional reforms, including altering sentencing practices.

Short of abolishing plea bargaining, reforming the criminal legal system to reduce the likelihood of false guilty pleas may encounter difficult obstacles. Bibas (2014) has offered several possible reforms, many of which relate to the collection and disclosure of evidence. He suggests that police should do a better job of documenting evidence to ensure that both the prosecution and defense have access to more (and more reliable) information prior to the entry of a guilty plea. He also recommends that prosecutors should demand more evidence of guilt before formally charging arrestees. More rigorous screening would reduce the number of cases reaching adjudication by weeding out those supported by less convincing evidence, and such cases may be especially likely to involve innocent persons. When prosecutors do move forward with charges, they should ensure that they take precautions to disclose all exculpatory evidence, or *Brady* material, to the defense, and to do so in a timely manner. When a plea deal is offered and accepted, Bibas suggests that a supervisor review the evidence before the negotiated plea is finally approved.

Other suggested reforms relating to the quality of evidence concern the judge's role in plea bargaining. Judges often know little about a case before conducting the **"plea colloquy"** — where they are tasked with determining that the defendant is entering the plea knowingly, voluntarily, and intelligently (Redlich, 2010a). It has been recommended that judges request more information from defendants before accepting a guilty plea, and require prosecutors to disclose the specifics of plea offers in order to more fully evaluate defendants' decisions (Bibas, 2014).

A final suggestion concerns the fundamental culture underlying criminal prosecutions. Prosecutors may be evaluated and rewarded, or at least perceive that they are, based on their conviction rates. Such practices and perceptions can incentivize them to seek convictions rather than carefully evaluate cases based on the strength of evidence and their merit. Changing the culture in prosecutors' offices by eliminating or reducing such incentives would presumably lead to changed practices, including reducing the number of cases resolved by guilty pleas and limiting the discounts prosecutors would be authorized to offer to encourage guilty pleas, thereby reducing the likelihood that innocents will be charged and convicted by entering false guilty pleas (Bibas, 2014).

Conclusion

Guilty pleas are the primary mechanism through which the criminal legal system in the United States adjudicates cases, accounting for more than 90% of convictions in the federal and most state systems. While we cannot know for certain the number or incidence of wrongful convictions that result from guilty pleas, it is undeniable that some defendants are willing to plead guilty to crimes they did not commit. Further, as discussed earlier, psychological research suggests that the proportion of innocent defendants willing to falsely plead guilty may be considerably higher than traditionally suggested by legal commentators.

Research concerning guilty pleas has grown tremendously in recent years, and the potential for the practice to generate wrongful convictions has been more widely recognized. As noted earlier, Alschuler (2015/2016, p. 919) described plea bargaining as "a nearly perfect system" for producing such errors. A story in a popular magazine called the current·era "the age of the plea bargain," with a headline declaring that "innocence is irrelevant" (Yoffe, 2017). Clearly, guilty pleas are on the minds of many who are studying and writing about criminal justice in the United States, and we will only learn more in the coming years about how often and why they contribute to wrongful convictions.

Key Terms and Concepts

- **Plea**: the defendant's answer—guilty, or not guilty—in response to criminal charge(s)
- *Alford* **plea**: from *North Carolina v. Alford*, a guilty plea that allows the defendant to nevertheless maintain innocence
- *Nolo contendere* **plea**: also called a "no contest" plea, this allows the court to enter a guilty verdict but does not require the defendant to admit guilt
- **Plea bargaining**: negotiations between the prosecution and defense to reach an agreement about the terms of a defendant's conviction and recommended sentence

- **Pretrial incarceration:** The confinement prior to a trial of a person charged with a crime, often resulting from an inability to post bail
- **Plea colloquy:** a conversation in court and under oath between the judge and the defendant, during which the judge must determine that the defendant is entering a plea of guilty knowingly, voluntarily, and intelligently

Discussion Questions

1. What proportion of convictions typically result from guilty pleas? Could our criminal justice system function without plea bargaining? How could we maintain our criminal justice system without the use of plea bargaining?

2. How might we protect populations that are most vulnerable to persuasion, and thus might be especially inclined to falsely plead guilty, during plea negotiations?

3. What are various advantages and disadvantages of abolishing plea bargaining as a mechanism for settling criminal cases?

References

Acker, J. R. (2017). Taking stock of innocence: Movements, mountains, and wrongful convictions. *Journal of Contemporary Criminal Justice, 33,* 8–25.

Alschuler, A. W. (2015/2016). A nearly perfect system for convicting the innocent. *Albany Law Review, 79*(3), 919–940.

Appleman, L. I. (2012). Justice in the shadowlands: Pretrial detention, punishment, and the Sixth Amendment. *Washington & Lee Law Review, 69,* 1297–1369.

Bibas, S. (2003). Harmonizing substantive-criminal-law values and criminal procedure: The case of *Alford* and nolo contendere pleas. *Cornell Law Review, 88,* 1361–1411.

Bibas, S. (2014). Plea bargaining's role in wrongful convictions. In A. D. Redlich, J. R. Acker, R. J. Norris, & C. L. Bonventre (Eds.), *Examining wrongful convictions: Stepping back, moving forward* (pp. 157–167). Carolina Academic Press.

Bordenkircher v. Hayes, 434 U.S. 357 (1978).

Bordens, K. S., & Bassett, J. (1985). The plea bargaining process from the defendant's perspective: A field investigation. *Basic and Applied Social Psychology, 6,* 93–110.

Boykin v. Alabama, 395 U.S. 238 (1969).

Brady v. Maryland, 373 U.S. 83 (1963).

Brady v. United States, 397 U.S. 742 (1970).

Brooks, J., Simpson, A., & Kaneb, P. (2015/2016). If hindsight is 20/20, our justice system should not be blind to new evidence of innocence: A survey of post-conviction new evidence statutes and a proposed model. *Albany Law Review, 79*(3), 1045–1090.

Chaffin v. Stynchcombe, 412 U.S. 17 (1973).

Gazal-Ayal, O. (2006). Partial ban on plea bargains. *Cardozo Law Review, 27*, 101–155.

Green, B. A. (2013). The right to plea bargain with competent counsel after *Cooper* and *Frye*: Is the Supreme Court making the ordinary criminal process "too long, too expensive, and unpredictable ... in pursuit of perfect justice?" *Duquesne Law Review, 51*, 735–766.

Gross, J. P. (2013). What matters more: A day in jail or a criminal conviction? *William & Mary Bill of Rights Journal, 22*, 55–89.

Gross, S. R., & O'Brien, B. (2008). Frequency and predictors of false conviction: Why we know so little, and new data on capital cases. *Journal of Empirical Legal Studies, 5*(4), 927–962.

Helm, R. K., Reyna, V. F., Franz, A. A., & Novick, R. Z. (2018). Too young to plead? Risk, rationality, and plea bargaining's innocence problem in adolescents. *Psychology, Public Policy, and Law, 24*(2), 180–191.

Henderson, K. S., & Levett, L. M. (2018). Investigating predictors of true and false guilty pleas. *Law and Human Behavior, 42*(5), 427–441.

Hoffman, M. B. (2007). The myth of factual innocence. *Chicago-Kent Law Review, 82*(2), 663–690.

Krieger, S. A. (2011). Why our justice system convicts innocent people, and the challenges faced by innocence projects trying to exonerate them. *New Criminal Law Review, 14*(3), 333–402.

Lafler v. Cooper, 566 U.S. 156 (2012).

Missouri v. Frye, 566 U.S. 133 (2012).

Natapoff, A. (2012). Misdemeanors. *Southern California Law Review, 85*, 1313–1375.

Natapoff, A. (2018). *Punishment without crime: How our massive misdemeanor system traps the innocent and makes America more unequal.* Basic Books.

National Registry of Exonerations. (n.d.). *Interactive data display.* https://www.law.umich.edu/special/exoneration/Pages/Exonerations-in-the-United-States-Map.aspx.

National Registry of Exonerations. (n.d.a). Jonathan Adams. http://www.law.umich.edu/special/exoneration/Pages/casedetail.aspx?caseid=2981.

National Registry of Exonerations. (n.d.b). Robert Davis. http://www.law. umich.edu/special/exoneration/Pages/casedetail.aspx?caseid=2981.

NeMoyer, A., Kelley, S., Zelle, H., & Goldstein, N. E. S. (2018). Attorney perspectives on juvenile and adult clients' competence to plead guilty. *Psychology, Public Policy, and Law, 24*, 171–179.

Norris, R. J., & Redlich, A. D. (2014). Seeking justice, compromising truth? Criminal admissions and the prisoner's dilemma. *Albany Law Review, 77*, 1005–1038.

North Carolina v. Alford, 400 U.S. 25 (1970).

Possley, M. (2017, December 7). Lionel White, Sr. The National Registry of Exonerations. https://www.law.umich.edu/special/exoneration/pages/case detail.aspx?caseid=5053.

Possley, M. (2018a, November 14). Ben Baker. The National Registry of Exonerations. https://www.law.umich.edu/special/exoneration/pages/case detail.aspx?caseid=4863.

Possley, M. (2018b, November 14). Clarissa Glenn. The National Registry of Exonerations. https://www.law.umich.edu/special/exoneration/pages/case detail.aspx?caseid=4864.

Possley, M. (2019, September 10). Lionel White, Jr. The National Registry of Exonerations. https://www.law.umich.edu/special/exoneration/pages/case detail.aspx?caseid=5421.

Possley, M. (2021, March 2). Marc Giles. The National Registry of Exonerations. https://www.law.umich.edu/special/exoneration/Pages/case detail.aspx?caseid=5925.

Redlich, A. D. (2010a). False confessions and false guilty pleas: Similarities and differences. In G. D. Lassiter & C. Meissner (Eds.), *Interrogations and confessions: Current research, practice, and policy* (pp. 49–66). American Psychological Association.

Redlich, A. D. (2010b). The susceptibility of juveniles to false confessions and false guilty pleas. *Rutgers Law Review, 62*, 943–957.

Redlich, A. D., Summers, A., & Hoover, S. (2010). Self-reported false confessions and false guilty pleas among offenders with mental illness. *Law and Human Behavior, 34*, 79–90.

Reimelt, A. W. (2010). An unjust bargain: Plea bargains and waiver of the right to appeal. *Boston College Law Review, 51*, 871–904.

Roberts, J. (2011). Why misdemeanors matter: Defining effective advocacy in the lower criminal courts. *U.C. Davis Law Review, 45*, 277–372.

Roberts, J. (2013). Crashing the misdemeanor system. *Washington & Lee Law Review, 70*, 1089–1131.

Rose, M. (2017, September 7). The deal prosecutors offer when they have no cards left to play. *The Atlantic*. https://www.theatlantic.com/politics/archive/2017/09/what-does-an-innocent-man-have-to-do-to-go-free-plead-guilty/539001/.

Russano, M. B., Meissner, C. A., Narchet, F. M., & Kassin, S. M. (2005). Investigating true and false confessions within a novel experimental design. *Psychological Science, 16*, 481–486.

Schneider, S. (2013). When innocent defendants falsely confess: Analyzing the ramifications of entering *Alford* pleas in the context of the burgeoning Innocence Movement. *Journal of Criminal Law & Criminology, 103*, 279–308.

United States Sentencing Commission. (2020). *Statistical information packet: Fiscal year 2019*. https://www.ussc.gov/sites/default/files/pdf/research-and-publications/federal-sentencing-statistics/state-district-circuit/2019/1c19.pdf.

United States v. Ruiz, 536 U.S. 622 (2002).

Viljoen, J. L., Klaver, J., & Roesch, R. (2005). Legal decisions of preadolescent and adolescent defendants: Predictors of confessions, pleas, communication with attorneys, and appeals. *Law and Human Behavior, 29*, 253–277.

West, E., & Meterko, V. (2016). Innocence Project: DNA exonerations, 1989–2014: Review of data and findings from the first 25 years. *Albany Law Review, 79*, 717–795.

Wilford, M. M., & Khairalla, A. (2019). Innocence and plea bargaining. In V. A. Edkins & A. D. Redlich (Eds.), *A system of pleas: Social science's contributions to the real legal system* (pp. 132–150). Oxford University Press.

Wilford, M. M., Wells, G. L., & Frazier, A. (2020). Plea-bargaining law: The impact of innocence, trial penalty, and conviction probability on plea outcomes. *American Journal of Criminal Justice*, 1–22. http://doi.org/10.1007/s12103-020-09564-y.

Yoffe, E. (2017, September). Innocence is irrelevant. *The Atlantic*. https://www.theatlantic.com/magazine/archive/2017/09/innocence-is-irrelevant/534171/.

Zimmerman, D. M., & Hunter, S. (2018). Factors affecting false guilty pleas in a mock plea bargaining scenario. *Legal and Criminological Psychology, 23*(1), 53–67.

Zottoli, T. M., Daftary-Kapur, T., Winters, G. M., & Hogan, C. (2016). Plea discounts, time pressures, and false guilty pleas in youth and adults who pleaded guilty to felonies in New York City. *Psychology, Public Policy, and Law, 22*(3), 250–259.

Chapter 6

Forensic Science Evidence

Learning Objectives

After reading this chapter, you should be able to:

- Distinguish intentional misconduct from other types of forensic science issues that contribute to wrongful convictions.
- Understand the role that cognitive bias plays in the analysis of forensic science evidence.
- Discuss the rules of evidence and case law governing the admissibility and reliability of expert testimony, including *Daubert* and *Frye*.
- Understand the Sixth Amendment right of criminal defendants to confront and cross-examine forensic analysts.
- Discuss the National Research Council's 2009 critical report on forensic science in the U.S.
- Appreciate the value of forensic science oversight commissions.

Case Study: Santae Tribble

Santae Tribble was 17 years old when he was convicted of the murder of Washington, D.C. taxicab driver John McCormick in 1978. McCormick was shot and killed on his front porch during the course of a robbery after he had finished his shift and was returning home. The only witness to have seen the masked assailant was McCormick's wife, who had a view of the robber through a window while she was inside the home. Soon after the incident, a police officer found a stocking mask assumed to have been worn by the robber on a sidewalk near the McCormicks' home. Tribble and his friend, Cleveland Wright, were implicated in the robbery and shooting of John McCormick by an informant who told the police that Cleveland had sold her roommate a handgun that fit the description of the one used to kill McCormick. The informant also told the police that Tribble had made admissions of guilt to her related to the killings. Tribble and Wright were charged with the robbery-murder of McCormick as well as the separate robbery and murder of William Horn, whose prior killing had occurred under similar circumstances (*United States v. Tribble*, 2012).

The stocking mask found near the scene of McCormick's murder was sent to the FBI Crime Laboratory for analysis. The agent who conducted the analysis testified at Tribble's trial for McCormick's murder that one of the hairs found in the mask matched Tribble's hair "in every microscopic characteristic" (*United States v. Tribble*, 2012, p. 1). In addition, the prosecutor stated in closing arguments to the jury that there was "one chance ... in ten million" that the hair belonged to someone other than Tribble (*United States v. Tribble*, 2012, p. 1). Tribble was convicted in 1980 and sentenced to 20 years to life in prison. He was paroled in 2009.

In 2012, investigative journalist Spencer Hsu of the *Washington Post* began reporting on a federal task force that was convened in the 1990s to review deficiencies involving unreliable **forensic evidence** at the FBI Laboratory (Hsu, 2012). The task force review had focused on 13 laboratory examiners, one of whom, Michael Malone, worked in the hair and fibers unit. The crux of the *Washington Post* investigation was that scores of defendants were not made aware of findings that deficient analysis and testimony may have led to the convictions of innocent defendants. In addition, argued Hsu, the task force should have extended its focus in the Hair and Fibers unit to examiners beyond Malone, as the problems were widespread (Hsu, 2012).

What does all this have to do with our story of Santae Tribble? Tribble is one of three District of Columbia men (Donald Gates and Kirk Odom were the others) who were convicted based on overstated hair comparison testimony provided by FBI examiners and were later exonerated. These cases illustrate just one of the multiple ways in which forensic science evidence can contribute to wrongful convictions.

A Closer Look: Spencer Hsu's Investigation of Hair Evidence

- *The Washington Post*—Since 2012, Spencer Hsu has been writing for the *Washington Post* about flawed FBI hair testimony and other forensic science issues. His article, "Convicted Defendants Left Uninformed of Forensic Flaws Found by Justice Dept.," discusses the Tribble case and others.

- *History of U.S. Forensic Errors* (2012)—In this C-SPAN video, Hsu discusses his *Washington Post* articles on forensic errors and takes calls from the public.

Research on Forensic Science Errors

Tribble's case is one of many exonerations involving forensic science errors at the trial stage. Among the 325 DNA exonerations compiled by the Innocence Project that occurred from 1989 to 2014, 47% involved the misapplication of forensic science (West & Meterko, 2015/2016). West and Meterko defined this error as, "an instance in which we know that forensic evidence was used to associate, identify or implicate someone who was later conclusively proven innocent with post-conviction DNA testing, thereby demonstrating that the original forensic evidence was incorrect" (p. 743). The forensic science disciplines that appeared the most frequently in the dataset were forensic serology and microscopic hair comparison (West & Meterko, 2015/2016). Keep in mind that the Innocence Project cases include primarily sexual assault and homicide convictions, so these numbers may not represent the role of forensic science as a contributor to wrongful convictions more broadly. Indeed, false or misleading forensic evidence was a contributing factor in 24% of the 2,755 exonerations documented by the National Registry of Exonerations as of April 2021. In addition, forensic science is often one of many factors contributing to wrongful convictions in individual cases. For example, 98% of the 133 DNA exonerations analyzed by LaPorte (2018) involved multiple sources of error (e.g., eyewitness misidentification or official misconduct).

During the two decades that Santae Tribble was incarcerated, considerable changes were underway in the world of forensic science evidence. In 1980, when Tribble was convicted, the forensic use of **DNA** had yet to be established. Three years before Tribble was officially declared innocent in 2012, the National Research Council of the National Academies of Sciences published a report ("NRC Report") that scrutinized forensic science (National Research Council, 2009). In many ways, the NRC Report was not encouraging — it found that many of the forensic sciences, like the microscopic hair comparison used to convict Tribble, did not rest on solid scientific foundations.

Research has shown that problems with forensic science evidence can arise in many ways (see, Bonventre, 2020). There can be mistakes or intentional misconduct with regard to testing evidence in the crime laboratory. Likewise, mistakes or intentional misconduct may occur during expert witness testimony at trial. Researchers attribute these problems to a variety of factors, including pro-prosecution bias, cognitive biases, poor training, lack of oversight, and more. Furthermore, as noted above, there is limited scientific theory underlying many of the forensic science disciplines.

Mistakes and Intentional Misconduct in the Lab and at Trial

No national database systematically compiles instances of intentional misconduct among forensic analysts who conduct laboratory analyses or provide trial testimony. Giannelli (1997; 2007) documented several cases of forensic analyst misconduct across the country. One of the more well-known cases concerned Trooper Fred Zain, who was a serologist with the West Virginia State Police. **Serology** involves the identification and characterization of biological stains for forensic purposes, including ABO blood types. Over the course of a decade in West Virginia, Zain systematically engaged in misconduct in the laboratory and at trial. His misdeeds came to light when Glen Dale Woodall, wrongfully convicted of kidnapping and sexual assault, was exonerated. Zain provided the crucial testimony against Woodall at trial, stating that Woodall's blood type could only be shared with "six in ten thousand" members of the population and that a single red hair found in the victim's car was "highly unlikely" to have come from anyone else (Scheck et al., 2003, p. 143). Following Woodall's settlement with the state for $1,000,000, the Supreme Court of Appeals of West Virginia appointed a judge as a special investigator to investigate the allegations of Zain's misconduct. The judge's report found that Zain's misconduct included:

> (1) overstating the strength of results; (2) overstating the frequency of genetic matches on individual pieces of evidence; (3) misreporting the frequency of genetic matches on multiple pieces of evidence; (4) reporting that multiple items had been tested, when only a single item had been tested; (5) reporting inconclusive results as conclusive; (6) repeatedly altering laboratory records; (7) grouping results to create the erroneous impression that genetic markers had been obtained from all samples tested; (8) failing to report conflicting results; (9) failing to conduct or to report conducting additional testing to resolve conflicting results; (10) implying a match with a suspect when testing supported only a match with the victim; and (11) reporting scientifically impossible or improbable results (*In the Matter of an Investigation of the West Virginia State Police Crime Laboratory, Serology Division*, 1993).

By the time the judge's report was released, Zain had moved on to Texas, where his egregious misconduct continued to contribute to wrongful convictions of others, including Gilbert Alejandro (Scheck et al., 2003). At Alejandro's trial for aggravated sexual assault, Zain falsely testified about the DNA tests he had conducted on semen found on the victim. He stated that the DNA "only could have originated from [Alejandro]" (Scheck et al., 2003, p. 151). Zain also testified that, "There was no information whatsoever, beyond a scientific reasonable degree, that the particular semen stains that would show they originated other than from him" (Trial Transcript, 1995). Subsequent evaluation of Zain's work and testing of the evidence by another analyst showed that Zain's work had been deficient and that the DNA tests actually excluded Alejandro as the source of the semen.

More recently, Annie Dookhan, formerly a forensic chemist with the now-closed Massachusetts Department of Health Forensic Drug Laboratory, also engaged in systematic evidence tampering and report falsification. Like Zain, Dookhan engaged in "**drylabbing**" or fabricating results for laboratory tests that were not conducted. She also tampered with negative drug samples to make them positive. Dookhan tested drugs in the laboratory from 2003 to 2012. In 2013, she pleaded guilty to 27 counts related to her misconduct and was sentenced to three to five years in prison. She was paroled in 2016 after having been incarcerated for three years. The reach of Dookhan's misconduct extended to over 24,000 cases (Rosen, 2017). At the beginning of 2017, the state's highest court ordered prosecutors across the state to implement a protocol for dismissing cases involving "Dookhan defendants" (*Bridgeman v. District Attorney for the Suffolk District*, 2017). According to the National Registry of Exonerations' Groups Registry, over 18,000 Dookhan defendants have had their convictions reversed as of 2021 (National Registry of Exonerations, n.d.)

Forensic science errors can also occur at trial. As noted above, almost half of the DNA exonerations involved the misapplication of forensic science. One way in which research has sought to better understand the role that forensic science evidence plays in wrongful convictions, is to analyze the trial testimony provided by forensic analysis in cases where the defendants were convicted and subsequently exonerated through DNA testing. Law professor Brandon Garrett and Innocence Project co-founder Peter Neufeld examined 137 trial transcripts from the first 232 DNA exonerations (Garrett & Neufeld, 2009). They found that in 60% (n = 82) of the cases, the forensic analysts provided invalid testimony. Invalid testimony was defined as "a conclusion not supported by empirical data" (Garrett & Neufeld, 2009, p. 7), which included "the misuse of empirical population data, and conclusions regarding the probative value of evidence that were unsupported by empirical data" (Garrett & Neufeld, 2009, p. 9). Several forensic science disciplines, including serology and microscopic hair comparison, were represented in the testimonies provided by the analysts in the study. Thus, the primary ways in which the forensic evidence testimony in the study contributed to wrongful convictions were (a) interpreting forensic evidence that actually tended to show the defendant's innocence — or tended to prove nothing at all — as incriminating, and (b) overstating the incriminating nature of microscopic hair comparison evidence (Cole, 2012; Garrett & Neufeld, 2009).

Human Factors

There is growing recognition of the role that human factors play in contributing to wrongful convictions. For example, while intentional misconduct is a very important concern, some researchers argue that **cognitive biases** that can affect forensic analysis at the subconscious level may provide an even larger threat to accuracy and reliability (Risinger et al., 2002). Confirmation bias is a cognitive bias that occurs when people unwittingly select evidence that confirms or supports their existing beliefs or expectations (Nickerson, 1998). In the forensic laboratory, these expectations may arise from knowledge of case facts that are not essential to the forensic examination, that is, information that is not relevant to the task at hand. Experimental research has shown that forensic science analysis is subject to confirmation bias. For example, Dror and colleagues demonstrated that case-contextual information can influence the ways that latent fingerprint examiners (Dror et al., 2006) and DNA analysts (Dror & Hampikian, 2011) evaluate ambiguous evidence. Although not done intentionally, if the existing belief or expectation is that the defendant is guilty, or if the examiner has been exposed to other incriminating evidence in the case (e.g., the defendant confessed), the bias may shift the analysis toward a finding of inculpatory results (*see*, Dror et al., 2017). A recent systematic review found that the effects of cognitive bias on forensic decision making was supported by the available research (Cooper & Meterko, 2019).

Another important consideration is that organizational factors such as workplace stresses or pressures can lead to errors in forensic decision making. As Jeanguenat and Dror (2018) note:

> The forensic scientist is subject to many of these common triggers, as well as forensic-specific pressures. With technology advancements and forensic science being used in new ways especially on "lesser crimes," workload volume has increased in many laboratories. This is accompanied by pressure from law enforcement and prosecutors to return results quickly, often requesting rush services. Agencies that have successfully focused on increasing efficiency often find that as they meet demand, more samples are submitted. Thus, the culture is

under continuous pressures to do more, regardless of how efficient they are (p. 259).

Consequently, Jeanguenat and Dror suggest mitigating workplace stress should be included in efforts to reduce forensic error.

As we will discuss later in this chapter, recognition of cognitive bias in forensic science has implications for forensic science reform. Next, we consider in more depth how courts have grappled with forensic science issues.

Wrongful Convictions in Popular Culture: Forensic Failures and Successes

- *How to Fix a Drug Scandal* (2020) — a limited series produced by Netflix that explores the Massachusetts forensic misconduct scandals involving chemists Annie Dookhan and Sonja Farak.

- *6,149 Days: The True Story of Greg Taylor* (2012) — This documentary produced by news station WRAL in North Carolina portrays Greg Taylor's journey from wrongful conviction to being the first person exonerated by the North Carolina Innocence Inquiry Commission. Watch to see how the state crime lab contributed to Taylor's wrongful conviction.

- *The Blooding* (1989) — a true-crime account, written by Joseph Wambaugh, of the investigation of the murders of Lydia Mann and Dawn Ashworth in England in the 1980s. After the crime went unsolved for a time, police made an arrest, but DNA testing showed they had the wrong suspect. As part of one of the largest manhunts in English history, DNA tests were conducted on hundreds of British men, eventually leading to the conviction of Colin Pitchfork. It was the first time DNA fingerprinting was used to convict an offender.

- *Forensic Magazine: On the Scene and in the Lab* — an online magazine that follows news related to forensic science and crime laboratories, including the crime-solving successes of forensic science, wrongful convictions, and more.

Forensic Science Evidence and the Law

Forensic testimony can relate to vastly different disciplines and endeavors, including conclusions drawn from the analysis of DNA, fingerprints, handwriting, ballistics, blood, drugs, bite marks, paint, tool marks, and many others. In all such areas, some measure of expertise is considered essential to understand the underlying subject matter. The testimony, accordingly, is typically offered by an expert witness and will be governed by corresponding special rules of evidence. These special rules are in order because expert testimony differs in important ways from the testimony of lay witnesses.

One difference is that experts are usually allowed to express an opinion or draw conclusions about issues in a case, based on their specialized knowledge or field of study. In contrast, lay witnesses generally must limit their testimony to whatever they observed, heard, or otherwise directly perceived, and must avoid making inferences or offering their opinions. Moreover, although experts can offer unique insights about matters important to a trial, their testimony simultaneously can present various dangers or drawbacks. One concern, commonly referred to as "the aura of scientific infallibility," is that jurors will be so highly impressed with the credentials and superior knowledge of an expert that they will almost blindly defer to whatever the expert says rather than carefully scrutinizing or evaluating the testimony, as they would do with any other witness. Another concern is that so much attention may focus on what the expert says, the jurors will become preoccupied with that testimony and give insufficient consideration to other evidence that is presented. And finally, it often is true that when one side (prosecution or defense) offers expert testimony, the other side will counter with an expert of its own. The "battle of experts" may consume an inordinate amount of time, be expensive (experts frequently are paid for their time), and otherwise become administratively cumbersome.

Rules of evidence thus have been developed to help balance the potential benefits and costs associated with expert testimony, and hence to govern whether the testimony should be admitted in a trial. Four general requirements typically must be satisfied for expert testimony to be ruled admissible: (1) the witness must qualify as an "expert"; (2) the subject of the testimony must be "beyond the ken" (beyond the common knowledge base) of the average lay juror; (3) the testimony must satisfy a threshold level of reliability; and (4) the probative value of the testimony must not be substantially outweighed by the danger of unfair prejudice (including the drawbacks mentioned above).

One way a witness might qualify as an expert is through advanced education, such as attaining a PhD degree in a scientific discipline and intensively studying a relevant body of knowledge. But formal schooling in a subject is not always necessary. For example, the Federal Rules of Evidence (which apply in the federal courts, but often are similar to rules followed in different state courts) recognize that expert qualifications also can be established by special "knowledge, skill, experience, [or] training," (Federal Rule of Evidence 702, 2011). Before a witness is qualified as an expert, the parties to a case will have a chance to challenge the witness's credentials, although in many cases they will agree about the asserted expertise and stipulate to that effect. This can be a strategic decision by one side to avoid having the witness's impressive background recited chapter and verse before the jury, thus underscoring the witness's presumed competence and credibility.

There is no need to bring an expert to court to testify about what already is obvious, to explain, for example, that it is cold at the North Pole and hot at the equator, or that it is dark at night but the sun rises in the east each morning. Thus, only if the subject of the expert's testimony is "beyond the ken" of average, lay jurors or, as stated in the Federal Rules of Evidence (702, 2011), "will help the trier of fact to understand the evidence or to determine a fact in issue," will it be admissible. This sometimes becomes a point of contention for the admissibility of expert testimony that can be directly relevant to wrongful convictions. Such controversies may arise, for example, when a defendant wants to introduce a qualified psychologist to explain about factors that can undermine the reliability of eyewitness identification, that can help produce false confessions, or that help explain why a child who is the alleged victim of incest or sexual assault delayed reporting or continued to affiliate with her alleged abuser. Some courts have ruled that these matters are sufficiently well known that expert testimony is unnecessary to help jurors understand them, although courts in several jurisdictions authorize experts on these subjects to testify in appropriate cases (e.g., *Heath v. United States*, 2011; *People v. Bedessie*, 2012; *People v. Taylor*, 2018; *State v. Edelman*, 1999; *State v. Guilbert*, 2012; *State v. Rosales*, 2010; *State v. Wright*, 2009).

Courts use different tests to determine whether the body of knowledge that serves as the basis for expert testimony is sufficiently reliable to allow an expert to testify at a trial. One widely used test was first announced almost a century ago by a federal court of appeals in *Frye v. United States* (1923). The defendant in this case had been charged with murder. He sought to have an expert witness testify that he had passed a "systolic blood pressure deception test" — essentially, a primitive form of a polygraph exam. The trial court refused to admit the expert testimony into evidence, a ruling the court of appeals upheld. In doing so it announced what has become known as "**the *Frye* test**" for reliability.

> Just when a scientific principle or discovery crosses the line between the experimental and demonstrable stages is difficult to define. Somewhere in this twilight zone the evidential force of the principle must be recognized, and while courts will go a long way in admitting expert testimony deduced from a well-recognized scientific principle or discovery, the thing from which the deduction is made must be sufficiently established to have gained general acceptance in the particular field in which it belongs.

The *Frye* "general acceptance" test requires a trial judge to determine whether a particular methodology, theory, or technique has gained broad approval within the relevant discipline or scientific community. The judge might consult published studies or literature, hear from knowledgeable scholars or practitioners, or refer to prior court decisions in making this assessment. The *Frye* standard is considered a conservative test, in that it requires a measure of consensus among experts before a novel or emerging scientific technique is recognized as being sufficiently established to allow its use in court. It largely alleviates the judge, who, after all, is trained in law rather than science, from having to master the complexities of the body of knowledge in question. The judge instead can defer to the common wisdom of experts in the field.

The other widely used test governing the admissibility of expert scientific testimony was announced in *Daubert v. Merrell Dow Pharmaceuticals, Inc.* (1993). *Daubert* was decided by the Supreme Court, but the ruling is based on an interpretation of a Federal Rule of Evidence rather than the U.S. Constitution. As such, "**the *Daubert* test**" announced in the decision is binding in federal court trials, although approximately 38 states now also use the test or a closely related one (New York State Bar Association, 2019). Congress adopted the Federal Rules of Evidence in 1975, or more than a half century after the decision in *Frye v. United States* (1923). When *Daubert* was decided in 1993, Federal Rule of Evidence 702 (which has since been revised), provided:

> If scientific, technical, or other specialized knowledge will assist the trier of fact to understand the evidence or to determine a fact in issue, a witness qualified as an expert by knowledge, skill, experience, training, or education, may testify thereto in the form of an opinion or otherwise.

In a federal trial involving a civil suit brought by families against the manufacturer of an anti-nausea drug, the plaintiffs sought to introduce expert testimony supporting their claim that the drug could cause birth defects. The trial court refused to admit the testimony, relying on the *Frye* "general acceptance" test. The Supreme Court ruled in *Daubert* that the *Frye* test had been supplanted by F.R.Ev. 702.

> Faced with a proffer of expert scientific testimony, ... the trial judge must determine at the outset ... whether the expert is proposing to testify to (1) scientific knowledge that (2) will assist the trier of fact to understand or determine a fact in issue. This entails a preliminary assessment of whether the reasoning or methodology underlying the testimony is scientifically valid and of whether that reasoning or methodology properly can be applied to the facts in issue. We are confident that federal judges possess the capacity to undertake this review.

Many factors will bear on the inquiry, and we do not presume to set out a definitive checklist or test. But some general observations are appropriate.

Ordinarily, a key question to be answered in determining whether a theory or technique is scientific knowledge that will assist the trier of fact will be whether it can be (and has been) tested. "Scientific methodology today is based on generating hypotheses and testing them to see if they can be falsified; indeed, this methodology is what distinguishes science from other fields of human inquiry."

...

Another pertinent consideration is whether the theory or technique has been subjected to peer review and publication.... [S]ubmission to the scrutiny of the scientific community is a component of "good science," in part because it increases the likelihood that substantive flaws in methodology will be detected. The fact of publication (or lack thereof) in a peer reviewed journal thus will be a relevant, though not dispositive, consideration in assessing the scientific validity of a particular technique or methodology on which an opinion is premised.

Additionally, in the case of a particular scientific technique, the court ordinarily should consider the known or potential rate of error, and the existence and maintenance of standards controlling the technique's operation.

Finally, "general acceptance" can yet have a bearing on the inquiry. A "reliability assessment does not require, although it does permit, explicit identification of a relevant scientific community and an express determination of a particular degree of acceptance within that community." Widespread acceptance can be an important factor in ruling particular evidence admissible, and "a known technique which has been able to attract only minimal support within the community," may properly be viewed with skepticism.

The inquiry envisioned by Rule 702 is, we emphasize, a flexible one. Its overarching subject is the scientific validity and thus the evidentiary relevance and reliability—of the principles that underlie a proposed submission. The focus, of course, must be solely on principles and methodology, not on the conclusions that they generate.

Throughout, a judge assessing a proffer of expert scientific testimony under Rule 702 should also be mindful of other applicable rules.... Rule 403 permits the exclusion of relevant evidence "if its probative value is substantially outweighed by the danger of unfair prejudice, confusion of the issues, or misleading the jury ..."

The "*Daubert* factors" governing the admissibility of expert scientific testimony thus include whether the technique in question can be *tested*, whether it has been subjected to scrutiny via *publication* and *peer review*, and whether it has a known *error rate* and is governed by applicable *standards*, while the "*general acceptance*" of the technique or its methodology within the relevant scientific community (carried over from *Frye*) also remains of interest. Judges charged with applying these factors thus have a more active role as the gate-keepers who control whether expert testimony is admissible in a trial than is required under the *Frye* general acceptance test. The original *Daubert* factors remain relevant under the current version Federal Rule of Evidence 702 (2011), which was revised following the Supreme Court's decision. Federal Rule of Evidence 702 now provides:

> A witness who is qualified as an expert by knowledge, skill, experience, training, or education may testify in the form of an opinion or otherwise if:
> (a) the expert's scientific, technical, or other specialized knowledge will help the trier of fact to understand the evidence or to determine a fact in issue;
> (b) the testimony is based on sufficient facts or data;
> (c) the testimony is the product of reliable principles and methods; and
> (d) the expert has reliably applied the principles and methods to the facts of the case.

When *Daubert* was decided, many observers believed that judges would be more liberal in admitting expert testimony pertaining to the forensic sciences and other disciplines because their decisions no longer depended so heavily on a technique's having gained general acceptance within the relevant field. Ironically, perhaps, one consequence of *Daubert* has been courts' willingness to re-examine forensic testimony that was traditionally deemed admissible under *Frye's* general acceptance test, but appeared to be sorely lacking under other of the *Daubert* considerations. In retrospect, *Daubert* has stimulated reconsideration of the reliability of forensic testimony in several areas of importance to wrongful convictions, including forensic odontology (bite marks), microscopic hair comparison, handwriting analysis, comparative bullet lead analysis, and others (Beecher-Monas, 2009; Fabricant & Carrington, 2016; Findley, 2008; Gavin, 2008; Giannelli, 2008). The lesson has been that just because a technique traditionally has been accepted by practitioners in an area, this general acceptance is not necessarily a testament to the technique's reliability.

Among the law's challenges is how to keep pace with advances in scientific knowledge. In this context, one issue concerns what action, if any, should be taken when the scientific evidence used to support a criminal conviction later is determined to be of questionable reliability. For example, Eddie Lee Howard was convicted of murder and sentenced to death in 1994 in Mississippi for the rape and murder of an 84-year-old woman. His conviction was reversed on appeal, but he was again convicted and sentenced to death following a retrial in 2000. Both of Howard's convictions were supported by expert testimony offered by Dr. Michael West, a forensic odontologist. Dr. West testified that the victim's body contained bite marks that were "identical" to impressions made by Howard's teeth, and that he had "no doubt" that Howard was the source of the bite marks. In the ensuing years, Dr. West's credibility and the basis of his conclusions in Howard's and other cases were significantly undermined (see Balko & Carrington, 2018). Doubts also were raised about the reliability of bite mark evidence more generally. In 2020, the Mississippi Supreme Court invalidated Howard's conviction and death sentence, relying in part on DNA analyses conducted on evidence material to the case, and in part on changed professional standards regarding bite mark comparisons as well as mounting evidence about the general unreliability of human bite mark analysis. In reversing the conviction and ordering a new trial, the court cited "Howard's evidence as to the change in scientific understanding of identification through bite-mark comparisons," and concluded that "a forensic dentist would not be permitted to identify Howard today as Dr. West did at Howard's trial in 2000" (*Howard v. State*, 2020, p. 1019). The charges against Howard were dismissed, and he was exonerated in 2021, after spending more than a quarter century on Mississippi's death row (Forth & Waller, 2021).

In a related ruling, in 2018 the Texas Court of Criminal Appeals invalidated the 1987 murder conviction and life prison sentence of Steven Mark Chaney. Two forensic odontologists had testified for the prosecution at Chaney's trial, one of whom concluded "to a reasonable degree of dental certainty" that the victim's body contained bitemarks left by Chaney, and the other who testified that there was "a one in a million chance" that someone other than Chaney had left the bite marks, which were "a perfect match" to Chaney's (*Ex parte Chaney*, 2018, pp. 250–251). In vacating Chaney's conviction, the court relied on legislation which addressed the more general issue of reconsidering criminal convictions that were based on scientific evidence that no longer is considered reliable:

In 2013, the legislature enacted Article 11.073 of the Texas Code of Criminal Procedure, which allows a defendant to obtain post-conviction relief based on a change in science relied on by the State at trial. Tex. Code Crim. Proc. art. 11.073. That statute provides that an applicant is entitled to post-conviction writ relief if he can prove that:

(1) Relevant scientific evidence is currently available and was not available at the time of the convicted person's trial because the evidence was not ascertainable through the exercise of reasonable diligence by the convicted person before the date of or during the convicted person's trial;

(2) The scientific evidence would be admissible under the Texas Rules of Evidence at a trial held on the date of the application; and

(3) The court must make findings of the foregoing and also find that, had the scientific evidence been presented at trial, on the preponderance of the evidence the person would not have been convicted.

Id. art. 11.073(b)(1) & (2). When assessing reasonable diligence, courts consider whether "the field of science, a testifying expert's scientific knowledge, or a scientific method on which the relevant scientific evidence is based" has changed since the applicant's trial. *Id.* art. 11.073(d). "Scientific method is defined as '[t]he process of generating hypotheses and testing them through experimentation, publication, and republication.'" *Ex parte Robbins*, 478 S.W.3d 678, 691 (Tex. Crim. App. 2014). "Scientific knowledge" includes a change in the body of science (e.g., the field has been discredited or evolved) and when an expert's opinion changes due to a change in their scientific knowledge (e.g., an expert who, upon further study and acquisition of additional scientific knowledge, would have given a different opinion at trial). Tex. Code Crim. Proc. art. 11.073(d); *Robbins*, 478 S.W.3d at 691 (*Ex parte Chaney*, 2018, p. 255 [footnote omitted]).

The court concluded that "Chaney is entitled to relief under Article 11.073 on the grounds that, not only has the body of scientific knowledge underlying the field of bitemark comparisons evolved in a way that discredits almost all the probabilistic bitemark evidence at trial but also because [one of the expert's] new opinion that the bitemark was inflicted days before the murders based on his new scientific knowledge that was not available at Chaney's trial" (*id.*, p. 257).

In common with other items of evidence, expert testimony can be ruled inadmissible if its probative value is substantially outweighed by offsetting dangers, including "unfair prejudice, confusing the issues, misleading the jury, undue delay, wasting time, or needlessly presenting cumulative evidence" (Federal Rule of Evidence 403, 2011; see *Old Chief v. United States*, 1997, pp. 180–185; Porter, 2009, pp. 58–59). As noted earlier, the fact that an "expert" is testifying about matters deemed to be scientific—which can be mystifying to laypersons—can cloak the testimony with an aura of infallibility. Forensic experts sometimes overstate their conclusions, and jurors might not fully understand commonly used terms, for example, misinterpreting "consistent with" to mean "match" (Garrett, 2011, pp. 90–91). Forensic testimony, even if it is of dubious value, thus can be unduly persuasive and present a heightened risk of unfair prejudice (Jabbar, 2010, p. 2036).

A principal safeguard used to help evaluate witness testimony is cross-examination. Of course, a witness who does not appear in court cannot be cross-examined. In many jurisdictions, individuals who analyzed evidence relating to an alleged crime—for example, the laboratory scientists who test substances which might be an illegal drug such as heroin or cocaine, or who calculate blood-alcohol content following a suspect's arrest for driving while intoxicated—were excused from coming to court. Instead, a record of their findings was admitted into evidence. The Supreme Court put a stop to such practices, ruling that a criminal defendant has a Sixth Amendment right to confront and cross-examine the analyst who prepared reports of this nature for use in court (*Bullcoming v. New Mexico*, 2011; *Melendez-Diaz v. Massachusetts*, 2009). However, in a fractured decision, the justices ruled in *Williams v. Illinois* (2012) that the lab analyst who created a DNA profile from biological material, which later was matched to the defendant's DNA profile, was not required to testify and be cross-examined at a defendant's criminal trial. Although not agreeing about the rationale, five justices considered reference to the analyst's report by another witness to be permissible. Justice Alito's plurality opinion noted that a different analyst, the one who compared the first analyst's report to the defendant's DNA profile and determined that there was a match, did testify at the trial (which was conducted before a judge, rather than a jury) and was subjected to cross-examination.

In addition to cross-examination, another feature of the adversarial process considered important to test the reliability of evidence is the opportunity for both parties—the prosecution and the defendant—to offer witnesses to testify about important case issues. In criminal trials, the prosecution normally has ready access to expert forensic science witnesses, who often are employed by law enforcement offices or state or local crime laboratories. The defendant is unlikely to be able to enlist expert witnesses so easily. Those who can afford to retain an expert might do so, although expert witness fees can easily run into hundreds of dollars an hour (Jurs, 2016, pp. 363–364; Richmond, 2000, pp. 933–940). We will return to this issue, which is of particular significance to indigent defendants who lack the resources to hire expert witnesses, in chapter 9.

Forensic Science Reform

Considering all the issues discussed above, what reforms might be implemented to improve forensic science practice? The NRC Report that was introduced at the beginning of this chapter offers several recommendations. To step back for a moment, it should be noted that Congress called on the National Academy of Sciences to examine the state of forensic science in the United States in part due to growing concerns about the contributions of forensic science to wrongful convictions (National Research Council, 2009). As the report noted, "[I]f evidence and laboratory tests are mishandled or improperly analyzed; if the scientific evidence carries a false sense of significance; or if there is bias, incompetence, or a lack of adequate controls for the evidence introduced by the forensic scientists and their laboratories, the jury or court can be misled, and this could lead to wrongful conviction or exoneration" (National Research Council, 2009, p. 37).

The National Research Council extensively examined several aspects of forensic science including the reliability and validity of various forensic disciplines, training and education in forensic science, reporting and testimony, and oversight of crime laboratories. One of the most troubling findings of the report is encapsulated in the following statement:

> Although some of the techniques used by the forensic science disciplines—such as DNA analysis, serology, forensic pathology, toxicology, chemical analysis, and digital and multimedia forensics— are built on solid bases of theory and research, many other techniques have been developed heuristically. That is, they are based on observation, experience, and reasoning without an underlying scientific theory, experiments designed to test the uncertainties and reliability of the method, or sufficient data that are collected and analyzed scientifically (National Research Council, 2009, p. 128).

The forensic disciplines based on pattern matching or experience, such as hair, fingerprints, impressions (e.g., footwear), toolmarks, and handwriting fall within the disciplines with limited scientific foundations. Thus, as recommended by the NRC Report, research is underway to establish empirically the scientific validity and error rates of these disciplines.

The majority of publicly funded crime laboratories in the United States are administered by law enforcement agencies (U.S. Department of Justice, 2009 [authors' analysis]). To combat the potential for pro-law enforcement bias, the NRC recommended removing crime laboratories from the administrative control of law enforcement (National Research Council, 2009). In the words of the NRC Report, "The best science is conducted in a scientific setting as opposed to a law enforcement setting. Because forensic scientists often are driven in their work by a need to answer a particular question related to the issues of a particular case, they sometimes face pressure to sacrifice appropriate methodology for the sake of expediency" (National Research Council, 2009). Time will tell if this is a reform that states and municipalities will undertake. Indeed, it was a series of high-profile scandals — including exonerations of the wrongfully convicted — that led the city of Houston to create a local government entity to assume independent operation of the police department's crime laboratory (Cásarez & Thompson, 2018). The Houston Forensic Science Center (HFSC) is governed as a public corporation with a board of directors composed of community volunteers. A Technical Advisory Group of scientists advises the board on scientific best practices. The laboratory has an exceptional staff, increased productivity, reduced case backlogs, and a transparent relationship with the community (Thompson & Cásarez, 2016). The independent Houston HFSC has now become a model for other jurisdictions seeking to remove their crime laboratories from law enforcement control (Beety, in press; Garrett, 2020; Thompson & Cásarez, 2016).

Following publication of the NRC Report, numerous entities undertook efforts to address the issues raised in the report (Butler, 2015). For example, in 2013, the U.S. Department of Justice and the National Institutes of Standards and Technology created the **National Commission on Forensic Science** (NCFS).[1] Multiple interests were represented on the NCFS, ranging from attorneys and judges to forensic practitioners, victim advocates, and academics (National Commission on Forensic Science, 2017). The NCFS formed several subcommittees that studied many of the problems identified by the NRC Report. For example, the Human Factors subcommittee included academic experts on the role of cognitive biases in forensic analysis. That subcommittee adopted three views that addressed the biasing influence of contextual information discussed above. These views were: forensic analysts should draw conclusions about evidence based only on task-relevant information; the Organization of Scientific Area Committees (an entity created by NIST to develop forensic science standards) should make clear what is and is not task-relevant information; and forensic laboratories should develop procedures to

---

1. The National Commission on Forensic Science charter expired in 2017 with the advent of the Trump administration. Calls have been made for the resuscitation of the NCFS under the administration of President Biden (Sah, 2021).

shield analysts from task-irrelevant information (National Commission on Forensic Science, 2015). The Reporting and Testimony Subcommittee provides another example. This subcommittee expressed the view that the term "reasonable degree of scientific certainty" or variations of the term, should not be used by expert witnesses at trial. The subcommittee found that the term lacks a common definition across or within scientific disciplines as to what constitutes a reasonable certainty. Moreover, the use of the word "scientific" in the term implies that scientific rigor underlies the expert testimony, while the use of the word "reasonable" might be confused with the standard "beyond a reasonable doubt" (National Commission on Forensic Science, 2016).

A complete enumeration of all the views expressed by the NCFS is beyond the scope of this chapter. However, the examples provided illustrate the kinds of steps that must be taken to improve forensic science practice to avoid miscarriages of justice. Since the charter of the NCFS has expired, it is imperative for states to take efforts to reduce errors in forensic science. One way states have done so is to create forensic science oversight commissions. Such commissions, which are typically comprised of multiple stakeholders, exist in at least 20 states and have varying degrees of responsibility, including developing standards for forensic practice and investigating allegations of misconduct in crime labs (Norris et al., 2017). Among other initiatives, such entities could establish and/or enforce standards for accreditation of laboratories and certification of analysts. Some of the commissions were created in response to wrongful convictions. For example, the North Carolina Forensic Science Advisory Board and Office of the Ombudsman was created as a consequence of Gregory Flint Taylor's exoneration after serving 17 years in prison for the murder of Jacquetta Thomas—a crime he did not commit. During Taylor's exoneration process, irregularities came to light about the reporting on the forensic evidence introduced against him at trial. A subsequent audit of the state crime laboratory revealed numerous cases involving misleading reporting on forensic evidence (e.g., not reporting negative results of forensic examinations) (Swecker & Wolf, 2010). Creating such oversight commissions is a positive step, although researchers should study the extent to which these commissions help to reduce the risk of forensic science errors or misconduct (Norris et al., 2017).

Conclusion

Forensic science evidence and the crime laboratories that analyze it are important components of the criminal justice process. Society has learned through the DNA exonerations of wrongfully convicted people that the forensic sciences play a paradoxical role: both contributing to and revealing wrongful convictions (Cole, 2012; Thompson, 2008). This chapter has sought to highlight forensic science's role in contributing to erroneous convictions. Our focus on forensic science errors helps us understand where improvements might be made in the training and education of forensic analysts and the organization and culture of crime laboratories. Thus, we remain hopeful that reform efforts — particularly those designed to reduce the impact of cognitive bias and strengthen the scientific foundations of the forensic disciplines — will take hold in the nation's crime laboratories and reduce forensic science's role in precipitating wrongful convictions.

Key Terms and Concepts

- **Forensic evidence**: evidence obtained through the use of scientific methods and techniques for use in court
- **DNA**: deoxyribonucleic acid; the hereditary material in the nucleus of most cells that can be identified through the testing of biological material
- **Serology**: the identification and characterization of biological stains for forensic purposes; includes ABO blood typing
- **Drylabbing**: fabricating results for laboratory tests that were not conducted
- **Cognitive bias**: systematic errors in human judgment and decision-making that derive from subconscious mental processes; includes confirmation and disconfirmation biases
- **The *Frye* test**: from *Frye v. United States*, one standard used to determine the admissibility of expert testimony; requires the scientific technique to be generally accepted within the relevant scientific community
- **The *Daubert* test/factors**: from *Daubert v. Merrell Dow Pharmaceuticals, Inc.*, one set of considerations used to determine the admissibility of expert testimony; charges judges to serve as gatekeepers and evaluate several factors before admitting expert testimony
- **National Commission on Forensic Science**: created in 2013 by the U.S. Department of Justice and the National Institutes of Standards and Technology; included a variety of stakeholders who examined problems related to forensic science and made recommendations for reform

Discussion Questions

1. Do you agree with the National Research Council's recommendation to remove crime laboratories from the administrative control of law enforcement? Why or why not?

2. Consider your answer to Question 1. If you supported removing laboratories from law enforcement, how would you structure them? If you did not, what steps would you take to guard against the potential for pro-law enforcement bias?

3. How should courts treat wrongful conviction claims involving discredited forensic analysts?

4. Consider the Supreme Court's Confrontation Clause jurisprudence with respect to forensic analysts. What arguments can you make for and against allowing the defense to cross-examine forensic analysts?

References

Balko, R., & Carrington, T. (2018). *The cadaver king and the country dentist: A true story of injustice in the American South*. Public Affairs.

Beecher-Monas, E. (2009). Reality bites: The illusion of science in bite-mark evidence. *Cardozo Law Review, 30*, 1369–1410.

Beety, V. E. (2020). Forensic evidence in Arizona: Reforms for victims and defendants. *Arizona State Law Journal, 52*, 709–740.

Bonventre, C. L. (2020). Wrongful convictions and forensic science. *WIREs Forensic Science*. Advance online publication. https://doi.org/10.1002/wfs2.1406.

Bridgeman v. District Attorney for the Suffolk District, 476 Mass. 298 (2017).

Bullcoming v. New Mexico, 564 U.S. 647 (2011).

Butler, J. M. (2015). U.S. initiatives to strengthen forensic science & international standards in forensic DNA. *Forensic Science International: Genetics, 18*, 4–20.

Cásarez, N. B., & Thompson, S. G. (2018). Three transformative ideals to build a better crime lab. *Georgia State University Law Review, 34*(4), 1007–1072.

Cole, S. A. (2012). Forensic science and wrongful convictions: From exposer to contributor to corrector. *New England Law Review, 46*, 711–736.

Cooper, G. S., & Meterko, V. (2019). Cognitive bias research in forensic science: A systematic review. *Forensic Science International, 297,* 35–46.

Daubert v. Merrell Dow Pharmaceuticals, Inc., 509 U.S. 579 (1993).

Dror, I. E., Charlton, D., & Peron, A. E. (2006). Contextual information renders experts vulnerable to making erroneous identifications. *Forensic Science International, 156,* 74–78.

Dror, I. E., & Hampikian, G. Subjectivity and bias in forensic DNA mixture interpretation. *Science & Justice, 51*(4), 204–208.

Dror, I. E., Morgan, R. M., Rando, C., & Nakhaeizadeh, D. (2017). The bias snowball and the bias cascade effects: Two distinct biases that may impact forensic decision making. *Journal of Forensic Sciences.* http://doi.org/10.1111/1556-4029.13496.

Ex parte Chaney, 563 S.W.3d 239 (Tex. Crim. App. 2018).

Fabricant, M. C., & Carrington, T. (2016). The shifted paradigm: Forensic science's overdue evolution from magic to law. *Virginia Journal of Criminal Law, 4,* 1–115.

Federal Rule of Evidence 403 (2011). United States Code Annotated, title 28.

Federal Rule of Evidence 702 (2011). United States Code Annotated, title 28.

Findley, K. A. (2008). Innocents at risk: Adversary imbalance, forensic science, and the search for truth. *Seton Hall Law Review, 38,* 893–973.

Forth, J., & Waller, A. (2021, January 14). Man who sat on death row is cleared after bite-mark evidence is doubted. *New York Times.* https://www.nytimes.com/2021/01/14/us/eddie-lee-howard-freed.html.

Frye v. United States, 293 F. 1013 (D.C. App. 1923).

Garrett, B. L. (2011). *Convicting the innocent: Where criminal prosecutions go wrong.* Harvard University Press.

Garrett, B. L. (2020). The costs and benefits of forensics. *Houston Law Review, 57,* 593–616.

Garrett, B. L., & Neufeld, P. J. (2009). Invalid forensic science testimony and wrongful convictions. *Virginia Law Review, 95,* 1–97.

Gavin, S. F. (2008). No second chances: Best practices for expert practice. *Stetson Law Review, 38,* 41–74.

Giannelli, P. C. (1997). Essay: The abuse of scientific evidence in criminal cases: The need for independent crime laboratories. *Virginia Journal of Social Policy & the Law, 4,* 439–478.

Giannelli, P. C. (2007). Wrongful convictions and forensic science: The need to regulate crime labs. *North Carolina Law Review, 86,* 163–235.

Giannelli, P. C. (2008). Forensic science: Under the microscope. *Ohio Northern University Law Review, 34,* 315–339.

Heath v. United States, 26 A.3d 266 (D.C. 2011).

Howard v. State, 300 So.3d 1011 (Miss. 2020).

Hsu, S. (2012, April 16). Convicted defendants left uninformed of forensic flaws found by Justice Dept. *The Washington Post*. https://www.washingtonpost.com/local/crime/convicted-defendants-left-uninformed-of-forensic-flaws-found-by-justice-dept/2012/04/16/gIQAWTcgMT_story.html?utm_term=.4abc7028609c.

In the Matter of an Investigation of the West Virginia State Police Crime Laboratory, Serology Division, 438 S.E.2d 501 (W. Va. 1993).

The Innocence Project. (n.d.). Misapplication of forensic science. https://www.innocenceproject.org/causes/misapplication-forensic-science/.

Jabbar, M. (2010). Overcoming *Daubert*'s shortcomings in criminal trials: Making the error rate the primary factor in *Daubert*'s validity inquiry. *New York University Law Review, 85*, 2034–2064.

Jeanguenat, A. M., & Dror, I. E. (2018). Human factors affecting forensic decision making: Workplace stress and well-being. *Journal of Forensic Sciences, 63*(1), 258–261.

Jurs, A. W. (2016). Expert prevalence, persuasion, and price: What trial participants really think about experts. *Indiana Law Journal, 91*, 353–391.

LaPorte, G. (2018). Wrongful convictions and DNA exonerations: Understanding the role of forensic science. *National Institute of Justice Journal, 279*, 11–25.

Melendez-Diaz v. Massachusetts, 557 U.S. 305 (2009).

National Commission on Forensic Science. (2015). *Ensuring that forensic analysis is based upon task-relevant information*. United States Department of Justice and National Institute of Standards and Technology.

National Commission on Forensic Science. (2016). *Views of the Commission regarding use of the term "reasonable scientific certainty."* United States Department of Justice and National Institute of Standards and Technology.

National Commission on Forensic Science. (2017). *National Commission on Forensic Science: Reflecting back, looking toward the future*. National Institute of Standards and Technology.

National Registry of Exonerations (n.d.). The Groups Registry. https://exonerations.newkirkcenter.uci.edu/groups/group-exonerations.

National Research Council. (2009). *Strengthening forensic science in the United States: A path forward*. The National Academies Press.

New York State Bar Association. (2019). *Report of the task force on wrongful convictions*. https://nysba.org/app/uploads/2020/01/Wrongful-Convictions-Report-Feb.-2019.pdf.

Nickerson, R. S. (1998). Confirmation bias: A ubiquitous phenomenon in many guises. *Review of General Psychology, 2*(2), 175–220.

Norris, R. J., Bonventre, C. L., Redlich, A. D., Acker, J. R., & Lowe, C. (2017). Preventing wrongful convictions: An analysis of state investigation reforms. *Criminal Justice Policy Review.* http://doi.org/10.1177/088740341 6687359. ·

Old Chief v. United States, 519 U.S. 172 (1997).

People v. Bedessie, 970 N.E.2d 380 (N.Y. 2012).

People v. Taylor, 84 N.Y.S.3d 262 (App. Div. 2018).

Porter, W. R. (2009). Repeating, yet evading review: Admitting reliable expert testimony in criminal cases still depends on who is asking. *Rutgers Law Record, 36,* 48–70.

Richmond, D. R. (2000). Expert witness conflicts and compensation. *Tennessee Law Review, 67,* 909–948.

Risinger, D. M., Saks, M. J., Thompson, W. C., & Rosenthal, R. (2002). The *Daubert/Kumho* implications of observer effects in forensic science: Hidden problems of expectation and suggestion. *California Law Review, 90,* 1–56.

Rosen, A. (2017, January 18). State's highest court orders prosecutors to drop weak Dookhan cases. *The Boston Globe.* https://www.bostonglobe.com/ metro/2017/01/18/state-high-court-orders-prosecutors-drop-weak-dookhan-cases/SAvG09FT8lb6Mcv8cMMIKO/story.html.

Sah, S. (2021, Jan. 22). The Biden administration must put the science back into forensic science. *Forbes.* https://www.forbes.com/sites/sunitasah/2021/01/ 22/the-biden-administration-must-put-the-science-back-into-forensic-science/?sh=2c6c48151dbf.

Scheck, B., Neufeld, P., & Dwyer, J. (2003). *Actual innocence: When justice goes wrong and how to make it right.* New American Library.

State v. Edelman, 593 N.W.2d 419 (S.D. 1999).

State v. Guilbert, 49 A.3d 705 (Ct. 2012).

State v. Rosales, 998 A.2d 459 (N.J. 2010).

State v. Wright, 206 P.3d 856 (Idaho App. 2009).

Swecker, C., & Wolf, M. (2010). An independent review of the SBI forensic laboratory. https://forensicresources.org/resources/an-independent-review-of-the-sbi-forensic-laboratory/.

Thompson, S. G., & Cásarez, N. B. (2016). Building the infrastructure for "justice through science": The Texas model. *West Virginia Law Review, 119,* 711–748.

Thompson, W. C. (2008). Beyond bad apples: Analyzing the role of forensic science in wrongful convictions. *Southwestern Law Review, 37,* 1027–1050.

Trial Transcript, *State of Texas v. Gilbert Alejandro.* (1995). http://www.law. virginia.edu/html/librarysite/garrett_exoneree.htm.

United States Department of Justice. (2009). Office of Justice Programs. Bureau of Justice Statistics. *Census of Publicly Funded Forensic Crime Laboratories, 2009.* ICPSR 34340-v1. Inter-university Consortium for Political and Social Research [distributor], 2012-11-26. http://doi.org/10.3886/ICPSR34340.v1.

United States v. Tribble. (2012). Motion to vacate conviction and dismiss indictment with prejudice on the grounds of actual innocence under the Innocence Protection Act. http://www.pdsdc.org/docs/default-source/default-document-library/motion-to-vacate-conviction-on-the-grounds-of-actual-innocence-january-18-2012.pdf?sfvrsn=0.

West, E., & Meterko, V. (2015/2016). Innocence Project: DNA exonerations, 1989–2014: Review of data and findings from the first 25 years. *Albany Law Review, 79,* 717–795.

Williams v. Illinois, 567 U.S. 50 (2012).

Chapter 7

Incentivized
Informants and Snitches

Learning Objectives

After reading this chapter, you should be able to:

- Distinguish the various types of informants and the incentives that induce informant testimony.
- Understand prosecutors' disclosure obligations regarding incentivized informant testimony.
- Appreciate the need for the systematic collection by law enforcement agencies of data on informant usage.
- Understand the value of establishing guidelines and limits on the use of informants.
- Discuss reform efforts aimed at improving the use of informants.

Case Study: William Dillon

On the morning of August 17, 1981, a driver picked up a hitchhiker near Canova Beach in Florida. The driver saw the man under the interior light of his truck; he reported that the hitchhiker was sweaty and had blood on his yellow T-shirt and smeared on his shorts and his leg. He described the man as six feet tall, with a mustache. The driver said that he performed oral sex on the man before dropping him off at a nearby tavern. After dropping him off, the driver realized the man had left his bloody shirt in the car, so he threw it away in a trashcan.

Only hours before the hitchhiker had been picked up, a man named James Dvorak was beaten to death near Canova Beach. Dvorak's body was found in a wooded area near the beach. He was nude and badly beaten. Police collected his clothes and several other items from the crime scene. After the murder was reported on the news, the driver called police, told them about the hitchhiker he'd picked up, and police found the T-shirt that had been discarded.

Five days later, William Dillon and his brother were near the beach when they were questioned by police. The officers were suspicious that Dillon knew about the crime—despite its coverage on the news—and took him into custody. Police enlisted the assistance of John Preston, a supposed expert in working with scent-tracking dogs, who claimed that his dog linked the bloody T-shirt to the crime scene and linked Dillon to the T-shirt. The police later conducted a "paper lineup," in which the dog sniffed the shirt and then identified a piece of paper Dillon had touched. William Dillon was charged with murder.

By the time trial began, four key witnesses appeared against Dillon. One was Preston, who said that the dog linked Dillon to the crime scene. A second was the driver of the car who reported having picked up a hitchhiker. Although Dillon did not match the description the driver had given—he was 6'4" and had no mustache—the driver identified Dillon as the man he had picked up. The third witness was Dillon's ex-girlfriend, who said she was with him on the night of the murder and saw him standing over the body while wearing a yellow T-shirt. The final witness was a man who was in jail with Dillon while he awaited trial. The man served as a jailhouse informant; he reported that, while they were in jail together, Dillon admitted to him that he committed the murder. Specifically, he said Dillon reenacted the murder, including how he held the victim down and punched him (Garrett, 2011). This informant was the only one who reported hearing Dillon's confession and witnessing his reenactment of the killing, although others were incarcerated and present at the time. Dillon testified on his own behalf, claiming that he was miles away from the beach on August 17. Although several alibi witnesses corroborated his story, he was convicted of murder and sentenced to life in prison.

After Dillon's trial, the jailhouse informant's own rape charges were dropped by prosecutors. Furthermore, Dillon's ex-girlfriend recanted her testimony, saying that she fabricated the story after being threatened with a charge of accessory to murder, which carries a 25-year sentence, if she did not cooperate with the authorities. It also was discovered later that she had sexual intercourse with the lead officer during the investigation of the case. The officer subsequently was suspended and resigned. And, two years after Dillon's conviction, questions began to arise about John Preston and the reliability of his dog. Preston had testified in hundreds of cases, including that of Wilton Dedge, who was convicted of murder in Florida shortly after Dillon's trial. Dedge was exonerated by DNA testing after serving more than two decades in prison.

Dillon lost his appeals during the five years following his conviction. In 1996, he sought DNA testing, but was denied. It was not until 2007—by which time most of the biological evidence had been lost or destroyed, but the bloody T-shirt had been saved—that a judge ordered testing on the remaining evidence. The DNA tests on the T-shirt purportedly worn by the killer provided no link to William Dillon. The blood matched the victim, and biological material found on the collar and armpit belonged to neither the victim nor Dillon. In November 2008, following the DNA exclusion, Dillon was released from prison and he was formally exonerated the next month, 27 years after he was wrongfully convicted of James Dvorak's murder.

At a later hearing to determine whether the state of Florida would provide him with any compensation, Dillon met the jailhouse informant who had testified against him. The man apologized, in tears, claiming that police officers sat with him and coached him on what to say and wrote down the words he repeated back to them. After he offered his apology, the man and Dillon shook hands (Garrett, 2011).

A Closer Look: William Dillon's Story

- *I Didn't Do It*, Episode 7, "William Dillon: Battered on the Beach"—This is another episode from the documentary series produced by Canadian production company Lively Media for the Investigation Discovery cable channel. Episode 7 is a fascinating retelling of Dillon's story through dramatizations and interviews with Dillon and others.

- *Black Robes and Lawyers* (2011)—This full-length CD features original songs written by Dillon about his struggles as a wrongfully convicted man.

Incentivized Informants: Overview and Research

In William Dillon's case, both his ex-girlfriend and a jailhouse snitch served as key informants at trial, for different but related reasons. One was threatened with a criminal charge and sought to avoid prosecution and punishment; the other was a suspected criminal, in custody and facing a rape charge, who avoided punishment after providing his information. Both were given a strong incentive to cooperate with police and provide information against Dillon.

Informants such as these play a critical role throughout the criminal legal process, from police investigation to prosecutors' charging decisions and through sentencing. As Natapoff (2009, p. 1) wrote, "criminal informant use is everywhere in the American legal system." In some circumstances—particularly in cases involving drugs or organized crime—informants can be an effective, even necessary, tool for law enforcement in their pursuit of criminals. Drug cases are particularly important; Natapoff (2006, p. 110) suggests that there is a "thriving market for information" in which snitches are given leniency in exchange for information provided to police and prosecutors. However, this market has not been heavily scrutinized. Given the substantial incentives informants often have to be of assistance to law enforcement, there is good reason to question, if not doubt the reliability of the information they provide. At a minimum, skepticism is warranted.

Inaccurate information provided by an incentivized informant can pose a stark danger to the innocent. According to Innocence Project data, informants were involved in nearly 15% (n = 48) of the first 325 DNA exonerations. Most of these cases involved jailhouse informants (people who were in police custody when they provided information, such as the man in Dillon's case), although nine of them involved other **incentivized informants** (those who were not in custody, but were provided an incentive in exchange for information, such as Dillon's ex-girlfriend). These informants often received money, or had their charges dropped or sentences reduced in exchange for information. Interestingly, the majority (83%) of informant cases involved homicide, and many cases were eligible for capital punishment (West & Meterko, 2016).

The National Registry of Exonerations does not have an explicit category for "informants," but instead uses a broader category: "Perjury or False Accusation." In these cases, someone "other than the exoneree committed perjury by making a false statement under oath that incriminated the exoneree in the crime for which the exoneree was later exonerated, or made a similar unsworn statement that would have been perjury if made under oath" (National Registry of Exonerations, n.d.). As conceptualized, this was the leading factor contributing to wrongful convictions in the first 2,754 exonerations (59.9%, or 1,649 cases). It was most common in child sex abuse (249/293, or 85%) and homicide (788/1108, or 71.1%) cases, and least common in sexual assault cases (147/341, or 43.1%). A closer look at the NRE data reveals that jailhouse informants figured into 200 of the 1,649 perjury/false accusation cases (12.1%), and more than 80% of those 200 jailhouse informant cases involved murders.

These findings concerning the prevalent use of informants in murder cases are in line with a 2005 report by Northwestern University School of Law's Center on Wrongful Convictions, which concluded that snitches contributed to nearly 46% of cases that resulted in death row exonerations, "mak[ing] snitches the leading cause of wrongful convictions in U.S. capital cases" (Center on Wrongful Convictions, 2005, p. 3). This may be due, at least in part, to the fact that unlike a rape or assault, murder cases do not leave a living victim to identify the perpetrator. To investigate homicides, police typically must rely on other evidence, such as a confession (see chapter 4 of this book), but when a confession cannot be secured, they may depend more heavily on information provided by informants or jailhouse snitches. And in capital murder cases, which frequently involve highly aggravated and publicized killings, informants may receive even better deals (Garrett, 2011).

Clearly, law enforcement's reliance on incentivized informants can be problematic. Part of the reason is obvious: "when the criminal justice system offers witnesses incentives to lie, they will" (Center on Wrongful Convictions, 2005, p. 2). However, it is not just the fact that informants lie, but "how and why they lie, and how the government depends on lying informants, that makes snitching a troubling distortion of the truth-seeking process" (Natapoff, 2006, p. 108). As indicated by the phrase, "*incentivized informants*," these individuals provide information in exchange for anticipated or actual benefits, or incentives. In some cases, the benefit may be monetary. Take, for example, the case of Kenny Waters, in which a murder investigation had gone cold for two years. Police only turned their attention to Waters after another man, Robert Osborne, offered his name to the police in exchange for money (although it is unclear whether he ultimately received a payment). Waters spent 18 years incarcerated before being exonerated through DNA testing.

Perhaps more troubling than monetary incentives are those provided to criminal informants, such as the jailhouse snitch in William Dillon's case, who often receive leniency in their own cases in exchange for information. While many informants deny receiving any benefit, one analysis of informant testimony in exoneration cases found that, of those who do admit to receiving a benefit, the most common is leniency in their own case, followed by assistance in relocating (Fessinger et al., 2020). Receiving a break in their own case not only rewards suspected or known criminals who provide information, it supplies added motivation for them to ensure that their story is believable. If the informant's story is the main piece of evidence against a defendant, the government may not be able to thoroughly vet the informant's information. Even if they can, police and prosecutors may not carefully and objectively scrutinize the informant's story, because they may be heavily invested in accepting it as credible. They consequently may pass over small yet important details or inconsistencies, and even secure information by questioning informants in leading or suggestive ways (Gershman, 2014; Yaroshefsky, 1999). This creates a "disturbing marriage of convenience" (Natapoff, 2006, p. 108), whereby both the informant and the government agents involved in the case benefit from the information and neither side has a strong incentive to establish its veracity. Incentivized informants thus can be quite dangerous to innocent suspects, as they have stronger incentives to lie to, deceive, and manipulate law enforcement than virtually any other type of witness (Gershman, 2014).

Informants often produce detailed accounts of the crime being investigated that appear to be quite believable. This is also true of jailhouse informants who claim to have heard a confession while incarcerated with the suspect — such "secondary confessions" are common features of informant testimony in exoneration cases (Fessinger et al., 2020) — even if they were not previously acquainted. The details may be available because, by definition, such an informant can only work with police after a suspect already is in custody. The police thus will have completed some investigation and developed a working theory of the crime. The informant therefore can acquire information by interacting with the police and prosecutors and as more details are made publicly available. It is also possible that innocent suspects may have discussed aspects of their case with other inmates without actually confessing, thus revealing details that were then repeated by the informant (Garrett, 2011).

Another type of informant may be a co-defendant or alleged accessory, that is, someone charged with participating in the same crime. Whether innocent or guilty, co-defendants may know something about the crime simply because they are also under investigation. In some cases, the co-defendant may actually be guilty and will work to shift responsibility to an innocent third party. In other cases, both co-defendants might be innocent (Garrett, 2011). Situations with co-defendants can be particularly challenging because there are unique incentives and opportunities to lie. One experimental study by Norris and Redlich (2014) used a variation of the **Prisoner's Dilemma** — a situation in which two suspects are separated, questioned independently, and each told that the other is implicating them in the crime — to determine admissions of guilt. They found that, under some circumstances, people may be willing to throw an innocent person "under the bus" in exchange for a favorable deal in their own case. Specifically, up to 63% of guilty suspects and 13% of innocent suspects who had an innocent acquaintance as a co-defendant were willing to implicate the other person in exchange for a deal where they were promised benefits.

Informants thus can supply important information in support of criminal investigations, and the incentives for informants to testify on behalf of the prosecution are clear. The connection between informants and the investigative practices of police and prosecutors is particularly close for certain crimes. One analysis of cases in the National Registry of Exonerations found that the "use of jailhouse informants … is especially strongly correlated with allegations or findings of official misconduct" (Covey, 2018, p. 539). Moreover, informant testimony may have implications for other aspects of a case. For instance, one study found that jailhouse informant testimony can influence the confidence of eyewitnesses who learn about the informant, in some cases even leading them to alter their identification decision (Mote et al., 2018). Juries may find informant testimony to be persuasive for a number of reasons. First, the incentives provided to the informant may not be clear to the jury. In many cases, deals discussed with the informant may not be finalized until after the trial testimony is completed (West & Meterko, 2016). Prosecutors often will not make promises before trial because doing so could hurt the credibility of their key informant. Even if a deal is made, informants may dispute its relevance and claim that they cooperated for more altruistic reasons (Garrett, 2011).

Second, as noted earlier, informants who are receiving benefits in exchange for their testimony have good reasons to ensure that their story sounds believable. After all, if their story is unhelpful or seems implausible, it may not be used; in such cases, they will fail to realize the anticipated benefits. Not only must the story be plausible on its face, but it ideally will be presented to the jury in a way that seems persuasive. While in many cases it is unclear if an informant has been "coached" to present information in a specific way, their stories are often neatly crafted to fit the prosecution's theory of a case. Indeed, Garrett (2011, p. 124) wrote that he "was most amazed by how the most aggressive informants delivered 'made to order' statements neatly molded to the litigation strategy of the State," including details that both bolstered the prosecution's own story and critically challenged that of the defense. In short, by the time a trial occurs, the informant may have a well-rehearsed story that fits cleanly with the prosecution's theory of the crime, thus presenting a veneer of accuracy and reliability.

Finally, even when jurors are made fully aware of the incentives given to secure informants' cooperation, that knowledge may have little impact on their assessment of the testimony's reliability. One study found that while knowledge about whether an incentive was offered (as opposed to no incentive being offered) did influence jury decisions, the size of the incentive (how large of a sentence reduction the informant received) had little or no effect (Maeder & Pica, 2014). Not surprisingly, perhaps, it may be difficult for trial jurors to discount testimony that is delivered under oath, particularly when the informant's story corroborates other evidence offered by the prosecution.

Wrongful Convictions in Popular Culture:
Informants and Snitches

- *The Innocent Man: Murder and Injustice in a Small Town* (2006) — a non-fiction book by famed author John Grisham about the case of Ron Williamson. Williamson was wrongly convicted, along with his friend Dennis Fritz, of the rape and murder of Debra Sue Carter in Ada, Oklahoma, and sentenced to death. He served more than a decade before being exonerated through DNA evidence.

- *The Innocent Man* (2018) — a documentary adaptation of Grisham's book, produced as a series on the streaming platform, Netflix.

Incentivized Informants and the Law

The legal procedures governing trial evidence function largely to promote reliable fact-finding. Some evidence is so inherently untrustworthy that it will be ruled inadmissible and hence will be excluded altogether from a trial and not presented to the jury. Evidence that is deemed admissible may or may not be considered credible by the jury (or the judge in a bench trial). Its reliability will be tested by the standard tools of the adversarial process, chief of which is cross-examining witnesses so their testimony can be critically evaluated. The law thus has options regarding the testimony of incentivized informants. It could flatly prohibit such testimony because of the numerous threats to such witnesses' trustworthiness. Alternatively, the law could allow juries to hear the testimony of jailhouse snitches and other witnesses whose testimony is provided in exchange for or in contemplation of some reward or benefits, as long as the threats to reliability can be fully exposed and assessed. The latter approach is far and away the dominant one in the nation's courts.

It is not impossible to imagine a rule that would prevent a jury hearing from a witness whose testimony has been conditioned on the promise of receiving significant benefits. Consider, for example, whether defense lawyers should be allowed to offer a witness a large sum of money, or something even more meaningful — such as freedom from incarceration — in exchange for trial testimony that will benefit their client. Although the promised reward is sure to be subject to an agreement that the witness will testify truthfully, such an arrangement sounds perilously close to bribery. At a minimum, it is fraught with danger that the "agreement to testify truthfully" simply cannot be trusted. Yet this description captures the essence of the practice of allowing the prosecution to offer incentives to informants in exchange for testimony that can be expected to bolster the chances of securing a guilty verdict.

Indeed, one appeals court issued a short-lived ruling which barred federal prosecutors from presenting the trial testimony of an informant which had been secured in exchange for a promise to recommend a reduction in sentence on an outstanding charge. The court concluded that "the government had impermissibly promised [the informant] something of value — leniency — in return for his testimony, in violation of" a federal statute, 18 U.S.C. § 201 (c)(2) (*United States v. Singleton*, 1998, p. 1334). The statute provides:

> Whoever ... directly or indirectly, gives, offers or promises anything of value to any person, for or because of the testimony under oath or affirmation given or to be given by such person as a witness upon a trial, hearing, or other proceeding, before any court ... authorized by the laws of the United States to hear evidence or take testimony ... shall be fined under this title or imprisoned for not more than two years, or both.

Its purpose, the court reasoned, is "deterring corruption" (p. 1345), and thus it applies to governmental representatives as well as to private parties.

This decision sent shockwaves through the legal community because it significantly compromised federal prosecutors' ability to rely on the testimony of incentivized informants. But the ruling was quickly vacated on rehearing before a larger panel of judges. The law in question, the court declared, "does not apply to ... an Assistant United States Attorney functioning within the official scope of the office" (*United States v. Singleton*, 1999, p. 1298).

The Supreme Court has found no constitutional barrier to the prosecution's reliance on the testimony of incentivized informants. Justice Stewart explained why in *Hoffa v. United States* (1966, pp. 311–312):

> In the words of Judge Learned Hand, "Courts have countenanced the use of informers from time immemorial; in cases of conspiracy, or in other cases when the crime consists of preparing for another crime, it is usually necessary to rely upon them or upon accomplices because the criminals will almost certainly proceed covertly. * * *" *United States v. Dennis*, 2 Cir., 183 F.2d 201, at 224.

This is not to say that a secret government informer is to the slightest degree more free from all relevant constitutional restrictions than is any other government agent. It is to say that the use of secret informers is not per se unconstitutional.

The petitioner is quite correct in the contention that [the informant in this case], perhaps even more than most informers, may have had motives to lie. But it does not follow that his testimony was untrue, nor does it follow that his testimony was constitutionally inadmissible. The established safeguards of the Anglo-American legal system leave the veracity of a witness to be tested by cross-examination, and the credibility of his testimony to be determined by a properly instructed jury. At the trial of this case, [the informant] was subjected to rigorous cross-examination, and the extent and nature of his dealings with federal and state authorities were insistently explored. The trial judge instructed the jury, both specifically and generally, with regard to assessing [the informant's] credibility. The Constitution does not require us to upset the jury's verdict.

As noted in Justice Stewart's opinion, "relevant constitutional restrictions" could bar an informant (incentivized or other) from testifying at a criminal trial. For example, if a defendant has been indicted, and thus is entitled to the assistance of counsel under the Sixth and Fourteenth Amendments, the government is not allowed to circumvent defense counsel by arranging for an informant to actively elicit incriminating statements from the defendant (*Massiah v. United States*, 1964; *United States v. Henry*, 1980). This rule does not prevent a government informant from testifying after serving as a passive "listening post" — i.e., from simply listening while a talkative defendant offers information (*Kuhlmann v. Wilson*, 1986) — even if the defendant has been indicted or is represented by counsel. Nor does it bar a government agent, including an undercover police officer, from trying to pry incriminating information from a defendant whose Sixth Amendment right to counsel has not attached (*Illinois v. Perkins*, 1990). And if the informant is operating on their own, without involvement or encouragement from the government, the informant is not subject to any constitutional constraints.

In many jurisdictions, the testimony of a defendant's alleged accomplices or co-defendants is so highly suspect that it is inadmissible unless it is supported by some type of corroborating evidence (Giannelli, 2007, p. 613; Kruse, 2015, p. 389). **Corroboration** requirements have been adopted in some states with respect to jailhouse informant testimony because of analogous doubts concerning its reliability. The Constitution does not mandate such corroboration, and statutory provisions of this nature have been criticized as not providing meaningful safeguards because corroboration typically can be supplied by minimal evidence (Covey, 2014, pp. 1416–1420; Roth, 2016, pp. 760–761).

If a witness's credibility is suspect because the prosecution has offered a reward in exchange for the testimony, it seems clear that this information should be made known to the jury (or the judge, in a bench trial) whose job it is to carefully evaluate the reliability of evidence. The Supreme Court has ruled that a defendant's due process rights are violated when a prosecutor knowingly allows a witness to misrepresent that no promises have been made to secure his trial testimony. In *Napue v. Illinois* (1959), an assistant district attorney asked a prosecution witness in a murder trial, "Have I promised you that I would recommend any reduction of sentence to anybody?" The witness replied, "You did not," although in fact, the prosecutor had promised to make such a recommendation to the judge following the witness's testimony. Chief Justice Warren's opinion for a unanimous Supreme Court invalidated the defendant's conviction.

> The principle that a State may not knowingly use false evidence, including false testimony, to obtain a tainted conviction, implicit in any concept of ordered liberty, does not cease to apply merely because the false testimony goes only to the credibility of the witness. The jury's estimate of the truthfulness and reliability of a given witness may well be determinative of guilt or innocence, and it is upon such subtle factors as the possible interest of the witness in testifying falsely that a defendant's life or liberty may depend.

Prosecutors' constitutional obligations extend beyond not allowing false testimony about promises extended to incentivized informants to go uncorrected. They have an affirmative duty to divulge to defense counsel the terms and conditions of any deals made to secure a witness's testimony. Only through such disclosure is defense counsel able to probe the informant's motivation for testifying through cross-examination and thus raise questions about the witness's credibility. As explained by Chief Justice Burger in *Giglio v. United States* (1972), this duty applies to the district attorney's office generally, and is not restricted to the individual prosecutor who participates in a trial.

> [W]hether the nondisclosure [of the promise made to the witness] was a result of negligence or design, it is the responsibility of the prosecutor. The prosecutor's office is an entity and as such it is the spokesman for the Government. A promise made by one attorney must be attributed, for these purposes, to the Government. To the ex-

tent this places a burden on the large prosecution offices, procedures and regulations can be established to carry that burden and to insure communication of all relevant information on each case to every lawyer who deals with it.

Here the Government's case depended almost entirely on [the testimony of the witness in question, the defendant's alleged co-conspirator in passing forged money orders to a bank]; without it there could have been no indictment and no evidence to carry the case to the jury. [His] credibility as a witness was therefore an important issue in the case, and evidence of any understanding or agreement as to a future prosecution would be relevant to his credibility and the jury was entitled to know of it.

For these reasons, the due process requirements enunciated in *Napue*... require a new trial, and the judgment of conviction is therefore reversed and the case is remanded for further proceedings consistent with this opinion.

Problems can arise with the enforcement of these rules when a firm agreement has not been made before a trial begins, but the prospect of a charge or sentence reduction nevertheless exists and hinges on the witness's testimony. Such arrangements, which involve implied or hoped-for consideration in exchange for testimony, are not uncommon. They are sometimes referred to as deals made by "a wink and a nod" to distinguish them from more specific promises which clearly must be disclosed (Alter, 2005, p. 227; Cassidy, 2004; Giannelli, 2007, p. 607). Revealing to the jury that the prospect of potential favors might motivate a witness's testimony is important for the same reasons that require the disclosure of a firm agreement. Thus, in *Wearry v. Cain* (2016, p. 1007), the Supreme Court described its earlier holding in *Napue v. Illinois* (1959) as encompassing the proposition that "even though the State had made no binding promises, a witness' attempt to obtain a deal before testifying was material because the jury 'might well have concluded that [the witness] had fabricated testimony in order to curry the [prosecution's] favor.'" Such implicit "wink and a nod" agreements may nevertheless frequently elude disclosure and detection because of their nebulous nature.

The Supreme Court has ruled that prosecutors are immune from civil liability for providing inadequate training to their staff and failing to supervise the sharing of information regarding the use of informants, even when such maladministration contributes to unreliable testimony and wrongful convictions (*Van de Kamp v. Goldstein*, 2009). Motivated by revelations of wrongful convictions linked to the false and unreliable testimony of jailhouse informants, some states have enacted legislation aimed at curbing such abuses. For example, Connecticut (Conn. Gen. Stat. Ann. §§ 51-286k, 54-86o, 2019), Nebraska (Neb. Stat. Ann. §§ 29-4702 through 29-4705, 2019), and Texas (Tex. Code Crim. Proc. Art. 2.024, 2019; Tex. Code Crim. Proc. Art. 39.14 (h-1), 2017) have adopted statutes that require prosecutors to maintain databases of cases in which jailhouse informants have provided testimony and to make pretrial disclosure of information to defense counsel about such matters as the benefits the informant has received or is expected to receive, the specific statements the defendant allegedly made, including the time, place, and manner in which they were made, prior cases in which the informant has testified, the informant's criminal record, and whether the informant at any time recanted any information they provided (see Allen, 2020). Illinois has gone even farther, not only requiring advance disclosure of relevant information, but also requiring a pretrial hearing in cases involving serious crimes so a judge can rule whether the informant's planned testimony has sufficient indicia of reliability to be admissible in evidence. The Illinois statute governing informant testimony provides:

725 Ill. Compiled Stat. Ann. 5/115-21 (2019)

(a) For the purposes of this Section, "informant" means someone who is purporting to testify about admissions made to him or her by the accused while detained or incarcerated in a penal institution contemporaneously.

(b) This Section applies to any criminal proceeding [involving specified offenses] ... in which the prosecution attempts to introduce evidence of incriminating statements made by the accused to or overheard by an informant.

(c) Except as provided in subsection (d-5), in any case under this Section, the prosecution shall disclose at least 30 days prior to a relevant evidentiary hearing or trial:

(1) the complete criminal history of the informant;

(2) any deal, promise, inducement, or benefit that the offering party has made or will make in the future to the informant;

(3) the statements made by the accused;

(4) the time and place of the statements, the time and place of their disclosure to law enforcement officials, and the names of all persons who were present when the statements were made;

(5) whether at any time the informant recanted that testimony or statement and, if so, the time and place of the recantation, the nature of the recantation, and the names of the persons who were present at the recantation;

(6) other cases in which the informant testified, provided that the existence of such testimony can be ascertained through reasonable inquiry and whether the informant received any promise, inducement, or benefit in exchange for or subsequent to that testimony or statement; and

(7) any other information relevant to the informant's credibility.

(d) Except as provided in subsection (d-5), in any case under this Section, the prosecution shall timely disclose at least 30 days prior to any relevant evidentiary hearing or trial its intent to introduce the testimony of an informant. The court shall conduct a hearing to determine whether the testimony of the informant is reliable, unless the defendant waives such a hearing. If the prosecution fails to show by a preponderance of the evidence that the informant's testimony is reliable, the court shall not allow the testimony to be heard at trial. At this hearing, the court shall consider the factors enumerated in subsection (c) as well as any other factors relating to reliability.

(d-5) The court may permit the prosecution to disclose its intent to introduce the testimony of an informant with less notice than the 30-day notice required under subsections (c) and (d) of this Section if the court finds that the informant was not known prior to the 30-day notice period and could not have been discovered or obtained by the exercise of due diligence by the prosecution prior to the 30-day notice period. Upon good cause shown, the court may set a reasonable notice period under the circumstances or may continue the trial on its own motion to allow for a reasonable notice period, which motion shall toll the speedy trial period under Section 103-5 of this Code for the period of the continuance.

(e) If a lawful recording of an incriminating statement is made of an accused to an informant or made of a statement of an informant to law enforcement or the prosecution, including any deal, promise, inducement, or other benefit offered to the informant, the accused may request a reliability hearing under subsection (d) of this Section and the prosecution shall be subject to the disclosure requirements of subsection (c) of this Section.

Increasing Informant Reliability: Policy Reforms

The law provides limited protections against problems involving incentivized informants. However, experts have suggested several additional reforms to agency policies and criminal procedure that might help alleviate concerns associated with unreliable snitches and informants.

Data Collection

Despite the frequency with which police and prosecutors rely on informants, there is rarely any way to systematically keep track of those individuals. Therefore, Natapoff (2009) suggests that law enforcement agencies develop mechanisms for collecting and reporting data on informants. She proposes that departments maintain aggregate data on how many informants they use, the crimes in which they are used, the crimes the informants commit, and the benefits provided to those informants in exchange for information. She also suggests that while identifying information not be included, the data include informants' race, sex, and location. Better data collection and reporting would not single-handedly solve the problems associated with informants and snitches, but it would allow for analysis of informant use. For both government actors and the public, this would promote a greater understanding of and a more informed discussion about the practice. Connecticut, for example, has enacted the following legislation.

Conn. Gen. Stat. Ann. §51-286k (2019)
Tracking and reporting of use of testimony by jailhouse witnesses

(a) Each state's attorney's office shall track the following:
(1) The substance and use of any testimony of a jailhouse witness, as defined in section 54-86o, against the interest of a (A) person suspected as the perpetrator of an offense, or (B) defendant, regardless of whether such testimony is presented at trial; and
(2) The jailhouse witness's agreement to cooperate with the state's attorney and benefit, as defined in section 54-86o, that the state's attorney has provided, offered or may offer in the future to the jailhouse witness in connection with the testimony described in subdivision (1) of this subsection.
(b) Each state's attorney's office shall send the information described in subsection (a) of this section to the Criminal Justice Policy and

Planning Division within the Office of Policy and Management, which shall maintain a state-wide record of such materials. Such information shall be confidential and not be subject to disclosure under the Freedom of Information Act, as defined in section 1-200.

Establishing Guidelines

A relatively straightforward suggestion for reform is for all police departments and prosecutor offices to establish guidelines or standards for the use of criminal informants. For police departments, Natapoff (2009) suggests these policies should be modeled after the Department of Justice's guidelines, which encourage better documentation and review of informant use. Some local agencies already have guidelines, some more complex than others. They might restrict informant use in some ways, require certain types of documentation before supplied information is credited, and so forth. Such guidelines are recommended to be put in place in police departments and supplemented with training to ensure that officers abide by them. Similarly, prosecutors' offices can and should develop internal guidelines. Guidelines already exist at the federal level, and the American Bar Association has issued standards for prosecutorial investigations that include cooperating witnesses. While these standards are not binding, many offices tend to follow ABA guidelines, and prosecutors' offices are free to adopt additional formal policies regarding the use of informant testimony.

Limits on Informants and Prosecutors

A policy change that may help address some of the fundamental concerns regarding informants — namely, the incentives they have to be dishonest and the possibility that juries will not fully appreciate those incentives — is to place limits on the situations in which an informant may be used. For instance, informants in many cases that later ended in exoneration had lengthy criminal histories (Neuschatz et al., 2020). Legislatures might consider restricting benefits for informants who themselves have committed particularly serious or heinous crimes (Natapoff, 2009). In addition, prosecutors can be prevented from postponing finalizing deals with informants until after trial testimony has been presented, or from dangling implied benefits rather than making the consideration offered in exchange for testimony explicit (Garrett, 2011). Having information about arrangements made to secure informants' testimony formalized and in place in advance of trial would assist the defense in challenging informants' credibility and provide more complete information to allow the fact-finder (i.e., the judge and/or jury) to assess how much weight to place on informants' testimony. Such practices also would help guard against informants' falsely denying that they have received or been offered benefits for testifying, a common occurrence in exoneration cases (Neuschatz et al., 2020).

Recording Requirements

If informants are to be used, whatever conversations take place between them and state officials can be recorded (Center on Wrongful Convictions, 2005; Garrett, 2011). As discussed earlier, a key problem with criminal informants is the lack of knowledge about the deals they strike, how law enforcement interacts with them, and the like. Electronic recording of discussions or negotiations between informants and police or prosecutors can be immensely helpful. If carried out properly and in full, the sources and nature of the informant's information can be better assessed. For example, did law enforcement provide details about the crime that were then repeated by the informant? Were there any promises or implications of lenient treatment in exchange for testimony? How closely does the informant's original report to authorities conform to later versions, including the testimony offered at trial? If such recordings were made and provided to the defense, defense lawyers could better challenge the use of informants whose reliability is suspect. Judges and juries also would have more information at their disposal in evaluating the informant's information.

Discovery and Disclosure

Another proposed reform is to enhance discovery and disclosure requirements in cases involving the use of an informant, such as by clarifying them and extending them beyond the constitutional minima. Broadly, **discovery** and disclosure refers to the exchange of information between sides prior to trial; in a criminal case, information is exchanged between the prosecution and defense. In cases involving the use of an informant, some suggest that prosecutors should disclose to the defense all relevant factors pertaining to the informant's testimony. Such a requirement would encompass extensive information about the informant's statements, including what was said, when statements were made and to whom, when the information was shared with law enforcement, whether the statements were ever recanted by the informant, and so forth. The prosecution should also be required to disclose any information that bears on the informant's credibility, such as their criminal history, deals made with the state, promises or implications of leniency, money exchanged, and others. Information also should be provided about previous cases in which the person has served as an informant (Center on Wrongful Convictions, 2005; Garrett, 2011; Natapoff, 2009; Norris, et al., 2011). Such disclosure would promote transparency in general and would allow the defense to challenge informant testimony more effectively. As one recent laboratory study found, potential jurors' perceptions of an informant's motive for providing information can influence their interpretations of information supplied by the informant, including inconsistencies in their story, and ultimately can affect their decision to convict or acquit (DeLoach et al., 2020).

As we noted earlier, some states have adopted statutes which require pretrial disclosure of such information, and the Constitution makes obligatory the disclosure of promises made to secure and reward informants' testimony (*Giglio v. United States*, 1972). However, it is worth noting that as the practice of using informants currently stands, enhanced discovery and disclosure may be somewhat limited in their ability to improve the system. This is due, in part, to the fact that the use of snitches often relies upon implied benefits, rather than formal deals (Center on Wrongful Convictions, 2005). It is also because discovery and disclosure requirements are generally only relevant to trials, and the vast majority of cases are settled through guilty pleas (see chapter 5 of this book). The Supreme Court has ruled that information useful to impeach the credibility of witnesses, including informants, need not be disclosed in advance of the discussions leading to defendants' entering guilty pleas (*United States v. Ruiz*, 2002). Thus, some suggest that criminal procedure be revised to ensure that any information pertinent to an informant is provided during plea negotiations (Natapoff, 2009).

Pretrial Reliability Hearings

One broad suggestion for improving the use of informants is to increase the courts' role in screening potential informants. We earlier reproduced a ground-breaking Illinois statute that requires judges in serious criminal cases to conduct pre-trial hearings and make findings that informants are sufficiently reliable before their testimony is admissible at trial. Natapoff (2006, 2009) has suggested that such pre-trial **reliability hearings** for informants should be conducted more widely and that they be structured in a fashion similar to pretrial reliability hearings for the admissibility of expert testimony. In *Daubert v. Merrell Dow Pharmaceuticals, Inc.* (1993), the Supreme Court recognized that while expert witness testimony can be immensely powerful, it can also be dangerously misleading, and the traditional ways of challenging testimony—discovery, cross-examination, and jury instructions—are not always adequate to ensure that expert testimony is reliable. In that case, the Court positioned trial judges as "gatekeepers," charging them with determining the threshold reliability of scientific evidence before admitting it before a jury. Natapoff (2006) suggests that in light of similarities between expert witnesses and informants—namely, that both are essentially paid by one side in the case, their testimony is often coached and well-prepared and is presented by a witness presumed to possess insider knowledge—judges should similarly act as gatekeepers to assess the reliability of informants and snitches before trial. This would allow the courts to evaluate the informant's history and incentives, any corroborating evidence (or the lack thereof), and the government's effort to double-check the informant's story before deciding if the informant's testimony can be admitted as evidence at trial.

Corroboration Requirements

Informants are often key witnesses at trial and may serve as the prosecution's main source of evidence against a defendant. Given their incentives to lie, this can be highly problematic. For this reason, some have suggested requiring corroboration of informant testimony—consisting of other evidence that supports or tends to confirm the informant's story—as a prerequisite to the informant's testimony being admissible at trial. Although corroboration requirements are minimal, and provide only limited protection against false testimony, they would at least help ensure that the informant's incentivized testimony is not the only piece of evidence supporting the prosecution's case. A number of states have such policies in place for accomplices, who often become key informants. Experts suggest that this requirement be expanded to any informant who receives some type of compensation or benefit in exchange for their testimony (Natapoff, 2009; Norris et al., 2011).

Expert Testimony

Some have argued that expert witnesses should be permitted to testify in criminal trials to explain to the fact-finder the many dangers associated with jailhouse informant testimony, in a fashion similar to eyewitness identification cases (Bloom, 2019). The Connecticut Court of Appeals agreed, ruling that the trial court in a murder case erroneously excluded expert testimony offered by the defendant about such matters (Professor Natapoff was prepared to testify as the expert witness) (*State v. Leniart*, 2016). The ruling was short-lived, as the Connecticut Supreme Court reversed the decision, holding that the reliability threats connected with jailhouse informant testimony are well known and not beyond the ken of lay jurors (*State v. Leniart*, 2019). A federal district court reached a similar conclusion (*United States v. Noze*, 2017), as have other state courts (e.g., *People v. Curl*, 2009).

Cautionary Jury Instructions

A final common suggestion is for judges to provide cautionary instructions about informant testimony to trial juries before they deliberate and reach verdicts. The goal ultimately is to encourage the jury to examine informant testimony critically before deciding how much weight to place on it. Such instructions would not advise jurors to disregard an informant's testimony, but rather would inform them that there may be good reasons to view such testimony cautiously, if not skeptically (Natapoff, 2009).

It is worth noting that the benefits of such cautionary **jury instructions** are unclear. Research has been somewhat mixed regarding the effects of cautionary instructions on jury decision-making in several areas (e.g., Cutler et al., 1990; Maeder & Pica, 2014; Marder, 2006). One recent study found that jury instructions regarding jailhouse informant testimony had no effect on mock jurors' decisions (Wetmore et al., 2020). Standing alone, cautionary jury instructions clearly are insufficient to eradicate the risks associated with testimony provided by incentivized informants (Norris et al., 2011).

Conclusion

People commonly act in their own self-interests. When someone is offered a financial reward or leniency with respect to criminal charges or punishment in exchange for providing information against another person, it is not hard to understand why informants can and sometimes do supply inaccurate information that contributes to miscarriages of justice. This is not a new problem, but rather one that dates back to the earliest documented wrongful convictions in the United States. Unfortunately, the fundamental challenges concerning incentivized informants are rooted in basic human behavior and therefore cannot be eliminated completely. Nevertheless, some of the problems related to unreliable informants can at least be alleviated through judicial and legislative remedies as well as through policy reforms adopted by prosecutors and police departments.

Key Terms and Concepts

- **Incentivized informant**: a person who agrees to provide information in a criminal case in exchange for some type of anticipated or promised benefit or other incentive
- **Prisoner's Dilemma**: a decision-making scenario in which two suspects are separated, questioned independently, and each told that the other is implicating them in the crime
- **Corroboration**: evidence that tends to support or confirm information, such as that provided by an informant
- **Discovery**: in a criminal case, the process involving the prosecutor's sharing or revealing evidence to the defense prior to trial; the defense sometimes has a reciprocal obligation to reveal evidence within its possession to the prosecutor
- **Reliability hearing**: a pre-trial hearing in which a judge determines whether an informant appears to be sufficiently trustworthy or credible to be allowed to testify at trial
- **Jury instructions**: a judge's charge to jurors about the law governing their deliberations as they attempt to reach a verdict; sometimes involving cautionary warnings regarding attorneys' questions or statements or a witness's testimony during a trial

Discussion Questions

1. What types of incentives are informants given in exchange for their testimony? How often do you think these incentives encourage informants to lie?

2. What was the original ruling in *United States v. Singleton*? Why was it reversed on reconsideration? Do you think the original *Singleton* ruling should have remained in place?

3. Should police and prosecutors be allowed to provide incentives in exchange for information from informants? If so, how can we help ensure the reliability of the provided information? If not, in light of how important informants are for many investigations, how can law enforcement make up for the information that might be lost?

4. Is a cautionary jury instruction enough to protect against unreliable informant testimony? How might jurors be better educated about informant testimony in order to fairly evaluate an informant's testimony?

References

Allen, L. G. (2020). Life behind bars: An analysis of the problematic reliance on jailhouse informant testimony in the criminal justice system and a Texas-sized attempt to address the issue. *Washington University Law Review*, 98, 257–280.

Alter, V. (2005). Jailhouse informants: A lesson in e-snitching. *Journal of Technology, Law & Policy*, 10, 223–241.

Bloom, R. M. (2019). What jurors should know about informants: The need for expert testimony. *Michigan State Law Review*, 2019(2), 345–373.

Cassidy, R. M. (2004). "Soft words of hope:" *Giglio*, accomplice witnesses, and the problem of implied inducements. *Northwestern University Law Review*, 98, 1129–1177.

Center on Wrongful Convictions. (2005). *The snitch system: How snitch testimony sent Randy Steidl and other innocent Americans to death row*. Bluhm Legal Clinic, Pritzker School of Law, Northwestern University. http://www.law.northwestern.edu/legalclinic/wrongfulconvictions/documents/SnitchSystemBooklet.pdf.

Connecticut General Statute Annotated § 51-286k (2019).

Connecticut General Statute Annotated § 54-86o (2019).

Covey, R. D. (2014). Abolishing jailhouse snitch testimony. *Wake Forest Law Review*, 49, 1375–1429.

Covey, R. D. (2018). Suspect evidence and coalmine canaries. *American Criminal Law Review*, 55(3), 537–584.

Cutler, B. L., Dexter, H. R., & Penrod, S. D. (1990). Nonadversarial methods for sensitizing jurors to eyewitness evidence. *Journal of Applied Social Psychology*, 20, 1197–1207.

Daubert v. Merrell Dow Pharmaceuticals, 509 U.S. 579 (1993).

DeLoach, D. K., Neuschatz, J. S., Wetmore, S. A., & Bornstein, B. H. (2020). The role of ulterior motives, inconsistencies, and details in unreliable jailhouse informant testimony. *Psychology, Crime, & Law*, 26(7), 667–686.

Fessinger, M. B., Bornstein, B. H., Neuschatz, J. S., DeLoach, D., Hillgartner, M. A., Wetmore, S. A., & Douglass, A. B. (2020). Informants v. innocents: Informant testimony and its contribution to wrongful convictions. *Capital University Law Review*, 48(2), 149–188.

Garrett, B. L. (2011). *Convicting the innocent: Where criminal prosecutions go wrong.* Harvard University Press.

Gershman, B. L. (2014). The prosecutor's contribution to wrongful convictions. In A. D. Redlich, J. R. Acker, R. J. Norris, & C. L. Bonventre (Eds.), *Examining wrongful convictions: Stepping back, moving forward* (pp. 109–121). Carolina Academic Press.

Giannelli, P. C. (2007). *Brady* and jailhouse snitches. *Case Western Reserve Law Review, 57,* 593–613.

Giglio v. United States, 405 U.S. 150 (1972).

Hoffa v. United States, 385 U.S. 293 (1966).

Illinois Compiled Statutes Annotated, Chapter 725 § 5/115-21 (2019).

Illinois v. Perkins, 496 U.S. 292 (1990).

Kruse, K. R. (2015). Wrongful convictions and upstream reform in the criminal justice system. *Texas A&M Law Review, 3,* 367–393.

Kuhlmann v. Wilson, 477 U.S. 436 (1986).

Maeder, E. M., & Pica, E. (2014). Secondary confessions: The influence (or lack thereof) of incentive size and scientific expert testimony on jurors' perceptions of informant testimony. *Law and Human Behavior, 38,* 560–568.

Marder, N. S. (2006). Bringing jury instructions into the twenty-first century. *Notre Dame Law Review, 81,* 449–511.

Massiah v. United States, 377 U.S. 201 (1964).

Mote, P. M., Neuschatz, J. S., Bornstein, B. H., Wetmore, S. A., & Key, K. N. (2018). Secondary confessions as post-identification feedback: How jailhouse informant testimony can alter eyewitnesses' identification decisions. *Journal of Police and Criminal Psychology, 33,* 375–384.

Napue v. Illinois, 360 U.S. 264 (1959).

Natapoff, A. (2006). Beyond unreliable: How snitches contribute to wrongful convictions. *Golden Gate University Law Review, 37,* 107–129.

Natapoff, A. (2009). *Snitching: Criminal informants and the erosion of American justice.* NYU Press.

National Registry of Exonerations. (n.d.). Glossary. https://www.law.umich.edu/special/exoneration/Pages/glossary.aspx.

Nebraska Statutes Annotated §§ 29-4702 through 29-4705 (2019).

Neuschatz, J. S., DeLoach, D. K., Hillgartner, M. A., Fessinger, M. B., Wetmore, S. A., Douglass, A. B., Bornstein, B. H., & Le Grand, A. M. (2020). The truth about snitches: An archival analysis of informant testimony. *Psychiatry, Psychology, and Law.* http://doi.org/10.1080/13218719.2020.1805810.

Norris, R. J., Bonventre, C. L., Redlich, A. D., & Acker, J. R. (2011). "Than that one innocent suffer": Evaluating state safeguards against wrongful convictions. *Albany Law Review, 74*(3), 1301–1364.

Norris, R. J., & Redlich, A. D. (2014). Seeking justice, compromising truth? Criminal admissions and the Prisoner's Dilemma. *Albany Law Review*, *77*, 1005–1038.

People v. Curl, 207 P.3d 2 (Cal. 2009), cert. den., 559 U.S. 1009 (2010).

Roth, J. A. (2016). Informant witnesses and the risk of wrongful convictions. *American Criminal Law Review*, *53*, 737–797.

State v. Leniart, 140 A.3d 1026 (Conn. App. 2016), reversed, 215 A.3d 1104 (Conn. 2019).

State v. Leniart, 215 A.3d 1104 (Conn. 2019).

Texas Code of Criminal Procedure, Article 2.024 (2019).

Texas Code of Criminal Procedure, Article 39.14 (h-1) (2017).

United States v. Henry, 447 U.S. 264 (1980).

United States v. Noze, 255 F.Supp.3d 352 (D. Conn. 2017).

United States v. Ruiz, 536 U.S. 622 (2002).

United States v. Singleton, 144 F.3d 1343 (10th Cir. 1998), *vacated on rehearing en banc*, 165 F.3d 1297 (10th Cir.), *cert. denied*, 527 U.S. 1024 (1999).

United States v. Singleton, 165 F.3d 1297 (10th Cir.) (*en banc*), *cert. denied*, 527 U.S. 1024 (1999).

Van de Kamp v. Goldstein, 555 U.S. 335 (2009).

Wearry v. Cain, 577 U.S. 385 (2016).

West, E., & Meterko, V. (2016). Innocence Project: DNA exonerations, 1989–2014: Review of data and findings from the first 25 years. *Albany Law Review*, *79*, 717–795.

Wetmore, S. A., Neuschatz, J. S., Fessinger, M. B., Bornstein, B. H., & Golding, J. M. (2020). Do judicial instructions aid in distinguishing between reliable and unreliable jailhouse informants? *Criminal Justice and Behavior*, *47*(5), 582–600.

Yaroshefsky, E. (1999). Cooperation with federal prosecutors: Experiences of truth telling and embellishment. *Fordham Law Review*, *68*, 917–964.

Chapter 8

Government Actors: Police and Prosecutors

Learning Objectives

After reading this chapter, you should be able to:

- Appreciate the role that cognitive and implicit biases play in the investigation and prosecution of crimes by law enforcement and prosecutors.
- Discuss the role of police misconduct in mass exonerations.
- Understand the limited federal constitutional obligation of the police to preserve evidence in criminal cases.
- Understand the prosecutor's duty to disclose material exculpatory evidence.
- Discuss the extent to which prosecutors are immune from civil liability for violating criminal defendants' constitutional rights.
- Appreciate the approaches that law enforcement agencies are taking to reduce the impact of implicit bias in investigations.

Case Study: Derrick Hamilton

When Derrick Hamilton was arrested in 1991 for the murder of Nathanial Cash in the Bedford-Stuyvesant neighborhood of Brooklyn, New York, he was already a formerly incarcerated person, having served six years in prison for a manslaughter conviction pursuant to his entry of an *Alford* plea (a kind of guilty plea that allows a defendant to proclaim innocence on the record) (Gonnerman, 2016). Hamilton was interrogated about Cash's murder by a detective named Louis Scarcella: "the New York Police Department's go-to investigator in some of Brooklyn's most crime-ridden precincts: a swaggering old-school character with a taste for cigars and a reputation for quickly solving murder cases" (Feuer, 2017). According to Hamilton, Scarcella told him that "he didn't care whether I did it or not, because I didn't serve enough time for my previous case, and I would be going back to jail" (Gonnerman, 2016). Although Hamilton maintained his innocence and had an alibi, a witness testified at trial that she had seen Hamilton shoot Cash. Prior to her testimony at Hamilton's trial, the witness had told Hamilton's attorney that she was not present when Cash was shot. What changed? The witness was Cash's girlfriend, and her association with him was a violation of the conditions of her parole. According to the witness, she provided false testimony at Hamilton's trial because Scarcella had threatened to incarcerate her and take her children away if she did not testify to witnessing Hamilton murder Cash. Hamilton was convicted and sentenced to 25 years to life in prison.

During his incarceration, Hamilton became an effective jailhouse lawyer — a skill he had begun developing during his earlier incarceration for manslaughter — helping other inmates win release. He also encountered other inmates who maintained their innocence and whose cases involved Detective Scarcella's investigative work, including Shabaka Shakur (Gonnerman, 2016). Hamilton was paroled in 2011 and exonerated in 2015 based on the Brooklyn district attorney's reinvestigation of the case (Possley, 2016a). Hamilton's case is one of many homicide convictions involving Detective Scarcella that have been reviewed and vacated through the Brooklyn district attorney's Conviction Review Unit (Possley, 2016a). Those cases include the friend Hamilton met while incarcerated, Shabaka Shakur, in whose case Scarcella purportedly fabricated a confession (Possley, 2016b). It is important to note that the Brooklyn district attorney's office recently acknowledged in a court filing that, notwithstanding the office's agreement to dismiss seven murder cases involving Detective Scarcella, they had no evidence that he engaged in any wrongdoing (Feuer, 2017). Detective Scarcella retired from the police department in 1999 and continues to maintain that he engaged in no wrongdoing, stating, "I never framed anybody in my life" (Samaha, 2014).

A Closer Look: Derrick Hamilton

- *CBS This Morning* (2017) — In a brief television segment, Derrick Hamilton and Shabaka Shakur discuss their wrongful convictions and the restaurant they opened in Brooklyn after they were exonerated.

- "Home Free: How a New York State Prisoner Became a Jailhouse Lawyer, and Changed the System" (2016) — Jennifer Gonnerman's fascinating article for *The New Yorker* chronicles Derrick Hamilton's struggle to free himself and other wrongfully convicted New York inmates.

- *The Leonard Lopate Show* (2016) — In an episode of this podcast produced by WNYC, Leonard Lopate talks with Derrick Hamilton and Jennifer Gonnerman about Hamilton's case.

Research on Government Actors

The primary government actors that participate in the investigation and prosecution of crimes are the police and prosecutors. These actors wield tremendous power. As noted below, the police provide the gateway through which individuals suspected of crimes enter the criminal justice process. Through their authority to impose criminal charges, prosecutors hold the ultimate power to turn suspects into criminal defendants. It is likely that most government actors wield their authority with the solemnity, care, and professionalism required when the liberty of citizens is at stake. However, as we saw in the case of Detective Scarcella, and the case of Sergeant Ronald Watts in chapter 5, sometimes the "often competitive enterprise of ferreting out crime" (*Johnson v. United States*, 1948, p. 14) can lead to mistakes or misconduct on the part of government officials. The National Registry of Exonerations defines **official misconduct** as follows: "Police, prosecutors, or other government officials significantly abused their authority or the judicial process in a manner that contributed to the exoneree's conviction" (National Registry of Exonerations, n.d.a). Under this definition, 55% of the first 2,776 exonerations in their database involved "official misconduct." However, as we shall see in our discussion below, even well-intentioned, ethically minded criminal justice actors can have ethical lapses.

Professor Marvin Zalman observed that "studying the police role in wrongful convictions needs to go beyond the paradigmatic innocence areas of identification, interrogation, and informants. Scholarship must consider police investigation *in toto*, in the context of police culture and organization, in order to better assess the police role in generating wrongful convictions, avenues of meaningful reform, and the possible outer limits of innocence reform" (Zalman, 2014, p. 148). In chapters 3, 4, and 7 we discussed the role that police officers occasionally play in producing erroneous eyewitness identifications, inducing false confessions, and eliciting unreliable informant testimony. Here, we step back and examine what research from psychology has to say about policing and the implications for wrongful convictions. Before we do, however, we should be mindful of an important point raised by Professor Dan Simon in his work on the psychology of police investigations. In acknowledging the difficulty of investigating crimes, Simon (2012, p. 21) observes, "Crimes that receive investigative attention lie mostly in the gray zone between easy cases and unsolvable ones." Moreover, difficulties abound with the amount of information available to investigators and the complications that arise from multiple sources including "departmental directives, public expectations, media exposure, and the passage of time, as well as by [factors including] limited resources and departmental politics" (Simon, 2012, p. 21). With these points in mind, let us examine the research.

Much has been written about the role of confirmation bias in producing or contributing to wrongful convictions. Recall our discussion in chapter 6 about the effects of this predisposition on forensic analysts. There we defined **confirmation bias** as a cognitive bias that occurs when people unwittingly select evidence that confirms or supports their existing beliefs or expectations (Nickerson, 1998). With respect to police investigations, or other aspects of criminal justice, this tendency is sometimes referred to as "**tunnel vision**" (Simon, 2012; *see also*, Findley & Scott, 2006). Martin (2002) describes tunnel vision as follows:

> Investigators focus on a suspect, select and filter the evidence that will "build a case" for conviction, while ignoring or suppressing evidence that points away from guilt. This drive to confirm a preconceived belief in guilt adversely impacts on witness interviews, eyewitness procedures, interrogation of suspects, and the management of informers in ways that have been identified in virtually all known cases of wrongful conviction (p. 848).

Confirmation bias affects all people. However, it can have a particularly insidious effect in police investigations. For example, Simon (2012) notes that, in investigations, confirmation bias tends to reaffirm belief in a suspect's guilt because most of the work is done once a suspect has been identified. In addition, existing pro-law enforcement attitudes and alignment with police as a peer group, motivation to solve the crime and make an arrest, the emotional arousal stemming from gruesome crime details, and commitment to the prevailing theory of the case can all interact to strengthen the bias. Simon additionally notes that even though investigators are also motivated by the goal of finding the actual perpetrator and not an innocent person, the adversarial nature of the process may implicitly outweigh truth-seeking goals. "Investigators get rewarded and recognized predominantly for making arrests, not for refraining from charging innocent people" (Simon, 2012, p. 32).

Stereotypes and unconscious, or implicit, biases can also affect how police officers perceive innocent individuals. **Stereotype threat** occurs when a person fears being judged by a negative stereotype concerning the group to which the person belongs. The stereotype of African American criminality—that African Americans, especially African American males, are prone to crime—may lead Blacks to experience stereotype threat in encounters with law enforcement. For innocent suspects, this is problematic. As Najdowski (2014) notes, "The threat of being accused of a crime not committed might lead African Americans to engage in nonverbal behavior that makes them appear nervous or suspicious before a police encounter even begins, but it is also important to understand how biased expectations influence African Americans and police officers *after* contact has been initiated.... [B]ased on the hypothesis that the African American criminal stereotype is true, a police officer might approach African American citizens with the presumption of guilt. An innocent African American citizen might perceive that the officer believes he or she is guilty, and, inadvertently, respond by behaving in ways that the officer perceives as deceptive or suspicious" (p. 63).

Likewise, prosecutors (and, in fact, all criminal justice actors) are subject to the same cognitive and implicit biases. As we discuss more fully below, prosecutors have a constitutional duty to disclose material exculpatory evidence ("*Brady* material") to the accused. Material exculpatory evidence is evidence that tends to show the defendant's innocence and that could influence the outcome of the case. Yet, a prosecutor's determination of whether evidence is material, and thus subject to disclosure, may be influenced by cognitive bias. Alafair Burke (2007) poses this concern in the form of a brainteaser. The *prosecutor* determines whether the evidence subject to disclosure is material—in light of all the evidence in the case and mindful of the potential for a subsequent appellate ruling on whether the evidence should have been disclosed under the *Brady* standard. Burke argues that cognitive biases can lead prosecutors to systematically undervalue materiality. Confirmation bias induces the actor to select information that supports the focal hypothesis (the defendant is guilty) and to discount or fail to rigorously scrutinize disconfirming information. Burke presents a hypothetical in which a prosecutor must decide whether the chronic alcoholism of a critical eyewitness to a robbery must be disclosed to the defense under *Brady*:

> To apply *Brady*, the prosecutor first has to envision the trial without the disclosure of the witness's alcoholism. Because of confirmation bias, as she retrieves the evidence in the case from memory, she is likely to recall facts that support her existing belief in guilt, such as the existence of another eyewitness, the defendant's inculpatory admissions, or the fact that the defendant was found in possession of some of the robbery proceeds in a search incident to arrest. In addition, selective information processing comes into play. While evaluating all of the evidence that suggests the defendant is guilty, the prosecutor will say to herself, "It sounds like very good evidence of guilt. I still believe he is guilty."
>
> In her analysis, the prosecutor is not likely to emphasize facts that might undermine her existing belief in the defendant's guilt. Perhaps the defendant's inculpatory admissions were accompanied by exculpatory denials. Maybe his statements were made under police pressure. Perhaps some of [the] robbery proceeds are missing, with no explanation for their whereabouts. Maybe the other eyewitness also suffers from memory or credibility problems. Because of confirmation bias, the prosecutor may not even consider these facts when she envisions her case. She may recall only the evidence that suggests the defendant's guilt. Even if she does consider these exculpatory facts, she may give them short shrift because of selective information processing. In short, she is going to overestimate the strength of her own case (Burke, 2007, p. 579).

Burke's hypothetical demonstrates that even well-intentioned prosecutors may systematically violate the *Brady* standard because of cognitive bias.

Prosecutors can and sometimes do engage in intentional misconduct such as purposefully withholding exculpatory evidence. For example, Michael Morton was exonerated after spending 25 years incarcerated for the murder of his wife (Morton, 2015; Possley, 2012). The prosecutor in his case, Ken Anderson, withheld evidence that tended to show someone other than Morton committed the crime. After Morton's exoneration, a court of inquiry determined that Anderson should face criminal charges for withholding evidence in Morton's case. Anderson was sentenced to ten days in jail and was disbarred. Focusing on "bad actor" cases like Anderson's, however, should not detract from the more ubiquitous impact of cognitive biases on conscientious prosecutors (Bandes, 2006).

Mass Exonerations and Police Misconduct

In some instances, purposeful or systematic misconduct can be a problem. The Scarcella case discussed at the beginning of this chapter is suggestive of this point. "**Mass exoneration**" or "group exoneration" cases vividly illustrate this problem. The National Registry of Exonerations defines a group exoneration as "[t]he exoneration of a group of defendants who were falsely convicted of crimes as a result of a large-scale pattern of police perjury and corruption" (Gross et al., 2017, p. 20). Recently, the NRE added an archive of group exonerations that "focuses on groups of defendants tied together by a common pattern of systematic official misconduct in the investigation and prosecution of these cases that undermined confidence in the defendants' convictions" (National Registry of Exonerations, n.d.b). The Groups Registry, as it is called, documents tens of thousands of cases — many of which stem from misconduct in the Massachusetts Department of Health drug laboratory, which we discussed in chapter 6. The number also includes many cases in which defendants were framed for drug crimes that did not happen (Gross et al., 2017, p. 20). For example, officers in the Rampart Division of the Los Angeles Police Department routinely engaged in extensive misconduct including evidence-planting, providing false testimony, beating suspects, and much more. Covey's (2013) empirical examination of the Rampart scandal and another scandal in Tulia, Texas, reminds us that the paradigmatic exoneration is not necessarily from a felony conviction and a lengthy incarceration. The mass exoneration cases depict defendants who rarely contested their guilt at trial — the majority pleaded guilty. Covey suggests three reasons for this outcome: "an outsized trial penalty, a lack of viable strategies to contest the charges, and presumptively or actually unsympathetic forums" (p. 1166). Contrasting the mass exonerations to DNA exonerations, Covey further observes:

> The offenses are generally less serious, and the sentences less severe, than those involved in the DNA exoneration cases. These cases involve drugs and guns, assaults on police officers, charges of disturbing the peace, resisting arrest, or other allegedly violent or aggressive conduct directed at the police. Hundreds of thousands, perhaps millions, of people have been convicted of such crimes. There is simply no way to know how many persons convicted of such offenses were actually innocent, but both Rampart and Tulia provide stark evidence that po-

lice misconduct can, and does, result in wrongful convictions (Covey, 2013, p. 1185).

Wrongful Convictions in Popular Culture: Prosecutorial Malpractice and Misconduct

- *An Unreal Dream: The Michael Morton Story* — Is the ghost of an innocent man an unreal dream? Not to Michael Morton. This documentary chronicles Morton's wrongful conviction for the murder of his wife and the prosecutor who was ultimately punished for his misconduct in Morton's case.

- *Getting Life: An Innocent Man's 25-Year Journey from Prison to Peace* — a memoir written by Michael Morton about his wrongful conviction. The book utilizes not just Morton's memories, but court documents and journals he wrote while incarcerated to describe his experiences leading up to his conviction, during his incarceration, and his experience after release.

- *Fantastic Lies* — an ESPN *30 for 30* documentary covering the accusations of sexual assault against members of Duke University's lacrosse team in 2006. The accusations were found to be baseless although they were fueled by the unethical behavior of the prosecutor, Mike Nifong. Nifong eventually resigned and was disbarred.

The Law

The Police and Probable Cause

The police commonly serve as gatekeepers in the criminal justice system. Their decisions at the front end of a criminal case to focus on and investigate possible suspects and make arrests are of extraordinary consequence. They can make the difference between an individual remaining free or, alternatively, being jailed and later prosecuted and convicted for a crime. In previous chapters we have noted that how the police conduct eyewitness identification procedures and how they interrogate persons suspected of committing a crime can influence the risk of wrongful convictions. Their arrest decisions may hinge on such investigations, although arrests often are made based on information and evidence that is gathered independently of the suspect. As we have discussed, the decision to arrest a particular suspect can be the product of tunnel vision, and the arrest is likely to curtail an investigation and consideration of the possibility that the wrong person has been arrested. The arrest of an innocent person is not inherently unlawful; an arrest is lawful if it is supported by probable cause to believe that the arrestee has committed a crime.

Probable cause — a standard embedded in the Fourth Amendment to the U.S. Constitution — does not require that the police be correct when they arrest a person for a crime. It is entirely possible for the police to have probable cause to arrest an innocent person (or, conversely, to lack probable cause for arresting someone who is truly guilty). Probable cause defies precise definition and quantification. It is a general test, objective in nature, which depends on the totality of the circumstances — the facts and the accompanying reasonable inferences — surrounding a particular situation. Although the police are entrusted to make arrests on their own authority, their probable cause determinations are subject to later review by a judge or magistrate. The Supreme Court has defined probable cause as follows:

> In dealing with probable cause…, as the very name implies, we deal with probabilities. These are not technical; they are the factual and practical considerations of everyday life on which reasonable and prudent men, not legal technicians, act. The standard of proof is accordingly correlative to what must be proved. "The substance of all the definitions" of probable cause "is a reasonable ground for belief of guilt." And this "means less than evidence which would justify condemnation" or conviction.… [I]t has come to mean more than bare suspicion: Probable cause exists where "the facts and circumstances within their [the officers'] knowledge and of which they had reasonably trustworthy information [are] sufficient in themselves to warrant a man of reasonable caution in the belief that" an offense has been or is being committed (*Brinegar v. United States*, 1949, pp. 175–176, quoting *Carroll v. United States*, 1925, p. 162).

An individual who is arrested without probable cause, in violation of the Fourth Amendment, can file a lawsuit against the police and seek money damages. The Supreme Court affirmed this principle in *Manuel v. City of Joliet* (2017), a case which involved the following:

> Shortly after midnight on March 18, 2011, Manuel was riding through Joliet, Illinois, in the passenger seat of a Dodge Charger, with his brother at the wheel. A pair of Joliet police officers pulled the car over when the driver failed to signal a turn. According to the complaint in this case, one of the officers dragged Manuel from the car, called him a racial slur, and kicked and punched him as he lay on the ground. The policeman then searched Manuel and found a vitamin bottle containing pills. Suspecting that the pills were actually illegal drugs, the officers conducted a field test of the bottle's contents. The test came

back negative for any controlled substance, leaving the officers with no evidence that Manuel had committed a crime. Still, the officers arrested Manuel and took him to the Joliet police station.

There, an evidence technician tested the pills once again, and got the same (negative) result. But the technician lied in his report, claiming that one of the pills was "found to be ... positive for the probable presence of ecstasy." Similarly, one of the arresting officers wrote in his report that "[f]rom [his] training and experience, [he] knew the pills to be ecstasy." On the basis of those statements, another officer swore out a criminal complaint against Manuel, charging him with unlawful possession of a controlled substance (*Manuel v. City of Joliet*, 2017, p. 915).

As previously noted, it is entirely possible for the police to have probable cause to arrest an individual who is not guilty of committing a crime. In such cases, the innocent person's rights have not been violated so there is no basis for damages. Moreover, the police, like many other government officials, are frequently insulated from civil liability by the doctrine of qualified immunity even when they violate individuals' rights. The Supreme Court has recognized two forms of immunity from civil damages. Absolute immunity, which we consider later in connection with constitutional violations allegedly committed by prosecutors, completely bars a claim for damages (*Harlow v. Fitzgerald*, 1982, p. 807). Qualified immunity shields officials from having to defend against a lawsuit under more limited circumstances.

[G]overnment officials performing discretionary functions generally are granted a qualified immunity and are "shielded from liability for civil damages insofar as their conduct does not violate clearly established statutory or constitutional rights of which a reasonable person would have known." *Harlow v. Fitzgerald*, 457 U.S. [800, 818 (1982)]. What this means in practice is that "whether an official protected by qualified immunity may be held personally liable for an allegedly unlawful official action generally turns on the 'objective legal reasonableness' of the action, assessed in light of the legal rules that were 'clearly established' at the time it was taken." *Anderson v. Creighton*, 483 U.S. 635, 639 (1987).

In *Anderson*, we explained that what "clearly established" means in this context depends largely "upon the level of generality at which the relevant 'legal rule' is to be identified." 483 U.S., at 639. "[C]learly established" for purposes of qualified immunity means that "[t]he contours of the right must be sufficiently clear that a reasonable official would understand that what he is doing violates that right. This is not to say that an official action is protected by qualified immunity unless the very action in question has previously been held unlawful, but it is to say that in the light of pre-existing law the unlawfulness must be apparent." *Id.*, at 640 (citations omitted) (*Wilson v. Layne*, 1999, pp. 614–615).

The overarching justification for the doctrine of qualified immunity concerns "an attempt to balance competing values: not only the importance of a damages remedy to protect the rights of citizens, but also 'the need to protect officials who are required to exercise their discretion and the related public interest in encouraging the vigorous exercise of official authority.' [*Butz v. Economou*, 438 U.S. 478, 506 (1978)]." (*Harlow v. Fitzgerald*, 1982, p. 807; see also *Mullenix v. Luna*, 2015; *Saucier v. Katz*, 2001). Although its impact on litigation may not be as substantial as some critics fear (Schwartz, 2020), the policy of affording police officers qualified immunity from civil liability has raised concerns that it is unduly insensitive to the rights of private citizens and overly protective of official misconduct (Armacost, 1998; Nemeth, 2019). Because the doctrine bars compensation when police officers violate individual rights unless their conduct violates "clearly established" legal rules (*District of Columbia v. Wesby*, 2018; *Kisela v. Hughes*, 2018; *Pearson v. Callahan*, 2009; *White v. Pauly*, 2017), it arguably undermines the objective of deterring misconduct that could help produce wrongful convictions.

If probable cause is established and a case then moves forward following arrest and it is not screened from prosecution, the risk of a wrongful conviction looms large for individuals who have not committed a crime. Preventive measures, including those designed to guard against the police prematurely focusing on a suspect and curtailing their investigation of a crime (tunnel vision), and from concluding that ambiguous evidence is necessarily supportive of the arrestee's guilt (confirmation bias), are much more likely to be effective in minimizing the risk of wrongful convictions than whatever deterrent function the threat of lawsuits might serve (see Acker, 2018/2019, pp. 732–735).

Police Investigations and the Preservation of Evidence

When a crime is reported, the ensuing investigation by the police may range considerably, from doing no follow-up work to intensively scouring the crime scene, interviewing witnesses, and searching for evidence. The police response will depend largely on the seriousness of the reported offense and the complexity of determining what happened. The police will make numerous judgments during the course of an investigation, including what evidence to seek out, and what evidence should be collected and preserved. Questions may arise concerning their decisions and conduct regarding evidence that might, alternatively, point to guilt or tend to exonerate a suspect. One such question was at the heart of a case that reached the U.S. Supreme Court, *Arizona v. Youngblood* (1988).

Larry Youngblood was arrested in December 1983 and charged with kidnapping and sexually assaulting a 10-year-old boy approximately six weeks earlier. The boy had been separated from his mother at a carnival and then abducted by a man who repeatedly sodomized him before turning him loose. The boy was treated in a hospital following the attack. Hospital personnel swabbed the boy's rectum and mouth to collect evidence of the assault. The swabbed material was turned over to the police, who refrigerated it to inhibit its deterioration. The police also took custody of the boy's T-shirt and underwear, which were stained with the assailant's semen, but they neglected to refrigerate these items. Nine days after the attack, the boy identified Youngblood from a photo array, which led to Youngblood's arrest.

Youngblood pled not guilty to the charges. The police did not examine the boy's T-shirt and underwear until January 1985. Because the clothing items had not been refrigerated, the semen deposited on them could no longer be analyzed. Not enough material was preserved on the refrigerated swabs to be analyzed. The forensic use of DNA evidence had yet to be developed, but had the police refrigerated the clothing, examining the semen could have revealed important information about the assailant. Youngblood, in common with roughly 80% of the population, was a "secretor," meaning that analysis of bodily fluids such as perspiration and semen will reveal the person's blood type as Type A, B, AB, or O. Had the semen been properly preserved, its analysis thus could have excluded him as the boy's assailant if it revealed either that the source of the semen was a non-secretor, or else was a secretor who had a different blood type than his own. Youngblood argued that the police's failure to properly preserve this crucial evidence in their possession cost him the chance to prove his innocence, and thus violated his due process rights. Chief Justice Rehnquist authored the majority opinion rejecting Youngblood's claim.

> The Due Process Clause of the Fourteenth Amendment, as interpreted in *Brady* [*v. Maryland*, 373 U.S. 83 (1963)], makes the good or bad faith of the State irrelevant when the State fails to disclose to the defendant material exculpatory evidence. But we think the Due Process Clause requires a different result when we deal with the failure of the State to preserve evidentiary material of which no more can be said

than that it could have been subjected to tests, the results of which might have exonerated the defendant. Part of the reason for the difference in treatment is ... that "[w]henever potentially exculpatory evidence is permanently lost, courts face the treacherous task of divining the import of materials whose contents are unknown and, very often, disputed." [*California v. Trombetta*, 467 U.S. 479, 486 (1984)]. Part of it stems from our unwillingness to read the "fundamental fairness" requirement of the Due Process Clause as imposing on the police an undifferentiated and absolute duty to retain and to preserve all material that might be of conceivable evidentiary significance in a particular prosecution. We think that requiring a defendant to show bad faith on the part of the police both limits the extent of the police's obligation to preserve evidence to reasonable bounds and confines it to that class of cases where the interests of justice most clearly require it, i.e., those cases in which the police themselves by their conduct indicate that the evidence could form a basis for exonerating the defendant. We therefore hold that unless a criminal defendant can show bad faith on the part of the police, failure to preserve potentially useful evidence does not constitute a denial of due process of law.

In this case, the police collected the rectal swab and clothing on the night of the crime; respondent was not taken into custody until six weeks later. The failure of the police to refrigerate the clothing and to perform tests on the semen samples can at worst be described as negligent.... [T]here was no suggestion of bad faith on the part of the police. It follows, therefore, from what we have said, that there was no violation of the Due Process Clause.

In his dissenting opinion, Justice Blackmun asserted that "[t]he Constitution requires that criminal defendants be provided with a fair trial, not merely a 'good faith' try at a fair trial." He continued:

[T]he State's conduct has deprived the defendant, and the courts, of the opportunity to determine with certainty the import of this evidence: it has "interfere[d] with the accused's ability to present a defense by imposing on him a requirement which the government's own actions have rendered impossible to fulfill." *Hilliard v. Spalding*, 719 F.2d [1443, 1446 (9th Cir. 1983)]. Good faith or not, this is intolerable, unless the particular circumstances of the case indicate either that the evidence was not likely to prove exculpatory, or that the defendant was able to use effective alternative means to prove the point the destroyed evidence otherwise could have made.

... Rather than allow a State's ineptitude to saddle a defendant with an impossible burden, a court should focus on the type of evidence, the possibility it might prove exculpatory, and the existence of other evidence going to the same point of contention in determining whether the failure to preserve the evidence in question violated due process. To put it succinctly, where no comparable evidence is likely to be available to the defendant, police must preserve physical evidence of a type that they reasonably should know has the potential, if tested, to reveal immutable characteristics of the criminal, and hence to exculpate a defendant charged with the crime....

Considered in the context of the entire trial, the failure of the prosecution to preserve this evidence deprived respondent of a fair trial. It still remains "a fundamental value determination of our society that it is far worse to convict an innocent man than to let a guilty man go free." *In re Winship*, 397 U.S. 358, 372 (1970) (concurring opinion). The evidence in this case was far from conclusive, and the possibility that the evidence denied to respondent would have exonerated him was not remote. The result is that he was denied a fair trial by the actions of the State, and consequently was denied due process of law.

Youngblood served several years in prison following his conviction and appeals. In 1999, when advances in technology allowed DNA analysis to be performed on the trace quantities of semen that still remained on the boy's clothing, the results excluded Youngblood. They instead matched the DNA profile of Walter Cruise, who had two prior convictions for the sexual abuse of children. Youngblood was formally exonerated and released from prison. Cruise subsequently pled guilty to the boy's assault (Bay, 2008, pp. 276–277). Nevertheless, the legal doctrine associated with Youngblood's case — that absent a showing of bad faith on the part of the police, law enforcement's failure to preserve potentially exculpatory evidence does not violate a criminal defendant's due process rights — remains good law.

The Prosecutor's Duty to Disclose Material Exculpatory Evidence

As the representative of the executive branch of government and its responsibilities in enforcing the law, the prosecutor occupies a special role in the adversarial system of justice. In *Berger v. United States* (1935), Justice Sutherland's opinion for a unanimous Supreme Court rebuked a federal prosecutor for his conduct during a trial, recounting that he was:

guilty of misstating the facts in his cross-examination of witnesses; of putting into the mouths of such witnesses things which they had not said; of suggesting by his questions that statements had been made to him personally out of court, in respect of which no proof was offered; of pretending to understand that a witness had said something which he had not said and persistently cross-examining the witness upon that basis; of assuming prejudicial facts not in evidence; of bullying and arguing with witnesses; and, in general, of conducting himself in a thoroughly indecorous and improper manner (p. 84).

These transgressions, the Court concluded, required reversal of the defendant's conviction for conspiracy.

The United States Attorney is the representative not of an ordinary party to a controversy, but of a sovereignty whose obligation to govern impartially is as compelling as its obligation to govern at all; and whose interest, therefore, in a criminal prosecution is not that it shall win a case, but that justice shall be done. As such, he is in a peculiar and very definite sense the servant of the law, the twofold aim of which is that guilt shall not escape or innocence suffer. He may prosecute with earnestness and vigor—indeed, he should do so. But, while he may strike hard blows, he is not at liberty to strike foul ones. It is as much his duty to refrain from improper methods calculated to produce a wrongful conviction as it is to use every legitimate means to bring about a just one.

If the prosecutor's duty is to see "that justice shall be done," and not to secure a conviction at all costs, it should be clear that a district attorney should not knowingly present the testimony of a witness who is committing perjury, nor allow false testimony to go uncorrected. We recognized these obligations in chapter 7, when we considered prosecutors' duties while presenting the trial testimony of incentivized informants (*Giglio v. United States*, 1972; *Napue v. Illinois*, 1959). The prosecutor's duty to serve justice was also breached in *Miller v. Pate* (1967), in which the Supreme Court reversed the conviction of Lloyd Eldon Miller, Jr., who had been sentenced to death in Illinois for raping and murdering an 8-year-old girl. A crucial item of evidence at Miller's trial was the testimony of a chemist for the State Bureau of Crime Identification. The chemist falsely reported that a reddish stain on a pair of men's underwear found abandoned in the general vicinity of the crime and purportedly belonging to Miller, was analyzed and determined to be Type A blood—the blood type of the murdered child. When the defense gained access to the underwear six years after Miller's conviction and submitted it to testing, the testing revealed that the reddish stain was not blood, but was paint. It was further revealed that the prosecutor knew that the chemist had testified falsely when he identified the paint as Type A blood. In reversing Miller's conviction, Justice Stewart declared for a unanimous Supreme Court:

> The record of the petitioner's trial reflects the prosecution's consistent and repeated misrepresentation that People's Exhibit 3 [the underwear] was, indeed, "a garment heavily stained with blood." The prosecution's whole theory with respect to the exhibit depended upon that misrepresentation.... The prosecution deliberately misrepresented the truth.
>
>   More than 30 years ago this Court held that the Fourteenth Amendment cannot tolerate a state criminal conviction obtained by the knowing use of false evidence. *Mooney v. Holohan*, 294 U.S. 103 [(1935)]. There has been no deviation from that established principle. There can be no retreat from that principle here.

Four years after the Supreme Court ruling, all charges against Miller were dismissed and Miller was released from prison. Other evidence supporting his conviction also was discredited. He had been wrongfully convicted. At one point, Miller had come within seven and one-half hours of execution (Lassers, 1973; Radelet et al., 1992, pp. 141–152).

Another constitutional obligation of prosecutors, somewhat less obvious, perhaps, than refraining from knowingly presenting perjured testimony, is the duty to disclose evidence to defense counsel that can be expected to help the defendant's case. This duty is consistent with the prosecutor's adversarial role to "serve justice," and not merely to gain a conviction. Evidence available to the prosecutor which might benefit the defendant is known as "*Brady* material," named after the Supreme Court's decision in *Brady v. Maryland* (1963). The Court specifically ruled in *Brady* that "the suppression by the prosecution of evidence favorable to an accused upon request violates due process where the evidence is material either to guilt or to punishment, irrespective of the good faith or bad faith of the prosecution" (p. 87).

Several aspects of this ruling are important. Prosecutors are not required to turn over all evidence in their files to the defense. Rather, the potentially favorable evidence must be "material" to issues of guilt or punishment. Later cases clarified that "material" means that the evidence is sufficiently important that, had it been disclosed in a timely fashion, there is a "reasonable probability" that the outcome of the case (the guilty verdict or the sentence) would be different (*Kyles v. Whitley*, 1995, p. 433). Note also that it does not matter whether a prosecutor's failure to disclose material exculpatory evidence is intentional or inadvertent: the duty exists "irrespective of the good faith or bad faith of the prosecution" (*Brady v. Maryland*, 1963, p. 87).

The Supreme Court has ruled that the prosecutor is presumed to know about evidence that the police have collected. Even if prosecutors honestly are unaware of the evidence because the police didn't share it, they nevertheless have "a duty to learn of any favorable evidence known to the others acting on the government's behalf in the case, including the police" (*Kyles v. Whitley*, 1995, p. 437). And finally, although in *Brady* the defendant's lawyer had made a specific request for the evidence that had not been disclosed (an incriminating statement made by Brady's co-defendant), the justices later ruled that the prosecutor's obligation to disclose material exculpatory evidence to the defense exists whether or not it has been requested (*Kyles v. Whitley*, 1995; *United States v. Bagley*, 1985).

We need not belabor the obvious link between the breach of a prosecutor's duty to disclose *Brady* material and the potential for convicting an innocent person. When a prosecutor withholds material exculpatory evidence, not only might the trial judge's or jury's evaluation of evidence supporting guilt be affected, but the defense's investigation of a case and its entire trial strategy might be fundamentally altered (*United States v. Burke*, 2009). In light of how important *Brady* violations can be in contributing to the wrongful conviction and punishment of innocents, we next ask what legal consequences in addition to invalidating a conviction or sentence, if any, should follow when prosecutors breach their constitutional obligations in this regard. What if the prosecutor not only failed to disclose potentially exculpatory material, but knowingly presented perjured testimony which led to the conviction of an innocent person?

Prosecutorial Immunity from Civil Liability

A federal statute, 42 U.S.C. § 1983, authorizes civil lawsuits to recover money damages against individuals who, while acting "under color of" state law, violate another person's constitutional rights. Prosecutors are governmental officials who act under color of state law. If they violate a criminal defendant's due process rights by securing a conviction by knowingly presenting perjured testimony or violating *Brady* obligations, should they be liable for damages under § 1983? Would such damages help provide justice for innocent persons whose convictions stem from prosecutorial misconduct? Would the threat of civil liability help deter prosecutors from violating defendants' rights? The Supreme Court considered the question of prosecutorial liability for trial-related misconduct under § 1983 in *Imbler v. Pachtman* (1976).

Paul Imbler was convicted of murder in California and spent several years in prison before a federal judge vacated his conviction. The judge found that the prosecutor at Imbler's trial had failed to disclose exculpatory evidence and knew or should have known that witnesses' testimony was misleading or false. The charges against Imbler were dismissed after he was released from prison. Imbler then sued Richard Pachtman, the prosecutor at his trial, seeking $2.7 million in damages from him and other officials. The Supreme Court ordered the lawsuit dismissed, ruling that a prosecutor is absolutely immune from civil liability under § 1983 for misconduct during a trial or otherwise intimately associated with the judicial process. Justice Stewart's majority opinion explained that § 1983 did not alter the long-standing common law rule protecting prosecutors from lawsuits based on such allegations:

> The common-law immunity of a prosecutor is based upon the same considerations that underlie the common-law immunities of judges and grand jurors acting within the scope of their duties. These include concern that harassment by unfounded litigation would cause a deflection of the prosecutor's energies from his public duties, and the possibility that he would shade his decisions instead of exercising the independence of judgment required by his public trust....
>
> We now must determine whether the same considerations of public policy that underlie the common-law rule likewise countenance absolute immunity under § 1983. We think they do.
>
> If a prosecutor had only a qualified immunity, the threat of § 1983 suits would undermine performance of his duties no less than would the threat of common-law suits for malicious prosecution. A prosecutor is duty bound to exercise his best judgment both in deciding which suits to bring and in conducting them in court. The public trust of the prosecutor's office would suffer if he were constrained in making every decision by the consequences in terms of his own potential liability in a suit for damages. Such suits could be expected with some frequency, for a defendant often will transform his resentment at being prosecuted into the ascription of improper and malicious actions to the State's advocate. Further, if the prosecutor could be made to answer in court each time such a person charged him with wrongdoing, his energy and attention would be diverted from the pressing duty of enforcing the criminal law.
>
> Moreover, suits that survived the pleadings would pose substantial danger of liability even to the honest prosecutor. The prosecutor's possible knowledge of a witness' falsehoods, the materiality of evidence

not revealed to the defense, the propriety of a closing argument, and ultimately in every case the likelihood that prosecutorial misconduct so infected a trial as to deny due process, are typical of issues with which judges struggle in actions for post-trial relief, sometimes to differing conclusions. The presentation of such issues in a § 1983 action often would require a virtual retrial of the criminal offense in a new forum, and the resolution of some technical issues by the lay jury. It is fair to say, we think, that the honest prosecutor would face greater difficulty in meeting the standards of qualified immunity than other executive or administrative officials. Frequently acting under serious constraints of time and even information, a prosecutor inevitably makes many decisions that could engender colorable claims of constitutional deprivation. Defending these decisions, often years after they were made, could impose unique and intolerable burdens upon a prosecutor responsible annually for hundreds of indictments and trials.

The affording of only a qualified immunity to the prosecutor also could have an adverse effect upon the functioning of the criminal justice system. Attaining the system's goal of accurately determining guilt or innocence requires that both the prosecution and the defense have wide discretion in the conduct of the trial and the presentation of evidence. The veracity of witnesses in criminal cases frequently is subject to doubt before and after they testify.... If prosecutors were hampered in exercising their judgment as to the use of such witnesses by concern about resulting personal liability, the triers of fact in criminal cases often would be denied relevant evidence.

The ultimate fairness of the operation of the system itself could be weakened by subjecting prosecutors to § 1983 liability. Various post-trial procedures are available to determine whether an accused has received a fair trial. These procedures include the remedial powers of the trial judge, appellate review, and state and federal post-conviction collateral remedies. In all of these the attention of the reviewing judge or tribunal is focused primarily on whether there was a fair trial under law. This focus should not be blurred by even the subconscious knowledge that a post-trial decision in favor of the accused might result in the prosecutor's being called upon to respond in damages for his error or mistaken judgment.

We conclude that the considerations outlined above dictate the same absolute immunity under § 1983 that the prosecutor enjoys at common law. To be sure, this immunity does leave the genuinely wronged defendant without civil redress against a prosecutor whose malicious or dishonest action deprives him of liberty. But the alternative of qualifying a prosecutor's immunity would disserve the broader public interest. It would prevent the vigorous and fearless performance of the prosecutor's duty that is essential to the proper functioning of the criminal justice system. Moreover, it often would prejudice defendants in criminal cases by skewing post-conviction judicial decisions that should be made with the sole purpose of insuring justice. With the issue thus framed, we find ourselves in agreement with Judge Learned Hand, who wrote of the prosecutor's immunity from actions for malicious prosecution:

"As is so often the case, the answer must be found in a balance between the evils inevitable in either alternative. In this instance it has been thought in the end better to leave unredressed the wrongs done by dishonest officers than to subject those who try to do their duty to the constant dread of retaliation." *Gregoire v. Biddle*, 177 F.2d 579, 581 (C.A.2 1949), cert. denied, 339 U.S. 949 (1950).

We emphasize that the immunity of prosecutors from liability in suits under § 1983 does not leave the public powerless to deter misconduct or to punish that which occurs. This Court has never suggested that the policy considerations which compel civil immunity for certain governmental officials also place them beyond the reach of the criminal law. Even judges, cloaked with absolute civil immunity for centuries, could be punished criminally for willful deprivations of constitutional rights on the strength of 18 U.S.C. § 242, the criminal analog of § 1983. The prosecutor would fare no better for his willful acts. Moreover, a prosecutor stands perhaps unique, among officials whose acts could deprive persons of constitutional rights, in his amenability to professional discipline by an association of his peers. These checks undermine the argument that the imposition of civil liability is the only way to insure that prosecutors are mindful of the constitutional rights of persons accused of crime.

As Justice Stewart's opinion notes, protecting prosecutors from civil liability — even those who purposefully or recklessly violate a criminal defendant's constitutional rights, resulting in a wrongful conviction and punishment — is thought, on balance, to serve public interests that outweigh the harm suffered by private individuals. In an effort to reassure that unscrupulous prosecutors cannot violate defendants' rights with impunity, the opinion reminds that criminal prosecution is available in egregious cases of misconduct, and also that prosecutors can be disciplined (e.g., disbarred or suspended from practicing law) for ethical violations. In practice, such repercussions have rarely followed (McKay, 2012, pp. 1227–1231; Sullivan & Possley, 2015), although more stringent oversight and enforcement of rules violations in cases of prosecutorial misconduct may be emerging (Green & Yaroshefsky, 2016).

Prosecutors' **absolute immunity** from civil liability under 42 U.S.C. § 1983 extends only to "conduct closely associated with the judicial process" (*Burns v. Reed*, 1991, p. 494). For example, a prosecutor cannot successfully be sued for activities directly related to preparing and filing criminal charges (*Kalina v. Fletcher*, 1997) or participating in a probable cause hearing (*Burns v. Reed*, 1991). However, absolute immunity does not extend to a prosecutor's pre-indictment investigative activities or statements made at a press conference (*Buckley v. Fitzsimmons*, 1993), advising the police as they conduct their investigations (*Burns v. Reed*, 1991), or certifying that an arrest warrant is supported by probable cause (*Kalina v. Fletcher*, 1997). The Supreme Court has rejected civil liability for prosecutors in cases involving prosecutors' alleged failure to train staff regarding their *Brady* obligations (*Connick v. Thompson*, 2011) and in failing to implement safeguards to avoid making use of unreliable incentivized informants (*Van de Kamp v. Goldstein*, 2009).

Key Case: Prosecutorial Immunity and John Thompson's Case

- *One for Ten: John Thompson* (2013) — One for Ten is an online documentary series that focuses on ten individuals who were freed from death row. Over the course of five weeks, filmmakers Will Francome and Mark Pizzey traveled across the U.S. and filmed, edited, and uploaded the documentaries. In this short video, exoneree John Thompson discusses how the prosecutors in the Orleans Parrish district attorney's office withheld crucial evidence leading to his wrongful conviction. Thompson won a $14 million judgment in his § 1983 lawsuit against the district attorney's office, which the U.S. Supreme reversed, concluding that there could be no civil liability for failing to train prosecutors about their *Brady* duties absent a showing of a widespread pattern or practice amounting to a policy decision, as opposed to a single incident where the alleged failure to train resulted in a miscarriage of justice.

- *CNN Death Row Stories*, Episode 5, "Rough Justice in the Big Easy" (2014) — *Death Row Stories* is a CNN TV series that examines death row cases. This episode features John Thompson's journey from death row to exoneration.

Policy Implications and Reforms

There is growing recognition among law enforcement and prosecutors that wrongful convictions may happen with more regularity than previously acknowledged. This is an important step toward reform. Recently, the International Association of Chiefs of Police convened a summit of experts and criminal justice stakeholders to examine issues around wrongful arrests and convictions with the goal of developing recommendations for law enforcement. Their recommendations were documented in a summit report and grouped into four thematic areas: making rightful arrests, correcting wrongful ones, maximizing the use of technology, and openness to new information in closed cases. A summary of all their recommendations is beyond the scope of this chapter, however it is encouraging to note that preventing investigative bias is among them. For example, the report recommended that law enforcement agencies develop protocols to address and limit investigative bias. The report also included the following hopeful and encouraging statement:

> With a cultural shift, law enforcement and the entire justice system can leverage cutting edge research, promising practices, and forensic science to re-envision its approach to preventing wrongful arrests, prosecutions, and convictions. Part of this cultural shift must also allow law enforcement to stand ready to change course in the midst of an investigation, if new information deems that necessary. The prosecutorial culture is likely to shift as well, through close collaboration with law enforcement. Ultimately, the courts and their stakeholders, including judges and juries, will become more attuned to evidentiary strengths and weaknesses in individual cases, allowing potential wrongful convictions to be identified before they occur (International Association of Chiefs of Police, 2013, p. 21).

In fact, **implicit bias** training—training designed to educate law enforcement on the pernicious effect of unconscious biases related to racial, ethnic, gender, and other stereotypes—is gaining traction. The U.S. Department of Justice recently announced that it would train all of its agents and prosecutors to recognize and address implicit bias (U.S. Department of Justice, 2016). In addition, the American Bar Association offers multi-media resources on its website aimed at helping prosecutors (as well as judges and defense attorneys) understand implicit biases. On the one hand, these are promising steps; on the other hand, the effects of these and other interventions remain to be seen. For example, a recent randomized controlled evaluation study of implicit bias training adopted by the New York City Police Department showed that while officers' awareness of implicit bias was elevated, there was no detectable change in enforcement disparities (Worden, et al., 2020).

In 2019, New York enacted legislation creating the nation's first "state commission on prosecutorial conduct" (N.Y. Jud. Law § 499-a, 2019; see Robinson, 2020). The 11-member commission was given broad power to investigate complaints of prosecutorial misconduct, subpoena witnesses, and conduct hearings "with respect to the conduct, qualifications, fitness to perform, or performance of official duties of any prosecutor and may determine that a prosecutor be admonished, or censured; and make a recommendation to the governor that a prosecutor be removed from office for cause, for, including, but not limited to, misconduct in office, as evidenced by his or her departure from his or her obligations under appropriate statute, case law, and/or New York Rules of Professional Conduct, … persistent failure to perform his or her duties, conduct prejudicial to the administration of justice, or that a prosecutor be retired for mental or physical disability preventing the proper performance of his or her prosecutorial duties" (N.Y. Jud. Law § 499-f, 2019). The District Attorneys Association of the State of New York filed a lawsuit challenging the constitutionality of the statute which created the commission on multiple grounds. A judge ruled that the legislation violated the state constitution because, among other reasons, it gave the commission the authority to discipline prosecutors when that authority resided exclusively with the judiciary (*Soares v. State*, 2020). A bill designed to correct the constitutional infirmities identified in the ruling and resurrect the planned commission remained pending in the New York Legislature in 2021 (N.Y. Assembly Bill A01634, 2021; see also N.Y. Sen. Bill 8815, 2020).

Conclusion

Wrongful convictions most directly affect the innocent individuals who suffer them, but they also are a significant public safety issue. As we have stressed elsewhere in this book, and discuss in detail in chapter 13, when someone is convicted of a crime they did not commit, the real perpetrator, in "wrong person" cases, remains unpunished and free to cause more harm. Because of the associated public safety issues, in addition to promoting justice, law enforcement officers and prosecutors should welcome the chance to take actions necessary to reduce their contributions to wrongful convictions.

Key Terms and Concepts

- **Official misconduct:** the abuse of authority by police, prosecutors, or other government officials that may contribute to a wrongful conviction
- **Confirmation bias:** the subconscious tendency to interpret new evidence in such a way as to confirm one's pre-existing beliefs
- **Tunnel vision:** an outcome of cognitive biases, such as confirmation and disconfirmation bias, in which investigators focus on a suspect, become convinced of their guilt, and build a case against the suspect by interpreting evidence to fit their beliefs and discounting contradictory evidence
- **Implicit bias:** unconscious attitudes or stereotypes that influence an individual's beliefs, understanding, and actions
- **Stereotype threat:** occurs when a person fears being judged by a negative stereotype or generalization about the group to which they belong
- **Mass exoneration:** cases in which a group of defendants were erroneously convicted, often due to official misconduct, and later exonerated; also called "group exoneration"
- **Probable cause:** required for arrests; a general standard of proof that involves an evaluation of objective observations and reasonable inferences, and an assessment of the totality of the circumstances to determine the legality of an arrest
- *Brady v. Maryland*: a 1963 Supreme Court case concerning the prosecutor's obligation to disclose to the defense material exculpatory evidence; a prosecutor's failure to do so is referred to as a "*Brady* violation"
- **Absolute immunity:** a long-standing practice providing prosecutors with immunity from civil damages for conduct directly related to the judicial process

Discussion Questions

1. Recall the discussion above regarding the federal statute, 42 U.S.C. § 1983, which authorizes civil lawsuits to recover money damages against individuals who, while acting "under color of" state law, violate another person's constitutional rights. Do you agree that prosecutors should be immune from liability under the statute, even when they engage in misconduct? Why or why not?

2. What mechanisms would you propose for deterring prosecutors from intentional misconduct? What would you propose with respect to deterring police officers from misconduct and rights violations?

3. What would you suggest agencies do to reduce the effects of cognitive and implicit biases?

4. Do you believe that wrongful convictions are likely to occur more frequently among felonies or misdemeanors? Why?

References

Acker, J. R. (2018/2019). Reliable justice: Advancing the twofold aim of establishing guilt and protecting the innocent. *Albany Law Review, 82*, 719–773.

Arizona v. Youngblood, 488 U.S. 51 (1988).

Armacost, B. E. (1998). Qualified immunity: Ignorance excused. *Vanderbilt Law Review, 51*, 581–680.

Bandes, S. (2006). Loyalty to one's convictions: The prosecutor and tunnel vision. *Howard Law Journal, 49*, 475–494.

Bay, N. C. (2008). Old blood, bad blood, and *Youngblood*: Due process, lost evidence, and the limits of bad faith. *Washington University Law Review, 86*, 241–311.

Berger v. United States, 295 U.S. 78 (1935).

Brady v. Maryland, 373 U.S. 83 (1963).

Brinegar v. United States, 338 U.S. 160 (1949).

Buckley v. Fitzsimmons, 509 U.S. 259 (1993).

Burke, A. (2007). *Brady's* brainteaser: The accidental prosecutor and cognitive bias. *Case Western Reserve Law Review, 57*, 575–580.

Burns v. Reed, 500 U.S. 478 (1991).

Carroll v. United States, 267 U.S. 132 (1925).

Connick v. Thompson, 563 U.S. 51 (2011).

Covey, R. (2013). Police misconduct as a cause of wrongful convictions. *Washington University Law Review, 90*(4), 1133–1189.

District of Columbia v. Wesby, 138 S.Ct. 577 (2018).

Feuer, A. (2017, May 25). Despite 7 scrapped convictions, prosecutors say ex-detective broke no laws. *The New York Times.* https://www.nytimes.com/2017/05/25/nyregion/louis-scarcella-murder-dismissals.html?_r=0.

Giglio v. United States, 405 U.S. 150 (1972).

Gonnerman, J. (2016, June 20). Home free: How a New York State prisoner became a jailhouse lawyer, and changed the system. *The New Yorker*. http://www.newyorker.com/magazine/2016/06/20/derrick-hamilton-jailhouse-lawyer.

Green, B., & Yaroshefsky, E. (2016). Prosecutorial accountability 2.0. *Notre Dame Law Review, 92*, 51–116.

Gross, S. R., Possley, M., & Stephens, K. (2017). Race and wrongful convictions in the United States. *National Registry of Exonerations*. https://www.law.umich.edu/special/exoneration/Documents/Race_and_Wrongful_Convictions.pdf.

Harlow v. Fitzgerald, 457 U.S. 800 (1982).

Imbler v. Pachtman, 424 U.S. 409 (1976).

International Association of Chiefs of Police. (2013). *Wrongful convictions: Building a systemic approach to prevent wrongful convictions*. https://www.bja.gov/publications/iacp-wrongful_convictions_summit_report.pdf.

Johnson v. United States, 333 U.S. 10 (1948).

Kalina v. Fletcher, 522 U.S. 118 (1997).

Kisela v. Hughes, 138 S.Ct. 1148 (2018) (per curiam).

Kyles v. Whitley, 514 U.S. 419 (1995).

Lassers, W. J. (1973). *Scapegoat justice: Lloyd Miller and the failure of the American legal system*. Indiana University Press.

Manuel v. City of Joliet, 137 S.Ct. 911 (2017).

McKay, A. L. (2012). Let the master answer: Why the doctrine of *respondeat superior* should be used to address egregious prosecutorial misconduct resulting in wrongful convictions. *Wisconsin Law Review, 2012*, 1215–1243.

Miller v. Pate, 386 U.S. 1 (1967).

Morton, M. (2015). *Getting life: An innocent man's 25-year journey from prison to peace*. Simon & Schuster.

Mullenix v. Luna, 577 U.S. 7 (2015).

Najdowski, C. J. (2014). Interactions between African Americans and police officers: How cultural stereotypes create a wrongful conviction pipeline for African Americans. In A. D. Redlich, J. R. Acker, R. J. Norris, & C. L. Bonventre (Eds.), *Examining wrongful convictions: Stepping back, moving forward* (pp. 55–70). Carolina Academic Press.

Napue v. Illinois, 360 U.S. 254 (1959).

National Registry of Exonerations. (n.d.a). *Glossary*. https://www.law.umich.edu/special/exoneration/Pages/glossary.aspx.

National Registry of Exonerations. (n.d.b). *The Groups Registry*. https://exonerations.newkirkcenter.uci.edu/groups/group-exonerations.

Nemeth, M. R. (2019). How was that reasonable? The misguided development of qualified immunity and excessive force by law enforcement officers. *Boston College Law Review, 60*, 989–1022.

New York Assembly Bill A01634 (2021). https://www.billtrack50.com/bill detail/1264321.

New York Judicial Law § 499-a (2019).

New York Judicial Law § 499-f (2019).

New York Senate Bill 8815 (2020). https://legislation.nysenate.gov/pdf/bills/ 2019/S8815.

Nickerson, R. S. (1998). Confirmation bias: A ubiquitous phenomenon in many guises. *Review of General Psychology, 2*(2), 175–220.

Pearson v. Callahan, 555 U.S. 223 (2009).

Possley, M. (2012). Michael Morton. National Registry of Exonerations. https://www.law.umich.edu/special/exoneration/Pages/casedetail.aspx? caseid=3834.

Possley, M. (2016a). Derrick Hamilton. National Registry of Exonerations. https://www.law.umich.edu/special/exoneration/Pages/casedetail.aspx? caseid=4601.

Possley, M. (2016b). Shabaka Shakur. National Registry of Exonerations. https://www.law.umich.edu/special/exoneration/Pages/casedetail.aspx? caseid=4701.

Radelet, M. L., Bedau, H. A., & Putnam, C. E. (1992). *In spite of innocence: Erroneous convictions in capital cases*. Northeastern University Press.

Robinson, D. (2020). Prosecuting misconduct: New York's creation of a watchdog commission. *Brooklyn Law Review, 85*, 1055–1081.

Samaha, A. (2014, August 5). The tragedy of Louis Scarcella. *The Village Voice*. https://www.villagevoice.com/2014/08/05/the-tragedy-of-louis-scarcella/.

Saucier v. Katz, 533 U.S. 194 (2001).

Schwartz, J. C. (2020). Qualified immunity's selection effects. *Northwestern University Law Review, 114*, 1101–1178.

Simon, D. (2012). *In doubt: The psychology of the criminal justice process*. Harvard University Press.

Sullivan, T. P., & Possley, M. (2015). The chronic failure to discipline prosecutors for misconduct: Proposals for reform. *Journal of Criminal Law & Criminology, 105*, 881–945.

United States v. Bagley, 473 U.S. 667 (1985).

United States v. Burke, 571 F.3d 1078 (10th Cir.), cert. denied, 558 U.S. 1016 (2009).

Van de Kamp v. Goldstein, 555 U.S. 335 (2009).

White v. Pauly, 137 S.Ct. 548 (2017).

Wilson v. Layne, 526 U.S. 603 (1999).

Worden, R. E., McLean, S. J., Engel, R. S., Cochran, H., Corsaro, N., Reynolds, D., Najdowski, C. J., & Isaza, G. T. (2020, July). *The impacts of implicit bias awareness training in the NYPD.* Official Website of the City of New York. https://www1.nyc.gov/assets/nypd/downloads/pdf/analysis_and_planning/impacts-of-implicit-bias-awareness-training-in-%20the-nypd.pdf.

Chapter 9

Defense Attorneys

Learning Objectives

After reading this chapter, you should be able to:

- List the three primary types of indigent defense systems.
- Understand that excessive caseloads in misdemeanor courts can lead to wrongful convictions.
- Understand what is meant by inadequate legal defense and appreciate its consequences for felony and capital defendants.
- Understand the scope and meaning of the right to counsel for criminal defendants under the Sixth and Fourteenth Amendments to the U.S. Constitution.
- Discuss the U.S. Supreme Court's framework for assessing ineffective assistance of counsel claims.
- Appreciate the importance of qualified expert testimony for defending against criminal charges.
- Discuss approaches to improving the quality of public defense, including increasing funding, more training, and statewide oversight.

Case Study: A Tale of Two Attorneys

Instead of telling one story, we begin this chapter by telling two, both of which share the common feature of poor defense lawyering. Leroy McGee was arrested for the robbery of a Florida gas station clerk when he was mistakenly identified by the victim (National Registry of Exonerations, n.d.). McGee's alibi was that he was at work when the robbery occurred and that his time-card would show it. In addition, he and a co-worker had been in regular contact during their shift. McGee shared this information with his defense attorney. During McGee's trial, his attorney failed to introduce his alibi evidence or to raise any objections. McGee was convicted and sentenced to four-and-a-half years in prison. After he served his sentence, McGee's conviction was eventually vacated on the grounds of his attorney's poor defense.

Now consider the following story:

> Jerry White was sentenced to death for the murder of a customer during a convenience-store robbery. At trial his attorney's drinking problem was so evident that each morning the judge had the prosecutor check the attorney's breath. A defense investigator "said he had witnessed the attorney shoot up with cocaine during trial recesses and saw him using speed, Quaaludes, alcohol, morphine and marijuana after court," according to a law review article. On appeal, even the trial prosecutor filed an affidavit saying the defense attorney "appeared confused or fatigued." The Florida Supreme Court affirmed White's death sentence in 1995, and he was executed that year (Armstrong, 2014).

We are not suggesting that Jerry White was innocent of murder — we do not know. However, we raise the case to illustrate the contrast between an outrageous case of "bad lawyering" and the (likely) more common failures of McGee's defense attorney. One would expect that having a skilled, competent defense attorney at one's side would provide a shield against a wrongful conviction. As we will see from the research below, that can make an important difference. The research also shows that sometimes defense attorneys are unskilled, incompetent, understaffed, and/or overwhelmed by large caseloads, and can contribute to producing wrongful convictions.

Research on Inadequate Defense Representation

Criminal defendants who are too poor (referred to as "**indigent**") to pay to hire a defense attorney may have a federal constitutional right to a court-appointed attorney at the government's expense. In addition, criminal defendants have the constitutional right to the *effective* assistance of their attorneys. We will discuss the legal landscape concerning these rights in the next section below. Our immediate task is to examine the standards against which defense attorneys are held and the empirical evidence that shows that they can fall short of these standards and contribute to wrongful convictions. We will begin with a very brief note on the manner in which public defense is delivered, which varies considerably in terms of structure, funding, and quality across the states. There are three general types of systems involving lawyers who represent poor defendants in criminal courts. **Public defender** offices are typically government-operated and focus exclusively on indigent defense. **Assigned-counsel** systems involve the ad-hoc appointment of private attorneys to represent poor defendants. Finally, under the **contract system**, attorneys contract with the government to accept a certain number of cases for a flat fee (Worden et al., 2010/2011). Collectively, these ways of providing legal representation in criminal cases to people who cannot afford to hire an attorney are referred to as indigent defense. It should also be kept in mind that defendants who can afford to do so, have the right to hire private attorneys.

The American Bar Association (ABA), a large and influential professional association of lawyers, develops standards of ethical conduct for attorneys. Rule 1.1 of their Model Rules of Professional Conduct states that, "A lawyer shall provide competent representation to a client. Competent representation requires the legal knowledge, skill, thoroughness and preparation reasonably necessary for the representation" (American Bar Association, 2016). In addition, Standard 4-1.2(b) of the ABA's Criminal Justice Standards for the Defense Function states, "Defense counsel have the difficult task of serving both as officers of the court and as loyal and zealous advocates for their clients. The primary duties that defense counsel owe to their clients, to the administration of justice, and as officers of the court, are to serve as their clients' counselor and advocate with courage and devotion; to ensure that constitutional and other legal rights of their clients are protected; and to render effective, high-quality legal representation with integrity" (American Bar Association, 2015). In general, the deficient contributions of defense attorneys may stem from incompetence, unethical conduct, lack of resources, or perhaps some combination thereof (Worden et al., 2014).

Wrongful Convictions in Popular Culture: Defense Attorneys, Bad and Good

- *One for Ten: Gary Drinkard* (2013) — An online documentary by filmmakers Will Francome and Mark Pizzey, this short film demonstrates the importance of competent, experienced criminal defense attorneys. Watch as Gary Drinkard describes how his court-appointed lawyers — who specialized in bankruptcy and commercial law — represented him in his trial for capital murder.

> • *The Trials of Darryl Hunt* (2006) — A gripping documentary from filmmakers Ricki Stern and Annie Sundberg chronicles the case of Darryl Hunt, who was convicted in North Carolina of raping and murdering a local newspaper editor. Hunt was appointed a defense attorney, Mark Rabil, who worked tirelessly on his behalf. However, Hunt was still convicted and sentenced to life in prison. Rabil worked on the case for two decades and eventually helped secure Hunt's exoneration through DNA testing in 2004.

Misdemeanor Defense

Although the majority of exonerations documented by the Innocence Project and the National Registry of Exonerations are from felony convictions, the majority of cases processed by the criminal justice system are for lower-level offenses, or **misdemeanors**. According to recent empirical estimates, over 13 million misdemeanor cases are filed in the United States each year (Stevenson & Mayson, 2018). In chapter 1, we addressed the difficulty in estimating the rate of wrongful convictions. This is especially the case with wrongful misdemeanor convictions. What we know about wrongful convictions stems primarily from felony exonerations. As of 2018, 4% of the exonerations in the National Registry were from misdemeanor convictions (Gross, 2018). That does not suggest, however, that wrongful misdemeanor convictions are rare. It is more likely that innocent people convicted of misdemeanors do not have a chance to pursue exoneration. As law professor Samuel Gross notes, "the scarce resources that are required to achieve an exoneration are generally allocated to innocent defendants with harsher punishments" (Gross, 2018, p. 1005).

As discussed in our legal section below, "petty" offenses are not petty in terms of their consequences. A few years ago, the National Association of Criminal Defense Lawyers (NACDL) conducted a comprehensive examination of misdemeanor courts in the United States. The study demonstrated several problems with misdemeanor defense practice (Boruchowitz et al., 2009). The research included an extensive review of the literature, interviews with criminal justice personnel, site visits in seven states across the country, an internet survey of criminal defense attorneys, and two conferences that collected input from criminal justice stakeholders. The study found that defense attorneys in misdemeanor courts carried yearly **caseload**s that far exceeded the national recommended maximum. For example, the report found that in three cities, defense attorneys carried loads of over 2,000 cases per year — well above the recommended maximum of 400 per year. The study estimated that a caseload of 2,000 per year would give a defense attorney about 70 minutes to spend on each case. Such exceedingly high caseloads make it difficult for defense attorneys to provide adequate representation for their clients, including having sufficient time to discuss cases with their clients, investigate and interview witnesses, conduct legal research, and more. As a result, "**meet and plead**" dispositions are common:

> In many jurisdictions, cases are resolved at the first court hearing, with minimal or no preparation by the defense. Misdemeanor courtrooms often have so many cases on the docket that an attorney has mere minutes to handle each case. Because of the number of cases assigned to each defender, "legal advice" often amounts to a hasty conversation in the courtroom or hallway with the client. Frequently, this conversation begins with the defender informing the defendant of a plea offer. When the defendant's case is called, he or she simply enters a guilty plea and is sentenced. No research of the facts or the law is undertaken. This process is known as meet-and-plead or plea at arraignment/first appearance (Boruchowitz et al., 2009, p. 31).

Structured this way, the misdemeanor process has serious implications for wrongful convictions. As the NACDL report observed:

> Legal representation for misdemeanants is absent in many cases. When an attorney is provided, crushing workloads often make it impossible for the defender to effectively represent her clients. Counsel is unable to spend adequate time on each of her cases, and often lacks necessary resources, such as access to investigators, experts, and online research tools. These deficiencies force even the most competent and dedicated attorneys to engage in breaches of professional duties. Too often, judges and prosecutors are complicit in these breaches, pushing defenders and defendants to take action with limited time and knowledge of their cases. This leads to guilty pleas by the innocent, inappropriate sentences, and wrongful incarceration, all at taxpayer expense (Boruchowitz et al., 2009, p. 7).

Felony Defense

The stakes are even greater for defendants facing **felony** or **capital charges**. The majority of the first 250 DNA exonerations involved convictions for serious violent felonies. For example, 68% (n = 171) of the convictions were for rape, 21% (n = 52) for rape and murder, and 9% (n = 22) were for murder (Garrett, 2011). A study of the first 255 DNA exonerations showed that in 21%

(n = 54) of the cases, exonerees argued in their appeals that their defense attorneys were ineffective (West, 2010). Common claims raised by the exonerees included the failure to present defense witnesses, the failure to seek scientific testing to exclude the defendant, the failure to object to prosecutors' statements, witness testimony, or other evidence introduced by the state, the failure to cross-examine witnesses, and more. The appeals courts rejected most of the claims, confirming only seven claims of **ineffective assistance** of counsel. For example, Willie Jackson's attorney failed to hire an expert witness to rebut the state's bite mark evidence because Jackson's parents could not pay for the expert, and the attorney did not request funds from the government to pay for one (West, 2010).

For defendants facing capital charges—crimes for which the death penalty may be imposed—an effective defense attorney is all the more critical. A search of the first 2,774 exonerations in the National Registry of Exonerations reveals 43 defendants who were sentenced to death and who were categorized as having had an inadequate legal defense at trial (National Registry of Exonerations, n.d.). The NRE defines inadequate legal defense as "The exoneree's lawyer at trial provided obviously and grossly inadequate representation" (National Registry of Exonerations, n.d.). For example, Glenn Ford was charged with murder and sentenced to death for the robbery and killing of a jewelry shop owner. He was exonerated after spending 30 years on Louisiana's death row. As the NRE describes his defense:

> Ford's lawyers at trial testified that they were very inexperienced in criminal cases and had no training in capital defense. One of the lawyers, who specialized in oil and gas law, had never tried a case to a jury—either civil or criminal—and the extent of his prior criminal work was handling two guilty pleas. The other lawyer was out of law school less than two years and was working at an insurance firm handling personal injury cases.
>
> Both said they were unaware they could seek court funding for defense experts and didn't hire any because they couldn't afford to pay out of their own pockets. Both were unaware of how to subpoena witnesses from out of state and so Ford's family members, who lived in California, did not testify for Ford at the guilt or punishment phase of the trial (National Registry of Exonerations, 2015).

Research comparing indicted defendants who were released before trial or acquitted based on their actual innocence ("near misses") with wrongfully convicted innocent defendants shows that "a poor defense increases the likelihood that an indicted, innocent defendant will be convicted" (Gould et al., 2014, p.

502). Many of the defense attorneys in the wrongful conviction cases in the study were inexperienced at handling serious felony cases, and many of the cases involved conflict of interest, poor preparation, or failure to call expert witnesses. As the study authors observed:

> By contrast, as evidenced by many of our near misses, an experienced, well-educated, and adequately funded defense attorney often plays a vital role in uncovering earlier flaws in the case so that charges are dismissed. Among the near misses, there were examples of defense attorneys establishing solid alibis for their clients by tracking down witnesses, finding receipts, or analyzing security footage. In some cases, defense attorneys made the crucial decision to retain an expert witness to examine the defendant's confession and eventually convince the judge or prosecutor that the confession was involuntary and/or false (Gould et al., 2014, p. 503).

In the next section, we will examine the constitutional underpinnings of criminal defendants' right to counsel and the standards by which courts hold them accountable for being effective.

Lawyering behind Bars

Once convicted, the innocent may struggle to find effective legal representation to help exonerate them. "Jailhouse lawyers" are incarcerated people who are (usually) self-taught in the law and help themselves or other incarcerated people with their cases.

- Derrick Hamilton — featured in chapter 8, Hamilton formed The Actual Innocence Team at Auburn Correctional Facility with fellow prisoners including Daniel Rincon, Shabaka Shakur, and Nelson Cruz. Hamilton's legal efforts led to the first appellate decision in New York State to recognize a freestanding claim of actual innocence. Hamilton's jailhouse lawyering has been featured in multiple media outlets including *The New York Times* and *The New Yorker*.

- Jabbar Collins — convicted of murder in 1995, Collins taught himself the law and conducted his own investigation, filing multiple appeals and petitions for post-conviction relief. Collins was exonerated in 2010 and obtained employment as a paralegal. Collins' jailhouse lawyering has been featured in *The Wall Street Journal* and other media outlets.

Defense Attorneys and the Law

The Right to Court-Appointed Counsel

In *Gideon v. Wainwright* (1963), one of the Supreme Court's landmark decisions during the tenure of Chief Justice Earl Warren, the justices ruled that defendants charged with committing a felony who are too poor to afford to hire a lawyer have the right, guaranteed by the Sixth and Fourteenth Amendments, to be represented by court-appointed trial counsel. Justice Black's opinion explained why this right is so fundamentally important.

[I]n our adversary system of criminal justice, any person haled into court, who is too poor to hire a lawyer, cannot be assured a fair trial unless counsel is provided for him. This seems to us to be an obvious truth. Governments, both state and federal, quite properly spend vast sums of money to establish machinery to try defendants accused of crime. Lawyers to prosecute are everywhere deemed essential to protect the public's interest in an orderly society. Similarly, there are few defendants charged with crime, few indeed, who fail to hire the best lawyers they can get to prepare and present their defenses. That government hires lawyers to prosecute and defendants who have the money hire lawyers to defend are the strongest indications of the widespread belief that lawyers in criminal courts are necessities, not luxuries.... From the very beginning, our state and national constitutions and laws have laid great emphasis on procedural and substantive safeguards designed to assure fair trials before impartial tribunals in which every defendant stands equal before the law. This noble ideal cannot be realized if the poor man charged with crime has to face his accusers without a lawyer to assist him. A defendant's need for a lawyer is nowhere better stated than in the moving words of Mr. Justice Sutherland in *Powell v. Alabama*, [287 U.S. 45, 68–69 (1932)]:

"The right to be heard would be, in many cases, of little avail if it did not comprehend the right to be heard by counsel. Even the intelligent and educated layman has small and sometimes no skill in the science of law. If charged with crime, he is incapable, generally, of determining for himself whether the indictment is good or bad. He is unfamiliar with the rules of evidence. Left without the aid of counsel he may be put on trial without a proper charge, and convicted upon incompetent evidence, or evidence irrelevant to the issue or otherwise inadmissible. He lacks both the skill and knowledge adequately to prepare his defense, even though he have a perfect one. He requires the guiding hand of counsel at every step in the proceedings against him. Without it, though he be not guilty, he faces the danger of conviction because he does not know how to establish his innocence."

Clarence Gideon had been charged with the felony of breaking into a pool hall in Florida. Unable to afford a lawyer, he was forced to represent himself at his trial. Although he "conducted his defense about as well as could be expected for a layman" (*Gideon v. Wainwright*, 1963, p. 337), he was convicted and sentenced to five years in prison. After the Supreme Court reversed his conviction, Gideon was tried once again, this time represented by court-appointed counsel. Following deliberations of just over an hour, the jury found him not guilty (Lewis, 1964, p. 249). In this regard, Justice Sutherland's observation in *Powell v. Alabama* (1932, p. 69), as quoted above, is particularly relevant: "Without [the guiding hand of counsel, a layperson], though he be not guilty, ... faces the danger of conviction because he does not know how to establish his innocence."

If this latter point is true in felony trials, it would appear to be true as well for laypersons charged with a misdemeanor. Jon Argersinger, who was indigent yet denied court-appointed counsel, was sentenced to 90 days in jail after representing himself at trial and being convicted in a Florida court for unlawfully carrying a concealed weapon. The charge was a misdemeanor, punishable by a maximum of six months incarceration and a $1,000 fine. The Supreme Court reversed his conviction. Justice Douglas's opinion acknowledged that: "Both *Powell* and *Gideon* involved felonies. But their rationale has relevance to any criminal trial, where an accused is deprived of his liberty" (*Argersinger v. Hamlin*, 1972, p. 32). "We are by no means convinced that legal and constitutional questions involved in a case that actually leads to imprisonment even for a brief period are any less complex than when a person can be sent off for six months or more [in jail or prison]" (p. 33).

Left unresolved in *Argersinger* was whether a poor person charged with a misdemeanor who does not receive a jail sentence, but is only fined and/or placed on probation, is entitled under the Constitution to court-appointed trial counsel. This question arose in *Scott v. Illinois* (1979). Justice Rehnquist answered it negatively for the Court majority, in a 5–4 ruling. Aubrey Scott had been charged with shoplifting, a misdemeanor punishable under Illinois law by up to one year in jail and a $500 fine. He pled not guilty and was tried before a judge. He could not afford a lawyer, so he represented himself. He was convicted, and the judge fined him $50. Citing historical limits on the right to counsel, ambiguity concerning the reach of the Sixth Amendment guarantee for the assistance of counsel, and the administrative and financial costs associated with requiring the appointment of counsel for indigents in all criminal trials, the majority opinion held that: "the Sixth and Fourteenth Amendments to the United States Constitution require only that no indigent criminal defendant be sentenced to a term of imprisonment unless the State has afforded him the right to assistance of appointed counsel in his defense" (pp. 373–374).

Justice Brennan's dissenting opinion charged that the majority's ruling could not be reconciled with the fundamental rationale of earlier right-to-counsel cases insofar as they emphasized the unreliability and unfairness of trials in which laypersons are required to defend themselves. It further argued that the rule was unworkable because judges would have to decide whether to appoint counsel for indigents charged with misdemeanors before hearing any evidence or knowing whether jail time would be imposed if the defendant was convicted. It finally disputed that requiring the appointment of counsel in all cases in which incarceration was a possible punishment would be unduly burdensome, noting that Scott would have been provided court-appointed counsel under the circumstances of his case pursuant to the laws of 33 states (*Scott v. Illinois*, 1979, p. 388).

Many states go beyond their constitutional obligation under the rule of *Scott v. Illinois* (1979) and have enacted statutes that provide court-appointed trial counsel for indigents in all cases where incarceration is possible. Implications of the ruling thus are not as far-reaching as they otherwise might have been. Moreover, the Supreme Court has clarified that indigent defendants who are denied court-appointed counsel, convicted, and then placed on probation and given a suspended jail sentence, cannot be required to serve the jail sentence if their probation is revoked (*Alabama v. Shelton*, 2002). This decision also has softened the ruling in *Scott* (Hashimoto, 2007, pp. 479–480).

Nevertheless, many poor people are still required to stand trial without legal counsel for low-level offenses. Lacking the skills and knowledge to mount a defense, deal with prosecutors, and navigate through the courts, they are likely at heightened risk of wrongful conviction (Acker, 2017, pp. 15–16). Even if they are appropriately found guilty, convictions in cases that do not directly result in jail time can have devastating consequences both within and outside of criminal justice systems. Later convictions can result in significantly harsher punishment because of a prior criminal record (*Nichols v. United States*, 1994). Collateral consequences ranging from compromising immigration status to disqualification from employment, public housing, parental rights, and firearms ownership, as well as other hardships can ensue (Buskey & Lucas, 2017; Clapman, 2011; King, 2013; Roberts, 2011).

The Sixth Amendment right to counsel does not extend beyond the trial stage of a criminal case. The justices nevertheless have ruled that Due Process requires that indigents be provided a lawyer to represent them on an initial appeal (*Douglas v. California*, 1963). However, the Constitution does not require the appointment of counsel to enable convicted, indigent defendants to seek discretionary review in higher courts (*Ross v. Moffitt*, 1974), pursue relief in state post-conviction proceedings (where matters outside of the record on appeal might be litigated, for example, alleged *Brady* violations and claims of ineffective assistance of counsel) (*Murray v. Giarratano*, 1989), or to petition the federal courts for habeas corpus relief. Although statutes in several jurisdictions authorize the appointment of counsel in many such circumstances, indigents who have suffered wrongful conviction can be handicapped in securing judicial review that could help correct miscarriages of justice (King, 2014).

Ineffective Assistance of Counsel

Where recognized, the constitutional right to the assistance of counsel contemplates more than that "a person who happens to be a lawyer is present at trial alongside the accused" (*Strickland v. Washington*, 1984, p. 685). Justice O'Connor's opinion for the Supreme Court in *Strickland v. Washington* continued:

> The Sixth Amendment recognizes the right to the assistance of counsel because it envisions counsel's playing a role that is critical to the ability of the adversarial system to produce just results. An accused is entitled to be assisted by an attorney, whether retained or appointed, who plays the role necessary to ensure that the trial is fair.
>
> For that reason, the Court has recognized that "the right to counsel is the right to the effective assistance of counsel." *McMann v. Richardson*, 397 U.S. 759, 771, n. 14 (1970)....
>
> The benchmark for judging any claim of ineffectiveness must be whether counsel's conduct so undermined the proper functioning of the adversarial process that the trial cannot be relied on as having produced a just result....
>
> A convicted defendant's claim that counsel's assistance was so defective as to require reversal of a conviction or death sentence has two components. First, the defendant must show that counsel's performance was deficient. This requires showing that counsel made errors so serious that counsel was not functioning as the "counsel" guaranteed the defendant by the Sixth Amendment. Second, the defendant must show that the deficient performance prejudiced the defense. This requires showing that counsel's errors were so serious as to deprive the defendant of a fair trial, a trial whose result is reliable.

Unless a defendant makes both showings, it cannot be said that the conviction or death sentence resulted from a breakdown in the adversary process that renders the result unreliable....

[T]he proper standard for attorney performance is that of reasonably effective assistance.... When a convicted defendant complains of the ineffectiveness of counsel's assistance, the defendant must show that counsel's representation fell below an objective standard of reasonableness....

More specific guidelines are not appropriate.... The proper measure of attorney performance remains simply reasonableness under prevailing professional norms.

An error by counsel, even if professionally unreasonable, does not warrant setting aside the judgment of a criminal proceeding if the error had no effect on the judgment. The purpose of the Sixth Amendment guarantee of counsel is to ensure that a defendant has the assistance necessary to justify reliance on the outcome of the proceeding. Accordingly, any deficiencies in counsel's performance must be prejudicial to the defense in order to constitute ineffective assistance under the Constitution....

[T]he appropriate test for prejudice [is that the] ... defendant must show that there is a reasonable probability that, but for counsel's unprofessional errors, the result of the proceeding would have been different. A reasonable probability is a probability sufficient to undermine confidence in the outcome.

While announcing the two-part test for establishing claims of constitutionally ineffective assistance of trial counsel, requiring a showing of both deficient performance and actual prejudice, the Court in *Strickland* emphasized that:

Judicial scrutiny of counsel's performance must be highly deferential. It is all too tempting for a defendant to second-guess counsel's assistance after conviction or adverse sentence, and it is all too easy for a court, examining counsel's defense after it has proved unsuccessful, to conclude that a particular act or omission of counsel was unreasonable. A fair assessment of attorney performance requires that every effort be made to eliminate the distorting effects of hindsight, to reconstruct the circumstances of counsel's challenged conduct, and to evaluate the conduct from counsel's perspective at the time. Because of the difficulties inherent in making the evaluation, a court must indulge a strong presumption that counsel's conduct falls within the wide range of reasonable professional assistance.

Strickland's loosely defined standards governing ineffective assistance of counsel, the Court's emphasis on the deference owed in reviewing defense counsel's tactical decisions, the demanding *post hoc* requirement for a showing of prejudice, and multiple factors endemic to the nation's indigent legal defense systems, including inadequate funding and overwhelming caseloads for public defenders, have resulted in some observers branding *Gideon's* constitutional mandate for court-appointed counsel as a "broken promise" (American Bar Association Standing Committee on Legal Aid and Indigent Defendants, 2004; see also, Allen, 2009; Dripps, 2012; Griffin, 2016; Hashimoto, 2016, pp. 1019–1020; Mallord, 2014; Metzger & Ferguson, 2015, pp. 1064–1065; Smith, 2009). Defense attorneys' failure to investigate potential defenses or mitigating circumstances that could affect sentencing will of course risk compromising their trial representation and contributing to miscarriages of justice. The Supreme Court has recognized as much in several death penalty cases, where more demanding scrutiny has recently been made of defense counsel's performance (*Porter v. McCollum*, 2009; *Rompilla v. Beard*, 2005; *Wiggins v. Smith*, 2003).

In one such case, Anthony Ray Hinton was charged in Alabama with two murders committed in 1985 during separate robberies of restaurants. There were no eyewitnesses to the murders and Hinton denied committing them. Hinton was arrested after he was identified as having robbed another restaurant by its manager, a man named Smotherman. The robber had fired two gunshots during that robbery, but Smotherman had not been killed. Hinton maintained that Smotherman's identification of him was erroneous, and he offered alibi witnesses in support of his claim that he had not robbed Smotherman. The testimony of two ballistics experts for the prosecution constituted "'the only evidence linking Hinton to the two murders'" (*Hinton v. Alabama*, 2014, p. 265). The expert witnesses had analyzed bullets from the murder scenes and from the Smotherman robbery, and opined that all of the bullets had been fired from a .38 revolver found at Hinton's house.

Hinton, who was not tried for the Smotherman robbery, was represented at his trial for the two murders by court-appointed counsel. In an effort to rebut the ballistics evidence offered by the prosecution experts, Hinton's lawyer sought funds to hire his own expert. The lawyer erroneously understood Alabama law to limit expert witness fees to $1,000; in reality, there was no such statutory cap. Hinton's attorney thus did not press for additional funding from the trial court. He could find only one expert, Andrew Payne, who was willing to analyze the ballistics evidence and testify for $1,000.

At trial, Payne testified that the toolmarks in the barrel of the Hinton revolver had been corroded away so that it would be impossible to say with certainty whether a particular bullet had been fired from that gun. He also testified that the bullets from the three crime scenes did not match one another. The State's two experts, by contrast, maintained that all six bullets had indeed been fired from the Hinton revolver.

On cross-examination, the prosecutor badly discredited Payne. Payne admitted that he'd testified as an expert on firearms and toolmark identification just twice in the preceding eight years and that one of the two cases involved a shotgun rather than a handgun. Payne also conceded that he had had difficulty operating the microscope at the state forensic laboratory and had asked for help from one of the state experts. The prosecutor ended the cross-examination with this colloquy:

"Q. Mr. Payne, do you have some problem with your vision?

"A. Why, yes.

"Q. How many eyes do you have?

"A. One."

The prosecutor's closing argument highlighted the fact that Payne's expertise was in military ordnance, not firearms and toolmark identification, and that Payne had graduated in 1933 (more than half a century before the trial) with a degree in civil engineering, whereas the State's experts had years of training and experience in the field of firearms and toolmark examination.

At the conclusion of the trial, Hinton was found guilty of both murders and sentenced to death. Much later, different attorneys assumed Hinton's representation and enlisted three new experts to evaluate the ballistics evidence that had been used to link Hinton to the murders. All three were of the opinion that the evidence did not support the conclusion that any of the recovered bullets had been fired from the gun taken from Hinton's home. Hinton argued that his trial lawyer's misinterpretation of Alabama law as limiting expert witness fees to $1,000, which resulted in his having to rely on Payne and his easily discredited expert testimony, constituted ineffective assistance of counsel. The Supreme Court's unanimous *per curiam* opinion vacated Hinton's conviction and death sentence.

> The trial attorney's failure to request additional funding in order to replace an expert he knew to be inadequate because he mistakenly believed that he had received all he could get under Alabama law constituted deficient performance. Under *Strickland*, "strategic choices made after thorough investigation of law and facts relevant to plausible options are virtually unchallengeable; and strategic choices made after less than complete investigation are reasonable precisely to the extent

that reasonable professional judgments support the limitations on investigation. In other words, counsel has a duty to make reasonable investigations or to make a reasonable decision that makes particular investigations unnecessary." 466 U.S., at 690–691. Hinton's attorney knew that he needed more funding to present an effective defense, yet he failed to make even the cursory investigation of the state statute providing for defense funding for indigent defendants that would have revealed to him that he could receive reimbursement not just for $1,000 but for "any expenses reasonably incurred." An attorney's ignorance of a point of law that is fundamental to his case combined with his failure to perform basic research on that point is a quintessential example of unreasonable performance under *Strickland*....

Having established deficient performance, Hinton must also "show that there is a reasonable probability that, but for counsel's unprofessional errors, the result of the proceeding would have been different...."

And if there is a reasonable probability that Hinton's attorney would have hired an expert who would have instilled in the jury a reasonable doubt as to Hinton's guilt had the attorney known that the statutory funding limit had been lifted, then Hinton was prejudiced by his lawyer's deficient performance and is entitled to a new trial.

That the State presented testimony from two experienced expert witnesses that tended to inculpate Hinton does not, taken alone, demonstrate that Hinton is guilty. Prosecution experts, of course, can sometimes make mistakes. Indeed, we have recognized the threat to fair criminal trials posed by the potential for incompetent or fraudulent prosecution forensics experts, noting that "[s]erious deficiencies have been found in the forensic evidence used in criminal trials.... One study of cases in which exonerating evidence resulted in the overturning of criminal convictions concluded that invalid forensic testimony contributed to the convictions in 60% of the cases." *Melendez-Diaz v. Massachusetts*, 557 U.S. 305, 319 (2009) (citing Garrett & Neufeld, Invalid Forensic Science Testimony and Wrongful Convictions, 95 Va. L. Rev. 1, 14 (2009)). This threat is minimized when the defense retains a competent expert to counter the testimony of the prosecution's expert witnesses; it is maximized when the defense instead fails to understand the resources available to it by law.

Because no court has yet evaluated the prejudice question by applying the proper inquiry to the facts of this case, we remand the case for reconsideration of whether Hinton's attorney's deficient performance was prejudicial under *Strickland*.

Following the Supreme Court's decision, Hinton was exonerated. He was released from Alabama's death row in April 2015, where he had spent nearly 30 years awaiting execution (Death Penalty Information Center, n.d.; Garrett, 2016, p. 1166; Green, 2016, pp. 526–527; Hinton & Hardin, 2018). Hinton's case suggests how important the services of a qualified expert can be in mounting a defense to a criminal charge. It also raises the question: If indigent defendants are entitled to the services of court-appointed trial counsel, are they also entitled to access to expert witnesses to assist with their defense?

Assistance of Counsel and Expert Witnesses

Glen Ake was charged with capital murder in Oklahoma. Ake's bizarre behavior when he appeared in court resulted in his commitment to a hospital for psychiatric evaluation. He was determined to be acutely psychotic and incompetent to stand trial. After several weeks and exhibiting some improvement, Ake was deemed fit for trial. He was represented by court-appointed counsel, who asked the trial court to authorize a psychiatric examination of Ake at state expense to help him prepare and present a defense of not guilty by reason of insanity. This request was denied. The only psychiatric testimony at Ake's trial was elicited from the doctors who had examined Ake for competency to stand trial. None of the testimony focused on Ake's mental state when he had killed his victims, the critical time relevant to his defense of insanity. The psychiatrists nevertheless did testify that Ake was dangerous. Ake was convicted and sentenced to death. Justice Marshall's opinion for the Supreme Court held that "when a defendant has made a preliminary showing that his sanity at the time of the offense is likely to be a significant factor at trial, the Constitution requires that a State provide access to a psychiatrist's assistance on this issue if the defendant cannot otherwise afford one" (*Ake v. Oklahoma*, 1985, p. 74).

> We recognized long ago that mere access to the courthouse doors does not by itself assure a proper functioning of the adversary process, and that a criminal trial is fundamentally unfair if the State proceeds against an indigent defendant without making certain that he has access to the raw materials integral to the building of an effective defense. Thus, while the Court has not held that a State must purchase for the indigent defendant all the assistance that his wealthier counterpart might buy, see *Ross v. Moffitt*, 417 U.S. 600 (1974), it has often reaffirmed that fundamental fairness entitles indigent defendants to "an

adequate opportunity to present their claims fairly within the adversary system," *id.*, at 612. To implement this principle, we have focused on identifying the "basic tools of an adequate defense or appeal," *Britt v. North Carolina*, 404 U.S. 226, 227 (1971), and we have required that such tools be provided to those defendants who cannot afford to pay for them.

To say that these basic tools must be provided is, of course, merely to begin our inquiry. In this case we must decide whether, and under what conditions, the participation of a psychiatrist is important enough to preparation of a defense to require the State to provide an indigent defendant with access to competent psychiatric assistance in preparing the defense. Three factors are relevant to this determination. The first is the private interest that will be affected by the action of the State. The second is the governmental interest that will be affected if the safeguard is to be provided. The third is the probable value of the additional or substitute procedural safeguards that are sought, and the risk of an erroneous deprivation of the affected interest if those safeguards are not provided.

Applying the three factors identified, the Court ruled that Ake's Due Process rights were violated when his lawyer was denied the requested court-appointed psychiatric evaluation. In *McWilliams v. Dunn* (2017) the Supreme Court did not reach the question of whether "a State must provide an indigent defendant with a qualified mental health expert retained specifically for the defense team, [and] not a neutral expert available to both parties" (p. 1799). It ruled, however, that McWilliams, an indigent defendant who had been convicted of murder and subsequently sentenced to death by an Alabama judge, was denied the minimum assistance which *Ake* required because he did not "receive the assistance of a mental health expert who is sufficiently available to the defense and independent from the prosecution to effectively 'assist in evaluation, preparation, and presentation of the defense'" (p. 1799, quoting *Ake v. Oklahoma*, 1985, p. 83). Although it generally is recognized that the ruling in *Ake* extends beyond capital cases and encompasses experts in disciplines other than mental health, courts frequently decline to authorize funding for court-appointed defense experts (Bailey, 2002; Giannelli, 2004; Giannelli, 2011, pp. 76–77; Groendyke, 2007). In light of the complicated issues that may arise in criminal cases, including DNA analysis, computer applications, medical diagnoses, accident reconstruction, arson investigation, and countless others, indigent defendants who are denied the assistance of court-appointed experts can be severely disadvantaged in preparing for and making a defense at trial

(Giannelli, 2011; Gilbert, 2013; Greeley, 2011). This is particularly so when experts are readily available to assist prosecutors in preparing and presenting their case. Such imbalances might clearly help tip the scales against innocents accused of crimes.

Attorney-Client Confidentiality

The confidential communications between lawyers and their clients generally are privileged. They ordinarily cannot be disclosed unless the client waives the privilege. The purpose of safeguarding the confidentiality of attorney-client communications is to ensure that individuals who consult with lawyers can freely disclose information which might be essential to the lawyer's ability to represent the person and assert their legal rights. In criminal cases, defense attorneys may learn from their clients that they indeed are guilty. Having this knowledge does not alter the lawyer's obligation to maintain confidentiality, zealously represent the client's interests, and present the best legal defense available to the charges.

Some attorneys have been presented with vexing ethical dilemmas pertaining to wrongful convictions which arise from the normal obligation to hold what their clients have shared with them in confidence. For example, what should a lawyer do if her client reveals to her that he, in fact, committed a crime for which another person—who is altogether innocent—has been convicted and faces punishment? If the lawyer reveals what she learned from her client in confidence, she risks not only violating ethical codes of professional responsibility but also exposing her client to conviction and punishment, which clearly is not in his best interests. She more generally conveys the message that the "promise" of confidentiality which attorneys make to their clients cannot be taken seriously, perhaps causing future clients to withhold information that might be essential to mounting a defense to the charges against them. Yet if she does not divulge what she knows, the innocent person who has been wrongly convicted will suffer punishment which might include years or a lifetime spent in prison, or even execution. These difficult issues are not purely hypothetical.

Alton Logan was convicted in Chicago in 1983 for the 1982 murder of Lloyd Wyckliffe, a security guard. Logan was sentenced to life imprisonment. Attorneys who represented Andrew Wilson in an unrelated murder case, in which he was convicted and sentenced to life in prison, learned from Wilson that he was responsible for Wyckliffe's murder and that Logan had nothing to do with it. Despite having this information, which they secured in the form of an affidavit sworn to and signed by Wilson, the attorneys did not come forward with it. They reasoned that doing so would expose Wilson to the risk of prosecution and conviction for the crime and violate the attorney-client privilege. Wilson authorized them to disclose his guilt for the killing but only after he died. The attorneys released the information upon Wilson's death in 2007, and Logan was exonerated—but not until 2008, after he had spent 26 years wrongfully imprisoned (Center on Wrongful Convictions, n.d.; Myers, 2018; *People v. Logan*, 1991; Rowe, 2015; Strutin, 2011). Logan's case is not unique. Criminal defense attorneys in other cases have learned from their clients that they have committed crimes for which innocent people have been convicted and imprisoned, and even sentenced to death (Acker & Brody, 2013, 513–515; Liptak, 2008; Rowe, 2015; Strutin, 2011). In relevant part, the American Bar Association's Model Rules of Professional Conduct (American Bar Association, 2016) address attorney-client confidentiality as follows:

Rule 1.6: Confidentiality of Information
(a) A lawyer shall not reveal information relating to the representation of a client unless the client gives informed consent, the disclosure is impliedly authorized in order to carry out the representation or the disclosure is permitted by paragraph (b).
(b) A lawyer may reveal information relating to the representation of a client to the extent the lawyer reasonably believes necessary:
(1) to prevent reasonably certain death or substantial bodily harm....

The rules do not explicitly address attorney-client confidentiality in the context we are considering: when lawyers learn from their clients that they are responsible for a crime for which another person has been wrongfully convicted and punished. Disclosing confidential information of this nature arguably is permissible under Rule 1.6 (b) (1), i.e., when it will "prevent reasonably certain death or substantial bodily harm"—an exception broad enough to encompass the risk of wrongful execution and, to the extent imprisonment occasions "substantial bodily harm," to apply in cases of wrongful incarceration, as well. At least two states, Alaska and Massachusetts, have adopted ethical codes that expressly permit (but do not require) lawyers to disclose confidential communications from their clients "to prevent the wrongful execution or incarceration of another" (see Myers, 2018, p. 109; Strutin, 2011, p. 546). Other solutions have been proposed, for example, allowing or requiring disclosure by attorneys when their client who has provided the information is given immunity from prosecution for the crime (see Myers, 2018). Perfect solutions to this problem, which presumably is rather rare, remain elusive.

Implications for Policy and Reform

What can be done to reduce the contribution of the defense function to wrongful convictions? Common themes among proposals for reform include reduced caseloads, adequate funding, and more or better training for defense lawyers. For example, the American Bar Association Criminal Justice Section (2006) recommends adequate workloads as well as compensation on par with prosecutors. There should be adequate resources and training so that defenders can thoroughly investigate and closely scrutinize their cases, especially those involving eyewitness identification, informant testimony, or confessions by defendants who are young or mentally impaired (American Bar Association Criminal Justice Section, 2006). In addition, defense attorneys should be required to "investigate circumstances indicating innocence regardless of the client's admissions or statements of facts constituting guilt or the client's stated desire to plead guilty or dispose of the case without trial" (American Bar Association Criminal Justice Section, 2006, p. 80).

Yaroshefsky and Schaefer (2014) argue that in a world of increasingly sophisticated scientific evidence, adequate training and funding are especially important so that defenders can develop the necessary competence to handle cases involving forensic science evidence. They also suggest that courts should authorize defense experts "without delay or undue burden" on defenders whenever forensic science is involved in cases (Yaroshefsky & Schaefer, 2014, p. 136). Finally, they argue for programs designed to ensure that defenders receive training in the forensic sciences, beginning with their law school education.

Policies regarding the organization and funding of public defense systems vary considerably across the states (Worden et al., 2010/2011). Advocates argue that organizing and funding at the state-level, rather than leaving these functions to localities, are crucial to improving the quality of public defense. Several states have developed oversight entities to monitor the quality of indigent defense delivery. As one study noted, "To be successful, an oversight body needs to be independent from political and judicial influence and able to assure the quality of representation provided. Proper construction and implementation of a statewide oversight body requires time, careful planning, and political fortitude. It is worth the effort, though, as meaningful state oversight can greatly enhance indigent defense representation" (National Right to Counsel Committee, 2009, p. 148).

It is important that policy proposals are supported by evidence that the suggested reforms are necessary and effective. Recently, a group of scholars and practitioners convened at the annual meeting of the American Society of Criminology to discuss their respective research endeavors in the field of public defense. Some of the functions of defense research are "documenting inequity, evaluating policy options, system monitoring, and pursuing a scientific agenda" (Davies, 2014/2015, p. 1185). Perhaps, this emerging field of research will make us "smarter" (Davies, 2014/2015, p. 1192) about policies aimed at reducing the role of defense attorneys in contributing to wrongful convictions.

Conclusion

Abbe Smith and Monroe Freedman, two well-known criminal law professors (and defense attorneys) edited a fascinating volume of essays directed at addressing the question, "How can you represent those people?" (Smith & Freedman, 2013). Although "those people" refers to "guilty" clients, the collection of essays offers insight into the meaning of zealous advocacy on behalf of criminal defendants that has implications for the guilty, the innocent, and indeed, all of us. Freedman writes:

> In a free society, it is vital that there be a counter to the overwhelming power of government because it is a power that can be easily abused by those who wield that power, individuals who may be more interested in advancing their own ambitions, venting their own hatreds, and satisfying their own prejudices, than they are in respecting our rights and protecting society. In representing "those people," therefore, even those who have committed the worst crimes against other people and against society, the criminal defense lawyer serves each of us by curbing official abuse and preserving the fundamental values of free society (Freedman, 2013, p. 78).

For some defenders, especially those with high caseloads and low resources, it may be difficult to keep this lofty ideal in mind given the daily exigencies of high-volume criminal defense. Nevertheless, the consequences of forgetting could be dire.

Key Terms and Concepts

- **Indigent defendants**: criminal defendants who are too poor to pay to hire their own defense attorney
- **Public defender offices**: government-financed offices in which criminal defense attorneys provide legal representation to indigents

- **Assigned-counsel system:** a method of providing indigent defense that involves the appointment of individual private attorneys to represent poor defendants
- **Contract system:** a method of providing indigent defense in which attorneys agree to a contract with the government to handle a certain number of criminal cases for a set fee
- **Misdemeanors:** lower-level criminal offenses (below felonies) that make up the majority of cases processed by the justice system
- **Caseload:** the number of cases for which a defense attorney has responsibility
- **"Meet and plead" disposition:** refers to a situation in which a case is resolved at the first court hearing, with little or no preparation by the defense attorney
- **Felony:** a more serious criminal offense (above misdemeanors), including most violent offenses, that are usually punishable by a year or more of imprisonment
- **Capital charge:** a charged crime for which the death penalty is a possible punishment
- **_Gideon v. Wainwright_:** a 1963 case in which the Supreme Court ruled that defendants charged with a felony and who cannot afford an attorney have the right to be represented at trial by court-appointed counsel
- **Ineffective assistance of counsel:** representation by a criminal defense lawyer that falls below constitutionally acceptable standards
- **_Strickland_ standard:** from _Strickland v. Washington_, provides a two-part test (based on deficient performance and demonstrated prejudice) for evaluating claims of ineffective assistance of criminal defense counsel

Discussion Questions

1. If you were a defense attorney, and you knew or suspected that your client was innocent, would you handle the case any differently than if you knew or suspected that your client was guilty? Why?

2. Should indigent defendants be provided with independent expert witnesses at the government's expense? Why or why not?

3. Some have argued that the _Strickland_ test for ineffective assistance of counsel sets the bar too low for acceptable representation. Do you agree or disagree? What standard would you propose?

4. Imagine you were writing a letter to your senator urging increased funding for public defense. What arguments would you make?

5. If you were a defense attorney and your client admitted to you, in confidence, to having committed the crime for which an innocent person was convicted and is being punished, what would you do: reveal this information, remain silent, or take some other course of action?

References

Acker, J. R. (2017). Taking stock of innocence: Movements, mountains, and wrongful convictions. *Journal of Contemporary Criminal Justice, 33*, 8–25.

Acker, J. R., & Brody, D. C. (2013). *Criminal procedure: A contemporary perspective* (3d ed.). Jones & Bartlett Learning.

Ake v. Oklahoma, 470 U.S. 68 (1985).

Alabama v. Shelton, 535 U.S. 654 (2002).

Allen, J. M. (2009). Free for all a free for all: The Supreme Court's abdication of duty in failing to establish standards for indigent defense. *Law & Inequality, 27*, 365–411.

American Bar Association. (2015). *Criminal justice standards for the defense function* (4th ed.). https://www.americanbar.org/groups/criminal_justice/standards/DefenseFunctionFourthEdition.html#1.2.

American Bar Association. (2016). *Model rules of professional conduct.* https://www.americanbar.org/groups/professional_responsibility/publications/model_rules_of_professional_conduct/rule_1_1_competence.html.

American Bar Association Criminal Justice Section. (2006). *Achieving justice: Freeing the innocent, convicting the guilty.* American Bar Association.

American Bar Association Standing Committee on Legal Aid and Indigent Defendants. (2004). *Gideon's broken promise: America's continuing quest for equal justice.* American Bar Association. http://www.americanbar.org/content/dam/aba/administrative/legal_aid_indigent_defendants/ls_sclaid_def_bp_right_to_counsel_in_criminal_proceedings.authcheckdam.pdf.

Argersinger v. Hamlin, 407 U.S. 25 (1972).

Armstrong, K. (2014, December 10). What can you do with a drunken lawyer? The Marshall Project. https://www.themarshallproject.org/2014/12/10/what-can-you-do-with-a-drunken-lawyer#.HsOhbumm6.

Bailey, C. (2002). *Ake v. Oklahoma* and an indigent defendant's "right" to an expert witness: A promise denied or imagined? *William & Mary Bill of Rights Journal, 10*, 401–458.

Boruchowitz, R. C., Brink, M. N., & Dimino, M. (2009). *Minor crimes, massive waste: The terrible toll of America's broken misdemeanor courts.* National Association of Criminal Defense Lawyers.

Buskey, B., & Lucas, L. S. (2017). Keeping *Gideon's* promise: Using equal protection to address the denial of counsel in misdemeanor cases. *Fordham Law Review, 85,* 2299–2339.

Center on Wrongful Convictions. (n.d.). Alton Logan. Bluhm Legal Clinic, Pritzker School of Law, Northwestern University. https://www.law.northwestern.edu/ legalclinic/wrongfulconvictions/exonerations/il/alton-logan.html.

Clapman, A. (2011). Petty offenses, drastic consequences: Toward a Sixth Amendment right to counsel for noncitizen defendants facing deportation. *Cardozo Law Review, 33,* 585–618.

Davies, A. L. B. (2014/2015). How do we "do data" in public defense? *Albany Law Review, 78,* 1179–1192.

Death Penalty Information Center. (n.d.). Innocence database: Anthony Hinton. https://deathpenaltyinfo.org/policy-issues/innocence-database?q=hinton.

Douglas v. California, 373 U.S. 353 (1963).

Dripps, D. A. (2012). Up from *Gideon. Texas Tech Law Review, 45,* 113–132.

Freedman, M. H. (2013). Why it's essential to represent "those people." In A. Smith & M. H. Freedman (Eds.), *How can you represent those people?* Palgrave Macmillan.

Garrett, B. L. (2011). *Convicting the innocent: Where criminal prosecutions go wrong.* Harvard University Press.

Garrett, B. L. (2016). Constitutional regulation of forensic evidence. *Washington & Lee Law Review, 73,* 1147–1187.

Giannelli, P. C. (2004). *Ake v. Oklahoma*: The right to expert assistance in a post-*Daubert*, post-DNA world. *Cornell Law Review, 89,* 1305–1419.

Giannelli, P. C. (2011). *Daubert* and forensic science: The pitfalls of law enforcement control of scientific research. *University of Illinois Law Review, 2011,* 53–90.

Gideon v. Wainwright, 372 U.S. 335 (1963).

Gilbert, L. (2013). Sharpening the tools of an adequate defense: Providing for the appointment of experts for indigent defendants in child death cases under *Ake v. Oklahoma. San Diego Law Review, 50,* 469–515.

Gould, J. B., Carrano, J., Leo, R. A., & Hail-Jares, K. (2014). Predicting erroneous convictions. *Iowa Law Review, 99,* 471–522.

Greeley, T. J. (2011). The plight of indigent defendants in a computer-based age: Maintaining the adversarial system by granting indigent defendants access to computer experts. *Virginia Journal of Law & Technology, 16,* 400–429.

Green, B. A. (2016). Access to criminal justice: Where are the prosecutors? *Texas A&M Law Review, 3,* 515–535.

Griffin, L. K. (2016). Criminal adjudication, error correction, and hindsight blind spots. *Washington & Lee Law Review, 73,* 165–214.

Groendyke, E. (2007). *Ake v. Oklahoma*: Proposals for making the right a reality. *New York University Journal of Legislation & Public Policy, 10,* 367–393.

Gross, S. R. (2018). Errors in misdemeanor adjudication. *Boston University Law Review, 98,* 999–1011.

Hashimoto, E. J. (2007). The price of misdemeanor representation. *William & Mary Law Review, 49,* 461–513.

Hashimoto, E. (2016). Motivating constitutional compliance. *Florida Law Review, 68,* 1001–1042.

Hinton, A. R., & Hardin, L. L. (2018). *The sun does shine: How I found life and freedom on death row.* St. Martin's Press.

Hinton v. Alabama, 571 U.S. 263 (2014).

King, J. D. (2013). Beyond "Life and Liberty": The evolving right to counsel. *Harvard Civil Rights-Civil Liberties Law Review, 48,* 1–49.

King, N. J. (2014). Judicial review: Appeals and postconviction proceedings. In A. R. Redlich, J. R. Acker, R. J. Norris, & C. L. Bonventre (Eds.), *Examining wrongful convictions: Stepping back, moving forward* (pp. 217–236). Carolina Academic Press.

Lewis, A. (1964). *Gideon's trumpet.* Random House.

Liptak, A. (2008, May 4). When law prevents righting a wrong. *The New York Times.* https://www.nytimes.com/2008/05/04/weekinreview/04liptak.html.

Mallord, J. (2014). Putting plea bargaining on the record. *University of Pennsylvania Law Review, 162,* 683–718.

McWilliams v. Dunn, 137 S.Ct. 1790 (2017).

Metzger, P., & Ferguson, A. G. (2015). Defending data. *Southern California Law Review, 88,* 1057–1123.

Murray v. Giarratano, 492 U.S. 1 (1989).

Myers, R. E. II. (2018). The attorney-client privilege, client confessions and wrongful convictions: Immunity as a statutory solution. *Cornell Law Review Online, 104,* 101–120.

National Registry of Exonerations. (n.d.) *Browse cases: Detailed view* (filters: death sentence and inadequate legal defense). http://www.law.umich.edu/special/exoneration/Pages/detaillist.aspx?View={FAF6EDDB-5A68-4F8F-8A52-2C61F5BF9EA7}&FilterField1=Sentence&FilterValue1=Death&FilterField2=ILD&FilterValue2=8%5FILD.

National Registry of Exonerations. (2015). *Glenn Ford.* https://www.law.umich.edu/special/exoneration/Pages/casedetail.aspx?caseid=4395.

National Right to Counsel Committee. (2009). *Justice denied: America's continuing neglect of our constitutional right to counsel.* http://www.constitutionproject.org/wp-content/uploads/2012/10/139.pdf.

Nichols v. United States, 511 U.S. 738 (1994).

People v. Logan, 586 N.E.2d 679 (Ill. App. 1991).

Powell v. Alabama, 287 U.S. 45 (1932).

Porter v. McCollum, 558 U.S. 30 (2009).

Roberts, J. (2011). Why misdemeanors matter: Defining effective advocacy in the lower criminal courts. *U.C. Davis Law Review, 45*, 277–372.

Rompilla v. Beard, 545 U.S. 374 (2005).

Ross v. Moffitt, 417 U.S. 600 (1974).

Rowe, G. (2015). Potential expansion, or modification, to the permissive exceptions of Model Rule 1.6: Client-lawyer confidentiality in criminal law and "the gap." *Journal of the Legal Profession, 39*, 291–302.

Scott v. Illinois, 440 U.S. 367 (1979).

Smith, A., & Freedman, M. H. (Eds.). (2013). *How can you represent those people?* Palgrave Macmillan.

Smith, S. F. (2009). Taking *Strickland* claims seriously. *Marquette Law Review, 93*, 515–544.

Strickland v. Washington, 466 U.S. 668 (1984).

Stevenson, M., & Mayson, S. (2018). The scale of misdemeanor justice. *Boston University Law Review, 98*, 731–777.

Strutin, K. (2011). Preserving attorney-client confidentiality at the cost of another's innocence: A systemic approach. *Texas Wesleyan Law Review, 17*, 499–563.

West, E. M. (2010). *Court findings of ineffective assistance of counsel claims in post-conviction appeals among the first 255 DNA exoneration cases.* https://www.innocenceproject.org/wp-content/uploads/2016/05/Innocence_Project_IAC_Report.pdf.

Wiggins v. Smith, 539 U.S. 510 (2003).

Worden, A. P., Davies, A. L. B., & Brown, E. K. (2010/2011). A patchwork of policies: Justice, due process, and public defense across American states. *Albany Law Review, 74*, 1423–1463.   .

Worden, A. P., Davies, A. L. B., & Brown, E. K. (2014). Public defense in an age of innocence: The innocence paradigm and the challenges of representing the accused. In M. Zalman & J. Carrano (Eds.), *Wrongful convictions and criminal justice reform: Making justice* (pp. 209–225). Routledge.

Yaroshefsky, E., & Schaefer, L. (2014). Defense lawyering and wrongful convictions. In A. D. Redlich, J. R. Acker, R. J. Norris, & C. L. Bonventre (Eds.), *Examining wrongful convictions: Stepping back, moving forward* (pp. 123–140). Carolina Academic Press.

Chapter 10

No-Crime Cases

Learning Objectives

After reading this chapter, you should be able to:

- Understand what is meant by a "no-crime" wrongful conviction.
- Discuss the kinds of cases in which no-crime wrongful convictions occur, including shaken-baby syndrome and child sex abuse cases.
- Understand how police misconduct and faulty forensic field tests can lead to no-crime wrongful convictions.

Overview of No-Crime Cases

The prototypical wrongful conviction is one in which a crime is committed, but the wrong person — an innocent person — is erroneously arrested, convicted, and punished for the act. Most of the cases discussed thus far in this book have been such "wrong-person" cases. There is, however, another type of wrongful conviction case: one in which *no* crime is ever committed, but someone is convicted anyway. That is, an innocent person is convicted and punished for a "crime" that *never actually took place*.

Such "no-crime" wrongful convictions have a long history. In fact, the first known wrongful conviction in the United States, the case of Stephen and Jesse Boorn (discussed in chapter 1 of this book), was a no-crime case: the brothers were convicted in 1819 of killing their brother-in-law, Russell Colvin, who later turned up very much alive. It might be easy for some to dismiss such a case as an artifact of its time. Surely, one might think, a person could not be convicted today if no crime were actually committed.

While seemingly unbelievable, no-crime wrongful convictions are not particularly rare in the modern criminal justice system. The National Registry of Exonerations defines a "no-crime" case as one in which: "The exoneree was convicted of a crime that did not occur, either because an accident or a suicide was mistaken for a crime, or because the exoneree was accused of a fabricated crime that never happened" (National Registry of Exonerations, n.d.). When the NRE published its first report in 2012, less than 15% of exonerations occurred in no-crime cases (Gross & Shaffer, 2012). As of March 2021, more than one-third of NRE cases (1,022 of 2,755) are categorized as no-crime cases. Remarkably, nearly three out of every four women exonerated since 1989 (73%) were convicted of crimes that never happened (Innocence Project, 2021). This startling proportion of no-crime cases is explained, in part, by the high incidence (roughly 40%) of these exoneration cases that involve women who were convicted of harming children or other loved ones in their care (Innocence Project, 2021), a topic we discuss in more detail later. Many no-crime exoneration cases involved drug-related charges, although these are far from the only cases represented. They run the gamut of crime types including arson, assault, child sex abuse, forgery, fraud, gun crimes, burglary, robbery, murder, and more. The Scottsboro Boys cases, which we discussed in chapter 1, involved false accusations of rape when no such crimes occurred.

The factors that are known to contribute to no-crime wrongful convictions overlap with those discussed throughout this book: forensic errors, false accusations, police and prosecutorial misconduct, poor defense lawyering, and the like (Henry, 2020). However, the prevalence of contributing factors among no-crime cases does differ somewhat from what is found in exonerations more broadly. According to the NRE, perjury or false accusation is the most common factor found across all exonerations (60%), and the same is true of no-crime cases (62%). However, other contributors are found less often in no-crime cases. For instance, official misconduct is present in nearly 55% of all exonerations but only 43% of no-crime exonerations. An even greater disparity is found with false confessions (12% in all exonerations vs. 5% in no-crime cases) and mistaken witness identification (28% vs. 0.3%). This makes some sense. If no crime is committed, we should expect few witnesses generally and hence fewer mistaken eyewitnesses, and one result may be that the police have less leverage to elicit a false confession.

How, then, are innocent people convicted of crimes that never occurred? Perhaps the best way to understand this phenomenon is through illustrative case studies. Below, we describe no-crime cases of several types, highlighting the variety of ways such wrongful convictions can occur.[1]

No-Crime Murder Convictions

Even in the modern justice system, people are occasionally convicted of murder when the alleged victim was, in fact, not killed. However, unlike the Boorn brothers' case already discussed, most no-crime wrongful murder convictions do not involve a victim who miraculously turns up alive. Instead, they tend to involve issues such as miscategorized suicides, shoddy arson investigations, the accidental or naturally caused deaths of children and infants, and rejected claims of self-defense.

Murder or Suicide?
The Case of Cesar Munoz

Magdaliz Rosario was killed by a gunshot wound to the head on September 8, 1997. She was in the bedroom of the Chicago, Illinois, apartment she shared with her common-law husband, Cesar Munoz, and another man named John Flores. Earlier that day, Flores had gone with Rosario to the security company where he worked so she could apply for a job, and she was hired on the spot. Munoz reported that he was annoyed with Rosario because she had left him to care for their children, so he drove with them to the business where she was interviewing. When they returned home, Munoz said they put two of the children to bed, and Rosario prepared a bath for the third. Then, Munoz said, Rosario went into their bedroom and locked the door, and he heard a gunshot. He tried opening the door lock with a nail and when he was unable to do so, he broke the door down. After Munoz screamed for help, Munoz's father entered the room while Munoz was dragging Rosario across the apartment to the stairs. Munoz said he had tossed the gun out of an open window and into a trash can, where police found the weapon under more than a foot of garbage. Munoz had two spots of blood on his shirt where he had seemingly cradled Rosario, and there was no other blood evidence to place him near her at the time of the shooting (Associated Press, 2013). Flores reported to the police that he and Rosario were having an affair. Munoz, he said, was jealous, and Rosario was unhappy with her relationship.

---

1. Unless otherwise noted, information about the cases was collected from the case profiles on the website of the National Registry of Exonerations.

Munoz was charged with first-degree murder. After his first trial ended in a mistrial, he was tried a second time in November 2000. Several witnesses testified against Munoz. Flores testified regarding his affair with Rosario and said she did not seem suicidal. The detectives testified to Munoz's statements, said that the gun was found buried in the trash can, rather than on top as would be expected, and that the bedroom door had not been locked as Munoz reported. A ballistics expert linked the fatal bullet to the gun, and a crime lab analyst found gun powder residue on Rosario's left hand, although testing on Munoz was inconclusive. Finally, a pathologist testified that the wound was from close contact, but was indicative of a homicide rather than a suicide.

For the defense, Munoz's brother testified that he heard Munoz scream for help and shout, "She shot herself!" He ran upstairs, saw Rosario on the floor and Munoz standing nearby, and then ran back down to call 911. Munoz's cousin also rushed to the apartment after hearing the screams and said he was told that Rosario shot herself. Munoz also testified on his own behalf. He said that after they returned home, Rosario went to the bedroom and was sobbing. She then prepared the bath for their third child, went to the bedroom, and slammed the door. He could not get in, but peeked through a crack and saw Rosario get the pistol out of the dresser. Munoz said he then heard the gunshot and broke the door down. He also admitted that he had reported to detectives that he struggled with Rosario over the gun, but said that was untrue. The defense also wanted to introduce testimony from a friend of Rosario's who reported that she had been suicidal a week before she died, and from a pathologist who would follow up with a report that the death was a suicide, but the friend's testimony was barred by the judge and the pathologist did not testify.

Munoz was convicted and sentenced to 45 years in prison. His conviction was reversed in 2004, but he was again convicted at his third trial. At that trial, a detective testified that he believed Munoz's story was a lie, and the prosecution further presented evidence that Munoz's jealousy about Rosario's affair was his motivation for killing her.

The conviction was again overturned in 2010 and for his fourth trial, Munoz decided on a bench trial—to have his case decided by a judge, rather than a jury. The defense introduced several new key pieces of evidence. First, a locksmith had examined photographs of the door and reported that it had been locked and it looked like it was scratched with a nail, as Munoz said. A child psychologist testified about Rosario's abandonment by her mother and the related depression she experienced. Finally, the defense introduced testimony about the gun powder residue on her left hand, which suggested that, although Rosario was right-handed, she had held the gun in her left hand and pulled the trigger with her right thumb.

On June 12, 2013—16 years after Rosario's death—Munoz was acquitted by Judge Rosemary Higgins. Although Munoz's innocence may not be as crystal clear as some of the other individuals we have discussed, his acquittal at retrial means that he was formally exonerated. At the very least, there is a clear lack of tangible evidence that Rosario's death was a homicide, let alone that it was committed by Munoz.

Death by Arson:
The Case of Han Tak Lee

When a cabin fire broke out at a camp in Halifax, Pennsylvania, on July 29, 1989, 20-year-old Ji Yun Lee was killed. Arson investigators reported that the fire was set intentionally. The victim's father, Han Tak Lee, was arrested a week later, after investigators said he made inconsistent statements about his rescue efforts. He went to trial in September 1990.

Three key witnesses testified for the prosecution: an expert on the origins and causes of fires, the investigating fire marshal, and a crime lab chemist. Their testimony suggested a number of reasons to believe the fire was the result of **arson**. The fire seemingly burned at an exceptionally high temperature, which suggested the use of an accelerant. They also identified what they believed was the point of ignition, based on the appearance of "crazed glass," or a series of cracks that were believed to be caused by a particularly hot fire. The collapse of furniture and bed springs also suggested an extremely hot fire, and chemical analysis apparently showed the use of fuel oil and another accelerant, such as gasoline, although the specific accelerant was not identified.

The defense consulted an arson expert who concluded that the fire appeared to be an accident, rather than a case of arson. However, he could not identify the cause of the fire, so the defense instead argued at trial that Ji Yun committed suicide by setting the fire herself. Lee testified that he woke up and left the cabin after smelling smoke and hearing electrical wires burning. He went back inside but could not find his daughter, and was forced to leave because of the smoke and flames.

Lee was convicted in September 1990 of arson and first-degree murder, and was sentenced to life without parole. At a hearing on a motion to vacate the conviction, an affidavit from arson expert John Lentini suggested that the original investigators had relied on outdated science to determine the cause of the fire, but the motion was denied. A later motion for a new trial, supported by Lentini's conclusion that the fire was accidental, requested the prosecution's lab reports and data, but it was also denied.

Eventually, in 2008, Lee filed a petition for a writ of habeas corpus. Lentini produced a 46-page report that discredited the state's arson evidence. For example, he noted that the "crazed glass" pattern is not an indication of an ignition point, but rather is usually produced when hot glass is rapidly cooled (such as being sprayed with a hose). Lentini "unequivocally" concluded that the state's evidence pointed to an accidental fire, not arson. The petition was denied in federal district court, but that ruling was overturned by a federal appellate court in 2011, which directed the lower court to hold a hearing and consider evidence in support of the habeas petition. A hearing was held in 2014, and Lee's convictions were vacated in August due to the lack of credible evidence that the fire was the result of arson. The ruling was upheld on appeal, and the prosecution did not pursue a retrial.

Lee's case does not stand alone as a questionable arson conviction that was later overturned based on new scientific knowledge. In recent years, progress in fire science has cast doubt on a number of arson convictions, which were based largely on outdated and unsubstantiated investigative techniques. How many of these cases involve wrongful convictions, we do not know. However, we do know that many of them involved accidental fires that were miscategorized, and the doubt seems substantial enough to warrant a reconsideration of many others.

Key Case: Cameron Todd Willingham

In December 1991, a house fire killed three young girls in Corsicana, Texas. Their father, Cameron Todd Willingham, escaped the blaze. Suspicion was cast on Willingham, with evidence that included neighbors' reports of his actions at the time of the fire and in the days after, a jailhouse informant who claimed that Willingham confessed to the crime, and, perhaps most importantly, an investigation that supposedly found indicators of arson. Willingham was convicted and sentenced to death in October 1992. Later analysis by independent fire scientists identified a variety of errors with the initial investigation, concluding that there was no factual basis for concluding that the fire was an arson, but rather that the evidence pointed toward an accidental fire. Despite the serious doubts about his guilt, Willingham was executed in 2004. His case was at the center of the national death penalty debate, raising questions about whether Texas executed an innocent man.

- *Death by Fire* (2010) — a PBS FRONTLINE documentary produced and directed by Jessie Deeter about the Willingham case.

> - *Trial by Fire: Did Texas Execute an Innocent Man?* (2009)—a full-length feature article in *The New Yorker* written by David Grann that provides an in-depth discussion and analysis of the Willingham case.
>
> - *Trial by Fire* (2018)—a feature film starring Laura Dern and Jack O'Connell about the Willingham case, with a focus on the relationship between him and Elizabeth Gilbert, a writer who helped bring attention to the case.

Infanticide:
The Case of Sabrina Butler

On April 29, 1989, 18-year-old Sabrina Butler returned from a short jog and found that her nine-month-old son, Walter Dean, had stopped breathing. She and others in her apartment complex attempted CPR to revive the child, but were unsuccessful. She rushed Walter to the hospital where he died shortly thereafter. Hospital staff believed that the baby had been abused and had internal injuries, and suspicion fell on Butler. She claimed that any injuries were the result of the attempted CPR, admitting that she and others had tried adult CPR techniques on the child. Butler was questioned at the hospital and again at the police station (Westervelt & Cook, 2012). Over the course of several hours, Butler told multiple versions of events. Eventually, she signed a statement that she had punched the baby.

At trial, the prosecution focused on Butler's statement and an autopsy showing that the baby had internal injuries and an internal infection that takes at least an hour to appear. The defense did not call any witnesses, but instead tried to argue that the injuries were the result of the CPR attempts. Medical experts testified that the injuries could not be the result of failed CPR methods (Westervelt & Cook, 2012). The prosecutor also claimed repeatedly that Butler's decision not to testify was evidence of her guilt. She was convicted on March 14, 1990, and sentenced to death.

Butler's conviction was overturned in August 1992 by the Mississippi Supreme Court due to the prosecutor's comments about her decision not to testify. Her defense attorney requested a change of venue, which was granted, but she was held for three years awaiting her retrial. At her second trial in December 1995, several neighbors testified that both Butler and a neighbor had attempted CPR on the child, and a medical expert testified that the infant's injuries, in fact, could have been caused by those CPR methods. The original physician who had performed the autopsy also testified that his work was not as thorough as it should have been.

The jury deliberated only briefly before acquitting Sabrina Butler on December 17, 1995. She was the first female death row exoneree, but is certainly not the only woman to be erroneously convicted of causing the death of a child.

Shaken Baby Syndrome:
The Case of Brandy Briggs

Brandy Briggs encountered a parent's worst nightmare on May 5, 1999: she found her two-month-old child, Daniel, unconscious in their Highlands, Texas, home. His body was limp, and he seemed to be barely breathing. The boy was rushed to the hospital but died four days later.

Forensic pathologist Patricia Moore performed the autopsy and determined the cause of death was craniocerebral trauma and reported that it was a case of "**shaken baby syndrome**" ("SBS"). This term (along with "abusive head trauma") refers to a "severe form of physical child abuse that results in an injury to the brain of an infant or toddler" (Center for Disease Control, n.d.). Three major symptoms are used to diagnose SBS: retinal hemorrhaging, which occurs when the blood vessels in a child's brain break, causing bleeding in the back of the eyes; subdural hematoma, or the tearing of the veins and nerve cells that bridge the brain's surface and the cerebral cortex; and brain swelling, which can change the shape of the brain and cause the loss of neurons (Cenziper, 2015; Szalavitz, 2012). Based on Dr. Moore's autopsy report, Briggs was charged with first-degree felony injury to a child.

Briggs maintained her innocence. However, according to her defense attorney, she was unable to afford to pay for expert witnesses who could refute Dr. Moore's testimony, and on the day before the trial, Briggs pled guilty to child endangerment. She was sentenced to 17 years in prison, although she said that her attorney told her she would get a probation sentence.

After her motion for a new trial was denied, Briggs's appellate attorneys had two pediatricians review Daniel's death. Both concluded that his death was not a result of SBS, but rather was due to complications from a urinary tract infection that he contracted shortly after birth. Furthermore, the chief medical examiner from Harris County, Texas, was critical of Dr. Moore's report, and a new medical examiner, Louis Sanchez, reviewed her work on the case. Dr. Sanchez found no evidence of abuse; instead, he reported that hospital personnel accidentally inserted the breathing tube into Daniel's stomach instead of his lung and concluded that the cause of death was asphyxia.

Based on the new evidence, Briggs's petition for a writ of habeas corpus was granted in December 2005, and her conviction was vacated. She was released on bail on Christmas Eve, and in September 2006 all charges were dropped.

Briggs is not the only caretaker to be exonerated in a shaken baby syndrome case. At least eight other women have been exonerated in cases where their convictions were based on evidence including testimony about shaken baby syndrome (Innocence Project, 2021). The science behind shaky baby syndrome has been challenged for some time and has emerged as a controversial topic in the courtroom. The three symptoms described above — retinal hemorrhaging, brain hemorrhaging, and brain swelling — were used by doctors to diagnose SBS for decades. It was long believed that SBS was the sole explanation for that combination of symptoms and that SBS victims became unresponsive quickly. Thus, SBS diagnoses not only helped doctors explain injuries to infants and children, but assisted prosecutors by suggesting that the last person to handle the child was responsible for their death. However, researchers have questioned whether shaking can even produce these symptoms, and other types of accidents, diseases, and genetic disorders have been found to generate the same symptoms (Bazelon, 2011; Cenziper, 2015; Szalavitz, 2012).

Shaken baby syndrome is therefore difficult to diagnose, particularly if the classic triad of symptoms are the only signs. Of course, this is not to say that all persons convicted of harming children by causing SBS are innocent. However, modern developments in medical research have called into question many convictions that rested solely on long-held beliefs about SBS that may simply not be true.

Wrongful Convictions in Popular Culture: Shaken Baby Syndrome

- *The Syndrome* (2016) — In this documentary, filmmaker Meryl Goldsmith and investigative journalist Susan Goldsmith follow doctors, scientists, and legal scholars in their work to disprove shaken baby syndrome.

- *Shaken Science* (2015) — Investigative journalists at the *Washington Post* collaborated with journalists at Northwestern University's Medill Justice Project to produce this multi-part series that examines the dispute surrounding shaken baby syndrome. The series includes an examination of 1,800 cases and includes interviews with doctors, defendants, and more.

No-Crime Drug Convictions

Not all no-crime wrongful convictions involve homicide. Perhaps the most widely reported no-crime cases in recent years involved convictions for various drug crimes. Although exonerations occur in cases involving everyday drug convictions, multiple scandals involving major drug busts have been reported widely. For example, in 1999, police in Tulia, Texas, arrested and charged more than 40 people for dealing drugs. Most were Black; in fact, those arrested made up 20% of the town's adult Black population. They included some people who were clearly innocent, some from families with no known legal issues, and others who were known drug users (Mosle, 2005). The arrests were based on information from one person, an undercover police officer named Tom Coleman. Despite a conspicuous lack of evidence to corroborate his claims, 38 of the people were convicted, many of whom pled guilty. After evidence of Coleman's questionable testimony was reviewed in 2003, a judge vacated all of the convictions, and Texas governor Rick Perry authorized the release of the remaining defendants.

The Tulia case received national media attention, but it does not rest alone. Drug-related wrongful convictions can occur in several ways. Some are broad scandals, such as occurred in Tulia, while others may involve isolated misconduct or faulty practices spread over many years.

Planted Evidence:
The Westbrooks-Cruz Case

In December 2005, two men were arrested in Brooklyn, New York, and charged with selling drugs to an undercover police officer. Lashane Westbrooks had stopped on his way to a store to talk to Jerome Cruz when the officers approached. Allegedly, they had sold drugs to Sean Johnstone, an undercover officer who was a member of the Brooklyn South Narcotics Unit.

At trial, Johnstone and the arresting officers testified against Westbrooks and Cruz. Both men were convicted in October 2007; the 29-year-old Westbrooks was sentenced to three-and-a-half years in prison while the 24-year-old Cruz was sentenced to one year.

Shortly after the Westbrooks-Cruz case was seemingly settled, Johnstone ran into trouble. A department recording from September was revealed in which Johnstone bragged about how he and fellow officer Julio Alvarez would keep drugs on them to give to informants. They had reported securing 17 Ziploc bags of cocaine from a suspect in Coney Island, when in fact they had retrieved 11 additional bags that were used to pay off informants. The recording also captured the officers using profanity and racial slurs (Gendar & Sherman, 2008). After this revelation about Johnstone's actions, the district attorney's office filed a motion to vacate Westbrooks's and Cruz's convictions in November 2007. Both cases were dismissed, and the men were released.

The next month, Johnstone and Alvarez were charged as a larger scandal was uncovered involving other Brooklyn police officers, some of whom were caught stealing drugs and money (Gendar & Sherman, 2008). Several officers, including Johnstone, were convicted of misconduct. One officer even testified that planting drugs on defendants was common practice. The scandal led to the dismissal of more than 150 pending cases and reinvestigations of many others (Baker, 2008; Gendar & Sherman, 2008).

Faulty Field Tests: Harris County Drug Cases

Harris County, Texas, (which includes Houston and environs) leads the United States in known wrongful convictions; in 2016 alone, the county was the origin of 48 of the state's 58 exonerations (Samuels, 2017). This incredible number is due to a spate of drug convictions that were based on substance tests performed in the field, which were later shown to be inaccurate in post-conviction lab tests. More than one-third of these drug convictions were misdemeanors, and they disproportionately involved African Americans, who constituted 20% of Harris County's population but 62% of drug case exonerees (Gross et al., 2017).

Over the past few years, there have been hundreds of wrongful convictions in drug possession cases in Harris County—298 cases as of July 2016, per an audit—and many have resulted in exonerations (Olsen & Hassan, 2016). After field testing suggested that people were in possession of illegal narcotics, many pled guilty (see chapter 5 of this volume for more on false guilty pleas), thinking it was their best option after being arrested, charged, and held in jail (Gross et al., 2017). Fortunately, Harris County tests materials from drug defendants even after they plead guilty, and in hundreds of cases, those tests revealed that the "narcotics" that were found in the possession of these defendants were not actually illegal drugs.

For instance, 29-year-old Danny Sweat was arrested in August 2009 after a field test on substances he was carrying tested positive for cocaine. He pled guilty just days later and was sentenced to 60 days in jail. In 2015, the Conviction Integrity Unit of the Harris County District Attorney's Office was informed that a lab test performed on the evidence in 2010 found no illegal drugs. Prosecutors informed Sweat's defense attorney, the conviction was vacated in September 2015, and the charges were dismissed in October. Similar circumstances led to the convictions and exonerations of Dequinncy Tyson, who pled guilty and was sentenced to 30 days in jail in 2012 after field tests showed he was in possession of methamphetamine, and Amber Upchurch, who pled guilty after tests indicated she was carrying controlled anti-anxiety medications. In both cases, lab tests later showed no illegal substances; Tyson was exonerated in 2015 and Upchurch in 2016.

The exonerations of Sweat, Tyson, Upchurch, and the hundreds of other defendants who were wrongly convicted of drug crimes in Harris County were largely due to the laudable policy which had been adopted there of testing evidence after the entry of guilty pleas. This is a rare practice, but it provides evidence about how easily wrongful convictions can occur. Thousands are convicted across the country for similar drug crimes. If testing evidence after guilty pleas were standard practice, it is likely that many, many more wrongful convictions would be unearthed.

No-Crime Child Sex Abuse Convictions

Widespread scandals and convictions in no-crime cases are not restricted to drug cases. In the 1980s and 1990s, a wave of child sex abuse prosecutions swept across the United States. The media and public frenzy over children's claims of being tortured and abused led to several group prosecutions, but also established a context in which law enforcement intensively focused on individual claims of child sexual abuse.

The Howard Dudley Case

In October 1991, Amy Moore's babysitter went to the girl's mother with a disturbing revelation: the nine-year-old girl reported that she had been abused by her father, Howard Dudley, multiple times, including that she had been raped the previous month. Amy allegedly told her babysitter that her father was "nasty," and when an explanation was sought, Amy revealed that he had "humped" her and "had S-E-X" with her.

Police in Kinston, North Carolina, along with the Department of Social Services, began an investigation. Dudley had no criminal record, and investigators found no evidence to corroborate Amy's story, but he was ordered not to have contact with Amy or her mother. A few months later, in February 1992, Dudley was indicted on charges of first-degree sexual offense and taking indecent liberties with a minor. By that time, he was married to another woman and had two other children.

Dudley refused an offer to plead guilty, saying that he would not admit to any wrongdoing because he was innocent (Neff, 2016b). At trial, no physical evidence pointed to Dudley's guilt, but the prosecution presented several witnesses, including Amy, her mother, the babysitter, and the lead investigator on the case. The accounts presented were inconsistent. Amy appeared confused while testifying, and the prosecutor corrected her several times. Dudley's defense attorney never objected to this practice, one of many inadequacies in his performance. The defense lawyer spent fewer than 30 hours working on the case, including the two days of trial. He never considered Amy's medical history nor consulted an independent medical expert. His defense was based on the testimony of a physician who had examined Amy at the prosecution's request. This doctor reported that he found no physical signs of abuse, but said that abuse was still possible and that children who were sexually abused often had normal exam results.

Dudley testified on his own behalf and denied the charges. He stated his belief that Amy had made the accusation in response to his disciplining her. Dudley's wife also testified, saying that they lived in a small mobile home and that she never heard anything suspicious during Amy's visits. Dudley was convicted on April 24, 1992, and sentenced to life in prison.

Shortly after the trial, Amy told another babysitter that she had made up the story. When the babysitter told Amy's mother, she became angry and Amy withdrew her recantation. Three motions were filed by Dudley's lawyers based on the original recantation, but all were dismissed. However, in 2005, a series of news reports about the case revealed exculpatory evidence that was never disclosed to Dudley's attorney. The evidence included a report from the juvenile court's guardian ad litem—the person appointed by the court to investigate and determine the needs of abused children and what is in their best interests—which concluded that Amy's story was false. When members of Duke University Law School's Wrongful Convictions Clinic investigated the case, they also found that police and social workers had improperly questioned Amy. They noted that in Amy's nine separate retellings of the abuse, her stories were inconsistent and implausible. Examinations of Amy showed that she was intellectually disabled—her IQ tested at 68—and that she suffered from depression, psychotic episodes, and an anxiety disorder. Owing to these conditions, she was highly suggestible, thus casting doubt on the reliability of her responses to leading questions (Neff, 2016b).

At a hearing in March 2016, Dudley again proclaimed his innocence. Expert witnesses testified regarding Amy's psychological and cognitive deficits, and Amy, now 33 years old, testified that she had fabricated the allegations against her father. She said she was raped when she was younger by two different men, but not by her father (Neff, 2016a). Dudley's lawyers also presented information from the Social Services reports that suggested that Dudley was innocent and that his alleged misconduct could not possibly have occurred. This information was never disclosed to his defense lawyer. With this new evidence presented and Amy's recantation considered credible, Dudley's convictions were vacated on March 2, 2016. He was released from prison after nearly 24 years. The prosecution dismissed the charges two months later.

Dudley's case occurred against the backdrop of several large child sex abuse scandals in the 1980s and 1990s, one of which took place in North Carolina at the same time. Robert Kelly, the owner of a day care center, was convicted of 99 counts of abusing children following an eight-month long trial. He was given 12 life sentences in April 1992. Like many of the child sex abuse scandals of the era, this case involved fantastical claims about children being tortured and abused in strange ways. Kelly's conviction was set aside in 1995, and he was exonerated subsequently. In all, more than 50 people were convicted in scandals involving claims of child sexual abuse. One of the largest occurred in Kern County, California.

Kern County Convictions

The child sex abuse scandal in Kern County, California, was one of the earliest and largest of several such cases that occurred in the 1980s and 1990s. Between 1984 and 1986, at least 30 people in the county were convicted of child sex abuse and sentenced to incarceration terms, while another 8 accepted plea deals to avoid imprisonment. The claims included satanic rituals of drinking blood, molestation, torture, and the murder and dismemberment of 27 infants (Burke, 2009; Corwin, 1990). From 1991 through 2008, at least 21 of those people were exonerated.

Investigations of sexual abuse were a high priority in Kern County in the 1980s. Most of the cases were group prosecutions involving multiple defendants. In one of them, several members of the Cox family were accused of running a child sex abuse ring. The case began when 12-year-old Teresa Modahl told her father that her uncles, Anthony and Leroy Cox, had molested her. When authorities questioned Teresa and her siblings, they accused their uncles of molestation, rape, and sodomy. The children were placed into shelter care and continually questioned by county authorities, who used suggestive interview techniques. The stories eventually changed to include accusations against their parents, grandparents, and other family members. The accusations led to the arrest of five people: Jeffrey Modahl, Ruth Taylor, Teresa Cox, Richard Cox, and Joanne Cox.

One of the children, Carla Jo Modahl, testified against each of the defendants. Before her testimony, prosecutors took her shopping for clothes and toys. Richard Cox and Ruth Taylor were the first defendants convicted following trial by a jury in 1985. Teresa Cox's trial and conviction followed. Jeffrey Modahl then chose a bench trial, but he was also convicted, in 1986.

The convictions of Richard Cox and Ruth Taylor were overturned on appeal, but both chose to accept a plea deal rather than risk a new trial. Teresa Cox was released on probation in 1990 and registered as a sex offender. Jeffrey Modahl's appeals and petitions for relief were denied. Joanne Cox died in prison following her conviction.

In 1997, Modahl's third habeas petition was granted after one of the accusers, Carla Jo Modahl, recanted her testimony for the second time. New evidence came to light that had never been disclosed to the defense: a medical exam which concluded that Carla Jo had never been sodomized, and a tape in which a social worker pressured one of the children, Teresa Modahl, to accept particular descriptions of sexual abuse. Based on this new evidence, a judge granted Jeffrey Modahl's petition. Jeffrey Modahl was released from prison in May 1999, and all charges were dropped.

Following his release, the other three living defendants filed petitions for writs of habeas corpus. They were all granted, charges were dropped, and their records were cleared. They later filed a lawsuit against Kern County and in 2003 received over $4 million. Many other defendants involved in the Kern sex abuse cases also sued; the last case was finally settled in March 2013 (Henry, 2013).

Wrongful Convictions in Popular Culture: Child Sex Abuse

- *Southwest of Salem: The Story of the San Antonio Four* (2016) — This documentary, directed by Deborah Esquenazi, tells the story of four Latina women who were wrongfully convicted and incarcerated for the rape of two young girls.

- *Indictment: The McMartin Trial* (1995) — A dramatic film, directed by Mick Jackson, that depicts the real-life case of the McMartin family's trial for child sex abuse.

Wrongful Convictions and Failed Affirmative Defenses

Defendants in criminal cases sometimes acknowledge that they engaged in conduct that normally is a crime, but raise an affirmative defense, in the form of justification or excuse, which they maintain should prevent their conviction. For example, while intentionally killing another person might ordinarily constitute murder or manslaughter, it would be *justified*, and entirely lawful, if it were a necessary act of self-defense against an unlawful, potentially lethal attack. And while it usually is a crime to point a gun at a bank teller and demand that she hand over a bag of money, a person who engages in such behavior while a terrorist has put a gun to her head and threatened to kill her, would be *excused* from criminal liability by asserting the defense of duress. For many types of affirmative defenses, defendants must ultimately persuade the judge or jury—typically by a preponderance of the evidence—that they qualify for the defense and thus should be found not guilty of committing a crime. We can easily envision cases in which defendants are convicted of crimes despite having a legitimate claim of self-defense, duress, or another affirmative defense (Acker & Wu, 2020). Yet in these cases, no crime actually was committed.

For instance, in 2011 Jacob Gentry was convicted of aggravated manslaughter and sentenced to 30 years in prison in New Jersey after the jury in his trial rejected his claim that he had killed another man in self-defense. His conviction was reversed on appeal, based in part on the trial judge's erroneous instructions to the jury on the law of self-defense. Gentry was re-tried in 2016 and was acquitted when the jury credited his self-defense claim. He spent four years in prison pursuant to the original conviction (Carlson, 2016; *State v. Gentry*, 2015).

Perhaps surprisingly, it is somewhat controversial whether individuals who were convicted of crimes after their affirmative defenses were rejected, but later are exonerated, are properly considered to be "factually innocent" and should be recognized as having been wrongfully convicted (Acker & Wu, 2020; Givelber, 1997, p. 1327; Risinger, 2007, p. 762). This classification can have considerable practical significance. Many states deny monetary compensation to individuals who were convicted of crimes in cases involving a failed affirmative defense, but later had their convictions vacated and were exonerated. Such wrongful convictions are often excluded from the category that qualify exonerees for compensation under state laws (Acker & Wu, 2020, pp. 157–166; see, e.g., *Marie v. State*, 2019).

Conclusion

When thinking about a *wrongful conviction*, many people envision a *wrong-person* case, where a crime is committed but the wrong person is arrested and convicted. However, as our knowledge of wrongful convictions expands, particularly beyond major crimes such as rape and murder, we are learning more about how people can be and sometimes are found guilty of a crime when no offense was actually committed. In this chapter, we have described a number of these convictions for different types of crimes. Some of these convictions involve serious, violent crimes, but many others — indeed, the majority of no-crime cases — involve non-violent crimes such as drug sale and possession.

The reforms needed to help reduce the occurrence of no-crime wrongful convictions are largely the same as those needed to minimize wrongful convictions generally (see generally Henry, 2020, pp. 173–195). In cases involving forensic evidence, caution must be taken to remain open to the possibility that the harm element of the alleged crime, for example, the death of a child, or the destruction of a building by fire, occurred by natural causes or by accident. Investigators, prosecutors, defense attorneys, and judges should be made aware of the cognitive biases that may lead them to prematurely assume that a crime has been committed in cases of this nature. There must also be a willingness to re-examine convictions supported by forensic testimony when evolving science or new technological developments cast doubt on the continued reliability of the original evidence. Early and open discovery would help defense attorneys and their clients arrive at more informed decisions before entering guilty pleas. Routine, complete testing of substances presumed to be illegal drugs should be conducted in all cases, including those resolved by guilty plea. Creating a culture among police that reinforces a respect for lawful behavior, combined with careful monitoring to deter and detect corrupt practices, would hopefully help avoid scandals such as the one that took place in Tulia, Texas. Recognizing the susceptibility of children to suggestive questioning, particularly in cases involving suspected sexual or physical abuse, could serve as another important check against potential wrongful convictions.

As with other types of wrongful convictions, the causes of no-crime wrongful convictions are complex and variable, and the essential measures needed to guard against and correct them are neither simple nor uniform. It is clear, however, that no-crime wrongful convictions occur with disturbing regularity and that they deserve more attention from innocence scholars and advocates.

Key Terms and Concepts

- **Arson:** a crime involving the deliberate setting of fire to property
- **Infanticide:** the crime of killing an infant
- **Shaken Baby Syndrome/Abusive Head Trauma:** a form of significant child abuse that leads to the brain injury of an infant or toddler

Discussion Questions

1. What proportion of exonerations involve "no-crime" cases? Why might it be especially difficult to identify wrongful convictions in cases where no crime occurred?

2. Why are crimes involving children disproportionately included among no-crime wrongful convictions?

3. How common do you think large-scale scandals like the ones in Tulia and Harris County, Texas, are? Is there a way to better "police the police" and protect against such situations?

4. Should there be consequences for officials—arson investigators, police officers, etc.—who make errors or engage in misconduct that leads to no-crime wrongful convictions?

References

Acker, J. R., & Wu, S. (2020). "I did it but ... I didn't": When rejected affirmative defenses produce wrongful convictions. *Nebraska Law Review, 98,* 101–167.

Associated Press. (2013, June 16). Chicago man acquitted of murder after fourth trial. *The Pantagraph.* http://www.pantagraph.com/news/state-and-regional/illinois/chicago-man-acquitted-of-murder-after-fourth-trial/article_542d6f1e-d6d1-11e2-9658-001a4bcf887a.html.

Baker, A. (2008, January 23). Drugs-for-information scandal shakes up New York police narcotics force. *The New York Times.* http://www.nytimes.com/2008/01/23/nyregion/23arrest.html.

Bazelon, E. (2011, February 2). Shaken-baby syndrome faces new questions in court. *New York Times Magazine.* http://www.nytimes.com/2011/02/06/magazine/06baby-t.html.

Burke, G. (2009, November 25). D.A. who wrongfully had dozens jailed to retire. *SF Gate.* http://www.sfgate.com/bayarea/article/D-A-who-wrongfully-had-dozens-jailed-to-retire-3210029.php.

Carlson, J. (2016, February 19). Gentry, who once faced 30 years, found not guilty on all counts. *New Jersey Herald.* https://www.njherald.com/article/20160219/NEWS/909012244.

Centers for Disease Control and Prevention. (n.d.). Preventing abusive head trauma in children. https://www.cdc.gov/violenceprevention/childmaltreatment/Abusive-Head-Trauma.html.

Cenziper, D. (2015, March 20). Shaken science: A disputed diagnosis imprisons parents. *Washington Post*. https://www.washingtonpost.com/graphics/investigations/shaken-baby-syndrome/.

Corwin, M. (1990, September 10). Court ruling forces new look at sex abuse case. *Los Angeles Times*. http://articles.latimes.com/1990-09-10/news/mn-278_1_molestation-abuse-case-investigators.

Gendar, A., & Sherman, W. (2008, January 27). 500 cases blown by narcotics cops. *Daily News*. http://www.nydailynews.com/news/crime/500-cases-blown-narcotics-cops-article-1.343387.

Givelber, D. (1997). Meaningless acquittal, meaningful convictions: Do we reliably acquit the innocent? *Rutgers Law Review, 49*, 1317–1396.

Gross, S. R., Possley, M., & Stephens, K. (2017). *Race and wrongful convictions in the United States. National Registry of Exonerations Report*. https://www.law.umich.edu/special/exoneration/Documents/Race_and_Wrongful_Convictions.pdf.

Gross, S. R., & Shaffer, M. (2012). *Exonerations in the United States, 1989–2012: Report by the National Registry of Exonerations*. https://www.law.umich.edu/special/exoneration/Documents/exonerations_us_1989_2012_full_report.pdf.

Henry, J. S. (2020). *Smoke but no fire: Convicting the innocent of crimes that never happened*. University of California Press.

Henry, L. (2013, March 25). Kern County settles last of molestation conviction suits. *Bakersfield Californian*. http://www.bakersfield.com/news/kern-county-settles-last-of-molestation-conviction-suits/article_49117483-79fe-5839-80c2-890937b88828.html.

The Innocence Project. (2021, March 1). 8 facts about incarcerated and wrongfully convicted women you should know. https://innocenceproject.org/women-wrongful-conviction-incarceration-facts-iwd2020/.

Marie v. State, 922 N.W.2d 733 (Neb. 2019).

Mosle, S. (2005, October 30). 'Tulia': The case of the Lone Star witness. *The New York Times*. http://www.nytimes.com/2005/10/30/books/review/tulia-the-case-of-the-lone-star-witness.html?_r=0.

National Registry of Exonerations. (n.d.). *Glossary*. https://www.law.umich.edu/special/exoneration/Pages/glossary.aspx.

Neff, J. (2016a, March 1). Howard Dudley's daughter says she lied about sexual assault. *News & Observer*. http://www.newsobserver.com/news/local/crime/article63342732.html.

Neff, J. (2016b, March 2). After 23 years in NC prison, Howard Dudley embraces his freedom. *News & Observer*. http://www.newsobserver.com/news/local/crime/article63564927.html.

Olsen, L., & Hassan, A. (2016, July 16). 298 wrongful drug convictions identified in ongoing audit. *Houston Chronicle.* http://www.houstonchronicle.com/news/houston-texas/houston/article/298-wrongful-drug-convictions-identified-in-8382474.php.

Risinger, D. M. (2007). Innocents convicted: An empirically justified factual wrongful conviction rate. *Journal of Criminal Law & Criminology, 97,* 761–806.

Samuels, A. (2017, March 7). Study finds Harris County leads nation in exonerations. *Texas Tribune.* https://www.texastribune.org/2017/03/07/report/.

State v. Gentry, 106 A.3d 552 (N.J. Super. Ct. App. Div. 2015).

Szalavitz, M. (2012, January 17). The shaky science of shaken baby syndrome. *Time.* http://healthland.time.com/2012/01/17/the-shaky-science-of-shaken-baby-syndrome/.

Westervelt, S. D., & Cook, K. J. (2012). *Life after death row: Exonerees' search for community and identity.* Rutgers University Press.

Chapter 11

Detecting and Correcting Miscarriages of Justice

Learning Objectives

After reading this chapter, you should be able to:

- Outline the stages of the appellate and post-conviction processes.
- Appreciate the limitations of appellate courts in correcting wrongful convictions.
- Understand the extent and limitations of state post-conviction review, federal habeas corpus, and executive clemency in addressing prisoners' claims of actual innocence.
- Appreciate the value of the proper preservation of evidence to post-conviction claims of innocence.

Case Study: The Norfolk Four

In 2017, Virginia Governor Terry McAuliffe gave absolute pardons to Danial Williams, Joseph Dick, Jr., Derek Tice, and Eric Williams (Jackman, 2017). The four men, U.S. Navy veterans who became known as the Norfolk Four, had been wrongly convicted of the 1997 rape and murder of a young woman, the wife of a Navy seaman, named Michelle Moore-Bosko (See Wells & Leo, 2008). All four men had falsely confessed to the crimes under harsh interrogations conducted by since-discredited Norfolk Police Department Detective Robert Glenn Ford. It was a long road from arrest to pardon for the four men. Along that road, there were many opportunities to detect and correct their wrongful convictions. Most notably, DNA testing excluded the four men and implicated another man, Omar Ballard, who confessed to committing the crime alone. These latter facts were known at the time of their trials. Yet, it took nearly 20 years for their innocence to be formally recognized and full corrective measures to be taken by the Commonwealth of Virginia. Throughout this chapter, we will return to the story of the Norfolk Four to illustrate the mechanisms through which erroneously convicted defendants attempt to secure their freedom and ultimately be relieved of responsibility for their wrongful convictions.

**Wrongful Convictions in Popular Culture:
Tales of the Exonerated ... and the Not-Exonerated**

- *Wrongful Conviction with Jason Flom*—a fascinating podcast, which began airing in 2016, features interviews with women and men who were exonerated after spending years in prison for crimes they did not commit.

- *The Wrong Carlos*—explore the website, watch the interviews, and read the book (2014)—all produced by Columbia Law professor James S. Liebman and the Columbia DeLuna Project. Then decide for yourself whether the state of Texas executed an innocent man.

The Courts

For innocent defendants convicted at trial, opportunities exist to detect and correct miscarriages of justice in the appellate and post-conviction process. In chapter 1, we provided an overview of the criminal process, including appeals and post-conviction remedies. We briefly outline the review process again here and describe it more fully below. After judgment is entered following a criminal trial, a convicted defendant will have a first appeal (usually as of right), which is taken in most states to an intermediate appellate court. If unsuccessful there, the defendant can ask the state high court to review the intermediate appellate court's decision. Thereafter, the unsuccessful defendant may request the U.S. Supreme Court to review the case via a petition for a writ of **certiorari**, but only if federal constitutional issues are involved in cases of individuals convicted of crimes in a state court. Petitions for writs of certiorari are rarely granted. Roughly 7,000 to 8,000 cert. petitions per year are filed with the U.S. Supreme Court, yet the Court typically only grants plenary review in about 80, or roughly 1% of the filings (U.S. Supreme Court, n.d.). If the Supreme Court refuses to hear the case, or if the defendant chooses not to file a petition for a writ of certiorari, the defendant may return to the state trial court for post-conviction proceedings, with another round of state court appeals, requests for discretionary review, and petition to the U.S. Supreme Court possible. Finally, if all these measures fail, the defendant may seek habeas corpus review of federal constitutional issues implicated in a state criminal conviction in a federal district court (trial court), with appeals possible to a federal court of appeals, followed again by a petition for writ of certiorari to the U.S. Supreme Court (Garrett, 2008).

Before beginning our discussion, we make three observations. First, although the process is primarily the same for innocent or guilty defendants convicted at trial, we focus here on the particular concerns of innocent defendants. Second, the United States has a federal system of government, and as such maintains both state and federal systems of criminal justice. States have the power to administer their justice systems in a manner they deem appropriate, as long as they do not violate federal constitutional mandates. Court systems and procedures vary widely across the states. In that regard, we use the term, "the process" loosely to capture the commonalities among the various systems rather than to imply that there is just *one* process. Third, options for those convicted upon a plea of guilty are more limited, in part because one of the conditions of entering a guilty plea often is the waiver or loss of the right to appeal (King, 2014; Miller, 2020). As a consequence, it is considerably more difficult for convictions based on false guilty pleas to be reversed.

Appeals

It may be surprising to know that the U.S. Constitution does not guarantee criminal defendants a right to appeal their convictions. Indeed, historically, many jurisdictions did not authorize a right of appeal from a criminal conviction. However, all of the states and the federal government now provide the right to a first appeal in the overwhelming majority of cases through statutory or state constitutional law (Robertson, 2013). Most, but not all states have both intermediate courts of appeal and **courts of final jurisdiction**, which normally are called supreme courts. Thus, in most states, the intermediate appellate court hears appeals as of right and the state's highest court has discretionary review, meaning it can by and large choose which cases it will hear (Waters et al., 2015).

Appeals serve several important functions, including correcting legal errors and articulating and developing governing legal principles through the precedential effect of appellate court decisions. To a much lesser extent, appellate courts can "play an additional role in guarding against wrongful conviction of the innocent" (Robertson, 2013, p. 1225). The appellate process arguably is poorly suited to correct wrongful convictions. Appeals courts almost exclusively concern themselves with issues of law, rather than re-examining the facts of a case. "Appeals and postconviction remedies in the United States were designed to ensure that police, lawyers, and judges follow the legal rules during the investigation or prosecution of the case. So long as the rules were followed, the adversarial process is presumed to produce reliable results" (King, 2014, p. 217).

Direct appeals from convictions are often referred to as being limited to "record review" because the appellate court only reviews the evidence and testimony preserved in the record made in the trial court. Appellate courts do not consider new evidence that may have come to light after the trial concluded (even evidence of innocence) or evidence of conduct that occurred outside of the trial record, such as ineffective assistance of defense counsel or misconduct on the part of government actors (King, 2014). For example, Derek Tice, of the Norfolk Four, recanted his false confession before his case went to trial. However, rather than focusing on whether his statements were or were not reliable, the issues on his direct appeal concerned whether the trial court properly instructed the jury on accomplice liability for capital murder and whether the court erred in refusing to admit Omar Ballard's confession to killing Moore-Bosko (*Tice v. Commonwealth*, 2002). Whether a defendant falsely confessed involves issues of fact, which standing alone do not serve as a basis for constitutional relief. In contrast, a claim that a confession was involuntary because of coercion raises an issue of law, which can be addressed on appeal, although it may be difficult to establish owing to the Supreme Court's rather demanding test for determining whether a confession was made involuntarily (Garrett, 2008).

King's observation above highlights an important question that researchers have attempted to answer: How effective is the appellate process at detecting and helping to guard against wrongful convictions? In general, appeals are not often successful for criminal defendants. For example, in 2010 in the United States, more than 69,000 criminal appeals were resolved, and of the 63% of those appeals that were reviewed on the merits, 81% of the trial court decisions were affirmed or upheld (Waters et al., 2015). Moreover, successful appeals almost always involve reversals based on procedural issues rather than on the factual issues that figure so heavily in cases of wrongful conviction. Analysis of the first 200 exonerations obtained through post-conviction DNA testing examined how the exonerees fared during the various stages of judicial review including direct appeal, state post-conviction, federal habeas corpus, and certiorari to the U.S. Supreme Court. Of the 200 exonerees, 133 received written published decisions in their appeals. Garrett found that exonerees were rarely successful with factual claims of innocence on direct appeal. As he noted, "[O]ur system of criminal appeals and postconviction review poorly addressed factual deficiencies in these trials. Few exonerees brought claims regarding those facts or claims alleging their innocence. For those who did, hardly any claims were granted by courts. Far from recognizing innocence, courts often denied relief by finding errors to be harmless" (Garrett, 2008, p. 55).

Appellate courts do have the power to reverse a conviction based on insufficient evidence of guilt, although they exercise that authority only in highly unusual circumstances. Thus, for example, in *Cavazos v. Smith* (2011, p. 2), upholding a defendant's conviction supported by evidence regarding the "shaken baby syndrome," the Supreme Court observed that "it is the responsibility of the jury—not the court—to decide what conclusions should be drawn from evidence admitted at trial. A reviewing court may set aside the jury's verdict on the ground of insufficient evidence only if no rational trier of fact could have agreed with the jury" (see also *Jackson v. Virginia*, 1979). In conducting such review, appellate courts show great deference to juries' and trial judges' determination of facts.

State Post-Conviction Review

In a state **post-conviction review** proceeding, defendants can challenge their conviction based on claims they were unable to raise on direct appeal (King, 2014). The claims that can be raised and to whom they are available, as well as the procedures for claiming them, are prescribed by statute. For wrongfully convicted individuals, a post-conviction review proceeding might provide a forum for bringing forth newly discovered evidence of innocence or evidence of misconduct that was not disclosed on the record. For example, Article 440 of New York's Criminal Procedure Law defines several grounds upon which defendants can move the court to vacate their judgment of conviction, including that: "Improper and prejudicial conduct not appearing in the record occurred during a trial resulting in the judgment which conduct, if it had appeared in the record, would have required a reversal of the judgment upon an appeal therefrom" (New York Criminal Procedure Law, § 440.10(1)(f)). Among other restrictions, this statute authorizes the review of claims for post-conviction review only in cases that were resolved following trials (New York Criminal Procedure Law, § 440.10(1)(g)). Defendants who pled guilty thus are ineligible to challenge their convictions, although the statute recognizes an exception in this regard for claims based on DNA testing (New York Criminal Procedure Law, § 440.10(1)(g-1)). Defendants who pled guilty yet seek to establish their innocence without reliance on new DNA evidence are not allowed to challenge their convictions on state-post conviction review under New York law (*People v. Tiger*, 2018). As we have discussed elsewhere, in light of the overriding importance of guilty pleas, which produce roughly 95% of criminal convictions in the courts, restrictions on raising claims of innocence in cases resolved by guilty pleas have tremendous implications. Such restrictions are justified in the interests of finality and because defendants who plead guilty typically admit under oath that they in fact are guilty. Nevertheless, as we discussed in chapter 5, defendants can and sometimes do plead guilty even though they are innocent. As a consequence, they can be denied re-examination of their convictions and thus of a chance to have their wrongful convictions invalidated (see Miller, 2020).

The showing required in state courts on post-conviction review to gain a new trial on grounds of actual innocence varies widely. Defendants typically must show that such claims are based on new evidence that could not reasonably have been produced at the trial through the exercise of due diligence. The new evidence must also be persuasive. Some states require "clear and convincing" evidence of innocence, while others use standards such as establishing a "reasonable probability of a different result," or that the evidence would "more likely than not" change the result (Brooks et al., 2015/2016).

In Garrett's (2008) study, less than half of the exonerees with written court decisions in their cases pursued state post-conviction relief. Overall, Garrett found that 14% (18) of the exonerees with published written decisions received a reversal on appeal or post-conviction review. Among those cases, the highest rate of reversal was for rape-murder.

Federal Habeas Corpus

Federal **habeas corpus** allows incarcerated prisoners to challenge a state court conviction on the ground that they are being held in violation of the United States Constitution or the laws or treaties of the United States. Petitioners must normally first exhaust all state court remedies before a petition for habeas review will be entertained by a federal court. The failure to raise claims in state court will be excused on federal habeas corpus review only in rare circumstances, including cases falling within the "actual innocence" exception recognized by the Supreme Court. A "defaulted" claimed violation of a federal constitutional right (one not fully pursued in the state courts) can be pursued on federal habeas corpus "only in the 'extraordinary' case.... [The petitioner must] demonstrate that more likely than not, in light of the new evidence, no reasonable juror would find him guilty beyond a reasonable doubt—

or, to remove the double negative, that more likely than not any reasonable juror would have reasonable doubt" (*House v. Bell*, 2006, p. 538). By vote of 5–4, the Supreme Court ruled that Paul House, the petitioner in *House v. Bell* (2006), succeeded in making that showing. It thus authorized the lower federal courts to consider the claim, which House failed to fully exhaust in the Tennessee state courts, that his trial attorney was constitutionally ineffective. House, who had been convicted of capital murder and sentenced to death, ultimately was exonerated. He was released from death row after his conviction was vacated and the charges against him were dismissed (see Innocence Project, 2009; National Registry of Exonerations, n.d.).

The Anti-Terrorism and Effective Death Penalty Act of 1996 (AEDPA) added substantive limitations to habeas review (Yackle, 1996). Under this statute, federal courts may not grant applications for the writ unless the state court decision "was contrary to, or involved an unreasonable application of, clearly established Federal law as determined by the Supreme Court of the United States; or [it] resulted in a decision that was based on an unreasonable determination of the facts in light of the evidence presented in the State proceeding" (28 U.S. Code § 2254(d)(1–2)). Stringent procedural requirements also must be observed for petitioners seeking habeas corpus relief. In addition, petitioners applying for habeas corpus relief must be in custody. Returning to the Norfolk Four, Eric Wilson had been released from prison and was on parole but under sex offender registration restrictions when he petitioned for habeas relief in federal court. Wilson unsuccessfully argued that the restrictions on his liberty were so substantial that they amounted to custody (*Wilson v. Flaherty*, 2012; see generally Calaway, 2018). His habeas corpus petition consequently was denied.

The Supreme Court has not definitively ruled whether the Constitution recognizes an independent, or freestanding, claim of actual innocence as a ground for federal habeas relief. Most challenges to criminal convictions on constitutional grounds involve *procedural* rights, such as whether a defendant's Sixth Amendment right to counsel or to confront accusing witnesses was violated, or whether a prosecutor's use of peremptory challenges violated the defendant's Fourteenth Amendment's Equal Protection rights. Yet innocent people can erroneously be convicted even if all trial-related procedures are scrupulously observed. To qualify for habeas relief, they consequently are left to argue that the Constitution prohibits the conviction and punishment of an innocent person. They generally make this claim by asserting that, *substantively*, such a result would violate the Eighth Amendment's prohibition against cruel and unusual punishments, or the Due Process right not to be deprived of life or liberty. In *Herrera v. Collins* (1993), a majority of the justices were willing to assume — without deciding — that the Constitution would not allow the execution of an innocent person, although Chief Justice Rehnquist took pains to point out that the "threshold showing for such an assumed right would necessarily be extraordinarily high" (p. 417). The Court ruled that the petitioner in this case, Leonel Herrera, had not met that threshold showing, and he subsequently was executed in Texas. In taking the almost unprecedented step of entertaining a writ of habeas corpus filed directly in the Supreme Court, the justices in the highly publicized case involving Troy Davis's murder conviction and death sentence returned in the state of Georgia, ordered a federal district court to "receive testimony and make findings of fact as to whether evidence that could not have been obtained at the time of trial clearly establishes [Davis's] innocence" (*In re Davis*, 2009, p. 952). The district court upheld Davis's conviction after conducting the required hearing, and Davis was later executed.

Actual innocence claims may serve as a "gateway" through which defaulted constitutional claims may be heard on the merits in habeas review under the standard announced in *House v. Bell* (2006), discussed above (see Leventhal, 2012/2013). In Garrett's (2008) study, none of the five exonerees who brought actual innocence claims were granted relief. It is worth noting, however, that states are slowly beginning to recognize freestanding claims of actual innocence as a matter of state constitutional, statutory, or case law (Kaneb, 2014; Leventhal, 2012/2013).

Wrongful Convictions in Popular Culture: Working in the Trenches

- *Truth Has Fallen* (2013) — a documentary film by Sheila M. Sofian that explores the work of James McCloskey, who founded Centurion Ministries as the first non-profit organization in the United States dedicated to innocence work. The film follows several of Centurion's cases to highlight how wrongful convictions occur, how the organization works to free the innocent, and what happens after release.

- *When Truth Is All You Have: A Memoir of Faith, Justice, and Freedom for the Wrongly Convicted* (2020) — a book written by Jim McCloskey and Philip Lerman, chronicling the origins and work of Centurion Ministries.

- *Time Magazine, Innocent: The Fight Against Wrongful Convictions* (2017) — a special edition of *Time* magazine dedicated entirely to wrongful convictions. Published on the 25th anniversary of the Innocence Project, many features focus specifically on the organization and its cases.

- *The Criminal Cases Review Commission: Hope for the Innocent* (2009) — a volume edited by Dr. Michael Naughton focusing on the United Kingdom's Criminal Cases Review Commission, the first publicly funded body to review potential wrongful convictions. Featuring chapters written by experts, the book covers a variety of issues related to wrongful convictions and the CCRC's work.

- *Just Mercy: A Story of Justice and Redemption* (2014) — a moving memoir written by attorney Bryan Stevenson about the founding and evolution of his Equal Justice Initiative, a non-profit that provides legal representation to death row inmates, and Stevenson's quest to free an innocent man — Walter McMillian — from death row.

Executive Clemency

Of the first 873 exonerations in the NRE database, pardons based on innocence were issued in 113 cases (National Registry of Exonerations, 2012, p. 8). Gould and Leo's (2016) systematic examination of a comparison set of wrongful convictions and near misses to determine the bases and methods of exoneration found that in 14% of the cases, the exonerees received gubernatorial pardons. However, this is not to say that clemency petitions necessarily led to the discovery of defendants' innocence. In many cases, governors have issued pardons after defendants had succeeded in overturning their convictions through the courts. For example, in the case of the Norfolk Four, Virginia Governor Tim Kaine granted conditional pardons to Joseph Dick, Derek Tice, and Danial Williams in 2009, reducing their sentences to the time they already had served, and the men were released from prison. Eric Wilson already had been freed from prison, and he did not benefit by this action. Tice's conviction was vacated later in 2009 when a federal district court ruled that he had been provided ineffective assistance of counsel because his trial lawyer did not attempt to suppress his confession (*Tice v. Johnson*, 2009). Dick's and Williams's convictions were vacated in 2016 when a federal district court concluded that "no sane human being could find them guilty" of raping and murdering Michelle Moore-Bosko (*Williams v. Brown*, 2016, p. 718). Only later, in 2017, did Virginia Governor Terry McAuliffe grant absolute pardons to all four men, thus officially exonerating them and entitling them to compensation for their wrongful convictions and incarceration (Associated Press, 2017; Innocence Project, 2017). In *Herrera v. Collins* (1993), the case described above involving a death-sentenced inmate's habeas corpus claim of actual innocence,

Chief Justice Rehnquist characterized executive clemency as a "fail-safe" against wrongful convictions and "the historic remedy for preventing miscarriages of justice where judicial process has been exhausted" (p. 415).

Commentators have nevertheless raised serious questions regarding the adequacy of executive clemency for identifying and remedying wrongful convictions (see Cooper & Gough, 2014; Dinsmore, 2002). Clemency hearings typically are conducted pursuant to minimal procedural safeguards and virtually non-existent standards. Speaking to the president's constitutional authority "to grant Reprieves and Pardons for Offences against the United States" (U.S. Const., Art. II, § 2[1]), Chief Justice John Marshall explained that "A pardon is an act of grace" (*United States v. Wilson*, 1833, p. 160). The Court later elaborated that "the executive's clemency authority would cease to be a matter of grace committed to the executive authority if it were constrained by the sort of procedural requirements" being sought by an Ohio prisoner who had been sentenced to death (*Ohio Adult Parole Authority v. Woodard*, 1998, p. 284). Clemency authority is vested in the president for federal offenses (Eckstein & Colby, 2019). Governors have exclusive clemency authority in most states, although in some states that power is dependent on the favorable recommendation of a pardons board, and in a few states a pardons board or similar commission is given the ability to issue pardons and commute sentences (Heise, 2003; Kobil, 1991). Clemency decisions can be fraught with political considerations, with chief executives risking a backlash for their unpopular commutation and pardoning decisions (Cooper, 2015; Larkin, Jr., 2016; Wolfe, 2007). For these and other reasons, clemency proceedings arguably are ill-suited to ensuring that evidence will be systematically collected, presented, and evaluated to ensure that errors of justice will be corrected.

Special Tribunals and Commissions

North Carolina is the only state in the country that offers a forum for relief for the wrongfully convicted outside of the appellate and post-conviction review process. The **North Carolina Innocence Inquiry Commission** ("NCIIC") was created by the state legislature in 2006. The NCIIC is an independent, neutral state agency that investigates claims of actual innocence from individuals convicted of felonies in North Carolina state courts. The NCIIC has the power to subpoena evidence and compel cooperation from criminal justice personnel and others. Claims are not limited to those supported by scientific evidence, such as DNA; nor are they limited by statutes of limitations or a requirement that the claimant be incarcerated (Mosteller, 2016). Credible claims of actual innocence are referred by the commission to a three-judge panel for adjudication. The NCIIC began operating in 2007. Of the first 2,914 claims received through 2020, 2,852 cases were closed, others remained under investigation, and 15 had resulted in exonerations (North Carolina Innocence Inquiry Commission, n.d.).

Preservation and Production of Evidence

The average time spent incarcerated for the 129 individuals exonerated in 2020 was 13.4 years. Twenty-five of those exonerees remained incarcerated for 25 years or more (National Registry of Exonerations, 2020). The average time spent in prison for the more than 2,400 exonerees identified between 1989 and early 2019 was eight years and eight months (National Registry of Exonerations, 2018). Many wrongfully convicted individuals have spent decades or more in prison before being exonerated. The appeals and post-conviction process can be quite protracted, and newly discovered evidence, particularly biological evidence (e.g., hair, tissue, blood, or other bodily fluids), can play an important role is establishing a person's innocence. Consequently, preservation of evidence can have a critical impact on dismantling an injustice. Rules and regulations regarding evidence handling and retention vary considerably across the states. More than half of the states require the preservation of evidence following criminal convictions, but the laws vary widely regarding how long and what types of evidence must be retained. In several states, evidence is not automatically preserved but rather convicted defendants must petition for its retention (Innocence Project, n.d.). Lost, misplaced, or mishandled evidence can contribute further to miscarriages of justice (see Jones, 2005, 2009). For example, in 1985, Alan Newton was convicted in New York of a rape he did not commit (National Registry of Exonerations, 2016). In 1994, he requested DNA testing on the biological evidence collected from the victim. His request for DNA testing was denied because the evidence collection kit could not be located. In 2005, another search for the evidence was conducted at the behest of the Innocence Project, and the evidence collection kit was located and tested, ultimately excluding Newton as the source of the biological evidence collected from the victim. Newton spent over a decade incarcerated because the evidence could not be found (*Newton v. City of New York*, 2015).

In this regard, the National Institutes of Standards and Technology and the National Institute of Justice have established a set of best practices for the handling and preservation of biological evidence to ensure its integrity and proper disposition.

> Across the nation, headlines tell the story of evidence that has been mishandled, misplaced, lost, or destroyed. Often the blame for these mishaps is directed toward property and evidence custodians housed in law enforcement agencies nationwide. Many law enforcement agencies do not properly address, recognize, or support the efforts of their property rooms. Although these agencies bear ultimate responsibility for maintaining the integrity of the evidence, the real problem lies with a systemic failure to properly account for evidence from collection through final disposition. This failure reduces the public's confidence in the criminal justice system to produce just results in criminal and civil proceedings (Technical Group on Biological Evidence Preservation, 2013, p. iv).

Alan Newton's case thus demonstrates the critical importance of the proper preservation of evidence.

Conclusion

As we have seen, the road to exoneration can be long and twisted. Wrongful convictions are difficult to overturn without clear evidence of innocence. Criminal justice actors are often highly resistant to revisiting or invalidating convictions throughout the exoneration process (Gould & Leo, 2016). Consequently, it is tragic, yet unsurprising, when we hear of exonerees who have spent years upon years in prison before finding justice.

Key Terms and Concepts

- **Certiorari**: a writ or order by which an appellate court exercises its discretion to review a case that was previously decided by a lower court
- **Courts of final jurisdiction**: refers to the highest court in a particular jurisdiction, typically state supreme courts or the U.S. Supreme Court
- **Direct appeal**: judicial review of a conviction that involves a review of the trial court record ("record review") for alleged legal errors committed at the trial

- **Post-conviction review/relief:** generally refers to challenges to a conviction or sentence based on matters not reflected in the trial record, and thus not considered on direct appeal
- **Habeas corpus:** Latin for, "you have the body"; allows incarcerated persons to challenge a criminal conviction or sentence on the grounds that they are being held in violation of the United States Constitution or the laws or treaties of the United States; typically filed in federal court after all state remedies have been exhausted
- **North Carolina Innocence Inquiry Commission:** an independent state agency that investigates claims of actual innocence from those convicted of felonies in North Carolina; credible claims are adjudicated by a panel of three judges

Discussion Questions

1. What are the fundamental differences between trial courts and appellate courts? How do these differences help explain why appellate courts are ill-equipped to resolve claims for relief based on actual innocence?

2. What is the purpose of federal habeas corpus review?

3. If you were a social scientist designing a survey for research on the judiciary and wrongful convictions, what kinds of questions would you ask the judges participating in your survey? Would your questions differ for trial court judges and appellate judges? Why or why not?

4. Why do you think it took so long for the Norfolk Four to be pardoned?

References

Associated Press. (2017, March 21). 20 years after being bullied into confessing, 'Norfolk 4' are pardoned. *The New York Times.* https://www.nytimes.com/ 2017/03/21/us/norfolk-four-sailors-rape-murder-mcauliffe.html.

Brooks, J., Simpson, A., & Kanch, P. (2015/2016). If hindsight is 20/20, our justice system should not be blind to new evidence of innocence: A survey of post-conviction new evidence statutes and a proposed model. *Albany Law Review, 79,* 1045–1090.

Calaway, W. R. (2018). Sex offenders, custody and habeas. *St. John's Law Review, 92,* 755–795.

Cavazos v. Smith, 565 U.S. 1 (2011).

Cooper, S. L. (2015). The state clemency power and innocence claims: The influence of finality and its implications for innocence. *Charlotte Law Review*, 7, 51–109.

Cooper, S. L., & Gough, D. (2014). The controversy of clemency and innocence in America. *California Western Law Review*, 51, 55–110.

Dinsmore, A. (2002). Clemency in capital cases: The need to ensure meaningful review. *U.C.L.A. Law Review*, 49, 1825–1858.

Eckstein, P. F., & Colby, M. (2019). Presidential pardon power: Are there limits and, if not, should there be? *Arizona State Law Journal*, 51, 71–108.

Findley, K. A. (2009). Innocence protection in the appellate process. *Marquette Law Review*, 93, 591–636.

Garrett, B. L. (2008). Judging innocence. *Columbia Law Review*, 108, 55–142.

Gould, J. B., & Leo, R. A. (2016). The path to exoneration. *Albany Law Review*, 79, 325–372.

Heise, M. (2003). Mercy by the numbers: An empirical analysis of clemency and its structure. *Virginia Law Review*, 89, 239–310.

Herrera v. Collins, 506 U.S. 390 (1993).

House v. Bell, 547 U.S. 518 (2006).

In re Davis, 557 U.S. 952 (2009).

The Innocence Project. (n.d.). *Preservation of evidence.* https://innocence project.org/preservation-of-evidence/.

The Innocence Project. (2009). Paul House and his elated mother celebrate exoneration with a trip to California. https://www.innocenceproject.org/paul-house-and-his-elated-mother-celebrate-exoneration-with-a-trip-to-california/.

The Innocence Project. (2017, March 22). Virginia governor pardons Norfolk Four. https://innocenceproject.org/virginia-governor-pardons-norfolk-four/.

Jackman, T. (2017, March 21). 'Norfolk 4' wrongly convicted of rape and murder, pardoned by Gov. McAuliffe. *The Washington Post.* https://www.washington post.com/news/true-crime/wp/2017/03/21/norfolk-4-wrongly-convicted-of-rape-and-murder-pardoned-by-gov-mcauliffe/?utm_term=.8723054dc4f8.

Jackson v. Virginia, 443 U.S. 307 (1979).

Jones, C. E. (2005). Evidence destroyed, innocence lost: The preservation of biological evidence under innocence protection statutes. *American Criminal Law Review*, 42, 1239–1270.

Jones, C. E. (2009). The right remedy for the wrongly convicted: Judicial sanctions for destruction of DNA evidence. *Fordham Law Review*, 77, 2893–2954.

Kaneb, P. (2014). Innocence presumed: A new analysis as a constitutional claim. *California Western Law Review*, 50, 171–231.

King, N. (2014). Judicial review: Appeals and postconviction proceedings. In A. D. Redlich, J. R. Acker, R. J. Norris, & C. L. Bonventre (Eds.), *Examining wrongful convictions: Stepping back, moving forward* (pp. 217–236). Carolina Academic Press.

Kobil, D. T. (1991). The quality of mercy strained: wresting the pardoning power from the king. *Texas Law Review, 69,* 569–639.

Larkin, P. J., Jr. (2016). Revitalizing the clemency process. *Harvard Journal of Law & Public Policy, 39,* 833–916.

Leventhal, J. M. (2012/2013). A survey of federal and state courts' approaches to a constitutional right of actual innocence: Is there a need for a state constitutional right in New York in the aftermath of CPL § 440.10(G-1)? *Albany Law Review, 76,* 1453–1515.

Miller, C. (2020). Why states must consider innocence claims after guilty pleas. *University of California-Irvine Law Review, 10,* 671–727.

Mosteller, R. P. (2016). N.C. Innocence Inquiry Commission's first decade: Impressive successes and lessons learned. *North Carolina Law Review, 94,* 1725–1870.

National Registry of Exonerations. (n.d.). Paul G. House. https://www.law.umich.edu/special/exoneration/Pages/casedetail.aspx?caseid=3307.

National Registry of Exonerations. (2012). *Exonerations in the United States, 1989–2012.* http://www.law.umich.edu/special/exoneration/Documents/exonerations_us_1989_2012_full_report.pdf.

National Registry of Exonerations. (2016). Alan Newton. https://www.law.umich.edu/special/exoneration/Pages/casedetail.aspx?caseid=3505.

National Registry of Exonerations. (2018). *Milestone: Exonerated defendants spent 20,000 years in prison.* http://www.law.umich.edu/special/exoneration/Documents/NRE.20000.Years.Report.pdf.

National Registry of Exonerations. (2020). *2020 annual report.* http://www.law.umich.edu/special/exoneration/Documents/2021AnnualReport.pdf.

New York Criminal Procedure Law, § 440.10(1)(f).

New York Criminal Procedure Law, § 440.10(1)(g).

New York Criminal Procedure Law, § 440.10(1)(g-1).

Newton v. City of New York, 779 F.3d 140 (2d Cir. 2015), cert. denied, 136 S.Ct. 795 (2016).

North Carolina Innocence Inquiry Commission. (n.d.). *About.* https://innocencecommission-nc.gov/about/.

Ohio Adult Parole Authority v. Woodard, 523 U.S. 272 (1998).

People v. Tiger, 110 N.E.3d 509 (N.Y. 2018).

Robertson, C. B. (2013). The right to appeal. *North Carolina Law Review, 91,* 1219–1281.

Technical Working Group on Biological Evidence Preservation. (2013). *The biological evidence preservation handbook: Best practices for evidence handlers*. National Institutes of Standards and Technology. http://nvlpubs. nist.gov/nistpubs/ir/2013/NIST.IR.7928.pdf.

Tice v. Commonwealth, 563 S.E.2d 412 (Va. App. 2002).

Tice v. Johnson, 2009 WL 2947380 (E.D. Va. 2009).

United States Constitution, Art. II § 2[1].

United States v. Wilson, 32 U.S. 150 (1833).

U.S. Supreme Court. (n.d.). *The Supreme Court at work: The term and caseload.* https://www.supremecourt.gov/about/courtatwork.aspx.

Waters, N. L., Gallegos, A., Green, J., & Rozsi, M. (2015). *Criminal appeals in state courts.* U.S. Department of Justice, Bureau of Justice Statistics. https://www.bjs.gov/index.cfm?ty=pbdetail&iid=5368.

Wells, T., & Leo, R. A. (2008). *The wrong guys: Murder, false confessions, and the Norfolk Four.* The New Press.

Williams v. Brown, 208 F.Supp.3d 718 (E.D. Va. 2016).

Wilson v. Flaherty, 689 F.3d 332 (4th Cir. 2012).

Wolfe, G. B. (2007). I beg your pardon: A call for renewal of executive clemency and accountability in Massachusetts. *Boston College Third World Law Journal, 27,* 417–454.

Yackle, L. W. (1996). A primer on the new habeas corpus statute. *Buffalo Law Review, 44,* 381–449.

Chapter 12

The Aftermath of Wrongful Convictions: Reintegration and Compensation

Learning Objectives

After reading this chapter, you should be able to:

- Appreciate the practical and psychological challenges faced by exonerees upon re-entering society following their incarceration.
- Conceptualize the wrongfully convicted as victims of state harm.
- Discuss the strengths and weaknesses of the various means of compensating exonerees.
- Identify ways to improve re-entry services for exonerees.
- Understand the limitations on holding criminal justice actors, especially prosecutors, accountable for wrongful convictions.

Case Study: Kirk Bloodsworth

On Wednesday, July 25, 1983, Elinor Helmick was watching five children: her own two children, her niece and nephew, and Dawn Hamilton, the daughter of a friend. The youngsters went out to play, but two of them went into the woods, which were off limits. Elinor sent her niece and Dawn to go find them and call them back. When only three of the four children returned, Elinor went looking for the missing Dawn.

Elinor ran into two neighborhood boys, Christian and Jackie, who said they had seen Dawn at a nearby pond. According to the boys, they were with Dawn at the pond when a man came up and asked what she was doing. She informed the man that she was looking for her friend, Lisa, and went with the man into the woods. They described the man as about 30 years old, white, with blond hair and a mustache.

Elinor called the police and within hours, more than 100 officers were on the search for Dawn. Her shorts and underwear were found hanging in a nearby tree, and her body was found shortly thereafter. The nine-year-old was naked from the waist down, with a stick penetrating her vagina and her head bloodied by a rock. Christian and Jackie, only 10 and 7 years old, worked with police to construct a sketch of the man they had seen with Dawn. The sketch was made public, and a few days later an anonymous tipster said it resembled a local man named Kirk Bloodsworth. Bloodsworth's wife, Wanda, had filed a missing person report; Kirk had left town on August 3 and had been sick before leaving.

Kirk Bloodsworth was arrested days later and was identified by Christian in a lineup despite having red hair, which did not fit Christian's prior description of the man he had seen with Dawn. Jackie could not identify Bloodsworth in a lineup, but Bloodsworth nevertheless was charged with the rape and murder. Despite having several alibi witnesses testify at his trial, Bloodsworth was convicted in March 1985 and sentenced to death. After his conviction was overturned on appeal the following year, he was retried, again convicted, and sentenced to life in prison.

In late 1992, evidence from the case was reexamined using the recently developed technique of forensic DNA testing. The results excluded Bloodsworth, and he was released from prison on June 28, 1993. The governor of Maryland issued him a full pardon in December. Bloodsworth stands as the first person in the United States to be sentenced to death and later exonerated through DNA testing.

Exoneration was not the end of the struggle for Kirk Bloodsworth, an honorably discharged Marine. After his release, he struggled with a number of issues. He dealt with periods of homelessness and substance abuse, and experienced **stigmatization** throughout the community. People in Cambridge, Maryland, avoided him, sometimes pulling their children closer and crossing the street with them when they encountered Bloodsworth in public. Many believed that he had been freed on a legal technicality and was not actually innocent of the horrific crimes. Someone even wrote the words "child killer" in the layer of dirt on the side of his truck (Junkin, 2004; Norris, 2014; Westervelt & Cook, 2012).

Bloodsworth also desired justice for the victim, Dawn Hamilton, and her family. In 2003, a forensic biologist identified stains from the crime scene evidence that had not yet been analyzed. The stains yielded a DNA profile and the results were run through the FBI's DNA database. A hit identified Kimberly Ruffner, who was in prison with Bloodsworth and lifted weights with him while they were both incarcerated. Ruffner was charged with Dawn's rape and murder in September 2003 and convicted in 2004 (Death Penalty Information Center, n.d.; Warden, n.d.).

For his troubles—a lost decade of his life and the unwarranted label of a child rapist and murderer—Bloodsworth was awarded $300,000 by the state of Maryland in compensation for the income he lost during the time of his arrest and incarceration. He has since become an advocate for criminal justice and death penalty reform. A part of the 2004's federal Justice for All Act was named after him: the Kirk Bloodsworth Post-Conviction DNA Testing Grant Program.

A Closer Look: The Kirk Bloodsworth Case

- *Bloodsworth: The True Story of the First Death Row Inmate Exonerated by DNA Evidence* (2005)—a book written by Tim Junkin that covers, in detail, the crime, investigation, trials, and experiences of Bloodsworth before, during, and after his wrongful conviction.

- *Bloodsworth: An Innocent Man* (2015)—a documentary memoir by director Gregory Bayne that covers the Bloodsworth case and provides an intimate look at the case and the failings of the criminal justice system.

Life after Exoneration

Kirk Bloodsworth's story is emblematic of many who are wrongly convicted. Exoneration is not the final step in their journey. The experiences faced by individuals who are unjustly imprisoned have effects that linger long after their release. Nearly every aspect of life is affected to some degree, from struggles with seemingly basic everyday tasks to complex emotional and psychological challenges.

Virtually all people who are incarcerated face difficult challenges when the time comes for them to reenter conventional society. This is true for the truly guilty former prisoners who have served their maximum sentences or have been released on parole, but many of the struggles are exacerbated for innocent individuals who were wrongfully convicted. Upon release, exonerees must deal with a diverse array of problems that affect them, their families, and others around them. A recent review of 20 published studies of the adverse psychological and psychosocial effects of wrongful conviction identified eight key themes (1) changes in self-identity; (2) stigmatization, including self-stigma and damage to exonerees' reputations; (3) psychological and physical health problems such as depression, anxiety, and other psychological symptoms; (4) relationship and family challenges, such as isolation, strained relationships, and family stigma; (5) negative attitudes toward the justice system; (6) adverse financial and employment consequences; (7) experiencing trauma while incarcerated; and (8) difficulties in adjustment to life outside of prison (Brooks & Greenberg, 2021).

Many of the post-release difficulties concern practical matters. Almost all exonerees face financial challenges, both short- and long-term. Many who are arrested for crimes are socioeconomically disadvantaged, and after their release from custody they generally return to similar circumstances. Many lack transitional funds for basic necessities such as housing, clothing, and food (Westervelt & Cook, 2010, 2012). They may turn to family or friends for assistance, although this can prove to be embarrassing or uncomfortable even when it is possible. Securing employment is a major challenge for nearly all exonerees. Many were incarcerated during their twenties and thirties, the period during which they would otherwise have been furthering their education, developing job skills, and building a career. Without a relevant knowledge base and skill set, and with a gap on their résumés for the period of incarceration, exonerees struggle to navigate the job market and secure meaningful employment. Further, the label of being an exoneree alone creates barriers to employment. In a recent study in which hiring professionals evaluated job applications, researchers found that exonerees may face negative stereotypes and employment discrimination similar to former offenders (Kukucka et al., 2020). In addition, exonerees often have gaps in their education and lack necessary resources to gain entry to and succeed in higher education.

The struggles faced by exonerees go far beyond education and employment, however. Prisons are physically challenging environments, characterized by violence, poor food, and substandard health care. Exonerees often must contend with physical ailments including malnutrition, muscular atrophy, asthma, and skin conditions, among others (Innocence Project, 2009; Westervelt & Cook, 2010, 2012). Following release, exonerees can have difficulty securing health insurance, which may be dependent on employment or otherwise be unaffordable.

Exonerees face both physical and mental health risks. Years of incarceration, during which many exonerees experienced repeated traumatic events, can have severe lingering psychological consequences (Alexander-Bloch et al., 2020; Brooks & Greenberg, 2021; Campbell & Denov, 2004; Grounds, 2004). Furthermore, while incarcerated, exonerees may have lost family members and friends, suffered broken relationships, and missed out on their children's growth and other significant opportunities in life. These familial and other difficulties can cause anxiety, depression, bitterness, and anger. Once disrupted, relationships can be difficult to repair. The experiences of a wrongful conviction may cause exonerees to have trouble connecting to others emotionally and building trust in their relationships. Even the experience of sleeping in a bed with another person can be challenging for someone accustomed to the prison environment (Westervelt & Cook, 2012). Indeed, a recent survey found that in addition to clinical levels of depression, anxiety, and **post-traumatic stress disorder (PTSD)**, exonerees reported limited sleep time and regular sleep disturbances (Alexander-Bloch et al., 2020).

Many exonerees are released into a world that is dramatically different from the one they left upon entering prison, making adjustment to life away from incarceration all the more difficult (Brooks & Greenberg, 2021). For example, some long-term incarcerated exonerees never used a computer or cell phone before being released. Such significant social and cultural changes can trigger discomfort and anxiety and create additional barriers to reintegration into a society so heavily reliant on new and evolving technology. Even small everyday tasks, such as grocery shopping or using standard eating utensils, can be a challenge for someone used to a highly limited, rigidly structured life inside prison (Westervelt & Cook, 2010). One exoneree, Calvin Johnson, Jr., described feeling like "a baby in a brand new world" after he was released from prison (Innocence Project, 2010).

The several difficult challenges identified above—those dealing with employment, education, mental and physical health, familial relationships, emotional wellbeing, and adaptation to change—are not confined to exonerees. They also are faced by other institutionalized people, including incarcerated and released individuals who presumably were guilty of committing crimes. Being innocent, however, increases the difficulty of dealing with such problems and creates some unique ones. Exonerees are victims of harmful actions taken by the government (Westervelt & Cook, 2010). While incarcerated, the wrongly convicted consequently must deal with their own victimization and fight the legal battles necessary to establish their innocence, while also enduring the hardships of prison. Despite their innocence, they commonly endure stigmatization following their release from incarceration. Some members of the public may even believe exonerees are responsible for their own wrongful conviction, particularly if their case involved a false confession (Savage et al., 2018). Even friends and family members may entertain doubts about an exoneree's innocence. In addition to the many practical difficulties they encounter, exonerees must also attempt to navigate and cope with the injustices they have suffered. Relative to other released inmates, the innocent tend to show an "increased intolerance of injustice" (Campbell & Denov, 2004, p. 154); they may be especially suspicious and cynical regarding figures of authority, but show an increased empathy for victims. They also must continue to fight for redress for the wrongs they experienced. Many exonerees desire an apology from government officials, or at least an acknowledgment of the errors that led to their suffering. They may also desire **compensation** or other assistance in rebuilding their lives. Ironically, as exonerees, the wrongly convicted frequently are not entitled to the **reentry** services that may be available to actual offenders who have been imprisoned and served their full sentences or released on parole; services such as halfway houses, rehabilitation programs, and more. Exonerees must therefore continue to pursue legal battles for compensation and the other **reintegration** assistance they so desperately need and deserve.

Wrongful Convictions in Popular Culture: The Aftermath of Exonerations

- *After Innocence* (2005) — Directed by Jessica Sanders, this documentary film tells the story of several exonerated men — Ronald Cotton, Scott Hornoff, Calvin Willis, Nicholas Yarris, Wilton Dedge, Herman Atkins, Vincent Moto, and Dennis Maher — as they navigate re-entry into society.

- *The Price of a Life* (2015) — This full-length feature written by Ariel Levy for *The New Yorker* examines the wrongful conviction of John Restivo, who was convicted along with Dennis Halstead and John Kogut of rape and murder in New York. The article discusses the struggles faced by exonerees after release and the shortcomings of current remedies.

- *Rectify* (2013–2016) — A dramatic TV series created by Ray McKinnon for Sundance TV depicts the struggles of character Daniel Holden, who has been released after spending 19 years on death row for the murder of his girlfriend and must cope with re-entering society and lingering doubts about his role in her murder.

Redress for Wrongful Conviction

As victims of **state harm** (Westervelt & Cook, 2010), exonerees are uniquely positioned in terms of deserving and qualifying for state assistance.

However, as noted above, exonerees often are not eligible for reintegration services that are made available to parolees and others who have been incarcerated. Instead, exonerees may seek compensation through various methods, although all entail impediments and limitations that make them less than ideal (Norris, 2012).

Methods of Compensation

In general, exonerees may obtain compensation in one of three ways: civil litigation, private legislation, and pursuant to general legislation (statutory compensation).

Civil litigation involves exonerees going to court to obtain compensation either through tort law or civil rights claims. Several exonerees have won large civil settlements that received extensive media coverage, but such stories are the exception rather than the rule. Suing the state or a criminal justice agency requires time and money that many exonerees simply do not have. They must hire a lawyer or find one willing to work pro bono, and then manage to get by while litigation works its way through the courts. Innocence Project exonerees who received compensation through civil lawsuits waited an average of roughly four years before receiving their awards (Innocence Project, 2009). Even if an exoneree has the necessary resources to pursue litigation, the success rate for winning such cases is low, in part because police and prosecutors have varying levels of immunity from liability for many discretionary decisions. Furthermore, successful claims require a showing of governmental culpability. Identifying a criminal justice agency or actor with the requisite level of culpability can be difficult, particularly for exonerees who may lack the resources to conduct extensive investigations (Griffiths & Owens, 2014).

A second method for gaining compensation that may be available to exonerees is **private legislation**. This method requires exonerees to petition their state legislature to pass a bill specially authorizing their compensation. Like litigation, however, winning individual compensation in this fashion is challenging. It requires political savvy and the legislature's willingness to pass the bill. An exoneree must convince a legislator to introduce the bill, then obtain the necessary votes for passage and the support of the governor to have it take effect (Griffiths & Owens, 2014). To succeed, exonerees and their supporters must intensively lobby and mobilize political support, necessitating the investment of time and resources which may not be available.

The unpredictable nature of civil litigation and private legislation may also lead to highly uneven reparations for exonerees. The attendant uncertainty and disparities create anxiety and may result in additional injustices for exonerees, heightening the disadvantages of these remedies.

Because of the shortcomings of litigation and private legislative compensation remedies, most experts and advocates support **statutory compensation**. These are duly enacted laws that establish a system for providing compensation to qualifying exonerees. Exonerees typically have to overcome several hurdles to receive compensation. They must show more than that they spent time in prison for a conviction that later was reversed. They normally must affirmatively demonstrate that they were factually innocent of the charged crime, a showing that demands more than demonstrating a procedural irregularity or simply that reasonable doubt exists about guilt (Gutman, 2017, p. 371; *Jefferson v. State*, 2012; Kahn, 2010; *State v. Ford*, 2016; Trivelli, 2016). Experts have argued that, at least in principle, compensation statutes provide the easiest, fairest, and most consistent form of redress for wrongful convictions (Bernhard, 1999, 2009). Advocates, scholars, and several prominent professional organizations, including the American Bar Association, have supported statutory compensation for individuals who have suffered wrongful conviction. As of mid-2021, at least 36 states, the District of Columbia, and the federal government have passed compensation statutes, although the scope and quality of those statutes varies widely.

Compensation Statutes: Strengths and Weaknesses

At least in theory, compensation statutes are the fairest and most consistent way to provide reentry assistance for the wrongly convicted following their release from prison. Not only does a compensation law offer a systematic form of redress for exonerees, it shows some level of acknowledgment by the government that an error was made and that the state bears some responsibility for assisting exonerees in rebuilding their lives.

The Innocence Project offers several suggestions for what a compensation policy should include. First, a set level of monetary compensation should be established based on the number of years a wrongfully convicted person was incarcerated. In addition to the base monetary award, exonerees should receive needed services, including immediate transitional finances for basic necessities, housing assistance, physical and mental health services, educational and/or vocational assistance, and legal services for other matters such as child custody disputes. These legal services should also include measures necessary for **record expungement**—the sealing or destruction of the exoneree's criminal record—which often does not occur automatically upon exoneration (Shlosberg et al., 2012).

While some of the Innocence Project's suggestions have been adopted in some states, compensation statutes vary widely in quality and are often lacking in important ways. For example, Kansas passed a compensation statute in 2018 that provides $65,000 per year of wrongful imprisonment and $25,000 per year spent on probation, parole, or as a registered sex offender. Exonerees are also eligible for additional compensation for attorney fees and are entitled to some social services such as housing and tuition assistance, counseling, health care, and more (Connolly, 2019). Similarly, Texas offers $80,000 per year of wrongful incarceration and $25,000 per year spent on parole, probation, or as a registered sex offender, with no cap on the maximum amount. Exonerees may also receive additional financial aid for child support payments and are eligible for services similar to those provided in Kansas. On the other end of the spectrum is a state such as Wisconsin, where exonerees are eligible for no more than $5,000 per year of wrongful incarceration, with a cap of $25,000. Thus, in Wisconsin, an exoneree who spent five years in prison and an exoneree who spent 25 years in prison are both only eligible for a maximum of $25,000 in compensation. Most states fall somewhere in between Texas and Wisconsin, while others, such as New York, do not offer a set amount, but determine compensation on a case-by-case basis. Montana is the only state which currently has a compensation policy that does not offer any financial award. Montana simply provides education aid to individuals who were wrongfully convicted and also limits such aid to those who were exonerated through DNA evidence (Gutman, 2017; Norris, 2014).

Even in states with a base financial award, other monetary and non-monetary assistance is often limited. Some states, as exemplified in the Kansas statute discussed above, offer additional financial assistance to make up for attorney fees, court costs, fines, restitution, detention facility costs, lost wages, or — as in Texas — reimbursement for child support payments, a provision that was added after Texas exoneree Clarence Brandley was not forgiven the debt he accrued as a result of missing child support payments while wrongfully incarcerated (Norris, 2014). Although enactment of this child support provision in Texas was a positive step, the state has attempted to block exonerees from receiving the full amount of payments missed while they were incarcerated (Innocence Project, 2014).

As discussed earlier, the struggles faced by exonerees after release from prison extend beyond financial challenges, and some state compensation policies contain provisions for additional support. As with the financial assistance offered, however, these supplemental provisions also are often lacking in comparison to the immense challenges that exonerees face. A few states provide educational assistance, usually including credits to attend a state college or university. A few also provide vocational training, counseling or mental health services, and/or physical health services. Given the ubiquity of challenges regarding health, employment, and education which confront exonerees, the fact that only a handful of states provide these services is disturbing, as these services are necessary for exonerees to successfully reenter and succeed in society. The lack of adequate reentry services often leaves exonerees on their own or reliant upon personal networks to deal with the challenges of post-incarceration life (Goldberg et al., 2020).

Several other important limitations accompany many existing statutory compensation policies. The vast majority of state laws do not provide for record expungement, which is critical for exonerees. A criminal record often represents a lingering negative label, and exonerees consequently find themselves in a particularly difficult situation when applying for jobs. Without their records expunged, they are in a catch-22 situation: if they indicate that they were convicted of a felony on a job application, they are unlikely to get the job; on the other hand, if they indicate that they were never convicted on a job application but a background check flags their criminal record, they will be viewed as having lied on the application and likely will not get the job. As exonerees have noted, they are not able to indicate on job applications that they were convicted but later exonerated (Westervelt & Cook, 2012). Record expungement may also be related to exonerees' post-release success in other ways. For instance, one study found that about one-third of exonerees did not have their records expunged, and that lack of expungement was associated with the commission of post-exoneration offenses (Shlosberg et al., 2014).

Another ambiguity in most statutes concerns whether compensation awards are subject to state taxes. The federal government has passed a law stipulating that federal compensation awards are not subject to taxes (Norris, 2017), but most state policies make no mention of the issue. This creates another layer of uncertainty and frustration for exonerees, who may have to pay taxes out of their compensation awards to the same government that wrongly imprisoned them.

Uncertainty also surrounds whether civil lawsuits can be pursued in addition to statutory compensation. Several states stipulate that exonerees who receive statutory compensation waive the right to pursue civil litigation. A few states explicitly allow both, but no specific policy is stated in most states. Similar uncertainty surrounds compensation policies concerning exonerees who die before receiving their awards. Several states have beneficiary provisions allowing recovery by a deceased exoneree's family or estate, and some policies allow an exoneree's family to file for compensation if an exoneree dies before applying. On the other hand, several state laws explicitly provide that only the exoneree is eligible for compensation and/or that compensation is terminated upon the exoneree's death.

In addition to limitations in the monetary awards and other services provided, many state policies contain limitations on which exonerees are eligible for compensation. As we discussed in chapter 10, exonerees who were convicted after an affirmative defense they asserted was erroneously rejected are foreclosed from statutory compensation in many states (Acker & Wu, 2020). A number of states limit compensation only to those who were wrongly convicted of a felony, notwithstanding the significant hardships associated with wrongful misdemeanor convictions. In several other states a pardon from the governor is a prerequisite to receiving compensation, even though pardons are notoriously difficult to obtain, which further politicizes the recovery process for exonerees.

Various other disqualifications are built into many current compensation statutes. For example, individuals serving a concurrent sentence for another crime in addition to the one for which they were wrongly convicted are ineligible for compensation in several states. Other states exclude those who falsely pled guilty (e.g., *Rhoades v. State*, 2016), who "contributed to" or "brought about" their own convictions, or who "fabricated evidence." Such provisions can be construed to disqualify exonerees who falsely confessed. In light of all that we know about how and why people falsely admit guilt (see chapters 4 and 5 of this book), it is regrettable that some states automatically exclude these exonerees from compensation. In particular, such restrictions disproportionately affect populations including juveniles and those suffering from mental illness or intellectual disabilities, who are particularly susceptible to making false confessions (Kassin et al., 2010).

Several states also have statutes of limitations, forcing exonerees to move expeditiously on their compensation applications. The time limits in current statutes range from one to ten years, with an average limit of less than three years (Norris, 2014). The immediate struggles faced by exonerees upon release and the common lack of basic life necessities can cause strict time limits on filing for compensation to be especially burdensome.

Florida's compensation statute also has a unique limitation, referred to as a "clean-hands provision." Under this policy, any exoneree who had a felony conviction prior to being wrongfully convicted is ineligible for compensation. For example, an exoneree who committed a felony drug crime at age 17 and was punished for it, but later suffered a wrongful conviction, would not be eligible for compensation because of the earlier conviction. When Florida included this provision in its 2008 compensation statute, it excluded virtually all exonerees in the state from being eligible for compensation (Norris, 2014).

Improving Reentry
Assistance for Exonerees

To improve the reentry process for exonerees, states could, with relative ease, pass new compensation statutes and improve their existing ones. The suggestions and models from organizations like the Innocence Project, as outlined above, would provide a sound starting point. However, several scholars have suggested that delivering statutory compensation as currently made available or envisioned is inadequate, and have called for other ways of thinking about solutions to the reentry problem.

Lonergan (2008) calls for comprehensive reentry assistance that is tailored to the specific needs and circumstances of each exoneree, structured similarly to individualized education programs for children with disabilities. She suggests that, as with individualized education programs, statutes should provide for an individualized assessment for each exoneree, since their needs and challenges are unique, and provide both monetary and non-monetary assistance as appropriate. Her proposal also involves periodic measurements of progress and reevaluations to determine continuing eligibility for services.

Cook and colleagues (2014) point out that in addition to immediate record expungement and comprehensive, accessible compensation packages, exonerees should be given an official apology and should be thought of as being analogous to the original crime victim and victims' survivors. More broadly, they speak about the need for reintegration efforts to be premised on "de-labeling" (p. 246) those who were previously incarcerated, and suggest that it is important for the state to acknowledge the error, attempt to learn why it happened, and improve the system to prevent future injustices.

Finally, Griffiths and Owens (2014) suggest conceptualizing compensation for the wrongfully convicted similarly to workers' compensation. Specifically, they suggest a no-fault system wherein "compensation is awarded to injured parties irrespective of any self-contribution to their harm" (p. 275). This would prevent exonerees from having to prove that they were not partially responsible for the harm they endured, and would help acknowledge that exonerees unambiguously are victims of harm who deserve redress. Potential shortcomings remain with no-fault compensation policies, but this approach may help provide more timely and consistent services for exonerees.

None of these approaches, standing alone, is a magic bullet for providing necessary reintegration services to exonerees. In light of all that they have endured and the uniqueness of each individual, exonerees face formidable challenges and have diverse needs. However, elements of various approaches can be integrated to better provide for exonerees after their release from prison. Individualized compensation and reentry assistance that acknowledges the state's creation of the harm and does not place blame on exonerees, that is provided as expeditiously as possible, and that helps overcome the stigma associated with conviction and imprisonment, would help exonerees navigate the post-exoneration waters more successfully than current compensation methods.

Official Accountability

Assisting exonerees as they reenter conventional society is of the utmost importance, and comprehensive compensation policies can help with the transition. But such compensation policies do not address another important issue concerning wrongful convictions: official accountability. As noted earlier, police and prosecutors are largely protected by immunity from civil liability, and courts for the most part have not been receptive to claims against government officials. The case of John Thompson (also discussed briefly in chapter 8) is indicative of this problem.

Thompson, a 22-year-old father of two, was convicted in 1985 of murder and sentenced to death in Louisiana. As his seventh scheduled execution date approached, a private investigator discovered exculpatory scientific evidence that had been hidden by the district attorney's office. After 18 years in prison, including 14 on death row, Thompson was exonerated in 2003. He was given $10 and a bus ticket on release from prison (Innocence Project, 2011).

Thompson sued the district attorney's office and was awarded $14 million by a jury. The district attorney appealed, and the United States Supreme Court ruled in 2011 that the prosecutor's office could not be held civilly liable under a federal civil rights statute, 42 U.S.C. § 1983, for failing to train its prosecutors properly when only a single violation of constitutional discovery obligations was established (*Connick v. Thompson*, 2011). Thompson therefore lost his large award and ultimately received $330,000 (Gross, 2017).

The Thompson case is an indication of how difficult it is to hold powerful government agents, particularly prosecutors, accountable for their actions. Some have suggested that officials who engage in deliberate misconduct should be criminally liable. As we discussed in chapter 8, in 2013, a prosecutor was jailed for the first time for conduct contributing to a wrongful conviction: Ken Anderson pled guilty to contempt of court after withholding exculpatory evidence in a Texas case that sent the innocent Michael Morton to prison for more than two decades for the murder of his wife. However, Anderson was released after only five days in jail, and was ordered to serve 500 hours of community service and pay a $500 fine (Osborn, 2013). In addition to criminal liability, stricter professional sanctions have been urged for prosecutors who engage in unethical behavior. For example, former Durham, North Carolina, district attorney Mike Nifong was disbarred after engaging in several ethics violations in the infamous Duke Lacrosse case (Setrakian, 2007), and Texas prosecutor Charles Sebesta was disbarred after withholding evidence and using false testimony in a case leading to the wrongful conviction of Anthony Graves (Crimesrider Staff, 2015).

All three of these avenues to hold officials accountable — professional sanctions, civil liability, and criminal charges — are employed relatively rarely. However, the growing awareness of wrongful convictions and how officials can contribute to them may bring increased pressure to hold officials accountable for the unethical and illegal actions that help produce wrongful convictions.

Key Terms and Concepts

- **Stigma/stigmatization**: a perception of negative attributes associated with a person's status or condition; often applied to formerly incarcerated individuals
- **Post-traumatic stress disorder (PTSD)**: a mental health condition suffered by those who have experienced traumatic or terrifying events, including a wrongful conviction and the associated punishment experiences
- **Compensation**: redress provided to exonerees for the loss, harm, and suffering caused by a wrongful conviction; used broadly to refer to both monetary and non-monetary assistance after exoneration
- **Reentry/Reintegration**: the process of returning to traditional civilian life following a conviction and period of incarceration
- **State harm**: actions or crimes committed by the state or by agents acting on behalf of the state that harm citizens
- **Civil litigation**: one method of compensation; involves the exoneree pursuing a civil lawsuit to recover damages suffered related to a wrongful conviction
- **Private legislation**: one method of compensation; involves the exoneree petitioning the state legislature to pass a bill to provide redress to the individual exoneree
- **Statutory compensation**: one method of compensation; a law of general application that provides a set level of compensation for exonerees who meet specified eligibility requirements

- **Record expungement:** the process of sealing an arrest and conviction record so as to make it inaccessible to the public and allow exonerees to lawfully report that they have not been convicted of a crime

Discussion Questions

1. What are the three main methods of compensating wrongfully convicted individuals? What are some of the potential strengths and weaknesses of each method?

2. Should exonerees be entitled to the same reintegration services that are available to guilty incarcerated offenders who served their sentences, parolees, and probationers?

3. In addition to monetary compensation, what types of services might help exonerees overcome the many challenges of reentry? How can we help exonerees rebuild their broken family relationships, overcome stigma, and successfully confront other challenges?

4. Should exonerees be held responsible if they were deemed to "contribute to" their own conviction by falsely confessing or pleading guilty? Should these exonerees be entitled to compensation for their wrongful conviction and incarceration? Why or why not?

5. Imagine that you were wrongly convicted and imprisoned for 10 years. What would you want from the state after you were exonerated?

6. Should police and prosecutors who contribute to wrongful convictions be protected by immunity from civil liability? Why might such immunity protections exist for law enforcement officials? Should culpable officials be exposed to professional and/or criminal sanctions?

References

Acker, J. R., & Wu, S. (2020). "I did it but … I didn't": When rejected affirmative defenses produce wrongful convictions. *Nebraska Law Review, 98*, 578–642.

Alexander-Bloch, B., Miller, M. A., Zeringue, M. M., & Rubens, S. L. (2020). Mental health characteristics of exonerees: A preliminary exploration. *Psychology, Crime, & Law, 26*(8), 768–775.

Bernhard, A. (1999). When justice fails: Indemnification for unjust conviction. *University of Chicago Law School Roundtable, 6*, 73–112.

Bernhard, A. (2009). A short overview of the statutory remedies for the wrongly convicted: What works, what doesn't, and why. *Public Interest Law Journal, 18*, 403–425.

Brooks, S. K., & Greenberg, N. (2021). Psychological impact of being wrongfully accused of criminal offences: A systematic literature review. *Medicine, Science, and the Law, 61*(1), 44–54.

Campbell, K., & Denov, M. (2004). The burden of innocence: Coping with wrongful imprisonment. *Canadian Journal of Criminology and Criminal Justice, 46*, 139–164.

Connick v. Thompson, 563 U.S. 51 (2011).

Connolly, S. (2019). Righting the wrongfully convicted: How Kansas's new exoneree compensation statute sets a standard for the United States. *St. John's Law Review, 93*(3), 883–911.

Cook, K. J., Westervelt, S. D., & Maruna, S. (2014). The problem of fit: Parolees, exonerees, and prisoner reentry. In A. D. Redlich, J. R. Acker, R. J. Norris, & C. L. Bonventre (Eds.), *Examining wrongful convictions: Stepping back, moving forward* (pp. 237–250). Carolina Academic Press.

Crimesrider Staff. (2015, June 12). DA disbarred for sending Texas man to death row. CBS News. http://www.cbsnews.com/news/charles-sebasta-prosecutor-of-wrongfully-convicted-man-anthony-graves-loses-law-license/.

Death Penalty Information Center. (n.d.). True murderer gets life 11 years after death row inmate is freed. https://deathpenaltyinfo.org/node/1167.

Goldberg, L., Guillen, N., Hernandez, N., & Levett, L. M. (2020). Obstacles and barriers after exoneration. *Albany Law Review, 83*(3), 829–854.

Griffiths, E., & Owens, M. L. (2014). Remedying wrongful convictions: Societal obligations to exonerees. In A. D. Redlich, J. R. Acker, R. J. Norris, & C. L. Bonventre (Eds.), *Examining wrongful convictions: Stepping back, moving forward* (pp. 267–280). Carolina Academic Press.

Gross, A. (2017, October 4). John Thompson. National Registry of Exonerations. https://www.law.umich.edu/special/exoneration/Pages/casedetail.aspx?caseid=3684.

Grounds, A. (2004). Psychological consequences of wrongful conviction and imprisonment. *Canadian Journal of Criminology and Criminal Justice, 46*, 165–182.

Gutman, J. S. (2017). An empirical reexamination of state statutory compensation for the wrongly convicted. *Missouri Law Review, 82*, 369–438.

The Innocence Project. (2009). *Making up for lost time: What the wrongfully convicted endure and how to provide fair compensation.* https://www.innocenceproject.org/wp-content/uploads/2016/06/innocence_project_compensation_report-6.pdf.

The Innocence Project. (2010). *Life after exoneration* [Video File]. https://www. youtube.com/watch?v=z8L8gxfM2Js.

The Innocence Project. (2011, August 31). Holding prosecutors accountable. https://www.innocenceproject.org/holding-prosecutors-accountable/.

The Innocence Project. (2014, November 5). Texas exoneree may be forced to pay $334,000 in back child support. https://www.innocenceproject.org/ texas-exoneree-may-be-forced-to-pay-334000-in-back-child-support/.

Jefferson v. State, 95 So.3d 709 (Miss. 2012).

Junkin, T. (2004). *Bloodsworth*. Algonquin Books.

Kahn, D. S. (2010). Presumed guilty until proven innocent: The burden of proof in wrongful conviction claims under state compensation statutes. *University of Michigan Journal of Law Reform, 44*, 123–168.

Kassin, S. M., Drizin, S. A., Grisso, T., Gudjonsson, G. H., Leo, R. A., & Redlich, A. D. (2010). Police-induced confessions: Risk factors and recommendations. *Law and Human Behavior, 34*, 3–38.

Kukucka, J., Applegarth, H. K., & Mello, A. L. (2020). Do exonerees face employment discrimination similar to actual offenders? *Legal and Criminological Psychology, 25*, 17–32.

Lonergan, J. R. (2008). Protecting the innocent: A model for comprehensive, individualized compensation of the exonerated. *NYU Journal of Legislation and Public Policy, 11*, 405–452.

Norris, R. J. (2012). Assessing compensation statutes for the wrongly convicted. *Criminal Justice Policy Review, 23*, 352–374.

Norris, R. J. (2014). Exoneree compensation: Current policies and future outlook. In M. Zalman & J. Carrano (Eds.), *Wrongful conviction and criminal justice reform: Making justice* (pp. 289–303). Routledge.

Norris, R. J. (2017). *Exonerated: A history of the innocence movement*. New York University Press.

Osborn, C. (2013, November 15). How Ken Anderson was released after only five days in jail. *Statesman*. http://www.statesman.com/news/local/how-ken-anderson-was-released-after-only-five-days-jail/UGpWcPAITgVFv W2R2S32xK/.

Rhoades v. State, 880 N.W.2d 431 (Iowa 2016).

Savage, M. E., Clow, K. A., Schuller, R. A., & Ricciardelli, R. (2018). After exoneration: Attributions of responsibility impact perceptions. *Canadian Journal of Law and Society, 33*(1), 85–103.

Setrakian, L. (2007, June 16). Former Duke prosecutor Nifong disbarred. ABC News. http://abcnews.go.com/TheLaw/story?id=3285862.

Shlosberg, A., Mandery, E., & West, V. (2012). The expungement myth. *Albany Law Review, 75*, 1229–1241.

Shlosberg, A., Mandery, E., West, V., & Callaghan, B. (2014). Expungement and post-exoneration offending. *Journal of Criminal Law and Criminology*, *104*(2), 353–388.

State v. Ford, 193 So.3d 1242 (La. App. 2016).

Trivelli, A. (2016). Compensating the wrongfully convicted: A proposal to make victims of wrongful incarceration whole again. *Richmond Journal of Law and the Public Interest*, *19*, 257–282.

Warden, R. (n.d.). Kirk Bloodsworth. National Registry of Exonerations. https://www.law.umich.edu/special/exoneration/Pages/casedetail.aspx?caseid=3032.

Westervelt, S. D., & Cook, K. J. (2010). Framing innocents: The wrongly convicted as victims of state harm. *Crime, Law, and Social Change*, *53*, 259–275.

Westervelt, S. D., & Cook, K. J. (2012). *Life after death row: Exonerees' search for community and identity*. Rutgers University Press.

Chapter 13

Actual Perpetrators: Public Safety and Monetary Considerations

Learning Objectives

After reading this chapter, you should be able to:

- Understand what is meant by "true perpetrators" in the context of wrongful convictions.
- Discuss research documenting the extent of preventable crimes committed by true perpetrators.
- Discuss the individual and societal costs incurred when true perpetrators remain at large while innocent individuals are wrongfully convicted.
- Understand that reforms aimed at improving justice system reliability and thus reducing wrongful convictions should outweigh ideological differences concerning justice system values.

Case Study: Levon Brooks and Kennedy Brewer

Three-year-old Courtney Smith was abducted from the bed she shared with her two sisters in rural Noxubee County, Mississippi, on the early morning of September 15, 1990. Two days later her body was found in a nearby pond. An autopsy revealed that she had suffered several injuries, including bruises about her head, tears in her vaginal wall and hymen, and abrasions on her wrist. The cause of death was drowning. Five-year-old Ashley Smith, one of Courtney's sisters, identified Levon Brooks, a former boyfriend of her mother, as the man who had taken Courtney from her bed. Brooks was arrested and charged with capital murder. He pled not guilty and was brought to trial in January 1992. Dr. Michael West, a forensic odontologist, testified for the prosecution. Dr. West identified the abrasions on Courtney's wrist as human bite marks and stated that "it could be no one else but Levon Brooks that bit this girl's arm" (quoted in *Brooks v. State*, 1999, p. 750). Brooks was convicted and sentenced to life imprisonment without possibility of parole.

In May 1992, a tragically similar crime occurred in Noxubee County, just three miles from where Courtney Smith had resided. Three-year-old Christine Jackson disappeared from her bedroom sometime before dawn on May 3rd. Kennedy Brewer, the boyfriend of Christine's mother and the father of two of her children, had been babysitting Christine and her two younger siblings during the night. Two days after Christine's disappearance, her body was discovered in a creek behind her house. She had been strangled and sexually assaulted. Brewer was charged with the crimes and brought to trial in March 1995. Dr. Michael West testified at the trial that multiple wounds found on Christine's body were human bite marks. He opined that five of the marks "were very good and [he] indicated within a reasonable degree of medical certainty that Brewer put them there" (*Brewer v. State*, 1998, p. 134). Brewer was convicted and sentenced to death. While affirming his conviction and death sentence, the Mississippi Supreme Court concluded that "[t]he evidence in this case, albeit circumstantial, sufficiently supported the jury's verdict" (*Brewer v. State*, 1998, p. 134).

Much later, the convictions against both Levon Brooks and Kennedy Brewer unraveled. Neither had committed the heinous crimes that resulted in Brooks spending 18 years in jail and prison, and Brewer remaining incarcerated for more than 15 years, including several spent on death row. DNA testing conducted in 2001 excluded Brewer as the source of semen recovered from Christine Jackson's body. Although his conviction was vacated, he was held in jail five more years pending a new trial. Attorneys for the Innocence Project pressed to secure Brewer's release. They also noted the similarity between the crimes for which Brewer and Brooks had been convicted. Their investigation linked the DNA evidence in Brewer's case to another man, Justin Albert Johnson (Innocence Project, 2008).

Johnson lived close to the homes of the murdered children in both cases. He had a history of sexually assaulting women and children. Although he had been a suspect in both crimes, and even provided blood and hair samples during one of the investigations, law enforcement authorities did not pursue him or the possible connection between the two sexual assaults and murders. They had focused instead on Brooks and Brewer. The same sheriff's officer had investigated the killings in both cases, and the same medical examiner had conducted the autopsies. The same prosecutor had filed charges in both cases. Dr. West had examined the bodies of both children and testified at both trials. Ironically, Johnson reportedly was excluded as a suspect in both cases based on bite-mark comparisons. After the DNA analysis led the police to Johnson, he confessed to murdering both Courtney Smith and Christine Jackson (Dewan, 2008; Lechliter, 2008; Innocence Project, 2008; Neufeld, 2008).

Levon Brooks and Kennedy Brewer were exonerated in 2008 (Mott, 2008). Justin Albert Johnson pled guilty to raping and murdering Courtney Smith and Christine Jackson in 2012. He was sentenced to two terms of life imprisonment without parole (Balko & Carrington, 2018, p. 319; Sisson, 2012). A lawyer from the Innocence Project observed: "If local law enforcement had properly investigated these crimes, they would have stayed focused on Albert Johnson from the beginning. In fact, if Albert Johnson had been apprehended for the first crime, the second one would never have happened—and the three-year-old victim would be approaching her 18th birthday" (Innocence Project, 2008).

A Closer Look: Kennedy Brewer and Levon Brooks

- *Mississippi Innocence* (2011). In this documentary film, director Joe York examines the wrongful convictions of Brewer and Brooks as well as their path to exoneration and return to society.

Additional Victims

Wrongful convictions produce a tsunami of harms. The harms begin, of course, with the innocent persons who suffer stigmatization and punishment for crimes they did not commit. As we discussed in chapter 12, they commonly entail fractured familial relations and lost friendships. They extend more broadly still, further victimizing original crime victims and their families, and tarnishing systems of justice and how citizens perceive them. Additional insidious harms loom in "wrong person" cases. When an innocent person is erroneously arrested, charged, convicted, and punished, the true offender has escaped prosecution and remains at large, all the while capable of committing more crimes and claiming new victims. As evidence of these grim truths, we need look no farther than the compounded miscarriages of justice in the cases of Levon Brooks, Kennedy Brewer, their families, and the young victims of Justin Albert Johnson's brutal crimes.

The new harms inflicted by the real offender when the wrong person is held responsible for a crime are an often-overlooked consequence of wrongful convictions. They represent "the flipside injustice" of wrongful convictions (Acker, 2012/2013). The most immediate and significant harm occurs in the form of new crime victims; victims whose lives, well-being, and property would have been spared had the crime's **true perpetrator** been arrested and prosecuted rather than the innocent person who instead suffered conviction and punishment. The Supreme Court observed many years ago that "the twofold aim of [the law] is that guilt shall not escape or innocence suffer" (*Berger v. United States*, 1935, p. 88). Although the focus throughout this book has been on miscarriages of justice in the form of wrongful convictions, we must keep in mind that justice is thwarted as well when those who commit criminal acts of violence and property loss elude detection and are not held accountable for their conduct. Few will quarrel with the desirability of achieving a system of "reliable justice, a perspective grounded in the dual objectives of fairly and accurately determining both guilt and innocence" (Acker, 2018/2019, p. 719).

One key benefit of post-conviction DNA testing is not only that it might help uncover and overturn wrongful convictions, but help identify the real offenders. In a study of the 325 DNA-based exonerations encompassing 1989 through 2014, West and Meterko (2015/2016, pp. 730–731) identified 159 (49%) in which the actual perpetrators were discovered.

> Tragically, many of these real perpetrators went on to commit additional violent crimes, leaving more victims and their families to suffer avoidable crimes.... 68 perpetrators went on to commit 142 violent crimes (based on convictions for subsequent violent crimes). Of these, 77 were rapes, 34 were homicides and 31 were other violent crimes (e.g., armed robbery, attempted homicide). These known additional crimes represent just a fraction of all subsequent criminal activity, as the real perpetrators have not been identified in half of these DNA exoneration cases and without a name we cannot know about their criminal activity (p. 731).

These figures doubtlessly represent a significant undercounting of the new crimes committed by the true offenders that occurred following the arrest of the individuals who were wrongfully convicted. Not only do they fail to capture crimes committed by the true perpetrators who were never identified, they only include the crimes known to have been carried out in the cases where the true offender ultimately was identified. Although we lack complete information about the nature and magnitude of the harms inflicted by the actual perpetrators of crimes for which others have been convicted and punished, we can be certain that many more innocent victims suffered damages to their lives and well-being while the true perpetrators eluded justice.

Several other researchers have collected information about the crimes committed by the truly guilty parties following the arrest and conviction of innocents. Two published studies focus on specific states — Illinois and North Carolina — and two others cast a wider net. Collectively, the Innocence Project data noted above and the studies described below offer some insight into the potential harms generated by actual offenders who escape apprehension when the innocent are arrested and convicted.

The Illinois study was completed in 2011 by the Better Government Association and the Center on Wrongful Convictions (BGA/CWC). It focused exclusively on wrongful convictions for the offenses of murder, attempted murder, kidnapping, sexual assault, and armed robbery, identifying 85 such cases in the state between 1989 and 2010. The wrongfully convicted individuals, on average, spent more than 10 years in prison before being exonerated. Meanwhile, "the actual perpetrators, left on the street, went on to commit at least 97 felonies, including 14 murders, 11 sexual assaults, 10 kidnappings, 19 armed robberies, and 43 other charges such as attempted murder of federal officers, aggravated battery, and various narcotics offenses." The true perpetrators were not identified in many of the cases, making the tally of new crimes committed far from complete: "the 85 exonerations left 35 murders, 11 rapes, and two murder-rapes with no identified perpetrators and thus no way to add up their accumulated crimes" (Conroy & Warden, 2011).

The stark statistics risk dehumanizing the full extent of the harms caused by the true offenders in the wake of others' wrongful convictions. For example, Jerry Miller was convicted in 1982 for beating, raping, and robbing a woman in Chicago in 1981. He was sentenced to serve 52 years in prison and was incarcerated for nearly 25 years before being paroled in 2006. Miller was exonerated in 2007 after DNA analysis linked Robin Weeks to the 1981 rape for which Miller had been convicted. While Miller stood wrongfully convicted and imprisoned for that offense, Weeks's known crimes included:

- In 1981, beating a man in the face and about his body with a chain in an attempt to steal his watch.
- In 1982, raping and robbing a woman in an alley, and in the process beating her, breaking her cheekbone while kicking her and pounding her head against the pavement.

- In 1982, hitting a woman in the face, choking and biting her, while attempting to force her into a car.
- In 1982, attacking four police officers who responded to arrest him for the above assault (Weeks was sentenced to 12 years in prison after pleading guilty to the crimes against the two women described above).
- In 1996, kicking the windows out of a police car after being arrested for breaking into cars.
- In 1999, violating sex offender registration requirements.
- In 2000, raping a woman and inflicting numerous injuries to her face, neck, ribs, and legs.
- In 2001, hitting a woman in the head with a rock, breaking her nose, orbital bone, and wrist, and raping her.
- In 2001, attacking five police officers while being booked on a battery charge, resulting in one officer's hospitalization.
- In 2004, attacking two police officers who had responded to a complaint about his public indecency. Weeks thereafter was sentenced to prison and a DNA sample was collected, leading to his identification for the 1981 rape for which Miller had been convicted, and for other crimes (Conroy & Warden, 2011).

In a study entitled, "The Mayhem of **Wrongful Liberty**: Documenting the Crimes of True Perpetrators in Cases of Wrongful Incarceration," Baumgartner and colleagues (2017/2018) identified 36 individuals in North Carolina who were exonerated after being wrongfully convicted of crimes. With the exception of one offense committed in 1942, resulting in a 1943 exoneration, all of the crimes and corresponding exonerations occurred between 1973 and 2007. The true perpetrators were identified in only ten of the 36 exoneration cases, and in one of the cases, involving Alan Gell, the real offender was arrested at the same time as the wrongfully convicted person. Thus, the researchers identified nine cases with known perpetrators who remained at liberty and capable of committing other crimes after the wrong person was erroneously arrested. They ascertained that the true perpetrators committed offenses in six of those cases following the arrest of the wrongfully convicted individual. More specifically, the authors explain that, "[t]hese six individuals collectively were arrested and convicted of ninety-nine subsequent crimes of which thirty-five were felonies and thirteen were violent crimes. These are all crimes that could have, should have, and would have never occurred if these true perpetrators had been in prison for their earlier crimes" (pp. 1281–82, footnote omitted). Baumgartner and colleagues note that the ninety-nine offenses known to have been committed by the actual offenders is a "very conservative" (p. 1284) estimate of the true incidence of criminality because many true offenders were never identified, and those who are known well may have committed additional offenses that were not linked to them.

The most active true perpetrator among the cases they identified was Albert Turner. Turner was responsible for the 1987 rape for which Willie Grimes was wrongfully convicted, resulting in Grimes serving 24 years in prison before being exonerated in 2012. While Grimes was imprisoned, over a 20-year period spanning 1988 to 2008, Turner committed at least seven additional crimes of assault on a female, two assaults with a deadly weapon, four simple assaults, two offenses of communicating threats, as well as other nonviolent crimes (Baumgartner et al., 2017/2018, pp. 1273–1274). Lamentably, Turner was a suspect for the original crime for which Grimes was arrested and convicted, but he was not arrested.

Another of the cases in their study involved the wrongful conviction of Ronald Cotton, which we highlighted in chapter 3 in our discussion of eyewitness misidentification (see Thompson-Cannino, Cotton, & Torneo, 2009). Cotton was erroneously convicted for committing two rapes while the true perpetrator of those crimes, Bobby Poole, remained at large. During his period of wrongful liberty Poole committed six additional rapes (Baumgartner et al., 2017/2018, p. 1264). As a result of his wrongful conviction, Cotton spent 11 years in prison. Collectively, the 36 North Carolina exonerees identified by the researchers spent approximately 387 years in prison for crimes committed by others (p. 1287).

One study identified sixty-two serial homicide offenders, who collectively were responsible for claiming the lives of 249 victims. Nearly half of those killings, 114, or 46%, were committed after an innocent person was incarcerated following the true offender's initial homicide and thus were deemed preventable. The researchers reported that thirty-nine of the serial homicide offenders were not apprehended for their first killing because an innocent person had been incarcerated for it, allowing 79 of the preventable homicides to be committed (Yaksic et al., 2021; see also Weintraub & Bernstein, 2020, p. 184).

Finally, relying on data supplied by the Innocence Project and other records, Norris et al. (2020) gathered information about the crimes committed by true perpetrators of offenses while they remained at large following the wrongful conviction of others for their crimes. They examined 109 cases of DNA-based exonerations in which the true offenders subsequently were identified through DNA evidence. Among the 109 true perpetrators, 102 were found to have committed a total of 337 new crimes during their period of wrongful liberty, or an average of 3.1 per person. Thirty-four of the offenders were linked to a single new crime, while the remainder committed multiple new offenses while free, ranging from two to twelve. Their new crimes included 43 homicides and 94 sex offenses. Projecting from these findings, the researchers estimated that nationally:

> [T]rue perpetrators may escape apprehension and conviction in an estimated 7,040 to 13,440 violent crime cases per year. Among the true perpetrators included in our analysis (n = 109), we found 337 crimes, or an average of 3.1 additional crimes per person. Thus, if 7,040 to 13,440 perpetrators remain free and each commits an average of 3.1 crimes during his or her period of wrongful liberty, the wrongful convictions that occur each year would ultimately enable true perpetrators to commit between 21,824 and 41,664 additional crimes (Norris et al., 2020, p. 375).

Noting that they doubtlessly had failed to uncover all crimes committed by the true offenders and that their sample involved only DNA-based exoneration cases in which the actual offenders were identified with the assistance of DNA evidence, they concluded: "These projections remain astounding.... Over time, the potential crime-related costs of wrongful conviction are tremendous" (Norris et al., 2020, p. 375).

Clearly, the harms caused nationwide by the true perpetrators of crimes while the wrong person has been arrested and suffers punishment represent a tragic compendium of lost lives, serious bodily injury, profound psychological damage, and extensive property loss. As worrisome as are the raw statistics, the narratives describing the new victimizations in such cases are particularly painful and sobering (Acker, 2012/2013). Mistakes in the administration of justice are inevitable. Not all wrongful arrests and convictions are avoidable. The harms suffered in cases such as those catalogued above are nevertheless especially tragic because at least some of them could have been prevented. They would not have been inflicted if the actual offender had been timely arrested and successfully prosecuted, and had justice not miscarried. Moreover, some of the harms inflicted by actual offenders could have been avoided if prosecutors and other criminal justice officials had been more willing to reinvestigate and correct cases in which wrongful convictions occurred (Weintraub, 2020).

Wrongful Convictions in Popular Culture: True Perps?

A Murder in the Park (2014) — Filmmakers Charles S. Rech and Brandon Kimber document the case of Anthony Porter, who was exonerated in 1999 after being sentenced to death for murder. His exoneration, spurred by the confession of Alstory Simon, was widely covered and was instrumental in Illinois's eventual abolition of the death penalty. However, recent events have led many to question Porter's exoneration and Simon's guilt, and investigators for Porter have been accused of engaging in unethical behavior. This case highlights the challenges with identifying actual innocence and true guilt.

Monetary Costs

The financial costs associated with the harms inflicted by actual offenders when innocent persons are erroneously arrested and convicted are substantial, although they defy precise calculation. No amount of money can adequately redress what the innocent have suffered, nor the loss of life, the serious injuries inflicted, and the multiple other harms caused when new crimes are committed. Nevertheless, no metric other than one based on dollars and cents is readily available. The estimated monetary costs are staggering. Nearly three-fourths (238/325, or 73%) of the individuals identified by the Innocence Project who were exonerated through 2014 with the help of DNA analysis received some type of compensation or damage awards stemming from their wrongful convictions. The aggregate sum paid to the exonerees was calculated at well in excess of half a *billion* dollars ($597,031,409) (West & Meterko, 2015/2016, pp. 773–774). Another study determined that between 1989 and September 2018, states paid some $545 million to wrongfully incarcerated exonerees pursuant to compensation statutes, and exonerees recovered an additional $1.7 billion by pursuing state and federal civil actions (Gutman & Sun, 2019, pp. 699–700; National Registry of Exonerations, n.d.). Many of these payouts, and the injuries they were meant to redress, would have been avoided if the crimes' true perpetrators had been identified at the outset and the wrongfully convicted innocents spared arrest and punishment.

The BGA/CWC study (Conroy & Warden, 2011) attempted to calculate the financial costs associated with Illinois wrongful convictions and exonerations between 1989 and 2010. As noted previously, the investigation was limited, focusing only on cases involving murder, attempted murder, kidnapping, sexual assault, and armed robbery. Total costs paid by taxpayers were estimated at $214 million. With several lawsuits related to the wrongful convictions still pending at the time the study was published, the researchers projected that the amount eventually would easily top $300 million. The $214 million in accrued costs included $155.9 million damages awarded to exonerees through litigation and settlements, $8.2 million paid as compensation through Illinois Court of

Claims filings, $31.6 million of public funds paid to the private attorneys representing governmental officials in civil suits, and $18.5 million spent incarcerating the wrongly convicted while they were housed for a total of 926 years in jail and prison (Conroy & Warden, 2011).

Direct costs of this nature do not begin to capture numerous additional fiscal consequences of wrongful convictions, most notably the injuries suffered by the new victims of the crimes' true perpetrators. These victim-related harms include the loss of life, serious physical injury, property damages, medical bills, lost wages, psychological counseling, and more. Such additional expenditures almost certainly total in the hundreds of millions of dollars or more when aggregated (Acker, 2012/2013).

Policy Implications

The defendants who suffer wrongful conviction are found guilty following contested trials and through pleas of guilty tendered in the face of prosecution. Defense attorneys who seek to overturn their unjust convictions and spare them further punishment must frequently engage in extended litigation while struggling to overcome prosecutors' strident opposition. Reform efforts designed to minimize the risk of wrongful convictions and help identify and correct miscarriages of justice are largely championed by organizations that represent convicted defendants or work closely with them. These alignments threaten to position the innocence movement within the traditional adversarial model, pitting the interests of pro-defendant, due process-oriented reformers against supporters who emphasize law and order and maintain a healthy crime control perspective (Acker, 2018/2019). For various reasons, "innocence advocates are generally lumped together with the defense community" (Norris, 2017, p. 186).

To the extent such perceptions prevail, they are sorely misguided. No one benefits when innocent people are convicted of crimes and when the guilty go free; no one, except the true perpetrators who elude justice while the wrongfully convicted suffer punishment instead. The commonality of interests shared by due process adherents, crime control proponents, and others who are concerned about errors of justice far outweighs the ideological differences that might otherwise separate them (see Norris et al., 2020). No one welcomes the punishment of innocent persons, the harms committed by true perpetrators, the attendant threats to public safety, or the undermining of community confidence in the administration of justice (Bowman, 2008; Forst, 2010/2011) that are among the consequences of wrongful convictions.

Several reforms that would help guard against wrongful convictions have the exclusive focus of enhancing reliability. They impose no significant costs on justice systems, including risking that guilty parties will somehow benefit by avoiding arrest, prosecution, and conviction (Acker, 2018/2019; Findley, 2008). One example of such reform efforts involves eyewitness identification procedures that are designed to prevent suggestiveness and related threats to accuracy. We discussed several recommended safeguards of this type in chapter 3, including having the police instruct witnesses that the actual offender may or may not appear in the line-up or photo array that they will observe, securing witnesses' contemporaneous statements regarding their degree of confidence in making an identification, advising witnesses following their attempt to make an identification that the investigation will continue, and using double-blind procedures to ensure that the participating officer is unaware of the suspect's identity and thus is prevented from transmitting cues that might influence the witness.

Criminal justice systems nevertheless serve multiple objectives. Although producing factually accurate decisions about guilt and innocence is among them, it is not the only one, as Simon (2011, p. 204) explained:

> The process must fulfill a broader array of objectives, which include promoting the public's acceptance of verdicts, expressing society's values, asserting the authoritative power of the state, bringing closure to victims, and finalizing disputes. The process must also comport with a number of constraints, such as expedience, cost-effectiveness, and timeliness, all the while protecting the privacy and autonomy interests of the people involved. A key challenge facing any criminal justice system is how to balance between and among the search for truth and these competing objectives and constraints.

It is undisputable that some measures that would help protect innocents against wrongful conviction would work at cross purposes with respect to other important interests, including bringing guilty parties to justice and protecting society from the crimes they might commit. Some reforms would also entail significant monetary and practical costs. For example, reducing the caseloads of public defenders by hiring more attorneys and investigators would almost certainly help avoid wrongful convictions by enhancing the quality of representation for indigents charged with both felonies and misdemeanors (American Bar Association Standing Committee on Legal Aid and Indigent Defendants, 2004). Yet such measures would also require a commensurate investment of resources. Similarly, separating crime laboratories from law enforcement agencies would promote independence and help ensure more equal access to services by the prosecution and defense (Gabel, 2014, pp. 336–337; Thompson, 2015), thus diminishing the risk of wrongful convictions, but taking such action would be quite expensive.

Various reforms that would reduce the likelihood of wrongful convictions would come at the expense of heightening the incidence of failed arrests and **wrongful acquittals**, i.e., of allowing factually guilty individuals to avoid prosecution and conviction (Bushway, 2010/2011; Clark, 2010/2011). In a rather extreme statement of this general principle, the British philosopher Jeremy Bentham observed: "[W]e must be on guard against those sentimental exaggerations which tend to give crime impunity, under the pretext of insuring the safety of innocence…. I know not how many writers, who hold, that, in no case, ought an accused person to be condemned, unless evidence amount to mathematical or absolute certainty. According to this maxim, nobody ought to be punished, lest an innocent man be punished" (Bentham, 1829, p. 169, quoted in Laufer, 1995, p. 333 n. 17).

The concern that measures designed to protect the innocent will occasion an unacceptably high risk of allowing the guilty to go free demands a careful assessment of the trade-offs envisioned in the famous proclamation by the prominent British jurist, Sir William Blackstone (1769, vol. 4, p. *358): "[I]t is better that ten guilty persons escape than that one innocent suffer." Whether the 10-to-1 "**Blackstone ratio**" represents the optimal balance between the respective undesirable outcomes has been extensively debated (Volokh, 1997). The weights assigned the different adverse consequences — having guilty offenders escape conviction and the wrongful conviction of an innocent person — in combination with estimates of the magnitude of the corresponding risks, have important policy consequences for justice system reforms (Allen & Laudan, 2008; Risinger, 2007).

In less abstract terms, the calculus embedded in the Blackstone ratio demands careful consideration of difficult questions that arise from cases such as those highlighted in this chapter. How many Justin Albert Johnsons should society risk remaining at large in order to spare the wrongful convictions of individuals such as Levon Brooks and Kennedy Brewer? How many Robin Weekses escaping conviction can be tolerated in return for guarding against the erroneous conviction and punishment of people like Jerry Miller? How many Albert Turners remaining free can be justified to avoid the conviction and punishment of Willie Grimes and other innocents? Of course, not all offenders will recidivate, and many of those who do will lack the vicious proclivities typified by Johnson, Weeks, and Turner. Nor does the Blackstone ratio, and variations of it, depend on the envisioned guilty offenders and the suffering innocents being linked with one another in the same or ensuing cases. Still, putting faces on the offenders, innocents, and injured victims requires confronting the underlying consequences and exquisitely difficult value judgments which depend on balancing the risk of having guilty parties escape justice to avoid erroneously punishing the innocent.

What should not be controversial is the wisdom of enacting reforms that would help protect the innocent against erroneous conviction without the accompanying, offsetting risk of enabling true perpetrators to go free, or the concern of overtaxing scarce resources (Acker, 2018/2019). At a minimum, legislative and administrative measures of this general type need not be derailed by ideological differences and the misconception that innocence-related protections must necessarily compromise law enforcement efforts to identify criminals and societal interests in prosecuting and punishing offenders (Norris et al., 2020). The Blackstone 10-to-1 ratio is misleading to the extent that it suggests that achieving justice is necessarily a zero-sum game. Some important safeguards can enhance reliability without occasioning reciprocal costs, and there is no reason to hold back on implementing them (Rosen, 2008; Zalman, 2010/2011).

Potential reforms that do entail costs, either in risking that some criminal perpetrators will remain at large, or in depleting fiscal and other resources, must be scrutinized more thoroughly. While virtually no one would knowingly countenance the conviction and punishment of an innocent person, there is no denying that highly significant costs are also incurred when criminal offenders remain at large, claim new victims, and otherwise cheat justice. The value judgments inherent in the Blackstone ratio and similar trade-offs — such as that it is better that 10 guilty offenders go free than that one innocent person suffer conviction and punishment — are unavoidable and must be confronted. There are no better solutions than candidly recognizing them, openly debating them, and ultimately attempting to reconcile them consistent with the multiple ends of justice.

Key Terms and Concepts

- **True perpetrator**: in a wrong-person case, the person who actually committed the offense for which an innocent individual was wrongly convicted
- **Wrongful liberty**: refers to the freedom of the true perpetrator who escapes arrest, conviction, and punishment for a criminal act, while an innocent person is wrongly convicted
- **Wrongful acquittal**: the acquittal (not guilty verdict) of a factually guilty individual

- **Blackstone ratio:** from Sir William Blackstone, the declaration that, "[I]t is better that ten guilty persons escape than that one innocent suffer"; suggests that the wrongful conviction of an innocent person should be weighed more heavily than the wrongful acquittal of a guilty person

Discussion Questions

1. What important individual and societal costs are incurred when the true perpetrators of crimes avoid apprehension and punishment, while innocent persons suffer arrest and wrongful conviction?

2. Why is it impossible to identify the full extent of the harms caused by actual offenders in cases of wrongful conviction?

3. What are examples of reforms that could be enacted that would help guard against wrongful convictions and that would be unlikely to entail countervailing costs, either in enabling more guilty offenders to remain free or in the form of requiring the investment of significant monetary or other resources?

4. What are examples of reforms that would help guard against wrongful convictions but, if enacted, would likely occasion trade-offs in allowing more guilty offenders to remain free or being prohibitively expensive?

5. Sir William Blackstone famously ventured that "it is better that ten guilty persons escape than that one innocent suffer." Do you believe that this 10-to-1 ratio works the right balance between the respective errors? If not, what ratio would better reflect the appropriate weighing of interests?

References

Acker, J. R. (2012/2013). The flipside injustice of wrongful convictions: When the guilty go free. *Albany Law Review, 76*, 1629–1712.

Acker, J. R. (2018/2019). Reliable justice: Achieving the twofold aim of establishing guilt and protecting the innocent. *Albany Law Review, 82*, 719–773.

Allen, R. J., & Laudan, L. (2008). Deadly dilemmas. *Texas Tech Law Review, 41*, 65–92.

American Bar Association Standing Committee on Legal Aid and Indigent Defendants. (2004). *Gideon's broken promise: America's continuing quest for equal justice.* http://www.americanbar.org/content/dam/aba/administrative/legal_aid_indigent_defendants/ls_sclaid_def_bp_execsummary.authcheck dam.pdf.

Balko, R., & Carrington, T. (2018). *The cadaver king and the country dentist: A true story of injustice in the American South.* PublicAffairs.

Baumgartner, F. R., Grigg, A., Ramirez, R., & Lucy, J. S. (2017/2018). The mayhem of wrongful liberty: Documenting the crimes of true perpetrators in cases of wrongful incarceration. *Albany Law Review, 81,* 1263–1288.

Bentham, J. (1829). *Principles of judicial procedure.* W. Tait.

Berger v. United States, 295 U.S. 78 (1935).

Blackstone, W. (1769). *Commentaries on the laws of England* (Vol. 4). Clarendon Press.

Bowman, L. E. (2008). Lemonade out of lemons: Can wrongful convictions lead to criminal justice reform? *Journal of Criminal Law & Criminology, 98,* 1501–1517.

Brewer v. State, 725 So. 2d 106 (Miss. 1998).

Brooks v. State, 748 So. 2d 736 (Miss. 1999).

Bushway, S. D. (2010/2011). Estimating empirical Blackstone ratios in two settings: Murder cases and hiring. *Albany Law Review, 74,* 1087–1104.

Clark, S. E. (2010/2011). Blackstone and the balance of eyewitness identification evidence. *Albany Law Review, 74,* 1105–1156.

Conroy, J., & Warden, R. (2011). *Special investigation: The high costs of wrongful convictions.* http://www.bettergov.org/news/special-investigation-the-high-costs-of-wrongful-convictions.

Dewan, S. (2008, February 8). New suspect is arrested in 2 Mississippi killings. *The New York Times.* http://www.nytimes.com/2008/02/08/us/08dna.html.

Findley, K. A. (2008). Toward a new paradigm of criminal justice: How the innocence movement merges crime control and due process. *Texas Tech Law Review, 41,* 133–173.

Forst, B. (2010/2011). Managing miscarriages of justice from victimization to reintegration. *Albany Law Review, 74,* 1209–1275.

Gabel, J. D. (2014). Realizing reliability in forensic science from the ground up. *Journal of Criminal Law & Criminology, 104,* 283–352.

Gutman, J. S., & Sun, L. (2019). Why is Mississippi the best state in which to be exonerated? An empirical examination of state statutory and civil compensation for the wrongfully convicted. *Northeastern University Law Review, 11,* 694–789.

The Innocence Project. (2008, February 15). *Two innocent men cleared today in separate murder cases in Mississippi, 15 years after wrongful convictions.* https://www.innocenceproject.org/two-innocent-men-cleared-today-in-separate-murder-cases-in-mississippi-15-years-after-wrongful-convictions/.

Laufer, W. S. (1995). The rhetoric of innocence. *Washington Law Review, 70,* 329–421.

Lechliter, J. (2008). Falsely accused: Prosecutor, forensic experts take heat for Mississippi "disaster." *The Forensic Examiner, 17*(2). https://issuu.com/acfei.media/docs/summer2008.

Mott, R. (2008, March 13). "The nightmare is over": Levon Brooks finally free. *The Jackson Free Press.* http://www.jacksonfreepress.com/news/2008/mar/13/the-nightmare-is-over-levon-brooks-finally-free/.

National Registry of Exonerations. (n.d.). Milestone: Exonerated defendants spent 20,000 years in prison. http://www.law.umich.edu/special/exoneration/Documents/NRE.20000.Years.Report.pdf.

Neufeld, P. (2008). Keynote address. *Southwestern Law Review, 37,* 1051–1063.

Norris, R. J. (2017). *Exonerated: A history of the innocence movement.* New York University Press.

Norris, R. J., Weintraub, J. N., Acker, J. R., Redlich, A. D., & Bonventre, C. L. (2020). The criminal costs of wrongful convictions: Can we reduce crime by protecting the innocent? *Criminology & Public Policy, 19,* 367–388.

Risinger, D. M. (2007). Innocents convicted: An empirically justified factual wrongful conviction rate. *Journal of Criminal Law & Criminology, 97,* 761–804.

Rosen, R. A. (2006). Reflections on innocence. *Wisconsin Law Review, 2006,* 237–290.

Simon, D. (2011). The limited diagnosticity of criminal trials. *Vanderbilt Law Review, 64,* 143–223.

Sisson, C. K. (2012, February 10). Noxubee man gets life sentence for rape, murder. *The Dispatch.* http://www.cdispatch.com/news/article.asp?aid=15589&TRACKER=1&TID=.

Thompson, S. G. (2015). *Curbing wrongful convictions through independent forensic laboratories.* Carolina Academic Press.

Thompson-Cannino, J., Cotton, R., & Torneo, E. (2009). *Picking Cotton: Our memoir of injustice and redemption.* St. Martin's Press.

Volokh, A. (1997). n guilty men. *University of Pennsylvania Law Review, 146,* 173–212.

Weintraub, J. N. (2020). Obstructing justice: The association between prosecutorial misconduct and the identification of true perpetrators. *Crime & Delinquency, 66,* 1195–1216.

Weintraub, J. N., & Bernstein, K. M. (2020). Identifying and charging true perpetrators in cases of wrongful convictions. *Wrongful Conviction Law Review*, *1*, 181–225.

West, E., & Meterko, V. (2015/2016). Innocence Project: DNA exonerations, 1989–2014: Review of data and findings from the first 25 years. *Albany Law Review*, *79*, 717–795.

Yaksic, E., Allred, T. B., Drakulic, C., Mooney, R., De Şilva, R., Geyer, P., Wills, A., Comerford, C., & Ranger, R. (2021). How much damage do serial homicide offenders wrought while the innocent rot in prison? A tabulation of preventable deaths as outcomes of sentinel events. *Psychology, Crime & Law*, *27*, 76–88.

Zalman, M. (2010/2011). An integrated justice model of wrongful convictions. *Albany Law Review*, *74*, 1465–1524.

Chapter 14

Wrongful Convictions: Continuing and Future Challenges

Learning Objectives

After reading this chapter, you should be able to:

- Discuss prosecutor-led initiatives to identify and correct wrongful convictions, including conviction integrity units.
- Understand the goals of the National Institute of Justice's Sentinel Events Initiative.
- Discuss what research has revealed about the risk of executing innocent persons and how such concerns have influenced capital punishment policies in the United States.
- Appreciate the importance of studying wrongful convictions for lower-level offenses.
- Understand how and why the juvenile justice system can produce miscarriages of justice.
- Identify under-examined areas of wrongful conviction research in need of further study.

Introduction

We have covered a great deal of territory to this point. We now consider a few additional issues of importance for students, researchers, policymakers, and activists who are concerned about wrongful convictions. Many of the themes explored below have surfaced in varying degrees throughout this volume. We touch on them in greater detail in this chapter.

A Focus on Justice Systems

Growing awareness about wrongful convictions has led to some innovative responses within the criminal justice system. System actors need not await legislation or court mandates to develop and implement reforms. We begin by focusing on two innovations undertaken at the initiative of officials in an effort to uncover wrongful convictions and gain a better understanding of why they occur: Conviction Integrity Units and the National Institute of Justice's Sentinel Events Initiative.

Conviction Integrity Units

The National Registry of Exonerations (2017) defines a **Conviction Integrity Unit** (CIU) as "a division of a prosecutorial office that works to prevent, identify, and remedy false convictions" (p. 10). The first CIU-facilitated exoneration occurred in 2003, when Quedillis Ricardo Walker was cleared of a 1991 murder in California. As of this writing, CIUs have been involved in 488 of the first 2,774 (17.6%) NRE exonerations, and their influence continues to expand. In 2020, there were 74 CIUs operating across the United States, compared to just 29 that were operating in 2016. (National Registry of Exonerations, 2017, 2021). In our adversarial system of justice, this is a welcome development, in light of the prosecutor's duty to seek justice. Nevertheless, not all CIUs are as well-staffed and are as thoroughly committed as others to uncover and correct errors. Although the growth of CIUs and their involvement in exonerating the wrongfully convicted are positive developments, whether these trends represent a fundamental change in prosecutors' efforts to rectify wrongful convictions remains to be determined.

Wrongful Convictions as Sentinel Events

When considering the misconduct of criminal justice actors like Detective Louis Scarcella (discussed in chapter 8) or forensic analyst Annie Dookhan (discussed in chapter 6), it may be tempting to attribute such misbehavior to "the one bad potato in every bag." Under this perspective, removing the bad potato leaves a perfectly serviceable remainder of a bag. Yet, it does not help us understand how the bad potato ended up in the bag in the first place. The sentinel events approach to examining adverse outcomes in criminal justice can help us understand how errors on the part of multiple individuals interact with system weaknesses to produce wrongful convictions. This type of analysis has been used effectively in other contexts, such as when investigators attempt to reconstruct why an airplane crashed or determine why a hospital error led to the death of a patient, with an eye toward avoiding future catastrophes of this nature (Doyle, 2010). The National Institute of Justice (2017a), the government agency leading the initiative to conduct sentinel event reviews, describes sentinel events as follows:

> When bad things happen in a complex system, the cause is rarely a single act, event or slip-up. More often, bad outcomes are "sentinel events." A sentinel event is a significant negative outcome that:
> • Signals underlying weaknesses in the system or process.
> • Is likely the result of compound errors.
> • May provide, if properly analyzed and addressed, important keys to strengthening the system and preventing future adverse events or outcomes.

A key aspect of sentinel event reviews is that they involve a non-blaming, forward-looking approach involving all stakeholders. Currently, the NIJ has three strategic priorities in the development and implementation of **sentinel events initiatives** across the country. These are:

1. Can non-blaming, all-stakeholder, forward-looking reviews of sentinel events be implemented in the criminal justice context?
2. If such reviews are implemented, can they provide jurisdictions with the information necessary to inform procedures and practice, and will this contribute to system improvement?
3. If these reviews can be implemented in the criminal justice context, and if these reviews do contribute to system improvements, can these reviews be routinized and sustained over time? (National Institute of Justice, 2017b)

It is important to note that the event review should not fully replace individual performance reviews, which may involve attributions of blame. That is, there have been several instances of misconduct and malpractice referenced throughout this book, and in some cases, individual actors should be held responsible. The review, however, should not stop with the individual, but should be coupled with an analysis that views the event through a wider lens, that seeks to understand the organizational and occupational factors that led to the event and the broader sociopolitical context in which the event took place. Hopefully, such practices will catch on in localities and encourage justice system officials to undertake probing reviews of the circumstances that contributed to the wrongful convictions that come to light. Sentinel event reviews have the potential to develop into a fruitful way to understand the systemic causes of wrongful convictions and how to reduce them.

Capital Punishment: The Risk of Wrongful Executions

"[T]he penalty of death," the Supreme Court has recognized, "is qualitatively different from a sentence of imprisonment, however long. Death, in its finality, differs more from life imprisonment than a 100-year prison term differs from one of only a year or two" (*Woodson v. North Carolina*, 1976, p. 305, plurality opinion). The implications of this truism for our study of wrongful convictions are obvious. The severity of punishment by death coupled with its irreversibility put miscarriages of justice in capital cases into a league of their own. As former New York Governor Mario Cuomo, who repeatedly vetoed death-penalty bills enacted by the legislature during his tenure as the state's chief executive, put it, in cases of wrongful execution, "mistakes cannot be corrected; there is no appeal from the grave" (Acker et al., 2001, p. 155).

After Virginia repealed its capital-punishment legislation in 2021, making life imprisonment without the possibility of parole the ultimate penalty for aggravated murder, 27 states, the federal government, and the United States Military continued to authorize the death penalty in the United States (Death Penalty Information Center, n.d.a). The "modern era" of **capital punishment** began in the United States in the mid-1970s, following the Supreme Court's invalidation of death-penalty laws nationwide in *Furman v. Georgia* (1972). The Court's 5–4 ruling in *Furman* voided capital punishment as violative of the Eighth Amendment's prohibition against cruel and unusual punishments. The decision was based largely on concerns that capital sentences were being imposed arbitrarily by juries that lacked the information and guidance necessary to reliably decide whether convicted offenders should be punished by death. Four years later, the justices approved revised legislation enacted in several jurisdictions that satisfied those concerns (*Gregg v. Georgia*, 1976; *Jurek v. Texas*, 1976; *Proffitt v. Florida*, 1976). In October 2020, more than 2,500 people inhabited death rows throughout our nation's prisons (NAACP Legal Defense and Education Fund, Inc., 2020), while more than 1,500 executions had been carried out since 1977 under the approved capital-sentencing legislation (Death Penalty Information Center, n.d.b).

Both support for capital punishment and its use have waned since the mid-1990s, when public opinion polls indicated that 80% of Americans approved of the death penalty, 38 states authorized capital punishment, and as many as 300 new death sentences were imposed annually across the country. In 2020, Gallup Poll results showed that support for the death penalty had dipped to just 55% (Gallup, n.d.), and a 2019 poll showed that a significant majority of Americans preferred life imprisonment (60%) to the death penalty (36%) (Jones, 2019). Further, only 18 new death sentences were handed out in 2020, and only 17 executions took place (Death Penalty Information Center, 2020).

The concern that innocent people risk wrongful conviction and execution has long been an important factor in debates about capital punishment. Motivated in large part by wrongful convictions in capital cases, in 2003 Illinois Governor George Ryan cleared the state's entire death row by commuting the death sentences of 167 inmates and pardoning four others (Gross, 2008; Sarat & Hussain, 2004). Illinois repealed its death penalty law eight years later (Death Penalty Information Center, n.d.a). The threat that innocent people will be executed has contributed to the decline in support for capital punishment and has been instrumental in its diminishing use in several jurisdictions (Baumgartner et al., 2008; Bowers & Sundby, 2009, pp. 51–52; Norris & Mullinix, 2019; Swift, 2014). Through April 2021, 185 individuals have been exonerated after being convicted of murder and sentenced to death in the United States during the modern death-penalty era, most of whom spent a decade or considerably more on death row before having their convictions overturned and being released (Death Penalty Information Center, n.d.c). The exonerees included at least ten who were freed after DNA evidence helped demonstrate their innocence (National Registry of Exonerations, n.d.).

Researchers have estimated that roughly 1 in 25 (4.1%) individuals sentenced to death between 1973 and 2004 were falsely convicted (Gross et al., 2014). Others have argued that there is no persuasive evidence that an innocent person has been executed during the modern capital-punishment era and have offered much lower estimates of the likelihood of innocent persons being sentenced to death. Justice Scalia did so in *Kansas v. Marsh* (2006), where he stated that "[o]ne cannot have a system of criminal punishment without accepting the possibility that someone will be punished mistakenly" (p. 199). He opined that "with regard to the punishment of death in the current American system, that possibility has been reduced to an insignificant minimum" (*id.*), although his calculation of a potential error rate fails the most rudimentary analytical review. In contrast, in 2015, Justice Breyer called for a wholesale reconsideration of whether the death penalty can be administered constitutionally, relying in part on evidence that innocent persons have been exposed to the risk of execution (*Glossip v. Gross*, 2015, pp. 909–915, dissenting opinion).

Because the consequences of error are so significant, the problems exposed in death-penalty cases tend to be especially noteworthy. Government misconduct figures heavily in capital case wrongful convictions, surfacing in an astounding 79% of such exonerations, a significantly higher proportion than in other types of cases (Gross et al., 2020, p. 15). Although capital cases involve heightened stakes and some unique procedural requirements, they share many features in common with other criminal prosecutions. The errors of justice that expose innocent people to the risk of execution in capital prosecutions thus offer a dramatically revealing window on the types and sources of error that occur in considerably more routine cases (see Acker & Bellandi, 2014).

For example, Henry McCollum was convicted and sentenced to death for the rape-murder of an 11-year-old girl in North Carolina in 1984. His half-brother, Leon Brown, also was convicted and received a death sentence but subsequently was resentenced to life imprisonment. McCollum was 19 years old at the time of the crime and Brown was 15. Both youths were compromised intellectually and each confessed to the crime—but falsely. DNA testing completed years later excluded them as the perpetrators. McCollum spent 30 years on death row while Brown was in service of his sentence of life imprisonment. The men were exonerated in 2014 (see National Registry of Exonerations, 2015; Neff, 2018). Walter McMillan's murder conviction and death sentence in Alabama, the subject of a best-selling book, *Just Mercy* (Stevenson, 2014), and a movie of the same name, unraveled after informants' untruthful testimony was exposed and egregious government misconduct came to light. McMillan, whose case was steeped in racial prejudices, was exonerated after spending six years under sentence of death. As we discussed in chapter 12, eyewitness misidentification and other errors marred Kirk Bloodsworth's murder trial and placed him on Maryland's death row before DNA evidence identified the actual killer in the case (see Junkin, 2004). Ron Williamson was convicted and sentenced to death in Oklahoma based on flawed forensic evidence and the testimony of unreliable informants (Grisham, 2006). He languished on death row for eleven years before he was exonerated with the assistance of DNA evidence. Racial bias and government misconduct figured prominently in Clarence Brandley's murder conviction and death sentence in Texas; Brandley was exonerated after spending more than nine years under sentence of death (see Davies, 1991).

The cataloguing of death row exonerees, and the roster of errors contributing to their wrongful convictions, could go on at much greater length. As we have emphasized, the problems plaguing erroneous capital convictions are not confined to death-penalty cases. Yet they are powerful reminders of the sources of miscarriages of justice that occur in other cases, ranging from misdemeanors to the most serious felonies.

Misdemeanors

In 2015, the National Science Foundation and the National Institute of Justice co-sponsored a workshop that focused on under-examined issues in wrongful convictions. One of the main themes at the workshop was the problem of wrongful misdemeanor convictions (Acker et al., 2015/2016). As we discussed in chapter 8, focusing on exonerations from serious felonies, for example, as typified by DNA exonerations, distracts attention from what may be an even larger problem: wrongful misdemeanor convictions. We noted in the introduction to this text that in the criminal justice system, the number of misdemeanor cases far surpasses the number of felony cases. The issues discussed in the text concerning guilty pleas and inadequate defense merge with misdemeanors to present a problem of potentially large magnitude.

Over four decades ago, Malcolm Feeley (1992 [1979]) observed a lower-level criminal court in Connecticut and found that, in a sample of more than 1,600 cases, no defendants went to trial and only half were represented by attorneys. Current research on misdemeanor courts is hardly more encouraging. As we saw in chapter 9, defense attorneys in misdemeanor courts frequently carry high caseloads and suffer from inadequate resources (Baruchowitz et al., 2009). Defendants in misdemeanor court, who are often poor and disempowered, and sometimes suffer from substance abuse or mental health issues, rarely contest their guilt. Regarding wrongful conviction, Natapoff (2015, p. 259) has observed, "[W]e have a process primed to generate formal criminal convictions based on arrest, i.e., the bare assertion of probable cause by a police officer. This is a system guaranteed to produce many wrongful convictions, because probable cause is by definition a low threshold of evidence. To put it another way, we can have confidence in the accuracy of misdemeanor convictions precisely to the extent that we are confident that police arrest only the guilty."

Russell Covey's research on mass exonerations discussed in chapter 8 represents a promising start to more systematic empirical analysis of wrongful misdemeanor convictions. The prevalence of guilty pleas to misdemeanor charges, the often hurried pace of business in misdemeanor courts and the lack of time and attention defense counsel may devote to those charged with misdemeanors, and the desire among many defendants to quickly resolve cases so they can gain release from jail while awaiting trial or otherwise avoid the disruption to employment and family life by making repeated appearances for court hearings, are among the factors that contribute to wrongful misdemeanor convictions (Gross, 2018; Roberts, 2018; Stevenson & Mayson, 2018). Even if the punishment imposed following a misdemeanor conviction is relatively light, having a criminal record for a misdemeanor can bring serious consequences, potentially jeopardizing immigration status as well as future employment and educational opportunities, compromising child custody and parental rights, requiring sex offender registration, preventing lawful gun ownership and residence in public housing, and heightening the punishment imposed for subsequent criminal convictions (Acker, 2017, p. 17). Additional research needs to be completed to more fully understand the extent, causes, correlates, and ramifications of these not-so-petty wrongful convictions.

Juvenile Justice

The **juvenile justice** system has traditionally maintained a different operating philosophy, employed different procedures, and relied on different terminology than used in the criminal courts. Juvenile courts originated with the objective of rehabilitating wayward youths rather than punishing them. Because their aim was benign, it followed that the procedures and safeguards observed in the criminal courts, which are designed to protect against government overreach and unjust punishment, could be relaxed. After all, it was reasoned, children did not require protection from being helped. The juveniles who were determined in court proceedings to have engaged in serious misconduct were not labeled convicted criminals but rather were considered to be adjudicated delinquents. These tenets and labels largely characterized juvenile court proceedings from their inception at the close of the nineteenth century into the mid-1960s, when the Supreme Court began to critically examine the juvenile justice system and question whether assumptions concerning its rehabilitative ideal and its loose procedures could be reconciled with actual practices. The Court's landmark ruling in *In re Gault* (1967) recognized that youths who were dispatched to reform school or a similar correctional facility after being adjudicated delinquent in juvenile court suffered a serious deprivation of liberty, and thus were constitutionally entitled to many of the same procedural rights observed in criminal trials.

Fifteen-year-old Gerald Gault appeared before a juvenile court judge in Gila County, Arizona, in 1964 to answer to a petition alleging simply that he was "in need of the [court's] protection" and that he "is a delinquent minor." What triggered this vague claim apparently was a phone call "of the irritatingly offensive, adolescent, sex variety" that Gerald and another boy allegedly made to a woman in the neighborhood, Mrs. Cook. Receiving no further notice of what he was charged with, Gerald arrived in court with his mother. He was not represented by a lawyer. In response to inquiries from the judge, Gerald admitted participating in the phone call by dialing Mrs. Cook's number but he blamed his friend for making the lewd remarks. Mrs. Cook, the complaining witness, did not appear in court; her account of the phone call was delivered by a probation officer who had spoken with her. "At the conclusion of the hearing, the judge committed Gerald as a juvenile delinquent to the State Industrial School 'for the period of his minority (that is, until 21), unless sooner discharged'" (*In re Gault*, 1967, p. 8). Had an adult been convicted in criminal court of the same offense, a misdemeanor, the maximum punishment would have been a jail sentence not to exceed two months and a fine of $5 to $50. Under Arizona law, no appeal was authorized from an adjudication of juvenile delinquency. The Gaults filed a petition for a writ of habeas corpus, which the Arizona Supreme Court rejected. The U.S. Supreme Court reviewed the case on a petition for a writ of certiorari. In a wide-ranging opinion authored by Justice Abe Fortas, the Supreme Court vacated the judgment resulting in Gerald's adjudication and confinement and mandated sweeping reforms in how juvenile courts heard delinquency cases in which youths were deprived of their liberty.

The Court ruled that in such cases due process requires that juveniles be given specific notice of the charges against them, that they have a right to counsel (court-appointed for those who cannot afford to hire a lawyer), a right against compelled self-incrimination, and a right to confront and cross-examine the witnesses against them. "Under our constitution," Justice Fortas admonished, "the condition of being a boy does not justify a kangaroo court" (p. 28). Without disparaging the rehabilitative ideal characterizing juvenile court proceedings, the justices emphasized the broad gap between these "highest motives and most enlightened impulses" (p. 17) and the practical reality that how children actually were treated in the juvenile justice system frequently fell far short of those ideals.

In re Gault thus imposed radically different procedures for juvenile courts' handling of juvenile delinquency cases than had previously been observed.

Three years later, the Court invalidated a New York juvenile court's determination "by a preponderance of the evidence" that 12-year-old Sam Winship be committed to reform school because he had stolen a purse, and ruled that juveniles cannot be adjudicated delinquent absent the more demanding standard of proof beyond a reasonable doubt (*In re Winship*, 1970). Although it then appeared that the justices were inclined to require juvenile courts to follow the same procedures used in the criminal courts, in *McKeiver v. Pennsylvania* (1971) the Court stopped short of mandating trial by jury in delinquency cases, ruling that judges could continue to preside over juvenile court proceedings. Although there is no constitutional requirement to do so, some states have enacted legislation to make jury trials an option in juvenile delinquency cases, and others have recognized that right under their state constitutions (Birckhead, 2012, pp. 87–88; Robinson, 2020, pp. 36–39).

Despite the juvenile justice reforms mandated by the Supreme Court, critics claimed that courts were slow to implement them and, when they came around to doing so, judges, probation officers, and lawyers often gave them lip-service rather than taking them seriously (see Duffee & Siegel, 1971; Feld, 1989). Others have charged that the rehabilitative ideal that characterized juvenile courts at their inception has increasingly yielded to a considerably more punitive orientation (Feld, 1999; Gardner, 2012; Sheffer, 1995). In tandem, these concerns have significant implications for the risk that juvenile delinquency proceedings will be plagued by error and produce wrongful adjudications. Indeed, some have questioned whether the juvenile courts are a "breeding ground" for miscarriages of justice (Drizin & Luloff, 2007).

Several considerations highlight this concern (Tepfer et al., 2010). As we discussed in chapters 4 and 5, juveniles are particularly vulnerable to falsely confess in the face of police interrogation and to enter false guilty pleas (see Luna, 2017; Redlich, 2010). Youths may well lack the competence to understand and intelligently forgo rights designed to protect them (Drizin & Luloff, 2007; Feld, 2017; Grisso, 1998). Defense attorneys may be less effective advocates, sometimes caused by their readiness to seek dispositions that spare their juvenile clients confinement rather than acting to zealously resist the charges against them (Armstrong & Kim, 2011; Birckhead, 2010; Feld, 1998). Prosecutors may fall short on their obligation to disclose exculpatory information to defense counsel (VanCleave, 2014). In short, the developmental state of juveniles, lax procedural safeguards in the juvenile courts, and a lack of meaningful oversight provide the ingredients for wrongful adjudications in the juvenile courts. More research is needed into this frequently overlooked segment of the justice system.

Politics, Policy, and Public Opinion

The intersection of criminal justice and popular culture has long attracted public interest, as stories involving crime, law, and justice have been abundant and remain in demand. While popular and celebrity attention has focused on wrongful convictions over a considerable period of time—famed novelist and lawyer Erle Stanley Gardner's "court of last resort" in the 1940s and 1950s, Muhammad Ali's and Bob Dylan's involvement in the campaign to free Rubin "Hurricane" Carter in the 1970s, and the popular documentary, *The Thin Blue Line* in the 1980s, to name a few—recent years have seen a dramatic increase in the cultural attention devoted to wrongful convictions. Cases of wrongful or otherwise questionable convictions have been among the most popular topics in different media outlets. Such stories have generated podcasts that have topped the charts (e.g., *Serial*) and have been among the most popular shows on streaming platforms (e.g., *When They See Us*); books by popular authors such as John Grisham and Tayari Jones have topped both fiction and nonfiction bestseller lists; major motion pictures starring mainstream actors have been produced (e.g., *Conviction*); and documentaries featuring wrongful conviction cases continue to flourish.

Without a doubt, wrongful convictions have captured the popular imagination. The fascination with wrongful convictions is not surprising; each case represents a powerful and dramatic narrative encompassing a host of emotions. Less well-understood is what effect these developments may have had on public opinion and on criminal justice policy. On the one hand, awareness of wrongful convictions may be tied to perceptions of legitimacy and/or trust in the criminal legal system and its actors, as well as on related policy preferences (e.g., Donovan & Klahm, 2018; Norris & Mullinix, 2019; Zalman et al., 2012). Indeed, as we discussed above, innocence may represent a compelling consideration for many with respect to capital punishment (Dardis et al., 2008), and a number of studies have demonstrated that wrongful convictions have played a significant role in reduced public support for the death penalty in recent decades (e.g., Baumgartner et al., 2008; Fan et al., 2002; Lambert et al., 2011; Norris & Mullinix, 2019). Yet, we still know relatively little about the dynamics of the relationship between wrongful convictions and public opinion (Norris, 2017).

To some extent, we might not expect that relationship to be especially dynamic, as advocacy on behalf of the wrongfully convicted has broad appeal. Indeed, some have argued that the innocence movement is somewhat unique in its ability to merge (typically conservative) crime control and (typically liberal) due process values (Findley, 2008). Others have suggested that "[w]rongful conviction is a one-sided or 'valence' issue in which political opposition seems unimaginable" (Smith et al., 2011, p. 680). These sentiments make sense, insofar as nobody would advocate for the conviction of the innocent (except for the actual offender, as discussed in chapter 13). However, this may be an oversimplified approach to thinking about how people and policies respond to wrongful convictions.

Research has consistently found that attitudes toward criminal justice issues are not shared universally, but instead differ across social (e.g., race, gender) and ideological (e.g., conservative, liberal) groups. Despite the presumed broad appeal of the innocence message, some early evidence suggests that social and ideological divisions also may be at work with respect to wrongful convictions, or at the very least, that the effects of wrongful convictions on public attitudes may not be as strong or consistent as sometimes has been assumed. For example, one study found that while an innocence frame reduced death penalty support by 16% among Black respondents, the reduction among white respondents was less than 1% (Peffley & Hurwitz, 2007). Another found that information about wrongful convictions had mostly small and inconsistent effects on (hypothetical) gubernatorial voting decisions (Bobo & Johnson, 2004). These findings suggest that much more research is needed to fully uncover how and why different people respond differently to wrongful convictions. Also of concern is the type and nature of information that people receive. A study by Norris and Mullinix (2019) found that learning about the number of exonerations reduced support for the death penalty, but hearing a single narrative about a wrongful conviction had almost twice the effect. Further, these different methods of conveying information influenced other attitudes differently; the numbers reduced people's trust in the justice system (while the narrative did not), and the narrative increased people's support for police reforms related to wrongful convictions and personal concern about being the victim of a wrongful conviction (while the numbers did not).

Uncovering how and why people may respond to the increasing coverage of wrongful convictions is important not only for understanding how people view the criminal legal system, but also may offer some insight into policy-making in this realm, which may be influenced by public opinion. Throughout this book, we have highlighted policy reforms that may reduce the likelihood of wrongful convictions occurring, increase the likelihood of discovering errors that have occurred, and provide redress after exoneration. A number of states and localities have passed some of these reforms, but here, too, we know relatively little about what influences the adoption of such policies. We might again assume that wrongful convictions have such broad appeal to stimulate reforms that necessary efforts to achieve them would not be highly politicized, but as with public opinion, the available evidence, limited as it is, suggests otherwise. A study of state policy adoption by Kent and Carmichael (2015) found that states with a Republican-controlled legislature and more Republican voters were less likely than other states to pass key laws related to wrongful convictions, including eyewitness identification reforms, recording interrogations, exoneree compensation, and more. More recently, Hicks and colleagues (2021) found that public opinion influences the adoption of wrongful conviction policies, but only when state lawmakers are vulnerable in upcoming elections. Both of these studies also found that the presence of organizations like the Innocence Project, which as advocacy organizations function in a manner akin to interest groups, increases the likelihood that states will adopt innocence-related policies.

Far more research is needed to fully understand the political dynamics that shape (and are shaped by) the innocence movement, but this is certainly a worthy pursuit. Stories of injustice may not alone be enough to persuade the public to support changes to policy and practice; facts and figures about the detrimental effects of wrongful convictions may not encourage state lawmakers to enact new legislation to improve the accuracy of the criminal process. Instead, a concerted and strategic effort may be needed to frame particular pieces of information in specific ways in order to generate change.

Those who work in and around the innocence movement are not entirely unaware of these dynamics. In addressing the American Society of Criminology in 2011, then-president of the organization, C. Ronald Huff, posed the question, "Why is wrongful conviction an important problem?" He then offered the following answer: "Most people can readily understand that convicting an innocent person is unjust, even though they might express more concern with the guilty who go free. A society that views itself as just and fair simply cannot afford to ignore this problem" (Huff, 2002, p. 3). The second part of his answer — that when innocents are convicted, the guilty go free — appeared to have a strategic frame to it. Huff observed that the politically expedient way to build "broad-based coalitions of interests" in addressing the wrongful conviction problem was to emphasize the risks to public safety when innocents are convicted, perhaps to appeal to political conservatives or others who tend to emphasize crime control or law-and-order. Other anecdotal support exists for the significance of framing issues of wrongful conviction to include concerns for the public safety in order to appeal to particular individuals or groups. For example, an article posted on a website dedicated to news events in New Jersey reported that "a bipartisan duo of New Jersey legislators wants to impanel a special commission to address wrongful convictions in the Garden State" (Sullivan, 2017). This brief excerpt from the article is telling:

"If we convict somebody wrongfully, that means the person who committed the crime is still out there," said state Sen. Joseph Pennacchio (R-Morris), a co-sponsor of a new criminal justice bill. "Nobody wins. Everybody loses."

The senator said in an interview he considers himself a "law and order conservative." But he teamed up with Sen. Shirley Turner (D-Mercer), a stalwart liberal, to introduce the measure, which would move to set up a formal state investigatory body charged with freeing the innocent (Sullivan, 2017).

There is still much to learn regarding how awareness of wrongful convictions influences public opinion and criminal justice policies, but it is clear that the increasing attention focused on wrongful convictions is having some effect. It now is up to researchers to further our understanding of those effects.

Researching Miscarriages of Justice

In a much-cited 2005 article, Professor Richard Leo called on social scientists to develop a "criminology of wrongful convictions." Leo's hope was to advance the field of wrongful conviction scholarship beyond case studies and legal analysis to rigorous analysis using social scientific methods. The goal of such analyses would advance understanding of the correlates of wrongful convictions beyond the standard list of eyewitness misidentification, false confessions, faulty forensic science evidence, and so on. A decade later, Leo revisited his earlier writing, concluding that although significant theoretical, substantive, and methodological progress had been made, much work remained to be completed by researchers investigating wrongful convictions, particularly in determining their fundamental or root causes (Leo, 2017). Norris and Bonventre (2015) also have called for deeper theoretical perspectives and suggested that scholars apply conceptual frameworks from the traditional criminal justice and other social scientific literatures to think more analytically about wrongful convictions. In that regard, Gould and colleagues' (2014) comparative analysis of near misses (innocent indicted defendants who were released before trial or acquitted) and wrongful convictions demonstrates the power of social scientific analysis in developing deeper and more nuanced knowledge.

From a substantive perspective, more research should be devoted to understudied areas of wrongful convictions. Many examples in addition to the ones we have discussed in this chapter merit consideration. For example, what is the nature and extent of wrongful convictions among immigrants? What is known about possible miscarriages of justice in military courts or specialized, problem-solving courts (e.g., drug courts, mental health courts)? How do the incarceration experiences of individuals who are wrongly convicted compare to those of others who are imprisoned? What else might we learn about the effects of wrongful convictions on exonerees' networks and communities, or on the original crime victims or the legal actors involved in a case? What are the short- and long-term effects of the reforms championed by innocence advocates, including those discussed throughout this book? In this growing area of scholarship, the questions are many; they extend far beyond those just asked and include many additional issues and questions yet to be identified, but which will certainly emerge and require systematic study and analysis. Students of the criminal justice system should have no trouble finding interesting avenues of inquiry to pursue.

Conclusion

We have come a long way. In 1985, the United States Attorney General — the highest prosecutor in the country — said in an interview, "[T]he thing is, you don't have many suspects who are innocent of a crime. That's contradictory. If a person is innocent of a crime, then he is not a suspect." The former attorney general's name was Edwin Meese, and the implication of his statement was that wrongful convictions are barely possible, a literal contradiction in terms. Now, many years later, the idea that the justice system is fallible is widely accepted, and we have developed a much greater understanding of how and why justice miscarries in the form of wrongful convictions. It is undeniable that wrongful convictions can and do occur, and this awareness has led to significant reforms in American systems of criminal justice. However, we continue to have a long way to go; there is much more to learn about how justice systems fail and what can be done to identify and correct those failures.

Key Terms and Concepts

- **Conviction Integrity Unit**: a division within a prosecutor's office that reviews questionable convictions and works to prevent, identify, and remedy wrongful convictions
- **Sentinel Events Initiative**: an initiative undertaken by the National Institute of Justice, designed to review undesirable outcomes in criminal justice, in-

cluding wrongful convictions, and study them in a non-blaming fashion to determine why they occurred and what can be done to prevent future injustices
- **Capital Punishment**: the penalty of death, currently authorized in 27 states and under federal and U.S. military law
- **Juvenile Justice**: the separate court system devoted to the offenses and misbehavior of young people, involving less severe sanctions than imposed by criminal courts, but potentially causing youths adjudicated as juvenile delinquents to be deprived of their liberty by confinement in youth correctional institutions

Discussion Questions

1. In your view, what is the most pressing issue related to wrongful convictions?

2. Do you believe that the risk of executing innocent persons is a sufficient reason to prohibit the use of capital punishment?

3. If the juvenile courts were created with the objective of helping and rehabilitating youths who run afoul of the law, why should juvenile courts be required to observe procedural protections of the type required by the Supreme Court in *In re Gault*?

4. Why do you think people of different social and political groups respond differently when learning about wrongful convictions? Can we bridge these gaps and develop a message with more universal appeal? How?

5. If you had limitless funds, what kind of research projects on wrongful convictions would you pursue?

6. The NRE has documented more than 2,700 exonerations as of April 2021. Do you think the number of exonerations will continue to rise? Why or why not?

References

Acker, J. R. (2017). Taking stock of innocence: Movements, mountains, and wrongful convictions. *Journal of Contemporary Criminal Justice, 33*, 8–25.
Acker, J. R., & Bellandi, R. (2014). Deadly errors and salutary reforms: The kill that cures? In M. Zalman & J. Carrano (Eds.), *Wrongful conviction and criminal justice reform: Making justice* (pp. 269–285). Routledge.

Acker, J. R., Brewer, T., Cunningham, E., Fitzgerald A., Flexon, J., Lombard, J., Ryn, B., & Stodghill, B. (2001). No appeal from the grave: Innocence, capital punishment, and the lessons of history. In S. D. Westervelt & J. A. Humphrey (Eds.), *Wrongly convicted: Perspectives on failed justice.* (pp. 154–173). Rutgers University Press.

Acker, J. R., Redlich, A. D., Bonventre, C. L., & Norris, R. J. (2015/2016). Foreword: Elephants in the courtroom: Examining overlooked issues in wrongful convictions. *Albany Law Review, 79,* 705–715.

Armstrong, G., & Kim, B. (2011). Juvenile penalties for "lawyering up": The role of counsel and extralegal case characteristics. *Crime & Delinquency, 57,* 827–848.

Baumgartner, F. R., De Boef, S. L., & Boydstun, A. E. (2008). *The decline of the death penalty and the discovery of innocence.* Cambridge University Press.

Birckhead, T. R. (2010). Culture clash: The challenge of lawyering across difference in juvenile court. *Rutgers Law Review, 62,* 959–990.

Birckhead, T. R. (2012). Delinquent by reason of poverty. *Washington University Journal of Law & Policy, 38,* 53–107.

Bobo, L. D., & Johnson, D. (2004). A taste for punishment: Black and white Americans' views on the death penalty and the war on drugs. *Du Bois Review, 1,* 151–180.

Bowers, W. J., & Sundby, S. E. (2009). Why the downturn in death sentences? In C. S. Lanier, W. J. Bowers, & J. R. Acker (Eds.), *The future of America's death penalty: An agenda for the next generation of capital punishment research* (pp. 47–67). Carolina Academic Press.

Dardis, F. E., Baumgartner, F. R., Boydstun, A. E., De Boef, S., & Shen, F. (2008). Media framing of capital punishment and its impact on individuals' cognitive responses. *Mass Communication and Society, 11,* 115–140.

Davies, N. (1991). *White lies: Rape, murder, and justice Texas style.* Pantheon Books.

Death Penalty Information Center. (n.d.a). State & federal info: State by state. https://deathpenaltyinfo.org/state-and-federal-info/state-by-state.

Death Penalty Information Center. (n.d.b). Executions overview. https://death penaltyinfo.org/executions/executions-overview.

Death Penalty Information Center. (n.d.c). Innocence. https://deathpenalty info.org/policy-issues/innocence.

Death Penalty Information Center. (2020). *The death penalty in 2020: Year end report.* https://reports.deathpenaltyinfo.org/year-end/YearEndReport 2020.pdf.

Donovan, K. M., & Klahm, C. F. (2018). How priming innocence influences public opinion on police misconduct and false convictions: A research note. *Criminal Justice Review, 43,* 174–185.

Doyle, J. M. (2010). Learning from error in American criminal justice. *Journal of Criminal Law & Criminology, 100,* 109–147.

Drizin, S. A., & Luloff, G. (2007). Are juvenile courts a breeding ground for wrongful convictions? *Northern Kentucky Law Review, 34,* 257–322.

Duffee, D., & Siegel, L. (1971). The organization man: Legal counsel in juvenile court. *Criminal Law Bulletin, 7,* 544–553.

Fan, D. P., Keltner, K. A., & Wyatt, R. O. (2002). A matter of guilt or innocence: How news reports affect support for the death penalty in the United States. *International Journal of Public Opinion Research, 14,* 439–452.

Feeley, M. (1992 [1979]). *The process is the punishment: Handling cases in a lower criminal court.* Russell Sage Foundation.

Feld, B. C. (1989). The right to counsel in juvenile court: An empirical study of when lawyers appear and the difference they make. *Journal of Criminal Law & Criminology, 79,* 1185–1346.

Feld, B. C. (1999). The transformation of the juvenile court — part II: Race and the "crack down" on youth crime. *Minnesota Law Review, 84,* 327–395.

Feld, B. C. (2017). Competence and culpability: Delinquents in juvenile courts, youths in criminal courts. *Minnesota Law Review, 102,* 473–576.

Findley, K. A. (2008). Toward a new paradigm of criminal justice: How the innocence movement merges crime control and due process. *Texas Tech Law Review, 41,* 133–175.

Furman v. Georgia, 408 U.S. 238 (1972).

Gallup. (n.d.). Death penalty. https://news.gallup.com/poll/1606/death-penalty. aspx.

Gardner, M. R. (2012). Punitive juvenile justice and public trials by jury: Sixth Amendment applications in a post-*McKeiver* world. *Nebraska Law Review, 91,* 1–71.

Glossip v. Gross, 576 U.S. 863 (2015).

Gould, J. B., Carrano, J., Leo, R. A., & Hail-Jares, K. (2014). Predicting erroneous convictions. *Iowa Law Review, 99,* 471–522.

Gregg v. Georgia, 428 U.S. 153 (1976).

Grisham, J. (2006). *The innocent man: Murder and injustice in a small town.* Doubleday.

Grisso, T. (1998). *Forensic evaluation of juveniles.* Professional Resource Press.

Gross, S. R. (2008). Convicting the innocent. *Annual Review of Law and Social Science, 4,* 173–190.

Gross, S. R. (2018). Errors in misdemeanor adjudication. *Boston University Law Review, 98,* 999–1011.

Gross, S. R., O'Brien, B., Hu, C., & Kennedy, E. H. (2014). Rate of false conviction of criminal defendants who are sentenced to death. *Proceedings of the National Academy of Sciences, 111,* 7230–7235.

Gross, S. R., Possley, M. J., Roll, K. J., & Stephens, K. H. (2020). *Government misconduct and convicting the innocent: The role of prosecutors, police, and other law enforcement.* https://www.law.umich.edu/special/exoneration/Documents/Government_Misconduct_and_Convicting_the_Innocent.pdf.

Hicks, W. D., Mullinix, K. J., & Norris, R. J. (2021). The politics of wrongful conviction legislation. *State Politics & Policy Quarterly.* Advance online publication. http://doi.org/10.1017/spq.2020.4.

Huff, C. R. (2002). Wrongful conviction and public policy: The American Society of Criminology 2001 presidential address. *Criminology, 40*(1), 1–18.

In re Gault, 387 U.S. 1 (1967).

In re Winship, 397 U.S. 358 (1970).

Jones, J. M. (2019). Americans now support life in prison over death penalty. https://news.gallup.com/poll/268514/americans-support-life-prison-death-penalty.aspx.

Junkin, T. (2004). *Bloodsworth: The true story of the first death row inmate exonerated by DNA.* Algonquin Books.

Jurek v. Texas, 428 U.S. 262 (1976).

Kansas v. Marsh, 548 U.S. 163 (2006).

Kent, S. L., & Carmichael, J. T. (2015). Legislative responses to wrongful conviction: Do partisan principals and advocacy efforts influence state-level criminal justice policy? *Social Science Research, 52,* 147–160.

Lambert, E. G., Camp, S. D., Clarke, A., & Jiang, S. (2011). The impact of information on death penalty support, revisited. *Crime & Delinquency, 57,* 572–599.

Leo, R. A. (2005). Rethinking the study of miscarriages of justice: Developing a criminology of wrongful conviction. *Journal of Contemporary Criminal Justice, 21*(3), 201–223.

Leo, R. A. (2017). The criminology of wrongful conviction: A decade later. *Journal of Contemporary Criminal Justice, 33,* 82–106.

Luna, M. (2017). Juvenile false confessions: Juvenile psychology, police interrogation tactics, and prosecutorial discretion. *Nevada Law Journal, 18,* 291–316.

McKeiver v. Pennsylvania, 403 U.S. 528 (1971).

NAACP Legal Defense and Education Fund, Inc. (2020, Fall). *Death row U.S.A.* https://www.naacpldf.org/wp-content/uploads/DRUSAFall2020.pdf.

Natapoff, A. (2015). Misdemeanors. *Annual Review of Law and Social Science,* *11,* 255–267.

National Institute of Justice. (2017a). *NIJ's sentinel events initiative.* U.S. Department of Justice. https://www.nij.gov/topics/justice-system/Pages/sentinel-events.aspx.

National Institute of Justice. (2017b). *NIJ strategic research and implementation plan: Sentinel events initiative.* U.S. Department of Justice. file:///Z:/Library/Sentinel%20Events/implementation%20plan.pdf.

National Registry of Exonerations. (n.d.). Browse cases: Detailed view (filters: sentence=death, DNA). http://www.law.umich.edu/special/exoneration/Pages/detaillist.aspx?View={faf6eddb-5a68-4f8f-8a52-2c61f5bf9ea7}&FilterField1=Sentence&FilterValue1=Death&SortField=_x002a_&SortDir=Asc&FilterField2=%5Fx002a%5F&FilterValue2=8%5F%2A.

National Registry of Exonerations. (2015). *Henry McCollum.* https://www.law.umich.edu/special/exoneration/Pages/casedetail.aspx?caseid=4492.

National Registry of Exonerations. (2017). *Exonerations in 2016.* https://www.law.umich.edu/special/exoneration/Documents/Exonerations_in_2016.pdf.

National Registry of Exonerations. (2021). *2020 Annual report.* http://www.law.umich.edu/special/exoneration/Documents/2021AnnualReport.pdf.

Neff, J. (2018, April 7). They did 30 years for someone else's crime. Then paid for it. *New York Times.* https://www.nytimes.com/2018/04/07/us/mccollum-brown-exoneration.html.

Norris, R. J. (2017). *Exonerated: A history of the innocence movement.* NYU Press.

Norris, R. J., & Bonventre, C. L. (2015). Advancing wrongful conviction scholarship: Toward new conceptual frameworks. *Justice Quarterly,* *32*(6), 929–949.

Norris, R. J., & Mullinix, K. J. (2019). Framing innocence: An experimental test of the effects of wrongful convictions on public opinion. *Journal of Experimental Criminology, 16,* 311–334.

Peffley, M., & Hurwitz, J. (2007). Persuasion and resistance: Race and the death penalty in America. *American Journal of Political Science, 51,* 996–1012.

Proffitt v. Florida, 428 U.S. 242 (1976).

Redlich, A. D. (2010). The susceptibility of juveniles to false confessions and false guilty pleas. *Rutgers Law Review, 62,* 943–957.

Roberts, J. (2018). The innocence movement and misdemeanors. *Boston University Law Review, 98,* 779–836.

Robinson, K. (2020). Juvenile in justice: A look at Maryland's practice of incarcerating children without a jury trial. *Maryland Law Review Online, 79,* 14–40.

Sarat, A., & Hussain, N. (2004). On lawful lawlessness: George Ryan, executive clemency, and the rhetoric of sparing life. *Stanford Law Review*, *56*, 1307–1344.

Sheffer, J. P. (1995). Serious and habitual juvenile offender statutes: Reconciling punishment and rehabilitation within the juvenile justice system. *Vanderbilt Law Review*, *48*, 479–512.

Smith, B., Zalman, M., & Kiger, A. (2011). How justice system officials view wrongful convictions. *Crime & Delinquency*, *57*, 663–685.

Stevenson, B. (2014). *Just mercy: A story of justice and redemption*. Spiegel & Grau.

Stevenson, M., & Mayson, S. (2018). The scale of misdemeanor justice. *Boston University Law Review*, *98*, 731–776.

Swift, A. (2014). Americans: "Eye for an eye" top reason for death penalty. https://news.gallup.com/poll/178799/americans-eye-eye-top-reason-death-penalty.aspx.

Tepfer, J. A., Nirider, L. H., & Tricarico, L. M. (2010). Arresting development: Convictions of innocent youth. *Rutgers Law Review*, *62*, 887–941.

VanCleave, A. (2014). *Brady* and the juvenile courts. *N.Y.U. Review of Law & Social Change*, *38*, 551–562.

Woodson v. North Carolina, 428 U.S. 280 (1976).

Zalman, M., Larson, M. J., & Smith, B. (2012). Citizens' attitudes toward wrongful convictions. *Criminal Justice Review*, *37*, 51–69.

Glossary

13th Amendment: the amendment to the U.S. Constitution that abolished the practice of slavery, "except as a punishment for crime"

Absolute immunity: a long-standing practice providing prosecutors with immunity from civil damages for conduct directly related to the judicial process

Absolute judgment: when a witness evaluates each lineup or photo array member individually to determine if that person matches their recollection of the offender

Alford **plea**: from *North Carolina v. Alford*, a guilty plea that allows the defendant to nevertheless maintain innocence

Arson: a crime involving the deliberate setting of fire to property

Assigned-counsel system: a method of providing indigent defense that involves the appointment of individual private attorneys to represent poor defendants

Battered woman syndrome: a psychological construct predicated on a controversial theory that posits that some women endure repeat cycles of violence from intimate partners and can experience a sense of psychological paralysis which severely limits their ability to leave the battering relationship

Bench trial: a trial in which the judge serves as the fact-finder and determines guilt or innocence in criminal cases

Blackstone ratio: from Sir William Blackstone, the declaration that, "[I]t is better that ten guilty persons escape than that one innocent suffer"; suggests that the wrongful conviction of an innocent person should be weighed more heavily than the wrongful acquittal of a guilty person

Blind/double-blind procedure: an identification procedure in which the officials administering the lineup or photo array do not know which person is the actual suspect

Brady v. Maryland: a 1963 Supreme Court case concerning the prosecutor's obligation to disclose to the defense material exculpatory evidence; a prosecutor's failure to do so is referred to as a "*Brady* violation"

Brathwaite factors: from *Manson v. Brathwaite*, the factors considered by courts in determining the admissibility of eyewitness identification testimony

Capital charge: a charged crime for which the death penalty is a possible punishment

Capital Punishment: The penalty of death, currently authorized in 27 states and under federal and U.S. military law.

Caseload: the number of cases for which a defense attorney has responsibility

Centurion Ministries: the first innocence organization in the United States, founded in 1983, that works to secure the exoneration of innocent defendants; now called only *Centurion*

Certiorari: a writ or order by which an appellate court exercises its discretion to review a case that was previously decided by a lower court

Civil litigation: one method of compensation, involves the exoneree pursuing a civil lawsuit to recover damages suffered related to a wrongful conviction

Cognitive bias: systematic errors in human judgment and decision-making that derive from subconscious mental processes; includes confirmation and disconfirmation biases

Community supervision: also referred to as community corrections, this refers to sentences that involve supervision in the community, rather than incarceration in a prison or jail; includes probation and parole

Compensation: redress provided to exonerees for the loss, harm, and suffering caused by a wrongful conviction; used broadly to refer to both monetary and non-monetary assistance after exoneration

Compliant false confession: a false confession prompted by the pressure and stress of police interrogation

Confession: an admission of guilt; in this chapter, referring to the admission of a person to a criminal act that is made to police officers either voluntarily or as the result of police interrogation

Confirmation bias: the subconscious tendency to interpret new evidence in such a way as to confirm one's pre-existing beliefs

Contract system: a method of providing indigent defense in which attorneys agree to a contract with the government to handle a certain number of criminal cases for a set fee

Conviction Integrity Unit: a division within a prosecutor's office that reviews questionable convictions and works to prevent, identify, and remedy wrongful convictions

Corroboration: evidence that tends to support or confirm information, such as that provided by an informant

Courts of final jurisdiction: refers to the highest court in a particular jurisdiction, typically state supreme courts or the U.S. Supreme Court

Critical stage: according to *Kirby v. Illinois*, a stage of the criminal process in which formal adversarial proceedings have begun, thus triggering the defendant's right to the assistance of counsel

Cross-racial identification: identifications in which the witness and perpetrator are of different races; tend to be less reliable than identifications within racial groups, a phenomenon often referred to as "own-race bias" or "the other-race effect"

Custodial interview and interrogation: questioning that occurs after a suspect is taken into custody, or when their liberty has been constrained in a significant way

***Daubert* test/factors:** from *Daubert v. Merrell Dow Pharmaceuticals, Inc.*, one set of considerations used to determine the admissibility of expert testimony; charges judges to serve as gatekeepers and evaluate several factors before admitting expert testimony

Death Penalty Information Center: a non-profit organization that compiles and analyzes information related to capital punishment

Direct appeal: judicial review of a conviction that involves a review of the trial court record ("record review") for alleged legal errors committed at the trial

Discovery: in a criminal case, the process involving the prosecutor's sharing or revealing evidence to the defense prior to trial; the defense sometimes has a reciprocal obligation to reveal evidence within its possession to the prosecutor

Dispositional risk factors: characteristics of the suspect that may affect the likelihood of the suspect giving a false statement

DNA: deoxyribonucleic acid; the hereditary material in the nucleus of most cells, that can be identified through the testing of biological material

Drylabbing: fabricating results for laboratory tests that were not conducted

Error rate: the rate at which innocent people are convicted, or the proportion of all convictions that involve innocent persons; estimates generally fall between 1–5%

Estimator variables: factors that may influence the accuracy of eyewitness identifications, but are beyond the control of the justice system

Exoneration: an official declaration that a person is innocent of the crimes for which they were convicted and/or relieved of the consequences of the criminal conviction

Exoneree: a person who has met the criteria for an exoneration as described above

Felony: a more serious criminal offense (above misdemeanors), including most violent offenses, that are usually punishable by a year or more of imprisonment

Fillers: the members of a lineup or photo array who are not the suspect

Forensic evidence: evidence obtained through the use of scientific methods and techniques for use in court

Frye **test:** from *Frye v. United States*, one standard used to determine the admissibility of expert testimony; requires the scientific technique to be generally accepted within the relevant scientific community

Gideon v. Wainwright: a 1963 case in which the Supreme Court ruled that defendants charged with a felony and who cannot afford an attorney have the right to be represented at trial by court-appointed counsel

Habeas corpus: Latin for, "you have the body"; allows incarcerated persons to challenge a criminal conviction or sentence on the grounds that they are being held in violation of the United States Constitution or the laws or treaties of the United States, typically filed in federal court after all state remedies have been exhausted

Implicit bias: unconscious attitudes or stereotypes that influence an individual's beliefs, understanding, and actions

Incentivized informant: a person who agrees to provide information in a criminal case in exchange for some type of anticipated or promised benefit or other incentive

Indigent defendants: criminal defendants who are too poor to pay to hire their own defense attorney

Ineffective assistance of counsel: representation by a criminal defense lawyer that falls below constitutionally acceptable standards

Infanticide: the crime of killing an infant

Innocence movement: the collection of international advocacy efforts centered on wrongful convictions and exonerations; includes casework, policy reform, public education, and popular culture

Innocence Network: an international affiliation of organizations that provide legal services to the wrongly convicted and work to reform justice systems

The Innocence Project: a non-profit organization founded in 1992 that works to secure exonerations through post-conviction DNA testing and advocates for criminal justice reform

Internalized/persuaded false confession: a false confession in which an innocent suspect comes to believe that they actually committed the crime

Investigative interviewing: a non-confrontational approach to suspect questioning that focuses on gathering information, rather than securing an admission of guilt

Jury instructions: a judge's charge to jurors about the law governing their deliberations as they attempt to reach a verdict; sometimes involving cautionary warnings regarding attorneys' questions or statements or a witness's testimony during a trial

Juvenile Justice: The separate court system devoted to the offenses and misbehavior of young people, involving less severe sanctions than imposed by criminal courts, but potentially causing youths adjudicated as juvenile delinquents to be deprived of their liberty by confinement in youth correctional institutions.

Live lineup: the presentation of multiple individuals, in-person, for purposes of identification

Mass exoneration: cases in which a group of defendants were erroneously convicted, often due to official misconduct, and later exonerated; also called "group exoneration"

Mass incarceration: the phrase used to rely on the United States' extensive use of incarceration as a form of criminal sanction

Maximization: interrogation techniques that involve exaggerating the strength of evidence against the suspect or the seriousness of the charges, and thus the benefit of confessing

"Meet and plead" disposition: refers to a situation in which a case is resolved at the first court hearing, with little or no preparation by the defense attorney

Minimization: interrogation techniques that involve downplaying the seriousness of the offense or the suspect's role in it

Miranda v. Arizona: a 1966 Supreme Court case announcing the procedures required to protect suspects' rights against compelled self-incrimination during custodial interrogation; requires law enforcement to advise suspects of their rights and secure a waiver of them

Misdemeanors: lower-level criminal offenses (below felonies) that make up the majority of cases processed by the justice system

National Commission on Forensic Science: created in 2013 by the U.S. Department of Justice and the National Institutes of Standards and Technology; included a variety of stakeholders who examined problems related to forensic science and made recommendations for reform

National Registry of Exonerations (NRE): a project founded in 2012 that provides information about wrongful convictions and exonerations in the United States; currently, the largest collection of known exonerations

Near misses: cases in which innocent individuals were arrested or charged with crimes but ultimately were not convicted

No-crime case: a case in which a factually innocent person is erroneously convicted, but no actual crime ever occurred

***Nolo contendere* plea**: also called a "no contest" plea, this allows the court to enter a guilty verdict but does not require the defendant to admit guilt

North Carolina Innocence Inquiry Commission: an independent state agency that investigates claims of actual innocence from those convicted of felonies in North Carolina; credible claims are adjudicated by a panel of three judges

Official misconduct: the abuse of authority by police, prosecutors, or other government officials that may contribute to a wrongful conviction

Photo array: a display constructed of multiple photographs, rather than individuals presented in an in-person lineup, for purposes of identification

Plea: the defendant's answer—guilty, or not guilty—in response to criminal charge(s)

Plea bargaining: negotiations between the prosecution and defense to reach an agreement about the terms of a defendant's conviction and recommended sentence

Plea colloquy: a conversation in court and under oath between the judge and the defendant, during which the judge must determine that the defendant is entering a plea of guilty knowingly, voluntarily, and intelligently

Post-conviction review/relief: generally refers to challenges to a conviction or sentence based on matters not reflected in the trial record, and thus not considered on direct appeal

Post-traumatic stress disorder (PTSD): a mental health condition suffered by those who have experienced traumatic or terrifying events, including a wrongful conviction and the associated punishment experiences

Pretrial incarceration: The confinement prior to a trial of a person charged with a crime, often resulting from an inability to post bail

Prisoner's Dilemma: a decision-making scenario in which two suspects are separated, questioned independently, and each told that the other is implicating them in the crime

Private legislation: one method of compensation, involves the exoneree petitioning the state legislature to pass a bill to provide redress to the individual exoneree

Probable cause: required for arrests; a general standard of proof that involves an evaluation of objective observations and reasonable inferences, and an assessment of the totality of the circumstances to determine the legality of an arrest

Procedural error: an error of process or procedure made in a court case, such as the denial of a fair hearing or an irregularity in the manner of enforcing a substantive legal right; a procedural error may be grounds for reversing a conviction but does not necessarily mean that a factual error has occurred or that a defendant has been wrongfully convicted

Public defender offices: government-financed offices in which criminal defense attorneys provide legal representation to indigents

Record expungement: the process of sealing an arrest and conviction record so as to make it inaccessible to the public and allow exonerees to lawfully report that they have not been convicted of a crime

Reentry/Reintegration: the process of returning to traditional civilian life following a conviction and period of incarceration

Relative judgment: when a witness decides which subject in a lineup or photo array most closely resembles the offender they saw compared to other members of the lineup or photo array, rather than basing an identification on the witness's recollection of the person viewed at the time of the crime

Reliability hearing: a pre-trial hearing in which a judge determines whether an informant appears to be sufficiently trustworthy or credible to be allowed to testify at trial

Sentinel Events Initiative: an initiative undertaken by the National Institute of Justice, designed to review undesirable outcomes in criminal justice, including wrongful convictions, and study them in a non-blaming fashion to determine why they occurred and what can be done to prevent future injustices.

Sequential lineup/photo array: an identification procedure in which lineup members or the pictures in a photo array are viewed one at a time and the witness is asked as each is presented to make an identification decision

Serology: the identification and characterization of biological stains for forensic purposes; includes ABO blood typing

Shaken Baby Syndrome/Abusive Head Trauma: a form of significant child abuse that leads to the brain injury of an infant or toddler

Show-up: a one-on-one identification procedure in which the witness is presented with a single person and asked if that person is the offender

Simultaneous lineup/photo array: an identification procedure in which all lineup members or pictures in a photo array are viewed at the same time

Situational risk factors: characteristics of the situation, or the criminal interrogation, that may affect the likelihood of a suspect giving a false statement

Southern Strategy: a strategy used largely by Republican politicians in the mid-20th century to appeal to Southern white voters by emphasizing issues of racial threat and states' rights

State harm: actions or crimes committed by the state or by agents acting on behalf of the state that harm citizens

Statutory compensation: one method of compensation, a law of general application that provides a set level of compensation for exonerees who meet specified eligibility requirements

Stereotype threat: occurs when a person fears being judged by a negative stereotype or generalization about the group to which they belong

Stigma/stigmatization: a perception of negative attributes associated with a person's status or condition; often applied to formerly incarcerated individuals

***Strickland* standard:** from *Strickland v. Washington*, provides a two-part test (based on deficient performance and demonstrated prejudice) for evaluating claims of ineffective assistance of criminal defense counsel

System variables: factors that may influence the accuracy of eyewitness identifications and are subject to control by actors in the justice system

True perpetrator: in a wrong-person case, the person who actually committed the offense for which an innocent individual was wrongly convicted

Tunnel vision: an outcome of cognitive biases, such as confirmation and disconfirmation bias, in which investigators focus on a suspect, become convinced of their guilt, and build a case against the suspect by interpreting evidence to fit their beliefs and discounting contradictory evidence

Voluntary false confession: a false confession made without prompting or pressure from police

***Wade* trilogy:** three Supreme Court cases (*United States v. Wade, Gilbert v. California*, and *Stovall v. Denno*) that decided important constitutional issues related to in-person eyewitness identification procedures

Weapon-focus effect: the phenomenon whereby the presence of a weapon used in the commission of a crime commands the attention of a witness and thus threatens to undermine the accuracy of an identification

Wrong-person case: a case in which a factually innocent person is erroneously convicted for crimes committed by someone else

Wrongful acquittal: the acquittal (not guilty verdict) of a factually guilty individual

Wrongful conviction: cases in which individuals are innocent of wrongdoing and have erroneously been convicted

Wrongful liberty: refers to the freedom of the true perpetrator who escapes arrest, conviction, and punishment for a criminal act, while an innocent person is wrongly convicted

Index

United States Department of Justice, 12
United States Sentencing Commission, 6, 115
United States Supreme Court
case law. *See* Case law
Due Process and, 190–192
federal habeas corpus, case reviews, 258–260
juvenile justice system and, 312–314
probable cause and, 13, 187–188
qualified immunity and, 188–189
Wade trilogy and, 57, 79
writs of certiorari, case review, 254–255
United States v. Ash, 69
United States v. Bagley, 195
United States v. Burke, 195
United States v. Dennis, 163
United States v. Henry, 164
United States v. Noze, 174
United States v. Ruiz, 121, 172
United States v. Singleton, 163
United States v. Tribble, 132
United States v. Wade, 57–61, 69–70, 334
United States v. Wilson, 262
Unreal Dream, An: The Michael Morton Story (documentary), 186
U.S. Constitution
Eighth Amendment, 259–260, 308
eyewitness testimony, rules governing, 56–71
federal habeas corpus review and, 258–260
Fifth Amendment, 95, 98
Fourteenth Amendment, 61, 95, 98, 164, 190–191, 214–217, 259
Fourth Amendment, 187

ineffective counsel, two-part test, 218–219
Sixth Amendment, 57–61, 62, 63, 69–71, 115, 145, 164, 214–217, 217, 218, 259
Thirteenth Amendment, 30, 40, 327
U.S. Department of Justice, 146, 147, 170, 200

V

Van de Kamp v. Goldstein, 199
VanCleave, A., 314
Victim-related harms, 296
Victims, additional, 289–295
Video recording
equal focus, 102
interrogations, 78, 98
reform recommendations, 101–102
Viljoen, J. L., 116
Vogelman, L., 36
Volokh, A., 298
Voluntariness principles, 97
Voluntary false confessions, 87–88, 105, 334
Vrij, A., 89
Vulnerable suspects, interrogation protections, 104

W

Wade trilogy, 57–61, 79, 334
Walker, Lenore, 37, 38
Wall Street Journal, The, 213
Waller, A., 143
Warden, R., 6, 34, 271, 291, 295–296
Warden, Rob, 34
War on Drugs, 37
Washington Post, 132
Waters, N. L., 255, 256
Waxman, S. P., 92